"With admirable breadth and lucidity, Craig Calhoun canvasses the most important debates in contemporary social theory. The result is an illuminating and important book." *Nancy Fraser*

"This is social theory at its very best. In a host of domains – concerning cultural difference, postmodernism, the politics of identity, and nationalism – Calhoun breaks new ground." *Charles Taylor*

"This is a very well-informed and very rigorous critical survey of Critical Social Theory." *Pierre Bourdieu*

"With this impressively wide-ranging and subtle exploration of the challenge posed by cultural diversity to the project of Critical Social Theory, Craig Calhoun makes an important contribution not only to the interpretation of that project, but also to its renewal and revitalization." *Rogers Brubaker*

"In recent years, the meaning of 'Critical Theory' and the contours of this approach have become more and more diffuse. Craig Calhoun's new book is perhaps the most important *sociological* attempt to breathe new life into this tradition." *Hans Joas*

"A brilliant synthesis of theory and history: Calhoun works at the cutting edge, facing the future but carrying his traditions with him." *Peter Beilharz*

"This book explores Critical Theory's origins, but more importantly it also shows how certain contemporary writers, despite not usually being recognized as such, have as much claim to the title 'critical theorist' as did Adorno and Horkheimer. It is this essential extension of critical analysis into today's body of theoretical concerns that gives the book its particular importance." *Alan Sica*

Twentieth-Century Social Theory

Series Editor: **Charles C. Lemert**

Twentieth-Century Social Theory invites authors respected for their contributions in the prominent traditions of social theory to reflect on past and present in order to propose what comes next. Books in the series will consider critical theory, race, symbolic interactionism, functionalism, feminism, world systems theory, psychoanalysis, and Weberian social theory, among other current topics. Each will be plain to read, yet provocative to ponder. Each will gather up what has come to pass in the twentieth century in order to define the terms of social theoretical imagination in the twenty-first.

Published
Critical Social Theory: Craig Calhoun
Feminist Thought: Patricia Clough
Symbolic Interactionism and Cultural Studies: Norman Denzin

In preparation
Neofunctionalism and After: Jeff Alexander
Politics and Social Theory: Richard and Mickey Flacks
Postmodernity and Social Theory: Charles Lemert
The Social Construction of Homosexual Desire: Steven Seidman
Weberian Social Theory: Alan Sica

Critical Social Theory

Culture, History, and the Challenge of Difference

Craig Calhoun

BLACKWELL
Oxford UK & Cambridge USA

First published 1995
Reprinted 1996

Blackwell Publishers Inc.
238 Main Street
Cambridge, Massachusetts 02142, USA

Blackwell Publishers Ltd
108 Cowley Road
Oxford OX4 1JF
UK

Library of Congress Cataloging-in-Publication Data
Calhoun, Craig J., 1952–
    Critical social theory: culture, history, and the challenge of difference/Craig Calhoun.
        p.   cm. – (Contemporary social theory)
    Includes bibliographical references and index.
    ISBN 1–55786–138–2 (acid-free paper). – ISBN 1–55786–288–5 (pbk: acid-free paper)
        1. Sociology – Philosophy.   2. Social sciences – Philosophy.
    3. Culture – Philosophy.   4. Critical theory.   5. Difference (Philosophy).   6. Identity.   I. Title.   II. Series: Twentieth-century social theory (Cambridge, Mass.)
    HM24.C228   1995
    301'.01 – dc20   94–44903
                                                                                      CIP

British Library Cataloguing in Publication Data

A CIP catalogue record for this book is available from the British Library.

Typeset in Sabon 10/12 pt
by Best-set Typesetter Ltd., Hong Kong
Printed in Great Britain by Hartnolls Limited, Bodmin, Cornwall

This book is printed on acid-free paper.

Contents

Dedicated to my children,
Salam and Jonah,
who think critical theory is hopelessly abstract,
but who have become critical thinkers by living in
a world where identity and difference must
be objects of struggle.

Series Editor's Preface

In the language world of social theory, "critical theory" is one of the most valuable coins of the realm. Among the more social scientific social theorists, the phrase stands for the important tradition of twentieth-century German thinkers in the lineage of Theodor Adorno and Max Horkheimer. Among the more literary and humanistic scholars, "critical theory" represents the genus of enterprises by which literatures and other cultural works are subjected to rigorous theoretical examination. Also, behind these two local usages stands the fact that critical thinking has itself come to be one of the more essential attributes of modern, Western cultures. To be a modern is at least to possess a capacity for critical judgment, one that allows the individual to stand sensibly apart from the dehumanizing forces of social life. So ubiquitous is the term in its several senses that its appearance is a sure sign one is in the presence of some or another important discussion of the nature of modern society itself.

When in the far future the definitive intellectual history of the modern age is written, the list of our culture's most decisive controversies will surely include the current one in which critical theories are central antagonists. At issue is the question of modernity's end and the supposed emergence of a postmodern era. Though the nuances of this cultural argument can be at times unbearably complicated, the most basic questions are comparatively straightforward, and of exacting importance. Will the ideal of a universal humanity survive? Should it?

On the one side are those who interpret the appearance of fragmentation in modern cultural and political forms as evidence of a major historical transformation. Hip hop culture, Madonna, Disney World, MTV, the AT&T (now Sony) building in midtown New York City, the velvet revolutions of 1989 in Eastern Europe, the rise of identity politics and ethnic rebellions world-wide, the collapse of state Marxisms in the

West — these are among the evidences put forth to argue that we are now in a postmodern era. Whether or not a series such as this, however composed, points to a world revolution is an open question — one that, in principle, cannot even be answered from within a postmodern "logic".

On the other side are those whose moral, political, and aesthetic judgments cause them to recoil from the very idea that evidences such as powerful social (and political) differences and confusing cultural expressions suggest anything new at all. Those on the modernist side of the controversy argue that the modern world over the last half-millennium has been continuously engaged in a struggle to come to terms with its own internal differences. The changes taking place today are, they insist, at best attenuations of the nature of the modern world. Modernists argue that the postmodern fad plays light and easy with the precious property of modern culture. In particular, they complain with cause that some postmodernisms flirt so loosely with differences as to produce a debilitating relativism that eliminates all prospects of action and debate on principles of good societies, just legal orders, and emancipatory politics.

This is a serious argument that is taken up with different purposes, though a core of common concern, by both the left and right wings of political and cultural life in the West, particularly in the United States. Left-modernists are accused, even by their friends, of being today's conservatives, while, in their view of themselves, they are the defenders of the most viable principles of political liberation. The cultural wars among high-minded social theorists, as among politicians and media stars, become complicated whenever combatants are retrofitted into one of the familiar categories. Insofar as the postmodernists are correct in some things, one of these may be that the categories by which modernity classifies its cultural and political entities may have outlived their usefulness. Here more than a few left-modernists would agree.

Curiously, the term "critical theory" has played a role on *both* sides of the cultural wars, at least as they have taken place among academic social theorists. "Critical theory" in reference to the inheritors and affines of the German school of social theory has referred to those who apply their critical attitudes to modern life for the evident purpose of saving it, Juergen Habermas, to mention the most mentionable example, is surely critical of modern society. He is also one of modernity's most articulate defenders. At the same time, "critical theory" in its references to theories of culture is commonly, if awkwardly, associated with postmodernism. The severe limitations of the expression "postmodernism" are well illustrated by the fact that cultural critics come in as many varieties as may exist on *both* the modernist and postmodernist sides. Yet, it is surely the case that the emergence of critical theories of literature and culture as they have developed in the last quarter century has been foremost among the driving forces of postmodern social theories generally. The uses and abuses of the ideas of earlier poststructuralist thinkers like Michel Foucault, Jacques Derrida, and Jacques Lacan have given life to fundamental changes in many academic fields. Whether or not those changes are somehow part of a transformation in world culture is a question yet to be answered. It may, at present, be unanswerable, just as it may be impossible to determine whether or not this new critical attitude in the study of culture is postmodern.

The feelings on these matters run deep because the issues at stake are so urgent. This may be why it is so painfully rare that one reads an account of the controversy in which an opposing position is given fair and coherent respect. Juergen Habermas's *The Philosophical Discourse of Modernity* (1987) is, however, one exception to this rule. Martin Jay's *Downcast Eyes* (1993) is another. Though it is a book of another kind, Craig Calhoun's *Critical Social Theory: Culture, History and the Challenge of Difference* is a welcome addition to a short list of writings that take their stand while evoking a nuanced and sensible, if not always friendly, view of those against whom they assert themselves. True to the tradition's founding faith in decent reason, these are among the books that come out more or less on the modernist side. Though there is foolishness on both sides, postmoderns are less inclined to read their theoretical Others with the same care, perhaps because they are on to other things.

Craig Calhoun is a man of many remarkable talents and energies. In his generation of social theorists there are few indeed who have embarked, as he has, on such a series of projects assessing the most important issues across the spectrum of current social thinking. The list of topics on which he has written is breathtaking — the new social movements, nationalism and ethnicity, civil society, radicalism in the industrial revolution, the public sphere, and more. It is clear that he is a social theorist more than willing to dig into the empirical depths many theorists deliberate only at abstract remove. This is a book in which Calhoun exhibits the breadth and depth of his learning to very satisfying effects for the reader.

Critical Social Theory breaks important new ground. Firstly, and most strikingly, it rethinks the tradition of German critical social theory in relation to subjects it is often accused of ignoring or, even, being incapable of handling. As the book's subtitle suggests, a major theme is the exploration of difference in respect to which Calhoun offers a truly original understanding of ways and means whereby critical theory both can and must consider social differences without giving up more fundamental commitments to principles of human emancipation. Secondly, and just as important, if slightly less striking, *Critical Social Theory* makes important connections among the major lines of social thought that for a good long while have called out for reconciliation. In composing his own social theory, Calhoun is one of a very few to draw as strongly on the work of Pierre Bourdieu and other cultural theorists as on the ideas of Habermas and the Frankfurt theorists. In this, and other, ways he demonstrates a certain grasp of the second important meaning of "critical theory" as a critique of culture.

But Calhoun refuses to keep within the safe precincts of sociology, his own disciplinary field. This book is one of the few in which a prominent sociological theorist gives serious and sophisticated attention to the contributions of feminist theory, in particular, and other theories associated with the New Social Movements that arose in the 1960s. This constitutes a third major contribution of the book — its encouragement to the revival of sociology's readiness to confront extra-sociological social theories.

Though there are still other riches to be mined in this wonderful book, these three alone make *Critical Social Theory* a book worth the time of its reading. Though Craig Calhoun is already widely recognized as a leading social theorist, this book will almost surely advance his strong reputation even more. *Critical Social Theory* is so compelling as to cause even those skeptical of the varieties of critical theories to think again. And, those who come to critical theory with an already warm appreciation will surely enjoy and benefit from the ways Craig Calhoun advances this important tradition of social thought.

Charles Lemert

Acknowledgments

One of the central arguments of this book is that the formation and reformation of identity is not given immutably by culture or history, does not stop with adulthood, and cannot be sharply divided into public and private elements. The same can be said of theory itself. This book started in reflections on problems that arose both in my other work and in my personal and political involvements. In early essays, I tried to think these issues through but never altogether satisfactorily. I kept at the task, benefitting from discussions with a number of colleagues and friends. Most important were faculty and graduate student colleagues in the Program in Social Theory and Cross-Cultural Studies at the University of North Carolina at Chapel Hill, and in the various working groups of the Center for Transcultural Studies (formerly the Center for Psychosocial Studies) in Chicago.

I also benefitted from chances to discuss these ideas in other settings. The second chapter was aired in draft as a presentation to the 1992 National Seminar of the Norwegian Sociological Association, and the American Sociological Association in 1993. The third began as a discussant's remarks in the conference on Prospects for General Theory sponsored by the Department of Sociology at SUNY Albany (later expanded for publication in S. Seidman and D. Wagner, eds: *Postmodernism and Social Theory*, Oxford: Blackwell, 1991). The fourth was first presented to the World Congress of Sociology in Madrid in 1990 (and published in an earlier version in *Theory, Culture and Society*, 1993). The fifth chapter was written for the Center for Psychosocial Studies conference on The Social Theory of Pierre Bourdieu, and published in *Bourdieu: Critical Perspectives* (edited by C. Calhoun, M. Postone and E. LiPuma; Cambridge: Polity; and Chicago: University of Chicago Press, 1993). Chapter 6 originated when – against my better judgment – I allowed Barbara Laslett to cajole me into participating in an American Sociological Association "author meets critics" session on the work of Dorothy Smith; an early draft of part of the chapter was also presented in a panel at the Tenth Anniversary celebration of the journal *Theory, Culture and Society*, on which occasion the audience debated for most of the allotted time the question of whether, as a man, I should have been allowed to speak on this issue (let alone to speak with any pretense or embodied manner of authority) and introduced me to Sandra Harding's description of the issue of men entering into feminist discourse as "the monster problem". A later discussion with the women's studies faculty and students of Uppsala University was also helpful. The seventh chapter started as the introduction to the miniconference on "Social Theory and the Politics of Identity" I organized as chair of the ASA Section on Social Theory in 1992 (published, under that title, by Blackwell in 1994); its revision benefitted from the helpful discussion after I presented it at UCLA and from the insights of a number of colleagues in Chapel Hill with whom I worked to develop a new course on "social theory and cultural diversity." The last chapter grew out of a series of discussions sponsored by the Center for Transcultural Studies, and was presented in multiple incarnations between 1991 and 1994; I am particularly grateful for the opportunity to present it as a Harney Professorship Lecture at the University of Toronto and in seminars at Copenhagen, Gothenberg, Lund, Stockholm, and Uppsala Universities.

In all these various settings – and others – I learned from those who asked me questions, challenged my arguments, and even claimed to support my positions in ways I found surprising. I am not sure whether my thinking was really public or private. None of the chapters now appears as originally written or previously published. All have been reworked in various ways; some have been substantially transformed, even in their basic arguments. Among the most important, and helpful, occasions for this has been my teaching in the Department of Sociology at the University of Oslo. Most chapters were presented as lectures there, and all received important commentary from students and colleagues. I am also grateful to Charles Lemert for helpfully reading a draft of the entire book and making useful editorial suggestions. I cannot name all the people who read one or more individual chapters and gave me helpful advice, but want to thank especially Peter Bearman, Rogers Brubaker, Nancy Fraser, and Moishe Postone. I owe a special debt to the Swedish Collegium for Advanced Study in the Social Sciences which gave me not only the time but the freedom from constant phone calls that enabled me to finish the writing, and the benefit of critical discussion with a group of colleagues who improved the thinking.

My debt is even greater to Leah Florence, who has labored for years to keep my professional life organized; and to my wife, Pamela DeLargy, my debt is beyond all calculation.

Introduction

I

The novelist Kurt Vonnegut studied anthropology at the University of Chicago after World War Two. He reports that "at that time, they were teaching that there was absolutely no difference between anybody."[1] Before the war, anthropology more often taught that everyone was different.

Anthropology – and the human or social sciences generally – have indeed had these two messages throughout their history. Anthropology – at least socio-cultural anthropology – has perhaps been the paradigmatic science of otherness and difference, but sameness, ethnocentrism, and explicit universalism have flourished there on occasion as well as predominating in sociology, economics, psychology, and most of the other human sciences. Today, the debate continues with particular vociferousness. On the one side stand poststructuralists, postmodernists, some feminists and others who would base an identity-politics on the absolute otherness, the radical incompatibility of different intellectual traditions, and even sometimes the impossibility of full communication across lines of cultural or other basic differences. On the other side stand defenders of Enlightenment universalism, modernism, and rationality as a basis for communication; Jürgen Habermas is most prominent among them.

Eventually a judgment day may come when all social theorists are summoned before the pearly gates to declare their allegiance. Were you with Habermas, the Archangel will ask, or with Deconstruction? So far, however, Gabriel has not blown his horn, I have not seen St Peter, and I refuse the presumption that there is no middle path. My path, readers will probably find, is closer to Habermas's Scylla than Derrida's Charybdis (to switch mythic metaphors). That is, forced to choose be-

tween the attempt at a liberating social project and endless warnings that
difference probably will be recuperated into sameness and order will turn
into tyranny, I will take the risk of trying for liberation, for equality,
justice, and all the other problematic terms that join with freedom (more
generally favored but very divergently understood) to make up the most
popular normative and political path for critical theory. But I think that
Habermas and many colleagues are acting prematurely as though they
have to choose, and very unfortunately sacrificing really serious attention
to the problems of identity and difference in both social theory and
ethical-political practice. There is more to learn from deconstruction,
poststructuralism, postmodernism, and the less academic politics of identity (and, what is to say much the same thing, difference) before the end
of this millennium or the Angelic summons.

   In short, the tension between universality and difference has come to
the fore once again as perhaps *the* central issue informing contemporary
debates in social and cultural theory, and I want to find a way out of
simple dualistic oppositions. Some postmodernists push their case
sharply enough to run the risk of stepping onto the slippery slope of
radical relativism; some, indeed, dive onto that slope head first.
Habermas defends the Enlightenment project by means of a rationalism
so thoroughgoing that it runs the risk of seeming vulnerable to the
charges Hegel leveled against Kant's moral philosophy: excessive formalism, abstract universalism, impotence of the mere ought, and the terror-
ism of pure conviction.[2]

   This is a debate in which social and cultural theory returns to face –
and perhaps, with luck, to contribute to – the great classical and modern
traditions in philosophy. Michel Foucault, for example, was at pains to
point out everything he was not: not a structuralist, not a historian, not
a philosopher. Yet, though there is ample evidence that his work can be
read with great enthusiasm by those for whom it is suggestive without
being understood, any deeper grasp of it – albeit a grasp that Foucault in
certain moods might have resisted – must recognize his arguments with
Hegel. His own great teacher Jean Hyppolyte, his philosophy teacher not
just at the Lycée Henri IV but later at the Sorbonne, perhaps did more
than anyone else to bring Hegel back into the forefront of French
intellectual attention after World War Two (even if Hegel was fated to
become more important as alter ego to the nascent structuralist movement than for his own positive theories).[3] As Allan Megill has commented, it is no accident that Foucault's first major publication, *Madness
and Civilization*, "should read like an oddly inverted Hegelian
Geistesgeschichte."[4] The Hegelian dialectic of the master and slave was

and is among the most powerful representations of the non-autonomy of self-recognition.

This theme of the politics of recognition was all but ubiquitous in certain segments of postwar avant-garde culture. It informed Sartrean existentialism, for example, and the way in which structuralists made Sartre their definitive other. It had not lost its force by the end of the student movement. As a graduate student in the early 1970s, I was taken along with my sometime mentor Max Gluckman, to see "The Living Theater," that slightly dated performance icon of the 1960s. Max's wife Mary did the taking, and he was already a bit disgruntled. We "spectators" gathered, most of us on the floor, in a large room with a cleared space at the front for Julian Beck, Judith Malina, and their colleagues. Predictably, the members of the Living Theater leapt beyond the bounds of that space, confronting members of the audience with a variety of challenges, many turning on our putatively complacent sense of who we were amid the evils and exploitations of the world. The production sought to unsettle identities and provoke action – even revolution – in the world beyond the theater. Nominally improvisational, it seemed to work with fairly set ideas of what should happen. A young women, naked but for a dirty rag or two, stuck her face in Max's, saying with some sense of drama, "Am I your slave?" "No, I'm bloody well yours," Max yelled as he leapt up, "but no longer." Living for himself, Max strode all gangly six feet four across the (ironically) more respectful crowd on the floor towards the door. Were he alive today, Max would no doubt be on the side of the modernists against the postmodernists, but he was in no way inclined to think the specificity of identity could be addressed adequately through so general a trope, or by such an apparently easy self-recognition. The master/slave image could backfire because it lacked nuance and attention to differences outside the polarity it posited. Hegel's dialectic more generally could always be reduced to slogans of thesis and antithesis despite its more basic concern for relations among the multifarious parts of any historical whole.

II

A sense of complexity remains important. We do not come to the issue of difference in a world that encourages simple, unconditional endorsement. "Difference" appears as importantly in the forms of violent ethnic nationalism, racism, and religious fundamentalism as in movements and personal choices about gender, sexual orientation, and ethnic pluralism. Some lines of difference, like national boundaries, are used not only to distinguish one human group from others but to demand internal conformity. The very rhetoric of difference, in other words, can be turned to the repression of differences. Recognition of difference can be the basis for mutual engagement, or for failure to appreciate and respect common humanity. And not all differences are equally valuable.

Social theorists are challenged by issues of difference precisely because they do not admit of easy answers. It is not so hard to suggest that there must be some "both/and" approach to human difference and commonality; it is very hard to make consistent sense of the approaches that have been offered. The problem is an eminently theoretical one, for it calls for going beyond the surface appeals of various immediate agendas of affirming difference (appeals from ethnic or lifestyle minorities in the US, for example) and recognizing common humanity (acting responsibly amid the tragedies in Rwanda and Bosnia) to grasping how different ways of invoking difference and identity affect our understanding of the world and shape the categories through which we make sense of it. This is above all an issue for critical social theory since it exists largely to facilitate a constructive engagement with the social world that starts from the presumption that existing arrangements – including currently affirmed identities and differences – do not exhaust the range of possibilities. It seeks to explore the ways in which our categories of thought reduce our freedom by occluding recognition of what could be.

Critical theory has come under widespread criticism, however, for its universalist tendencies and its failures to consider the full impact of the cultural diversity of human existence. This is not altogether without merit. In order to establish a ground for critical engagement, critical theorists have commonly claimed the basis of a more or less undifferentiated human condition. Their view of this human condition has been deeply, but not always with acknowledgement, shaped by the specifics of the Western intellectual tradition.

Even where critical theory has been radical, its tacit universalism has often allied it to aspects of the liberal political tradition. It has been disposed to speak of humanity in ways that obscured the multiplicity of actual human beings and human possibilities. Marxists, for example, found it hard to make adequate sense of the commitment of members of the international working class to specific national cultures. Marxist critiques of bourgeois liberalism focused on incomplete universalism, the ways in which putatively illegitimate differences among human beings were maintained despite allegedly universal political freedoms. Yet this is not the whole story. The founders of the "Frankfurt School" who made "critical theory" a catchword in the mid-twentieth century were passionate critics of administrative normalization and alienation, admirers of artistic individuality and resistance to convention. Adorno sought to develop a "many-sided theory of non-identity, or rather of the forms in which the non-identical could, paradoxically, be given consideration."[5] Even Habermas's more straightforwardly universalistic theories owe a good deal to Adorno, especially in their persistent pursuit of a move beyond the philosophy of the subject.[6]

Part of the problem is that a great deal of modern social science has tacitly assumed that human beings normally live in one social world at a time. Modern social science has produced a notion of bounded and internally integrated societies and has treated both cross-border relations and subcultures as problematic. It has presumed that the individual consciousness is itself integral and that it requires a stable and consistent social environment. Monolinguality and religious orthodoxy have been taken as normal, and multilinguality and religious syncretism or variation as deviant cases to be explained. Yet in these and a range of other ways, it does not seem obvious that people usually live in one social world at a time, but rather that it is now, and throughout human history often has been, common to inhabit multiple worlds simultaneously and even to grow as a person by the ability to maintain oneself in connection to all of them. This means that anyone's horizon of experience, to borrow the phenomenological term, is unlikely to be fixed by a single collectivity or categorial framework.[7]

Even where the charge of universalistic inattention to the politics of difference is justified, it does not seem to me a reason to abandon the venture of critical theory. It does seem a reason to change it. The present book explores the challenge of taking seriously the differences among human beings – a challenge not only to critical theories but to more conventional social science theories. I do not think that this challenge admits of an easy answer. Too often, self-proclaimed multiculturalists offer a sort of cheap celebration of the existence of difference without a serious grappling with the challenges posed both by difference in general and by specific differences.

In this book, I do not attempt any sustained exploration of particular cultures or the differences among them. Rather, I try to sort out something of what the challenge posed by difference is, why it is basic, and how it might be confronted without sacrificing commitment to theory or critique. The challenge is one that runs through many sorts of theory and many sorts of difference. Gender, race, and nationality figure prominently, for example. But the problem is apparent in class differences, differences among regions within countries, and cultural differences that no one has ever claimed should demarcate nations.

At the same time, it is important not to accept too restricted a view of critical theory. The label is sometimes claimed for the Frankfurt School as though it could be a sort of property right. I shall only introduce briefly the powerful but sometimes problematic contributions of the Frankfurt theorists – both the first generation of Theodor Adorno, Max Horkheimer, and their colleagues, and the second generation of Jürgen Habermas.[8] Their work shapes much of my approach, and much of this book implicitly engages Habermas's theory. A critical theory of exceptional scope and many advantages, Habermas's work brings together themes I think are crucial. Much as Weber said he was "unmusical" in matters of religious belief, however, so Habermas is unmusical on the theme of cultural difference. Though my arguments implicitly engage and attempt to advance the lines of work initiated by the Frankfurt theorists, I shall focus more on suggesting some of the ways in which other lines of theory might inform the project of critical theory.

In particular, I shall explore feminist and poststructuralist theory because these two discourses (they are not really the unified theoretical positions sometimes implied) have done a great deal to open up the issue of difference as a basic categorial problem rather than a merely contingent empirical issue. I shall pay special attention to the work of Pierre Bourdieu and especially his ideas of habitus and field. Bourdieu is not always seen as a poststructuralist, though I think he should be. His approach to knowledge was formed in the structuralist crucible of 1950s and early 1960s France, and remains deeply shaped by it. Yet like his classmate and exact contemporary Derrida, he moved beyond structuralist orthodoxies partly by recovering elements of a phenomenology that had been suppressed and by resisting the complete enclosure of system. Like Foucault he sought to recover the significance of human embodiment. But unlike Derrida or Foucault, Bourdieu has remained consistently sociological. Though trained initially as a philosopher, he has neither stayed within an almost entirely cognitive argument, like Derrida, nor attempted to claim the body as an extra-social standpoint for critique, like Foucault. Although Bourdieu's work is ambiguous about its cultural and historical specificity, it offers important possibilities for developing an approach to the concretely social and embodied dimensions of human life that are frequently slighted by those poststructuralists who are taken, especially in the English language countries, as intellectual sources for "postmodernism."

Finding a variety of problems with modernity, many feminists and others attentive to the politics of difference have been drawn to postmodernist ideas. This move raises problems, however, for a critical social theory. First, as I shall try to show in chapter 4, the idea of postmodernism commonly involves a pseudohistorical claim to an epochal transition that in fact cuts theorists off from the necessary analysis of the conditions and possibilities for truly transformative change in modern society. Second, postmodernists too often write as though all knowledge is discursive and therefore cut themselves off from understanding much of culture and practice. Too often they focus on certain sorts of culture – especially those that seem most like language – without attending to the construction and organization of social relations. Feminists are generally more attentive to embeddedness in social relations and to embodiment, but even within feminist theory there is an unfortunate split between thinkers who focus overwhelmingly on "ideas, symbols and forms of consciousness," as Iris Marion Young describes the significance of the category of gender, and those who undertake the analysis of concrete social relations – whether within families or on larger scales of societal organization.[9] Third, in many of its versions, postmodernist theory encourages a relativism that makes it hard to explain why feminist theories should be more persuasive than others, or on what basis feminists and other critical theorists can defend strong normative conclusions.

I shall try to show that we can draw on many of the positive achievements of poststructuralist thought without buying the problematic package sold as postmodernism. Likewise, then, we can avoid the notion of a forced choice between this postmodernism and a so-called modernism which turns out to be unusually rigid whether in outright universalism or in defense of certain essentialized differences. The problems of postmodernism have encouraged many feminists to stick to problematically fixed notions of standpoint (inherited from androcentric Enlightenment thought) as the basis for critique. For some, following Foucault and/or Lacanian psychoanalysis, this standpoint is an essentialized extrasocial and extra-linguistic notion of the body. It is very hard for such theory (as for conservative counterparts that rely on conventional biological determinism) to be opened to genuinely social and cultural argumentation. Feminist standpoints modeled on ideas of class standpoints are more readily sociological, but as I shall try to show in chapter 6, are not without serious drawbacks.

These different theoretical strategies have longstanding, if too often unrecognized, precursors. I shall also try to show something of the older roots of critical theory before the Frankfurt School, including the ways in which problems of cultural diversity and historical specificity have shaped social theory throughout the modern era.

III

Outside the realms of art, literature, and philosophy, the Frankfurt School's appropriation of history was largely (though not exclusively) a matter of knowing canonical European history – the product of good gymnasium educations, rather than a matter of involvement in actual historical research.[9] Breaking with the givenness and immediate facticity of the social world, however, calls not only for historical knowledge as a precondition of theory but for a continual engagement with history and rethinking of historical assumptions. To take a simple example, thus, it is remarkable to what extent the understanding contemporary sociologists have of the industrial revolution is based on the syntheses incorporated into theoretical discourses by Max Weber, Emile Durkheim and Karl Marx – and how little need most sociologists feel to allow their inherited ideas to be challenged by the enormous more recent production of historical research and analysis that puts the so-called industrial revolution in new light. Much the same could be said with regard to sociological neglect of anthropology and cross-cultural knowledge.

The lead of the classical social theorists has also been followed in the area of gender, though here the lead was more to ignore the significance of the matter than to appropriate any particular historical account. Developing ways to take seriously such fundamental categorial differences as gender is a basic and urgent project for critical social theory. There is no aspect of social life on which the contributions of Marx, Weber, and Durkheim are more strikingly unable to speak to current concerns. None of the most important sociological theorists at work today has written more than glancingly of gender – not Habermas, not Bourdieu, not Giddens, not Luhmann (though each has opened the door to serious gender concerns farther than most of their predecessors).[11] The issue is not just that these theorists (and most others) have ignored women, but that they have ignored the extent to which the category of gender exerts a basic influence over social thought and social life. Gender is like race – but even more basic and pervasive – in its structuring of a host of forms and dimensions of social understanding. In realms that seem quite separate from biological differences between sexes (let alone from sexual relations) the category of gender helps to give meaning to the world, even encouraging cultures in their common proliferations of binary oppositions (male sun to female moon).

Feminist theory, in turn, remains remarkably disconnected from this disciplinary mainstream of sociological theory. This is less true in the broader, interdisciplinary discourses of social, cultural, and political theory, where feminist theory is itself an important organizing theme and where it is in close relationship to other thematic clusters such as poststructuralism and postmodernism. Sociologists are, however, remarkably underrepresented in both feminist theory and these cognate discourses. Poststructuralists and postmodernists have played a crucial role in bringing themes of difference to the forefront, and this combined with the failure of mainstream sociological theory to take gender seriously perhaps accounts for some of the affinity many feminists feel for the poststructuralist and postmodernist currents. Unfortunately, however, these currents are in many cases refractory to sociology; they encourage analyses of culture and power shorn of serious attention to the constitution of social relationships and especially to problems of societal integration.

Taking the constitutive centrality of categorial differences seriously within a genuinely social theory offers the possibility of a kind of bridge across discourses in which not only does sociology stand to gain from taking gender seriously, but there is potential for a stronger notion of the social to be developed in feminist theory. This is why opening up the possibility of a sociology written from a feminist standpoint is of more than strategic interest, why it is not just a way of remedying an absence in conventional sociological theory but an attempt to remake uncritical theory as critical theory. As Dorothy Smith puts it, "It is not enough to supplement an established sociology by addressing ourselves to what has been left out or overlooked, or by making women's issues into sociological issues. That does not change the standpoint built into existing sociological procedures, but merely makes the sociology of women an addendum to the body of objectified knowledge."[12] Smith's point, rather, is to use the standpoint of women to reconstitute sociological inquiry as "a critique of socially organized practices of knowing."[13] Such a critique is, I think, deeply needed if sociology is to become truly adequate to the project of feminist theory. But, as I will suggest in chapter 6, there is some question about whether "the standpoint of women" is an adequate account of what makes feminist insights so pivotal, and about whether the experience of women can readily be claimed as a basis for knowledge without brooking a troubling essentialism. Whether standpoint theory is an unduly essentializing move or a way to recognize plurality and difference remains, in Charles Lemert's phrase, "the unsolved riddle of the standpoint."[14]

From Kant on, most critical theory has claimed, or at least aimed at, a standpoint of universal validity. This remains true of Habermas's theory of communicative action. But too often, the seemingly universal is the presentation of a partial view as though it were all encompassing.

Marx spoke in the "Theses on Feuerbach," for example, of the "this-sidedness" of all thought. He sought elsewhere to show how the seemingly universal categories of early liberal political thought in fact reflected bourgeois interests. The emancipation of man as citizen could never be more than partial, therefore, while man as laborer remained in chains. And if the term citizen implicitly meant property-owner even while it claimed a sort of universality, so did it also implicitly mean men. In many countries only men of European ancestry were included in the seemingly universal category. And though Enlightenment thought about citizenship treated nationality in universal terms, as something that everyone might have, this internationalism which was present at the birth of nationalism all too rapidly faded after Napoleon into a much more persistent invocation of the priority of certain identities at the expense of others. Socialism seemed at times the answer, but workers shooting each other from the trenches of World War One suggested that in and of itself, this answer was inadequate.

Ironically, it may even be the case that this very rhetoric of universality predisposed thinkers to use categorical terms – man, citizen, worker – in ways that obscured their own partiality and prejudice. The logic of market equivalents also encouraged a semblance of identity that made it hard and even made it seem dangerous to recognize difference. So difference became constituted as "other" to universality. The logic of "both/and," the possibility of recognizing simultaneously connection and distinction, was submerged. Advocates of difference became too often advocates of radical particularity, even while invoking universalistic rhetorics like the rights of national self-determination in support of their anti-universalist positions. The sharp opposition represented only a seeming clarity.

We should be equally cautious about treating the Enlightenment without complication as the era of universalism, succeeded then by a Romantic epoch of particularism. Neither era was so simple. Indeed, the Enlightenment and early modern social thought generally were shaped extraordinarily deeply by the confrontation with difference. The attempt to construct universal truths or norms followed from the rupture in unquestioned, "doxic" acceptance of traditions that constituted not multiple truths and commensurable values but simply Truth and Value.[15] This rupture was one made not merely by science or capitalism or industrialization, but by a whole congeries of factors that brought Europeans into new relationships across lines of difference. The Reformation and the later rise of deism and unbelief were crucial. Confrontations with difference were basic to the voyages of discovery and colonization, to the institution of slavery, to the expansion of interregional trade within what were to become nations, to the mobilization of citizen armies, and to the spread of printing and literacy. Ruptures in doxic assumptions and engagements across distances and differences brought the corresponding challenge of building relations recognizing both distinction and connection.

Today the sharp opposition of universalism and particularism has returned to the fore. Some writers, indeed, see the very possibility of a critical theory as impugned by the impossibility of a benign universalism. This issue is not of purely academic interest. In the final two chapters, I shall turn in more substantive form to the challenges posed by the "politics of identity." These involve the creation of collective movements that aim to reconcile personal positions in cultural and historical space with broader patterns of social organization. Feminism, the gay movement, and a range of racial, ethnic, and subcultural movements all figure prominently. Less commonly seen in this light but as important as any, I shall argue, is nationalism. All these movements and discourses reflect the extent to which the problems of critical theory and cultural difference extend beyond the abstract and academic to shape the immediate and practical.

Can critical theory reach beyond the purely particular yet remain sensitive to culture and difference? The present book is an attempt to think through this issue, and to think the possibility of a critical theory imprisoned by neither universalism nor particularism, speaking with some general moment and yet attending to difference. This is not a comprehensive review of critical theory nor a book about all the many and inherently specific forms – let alone contents – of cultural diversity. It is about the challenge such diversity poses to the task of critical social theory.

Notes

1   *Slaughterhouse Five*, p. 8.
2   Habermas, "Morality and Ethical Life," has recently noted the possible vulnerability but argued that discourse ethics is not much damaged by these criticisms.
3   Much of the French involvement with Hegel was based not on the original texts but on the powerful and more accessible readings of Hyppolyte and Kojève.
4   Megill, *Prophets of Extremity*, p. 187. Foucault's French title – *Histoire de la folie à l'âge classique* – evokes a bit more than this accurate English translation which loses the other senses of *folie*, folly and unreason generally, and both more and less than the published English title of *Madness and Civilization: A History of Insanity in the Age of Reason* – which is, in fact,

a very sharply abridged version of the French original, and one from which most of Foucault's structuralism has been expurgated.

5　Wiggershaus, *The Frankfurt School.*

6　See especially Habermas, *The Philosophical Discourse of Modernity.*

7　On the concept of social world, see Strauss, "A Social World Perspective." Aspects of this issue are discussed in several places in this book, but see especially chapter 2.

8　Several such reviews are available. Perhaps the best introductions in English are those of Martin Jay: *The Dialectical Imagination*, which is specifically on the Frankfurt School, and *Marxism and Totality*, which covers a broader range of thinkers with reference to one of the core ideas that has inhibited attention to difference. For a more detailed, indeed monumental, study of the Frankfurt founders of political theory, see Wiggerhaus's translated *The Frankfurt School.* One crucial dimension of critical theory which I do not take up in this book is political economy, including the role of technology in transforming the modern world and especially the role of capitalism in constituting it.

9　I draw both the quotation from Young's "Is Male Gender Identity the Cause of Male Domination," and much of the criticism of the privileging of the symbolic over the social in some recent feminist theory from Flax, *Thinking Fragments*, pp. 180–1.

10　By the Frankfurt School, I refer to the extraordinary cluster of scholars brought together at the Institute for Social Research in the 1930s under the direction of Max Horkheimer. The earliest members of the ISR under Carl Grünberg did focus largely on empirical research into the history of socialism and the labor movement.

11　Giddens (*Transformation of Intimacy*) and Luhmann (*Love as Passion*) have each written on love and sexuality, topics that bring sexual difference to their attention, but neither makes the category of gender basic to his more general social theory.

12　Smith, *Conceptual Practices*, p. 13.

13　Ibid., p. 12.

14　Lemert, "Subjectivity's Limit."

15　See Arendt, *Between Past and Future*, ch 1; see also Habermas, *Philosophical Discourse*, on Hegel's reconstruction of these "diremptions" as the organizing problem of modernity, which his philosophy sought to overcome.

1

Rethinking Critical Theory

I

A philistine has been defined as "someone who is content to live in a wholly unexplored world."[1] The philistine is not necessarily passive, for he or she may be quite actively engaged in making objects or gaining position in the world, but the philistine is unreflective, primarily utilitarian in orientation. The Biblical association suggests an enemy superior in numbers and into whose hands one might fall, and Hannah Arendt tells us that the term was first used in its modern sense to distinguish between town and gown in the student slang of German university towns.[2] But if this reproach was initially just intellectual snobbery (combined perhaps with genuine fear of attack), the notion of the philistine took on more subtle colorings as nonintellectuals began to manifest a substantial interest in "culture," particularly as part of the construction of a new form of elite status.[3] Nonacademic interest in the life of the mind and even in matters of culture more generally has been intermittent and uneven.

The fear that cultural objects and intellectual products would be reduced to mere use values or commodities through an insensitive appropriation by those outside universities has proved exaggerated. But at the same time, a certain philistinism has grown within universities themselves. Not only is academic life far from exclusively a life of the mind, the use of cultural objects (e.g. publications) as means of professional advancement exerts a distorting, perhaps even transformative effect. I do not mean to point to the crassness of this new philistinism, but to the way in which it undermines critical thought. To the extent that cultural production is remade into the means of accumulating a kind of academic-professional capital, cultural producers are encouraged to accept commonplace understandings of the world. To challenge these too deeply would be to court detachment from those whose "purchase" of their products enables them to accumulate capital.[4] The point, thus, is not that intellectuals lie to serve illegitimate masters, which they seem no more likely to do under contemporary conditions than at other times, but that in the spirit of professionalism they betray the calling truly and openly to explore the world.

Despite recurrent disappointments, one wants to hope that a social scientist could never in this sense be a philistine. Indeed, at some level all social scientists, like all novelists and a great many others, are engaged in exploring the world. Yet for most of us, and for social scientists more than novelists, our explorations are limited by the boundaries of the known world of convention. We discover new facts, to be sure, but they are already tamed within schemes of knowledge that we take as self-evident and beyond question. One of the enduring challenges for social science is to go beyond the affirmation and reconstitution of the familiar world to recognize other possibilities. New perspectives, new theories, and new empirical information all can enable us to see how things can be different from the ways they first present themselves to us, and how things even could be different from the ways they are. Seizing such possibilities, however, means rejecting the notion that either we must accept nearly everything as it is or we must enter into a radical disorganization of reality in which we can claim no bearings to guide us.[5]

Not just research but everyday life can be the source of challenges to complacency in our views of the world. Our ordinary relations with other people provide us with occasions for seeing the world from different angles and thinking it in different rhetorics. Our practical projects – even the project of growing up – confront us not only with the need for some continuous sense of identity but with the multiplicity of the world and of ourselves as creatures of that world. Not least of all, as creatures who exist fully only in our relations with others, we can never see our identities altogether directly; they inhere in the many-sided relations of our lives and actions to those of others. As Arendt suggested, the "who" of each person "which appears so clearly and unmistakably to others, remains hidden from the person himself, like the *daimon* in Greek religion which accompanies each man throughout his life, always looking over his shoulder from behind and thus visible only to those he encounters."[6]

So too, neither intellectual nor cultural traditions exist in such autonomous and self-contained fashions as are sometimes suggested; they are not knowable simply through internal reflection. "Cultural diversity" has recently become a hot academic topic, and "multiculturalism" has been discovered as though it was something altogether new in practical affairs.

Yet recurrent, sometimes everyday, dealings with cultural diversity have been common in human history, especially where that history has been marked by long-distance trade, cities, empires, and the great, literate religious traditions. It is the nationalist ideal of cultural homogeneity that is modern, a reflection of new forms of public life and new ideologies of solidarity.

Yet it is not easy to reach across these traditions and modes of understanding to grasp the relationship between our own thought or that of others, and it is especially hard to do so within the modality of theory. The modern venture of social theory – concerned since its origins in Machiavelli, Vico, and Hobbes critically to engage practical affairs – adopted at first a universalistic voice. However immediate and local theorists' inductions and concerns, they sought to speak to the general human condition. But with increasing emphasis, many recognized the challenges both historical changes and cross-cultural diversity posed for the unitary construct of the human condition.

II

Most social science is description of the familiar social world with slightly differing contexts and particulars – like romance novels that rehearse fairly standard plots in new settings and with new characters. We industriously accumulate facts, test them to be sure of their solidity, sort them into identifiable patterns.[7] For the most part this sorting is limited to taxonomy, rather like pre-Darwinian orderings of the biological universe in terms of phenotypic characteristics. Only occasionally do we systematize in a more theoretical way, one that argues for an underlying order that cannot be found in any of the surface characteristics of its objects. Nothing presses this theoretical venture on us more firmly than the experience of historical change and cross-cultural diversity.

Theory, in this sense, lies never in the facts themselves, not even those that demonstrate the statistical connection between various occurrences. In his distinction of mere correlation from true causality, Hume showed – almost despite himself, or to Kant rather than to himself – the essential place of theory and the limits of empiricism as a source of certain knowledge. At the same time he suggested the indeterminacy of theory, the impossibility of ever arriving at definite proofs based on empirical evidence. Hume turned away from theory to history as a guide for human understanding and action. Theory, after all, is not the only way to provide orientation to action; language and everyday culture provide us with enormous classificatory abilities, though as we move into analysis we become at least implicitly a bit theoretical. This is commonly equated with causal reasoning, but our idea of theory needs to make room also for the reasoning involved in narratives. Narratives need not be simply statements of progression or sequence. They can also be accounts of how prior events or actions limit and orient subsequent ones. Analysts can theorize variation of "plot" structures without introducing notions of causality *per se*.[8] Theory is important as the systematic examination and construction of knowledge – in the case of social theory, knowledge about social life. This may be causal or narrative in form, with each form suggesting different approaches to generalization and specification. While causal reasoning may be applied to discrete events, it is more commonly used in social science to refer to classes of phenomena, treated as internally equivalent, that influence other classes of similarly equivalent phenomena (an instance of x can be expected to produce or increase y in the absence of intervening factors). Narrative, conversely, is often described as inherently particularizing but (1) the particularities may be global (as in narratives of world history), and (2) comparisons among narratives facilitate a form of general, cross-situational knowledge.

The world that social theorists seek to understand is not just empirical, constituted of facts and propositions; it is the world also of phenomenological experience, reflective judgment, and practical action. Recognizing this makes more difficult, but perhaps more interesting, the key challenge theorists have faced ever since Hume: to develop systematic ways of understanding the world that are true to that world as the object of experience and action as well as of observation, that recognize the place of other subjects in that world, and that are rigorous yet recognize their own embeddedness in history.

This suggests that some common conceptions of theory are misleading. It is a mistake in particular to imagine that theory is altogether abstract while empirical knowledge is somehow perfectly concrete. This is wrong on both counts.

First, social science theories are always partly inductive, they depend on at least some information about how the world works and also on an orientation to the world induced from the culture and experience of the theorists (but usually left inexplicit). More than this, many of the best theories are "empirically rich." That is, they are compilations not solely of formal propositions or abstract speculations but of concrete explanations and narratives. They work very largely by empirical analogies, statements of similarity and contrast, rather than law-like universal statements.[9] The extent to which the most compelling theories are richly, densely empirical can be seen easily by a quick reflection on the theories that have proved most enduringly influential – those, for example, of Marx, Weber, Durkheim, and Freud.

Second, the idea of a theory-free, totally concrete empirical sociology is equally misleading. Even when empirical researchers leave their theoretical orientations completely inexplicit, and claim – like Sherlock Holmes – to be working with "nothing but the facts," they rely on concepts, ideas about causality, and understandings of where to look for empirical relationships that cannot be derived entirely from this realm of facts, and that are necessary to constitute both facts and explanations. One of the major jobs of theoretical sociology is to make explicit, orderly, consistent – and open to critical analysis – these "orientations" that are usually taken for granted by empirical researchers.

Perhaps it is useful to clarify the ways in which the term "theory" is used by sociologists – and indeed by social scientists generally – in order to see why our habitual ways of thinking about theory sometimes obscure understanding both of what is going on in academic science and how theory is important in the public sphere. First, "theory" is sometimes understood in a strongly empiricist fashion to refer to an orderly system of tested propositions. In such a usage of theory, the main elements are (1) potentially generalizable propositions, and (2) scope statements about where they do and do not fit. Generality and cumulation are key goals of theory thus conceived. This is often called positivism, by both critics and proponents, but that is really a misnomer. The "positivism" label comes from the scientism of early French social theorists like Comte, and Hegel's critique of "mere positivity" – seeing the surface existence of the world but not its internal tensions. The Frankfurt theorists, especially Horkheimer and Adorno, combined their appropriation of Hegel's dialectics (stressing the role of "determinate negation") with their critique of both social science empiricism and the philosophy of the Vienna Circle (which called its work "logical positivism").[10]

Logical positivism was far from a summation of tested propositions. It turned on the search for consistency and the power of logical (usually quite formal) expression, not just empirical generalization. Many logical positivists were (and are) interested in the theories of physics and mathematics, which are hardly empirical generalizations. The theory of relativity, for example, yields some testable propositions, but achieved recognition as a "beautiful" and powerful theory before very many of its key propositions could be tested. As Karl Popper, though only ambiguously part of the positivist grouping, summed up in a neat phrase, scientists should be interested in "conjectures and refutations," not mere generalizations.[11] This leads, then, to the second sense of "theory," a logically integrated causal explanation. It is only for this second sort of theory that criteria of praise like parsimony or power or completeness become relevant.

Finally, there is a third sense of theory, one Robert Merton tried to distinguish from the first two.[12] He called this third sort theoretical orientations or perspectives, rather than theories. He meant, I think, something like approaches to solving problems and developing explanations rather than the solutions and explanations themselves. While Talcott Parsons tried to consolidate functionalism as an integrated general theory, thus, Merton's own use of functionalism in middle-range theories was as an orienting perspective; so too has been most use of the broad traditions associated with Max Weber or Karl Marx. During the last thirty years, however, we have become aware that this third sense of theory cannot be kept altogether in the background of the first two. This is so for two reasons. First, we realize that the language our so-called theoretical perspectives provide for talking about various issues is itself dependent on theories. In other words, if we say that we think power and conflict play a larger role than functional integration in establishing social order, we presume understandings of what social order is that can only be achieved on the basis of some level of theorization, and which may not be the same as other understandings. Second, and for partly similar reasons, most of what we take to be the "facts" of social science, and indeed the criteria for evaluating both facts and explanations, are themselves constituted in part through theory. Theory does not only follow from and attempt to explain an inductively pre-given world of empirical observations, theory enables us to make observations and thus convert sensory impressions into understandings we can appropriate as facts. Theories thus offer us ways to think about the empirical world, ways to make observations, and ways to formulate tests, not just ways to explain the results of the tests and the correlations among the empirical observations.

Each of these three widespread senses of theory offers us insight into the ways sociological theory informs both scientific research and public life and practical action outside academia. Theoretical writings offer repositories and syntheses of empirical knowledge; they offer explanations, and they offer methods for thinking up new explanations. But this makes things seem too simple, and it obscures the potentially transformative role of theory in both academic sociology and public life. The three conventional ideas about how theory works, to put this another way, assume that all science is normal science in Kuhn's sense.[13] They leave no room for revolutionary science or even for smaller challenges to paradigms that we might not want to claim are revolutionary even though they bring significant changes to the way we see the world.

Consider, for example, the empiricist notion of theory I listed first. This rightly grasps the extent to which theory needs to be rich with empirical knowledge, but misleadingly presents empirical knowledge as though it could be simply an orderly summation of tested propositions. In the first place, this involves imagining that the empirical propositions can be constructed in ways that do not depend on theoretical (or metatheoretical) assumptions, that are not embedded within particular theoretical orientations and thus sometimes difficult to translate across theoretical discourses. More basically, this understanding fails to leave room for anomalies and lacunae that structure our knowledge alongside tested certainties and that perhaps do much more to drive knowledge forward. And last but not least, it misses the extent to which the best theories are not simply assemblages of propositions but analogical constructs comparing, contrasting, and identifying similarities among cases of various sorts, including narratives.

Even when we speak with more sophistication of theory as explanation and methods for constructing explanations, we fail to do justice to the role of theory in *constituting* our very access to the social world, including the facts about which we theorize and the practical actions through which we test propositions and understanding. Theoretical ideas – like for example the ideas of democracy or class – also become part of the world we study, changing it so that we are never able to achieve the complete closure envisaged by our conventional textbook notions of theoretical cumulation or the relationship between theory and research. And especially with regard to the relationship of social theory to the public sphere, but also in relation to the most academic science, we need to recognize that our theoretical innovations respond to problems in our efforts to achieve understanding or to offer normative guidance, but that in fixing one set of problems they may create new ones, or new ones may emerge as the social world changes. We do not move simply from false propositions to true ones; for the most part, we move from less adequate accounts to more adequate accounts, with our criteria of adequacy always shaped in part by the practical problems that command our attention.[14] Weber's and Durkheim's theories, thus, cannot be compared simply on the criterion of truth, as though with some imaginable data we could decide that one is right and the other wrong. Rather, they are best compared in terms of their potential usefulness for achieving different kinds of understandings or understandings of different issues.[15]

In this connection, one of the most important roles of theory lies in enabling us to ask new and different sorts of questions. A host of important questions arise from Marx's theories, for example, that would not arise from those of either Durkheim or Weber. Marxist theory urges us to study to what extent interests rooted in material relations of production shape people's identities and actions, and whether recognition of such interests makes for an international class consciousness strong enough to triumph over nationalism. We may learn more from Marx's questions in some cases than from his answers. Moreover, theories enable us to ask questions that didn't occur to the originating theorists themselves – as for example Marx's theory of alienation produced such insistent questioning of the conditions of communist societies that allegedly marxist governments attempted to suppress its use.

But the fact that theories enable us to ask new questions is not just a sign that our knowledge grows progressively better. It is, rather, a result of the many possible vantage points that one might achieve in consideration of a single set of social phenomena. Theories remain multiple not because we are confused or have not yet reached correct scientific understanding of the problems before us, but because all problems – like all people – can be seen in different ways. Or put another way, it is generally not possible to ask all the interesting questions about any really significant phenomenon within the same theory or even within a set of commensurable, logically integratable, theories. Noting this was one of the breakthroughs of modern physics, linked to the theory of relativity. As Heisenberg remarked:

> The most important new result of nuclear physics was the recognition of the possibility of applying quite different types of natural laws, without contradiction, to one and the same physical event. This is due to the fact that within a system of laws which are based on certain fundamental ideas only certain quite definite ways of asking questions make sense, and thus, that such a system is separated from others which allow different questions to be put.[16]

For this reason, we cannot expect theoretical cumulation to result in the development of *the* single, completely adequate theory. The field of sociological theory necessarily – and indeed happily – will remain a field of dialogue among multiple theories, each offering aspects of truth and none of them commanding truth entirely. This means also that theory needs to be seen crucially through its role in the process of interpretation, and that its empirical content is often best deployed not as universal truths or law-like generalizations but as analogies, contrasts, and comparisons.

III

To combat the cosy contentment of the philistine (or positivist-empiricist cousins), critical social theory makes the very givenness of the world the object of exploration and analysis. This suggests another reason why theory has a complex relationship to facts. It cannot merely summarize them, or be neatly tested by them, since theory of some sort is always essential to the constitution of those facts. Theory is not only a guide to action in the way in which engineering principles guide the construction of bridges. It is an aid in thinking through changed circumstances and new possibilities. It helps practical actors deal with social change by helping them see beyond the immediacy of what *is* at any particular moment to conceptualize something of what could be. This is not only true of utopian or other normative theorizing, though the same capacity facilitates normative theorizing. Rather, this is a crucial analytic ability that shows the limits of sheer empiricism.

The point is conceptualized differently but equally clearly by dialectical theorists following Hegel and by theorists in the structuralist movement emanating from the work of the linguist Ferdinand de Saussure. For the former, the key is the tensions and contradictions that underpin existing reality and point both to its situation in a larger historical reality and to the possibilities of its transcendence. For the latter, the key is to be able to see an underlying pattern of causes and constraints, not merely the more contingent surface pattern of actual occurrences. Actual occurrences always reflect elements of chance and arbitrariness, and thus are imperfect guides to the underlying structure of possibilities. This is why empirical knowledge needs to be complemented with theory and why theory cannot be a mere summation of empirical knowledge. Social scientists are familiar with the difference between an anecdote and a statistical pattern – and sometimes frustrated with students, colleagues, and politicians who insist on thinking in terms of particular cases rather than overall patterns and probabilities. But even a well-constructed statistical sample does not necessarily reach to underlying causality; it simply represents accurately the empirical pattern at one point in time. Causality always depends on inference that goes beyond the "facts" or numbers themselves. And in the deeper, theoretical sense, it depends on recognizing that the facts could have been otherwise.

The old contrast between idiographic (particularistic or singular) and nomothetic (generalized or typified) reasoning doesn't quite capture this point. It grasps, accurately, the extent to which typical history writing gives the story of a chain of particular events that lead to a singular result. History, thus, is the story of what has happened. We seek in addition, however, an account of what *could* have happened because this is crucial information for consideration of our current decisions. But nomothetic reasoning doesn't offer this either. It offers – at least in most versions and in the terms of the *Methodenstreit* – a generalization of the many specific cases of what has happened.[17] An additional step beyond mere generalization is involved in the move from empirical history to theory. It is said of generals that, based on experience, they are always preparing to fight the *last* war. One of the roles of theory is to enable us to recognize in what ways our future wars may be different.

None of the complexity in the relationship of theory to facts should be taken as license to make theory less empirically rich. Reaching to underlying causality is not simply a matter of abstraction. Moreover, if theory is not constantly opened to revision in the light of empirical inquiry, it is likely to become brittle, or to fall into disuse, or to become simply a repository of ideology. But the same is true not only of empirical investigation as organized by social science, but of experience and practical action which are also sources of the inductive content, meaning, and flexibility of social theory. Using theory to challenge the givenness of the social world and to enable researchers to see new problems and new facts in that world requires recognizing that knowledge is a historical product and always at least potentially a medium of historically significant action.

Since to theorize is to open up vistas of understanding, it can never be altogether neutral; it is necessarily perspectival. This obligates the theorist to take seriously both the historical sources of her/his theory and its orientation to the future. Arendt invoked a parable from Kafka to describe this necessary situation of theory – indeed of thinking – in a tension between past and future. It posits an individual:

> He has two antagonists: the first presses him from behind, from the origin. The second blocks the road ahead. He gives battle to both. To be sure, the first supports him in his fight with the second, for he wants to push him forward, and in the same way the second supports him in his fight with the first, since he drives him back. But it is only theoretically so. For it is not only the two antagonists who are there, but he himself as well, and who really knows his intentions? His dream, though, is that some time in an unguarded moment – and this would require a night darker than any night has ever been yet – he will jump out of the fighting line and be promoted, on account of his experience in fighting, to the position of umpire over his antagonists in their fight with each other.[18]

The protagonist gains his specific and determinate identity from his position in this conflict. The dream of being promoted to umpire over it is a somewhat dangerous one to which many thinkers have succumbed, the dream that theory can be set apart from both a retrospective analysis of the past – including its own past – and from a prospective engagement with the future. It is not surprising that theorists should have this dream, this hope of achieving perfect knowledge, but it is crucial that they should resist it. To leave the field of struggle for the umpire's chair is to try to adopt the Cartesian view from nowhere. Instead of a triumph of reason, this is simply a misrecognition. Instead of knowledge free from biased origins and undistorted by any practical purposes, it offers knowledge that cannot understand its origins or take responsibility for its effects.

A great deal of even very good social theory is produced and presented as though written from the umpire's chair. Its failure to take seriously both its own historical conditions of production and its implications as a practical action not only annoy those who call for more critical theory, but contribute to the frequent disappointments of traditional, mainstream or positivist theorists who expect a kind of straightforward cumulation in social science knowledge. Philosophical self-understandings rooted in empiricism or other metatheories of the sort loosely termed positivist actually lead many social theorists to keep bad faith with their own genuine accomplishments. Placing their hopes in the "discovery" of timeless and perspectiveless truths, they watch helplessly – or sometimes in bad humor lash out defensively and destructively – as their truths are overtaken by others. They are unable to appreciate the importance of their own work as more time-bound contributions to a process of practical reason rather than pure knowledge, to a conversation in which the construction of new understandings is continual. It is as though they identify only with the Socrates of the later dialogues (or the Plato of the non-dialogic writings) who insists on dominating the whole discussion and stating the whole truth; they don't see the virtue of Socrates' greater modesty in the early dialogues when his voice is only one, however brilliant, among several, each of which speaks aspects of the truth and alters the implications of what the others have to say.[19]

As this metaphor suggests, the issue is not only historical change but the multiplicity of voices, the differences among an indefinite range of different subject-positions and subjective identities. The very fact of natality, as Arendt called the unceasing renewal of the human world through the production of beings both mortal and unique, means that each child comes into the world as the potential source of radical novelty. In the common – but never fully common – world of human history, this is also the beginning of cultural diversity, though this flourishes only with the transmission of new ideas that allows some of them to become traditions.

Since so much theory seeks the umpire's chair, it seems useful to have a special term for theory that is self-conscious about its historicity, its place in dialogue and among cultures, its irreducibility to facts, and its engagement in the practical world. Deferring to Kant and a long tradition, not just to Horkheimer and Adorno, we can call it critical theory.

Kant firmly placed his philosophy in contrast both to Hume's skepticism and to the dogmatic rationalism of Leibniz. It was as untenable to reject the project of increasingly secure understanding and theoretical knowledge as to imagine it settled prematurely. Instead, Kant sought as systematically as he could to explore the limits as well as the grounds of different forms of reason, knowledge, and understanding, taking seriously not only pure reason but practical reason and aesthetic judgment. Kant was perhaps not fully successful in his quest, and indeed underestimated the extent to which his theory, like all others, was embedded in rather than able to leap beyond or beneath history and culture. Hegel sought to historicize – and socialize – Kant in one way; Durkheim in another. In our own day, it is no accident that both Pierre Bourdieu (in "The Categories of Professorial Judgement, or The Conflict of the Faculties") and Michel Foucault (in "What Is Enlightenment?") should have chosen to evoke Kant in their titles as well as aspects of their thought.[20] And in his more recent work especially, Jürgen Habermas appears increasingly as a neo-Kantian ethicist.

Kant is a useful figure to remind us also of the error involved in drawing oversharp boundaries between the Enlightenment and the Romantic movement (or the modern and the postmodern). Kant, who helped to name as well as complete the Enlightenment, admired no one more than Rousseau, whose bust he kept on his desk. Yet of all eighteenth-century thinkers, Rousseau most anticipated Romanticism. In an era when self-declared postmodernists scourge the Enlightenment as the foundation of a repressive modern consciousness, it is worth remembering that in their day, the philosophes were as surely the enemies of philistine complacency as the Romantics were a generation or two later. And if critical theory has as its focus the exploration of the social world beyond the dimensions which can be taken for granted as part of the contemporary consciousness of any era, then it must be a broad enough house to welcome – albeit not uncritically – the descendants of Romantics and Enlighteners alike, while avoiding both utter skepticism with its suggestion that we have no sources of intellectual security but tradition, and dogmatism with its affirmation of the positivity of the intuited world.

At the same time, while Kant was not a Cartesian subjective rationalist, content with a "view from nowhere," neither was he fully attentive to the importance of cultural and interpersonal difference in the constitution of understanding. Arendt, keen to see the maximal interest in human plurality in Kant, did rightly detect an opening to this concern in paragraph 40 of the Third Critique in which Kant considers the nature of the *sensus communis* that makes possible our shared capacity for judgment.

But it is a minimal opening. Kant explores what it means to have a broad rather than a narrow mind. This involves seeing things from the standpoint of others, but as a method of achieving universality rather than multiplicity of perspective:

> a man with a *broadened way of thinking* . . . overrides the private subjec-
> tive conditions of his judgment, into which so many others are locked, as
> it were, and reflects on his own judgment from a *universal standpoint*
> (which he can determine only by transferring himself to the standpoint of
> others).[21]

Ultimately, the test of this broadness lies in the capacity to make judgments "universally communicable."[22] Though Kant thus recognizes the existence of multiple standpoints, he in no way sees these as impeding or challenging the goal of universality. Though this section of the Third Critique was crucial for Arendt's consideration of Kant's political philosophy, in many ways it seems to evoke Habermas with his concern for universality and communication more than Arendt with her focus on plurality and action.[23] Arendt's own interest in plurality, in any case, is an interest in the distinctiveness of individual human beings as a crucial, defining attribute of the human condition, not in the differences among cultures. The implications of the matter of plurality, the multiplicity and difference of human individuals and cultures, remain central, and pose a critical challenge to critical theory.

IV

The idea of critique is obviously an old one in philosophy, but also a hard one to pin down. In many usages it stands on the side of "analysis" against "substance," on the side of discovering our limits rather than affirming our possibilities. I appropriate the term, however, not so much as to open these old discourses as to evoke and at the same time broaden a more recent one. Critical theory was the name chosen by the founders of the Frankfurt School in the period between two world wars to symbolize their attempt to achieve a unity of theory and practice, including a unity of theory with empirical research and both with an historically grounded awareness of the social, political, and cultural problems of the age. The attempt held an attractive promise, and remains important, but it also ran into problems that proved insurmountable, at least for those who initially undertook it.

Key figures in the first generation of the Frankfurt School included Max Horkheimer, the charismatic leader and academic entrepreneur who held the group together to the extent anyone did, Theodor Adorno, Herbert Marcuse, Friedrich Pollock, Franz Neumann, Leo Lowenthal, Erich Fromm, and – sometimes at arms length – Walter Benjamin. The prominence of these figures within the group waxed and waned, and some eventually severed ties completely. Other significant scholars were also linked in various ways to the core Frankfurt group, both in Germany and through its years of exile in America: Moses Finley, Alexander Mitcherlich, Paul Lazarsfeld, Karl Korsch. Aside from the endowment by which Felix Weil and his father created the Institute for Social Research, the group was held together by loyalty to Horkheimer and interest in a project that would bridge philosophy and the emerging human sciences.

The thought of the Frankfurt group combined influences from many quarters, including marxism, psychoanalysis, German idealist philosophy and theology, the Romantics, Nietzsche, and the nascent discipline of sociology. As Horkheimer suggested, they wanted to distinguish critical theory from the sort of "traditional theory" that accepted the self-definition of the familiar and failed to look more deeply at how the categories of our consciousness were shaped and how they in turn constituted both the world we saw and what we took to be possible.[24] In this sense, it is useful to recall that theology was among the important influences in their background, and to note how it too analyzed the existing world as the "proto-history" of a possibly better world to come, and as the surface reflection of contradictory underlying forces. But above all, the idea of critical theory as a distinctive project, and a project that would distinctively combine traditionally abstract and universal philosophy with historically concrete and empirical knowledge of the social world is rooted in Hegel and in the responses to Hegel begun by the "Young Hegelians," Marx and Kierkegaard.

It was Hegel, most specifically, who conceived of a "dialectic of enlightenment" in which reason that had turned against enlightenment might be deployed to redeem the potential of enlightenment. His philosophical project turned on achieving a reconciliation of internally contradictory modern life – as Habermas reminds us, "Hegel was the first philosopher to develop a clear concept of modernity."[25] This encompassing reconciliation included several more specific aspects of reconciliation: among the competing sorts of reason, among the fragmented pieces of the social whole, and among the disconnected moments of individual identities. In Hegel's terms, modernity was constituted by several "diremptions" in what had been whole; there was no attractive way to go back to previous unity, and therefore one must move forward to create out of the conditions of the historical present a new kind of social totality.

Working through the dialectic of enlightenment, then, was a way to try to achieve a capacity to make sense of and potentially bring transformation (or unification) to the modern age. Central to this modern age, for Hegel, were a subjectivity which he conceived both on the plane of individual freedom and on that of the singular subjectivity of the ideal social totality, and a critical awareness based on the tensions and contradictions introduced into social life and consciousness by the basic diremptions. Although reason helped to produce these diremptions through Renaissance, Reformation, and Enlightenment (and implicitly through enabling the revolutions of increased material productivity as well), reason remained the necessary way out. It was reason that could transform the mere longing for previous unity into a recognition of all the basic changes that had severed people from each other and reason which could lead these alienated people to see how the nature of each was denied in the split-off existence of the other. The young Hegel approached this in a way close to that of later critical theory, seeking a resolution that would combine freedom with societal integration, and one rooted in a sort of intersubjectivity rather than a philosophy of the subject as such.[26] But the mature Hegel accepted the necessity of one crucial social division – the differentiation of state and society. Granting the state a kind of higher level subjective rationality, he at the same time gave up the capacity for radical critique of existing conditions.

A number of other thinkers tried in various ways to recover the capacity for critique within schemes of thought influenced by Hegel. Karl Marx was undoubtedly the most important. Marx's critique of political economy followed the basic design of approaching the future through a history of the present which took the concrete specificity of its categories seriously – indeed, he did this more consistently than Hegel.[27] Marx shared with the young Hegel an attempt to conceptualize the absolute creativity of the human being through the example of art, but unlike Hegel he extended this into a more general analysis of labor. This is not the place to try to work out the nature or implications of Marx's analysis. The crucial connection to the tradition of critical theory came through Marx's defetishizing critique (developed especially in chapter 1 of *Capital*) of the way in which the historically specific and humanly created categories of capital – labor, commodity, value – came to appear as quasi-natural, and indeed to dominate over the apparently more contingent quality of human life. The reified categories of capital transform qualitatively differentiated human activity into oppressive uniformities and identities. This is the crucial basis for Lukacs' early-twentieth-century extension of Marx's critique, one which placed the emphasis more firmly on overcoming reification and which relied more consistently on aesthetic criteria for establishing what non-reified life could be like.[28]

The Frankfurt School pioneers drew on this line of critical theory, and retained the central reliance on aesthetics. To this they coupled Max Weber's analysis of bureaucracy as the completion of instrumental rationality. This aroused in them a fear of a totally administered society in which the very disunity and alienation that Hegel and Marx thought must lead to the transcendence of modern society would instead be stabilized. "What is new about the phase of mass culture compared with the late liberal stage is the exclusion of the new."[29] At the same time, Horkheimer and Adorno linked the notion of dialectical critique to a more positive appreciation of non-identity, not just as the tension in every subject's relation to itself, but as the source of creativity and autonomous existence for the human individual.

At both the level of theory and the level of biographical motivation, the Frankfurt theorists were deeply concerned that transcendence of alienated society not mean the fixation of the individual as mere moment of an administered totality. "The perfect similarity is the absolute difference. The identity of the category forbids that of the individual cases. . . . Now any person signifies only those attributes by which he can replace everybody else: he is interchangeable, a copy. As an individual he is completely expendable and utterly insignificant."[30] They challenged the traditional philosophy of individual consciousness, the reliance on the presumed absolute identity of the individual as knower embodied famously in the Cartesian cogito ("I think, therefore I am"). Influenced by Freud, Romanticism, and thinkers of the "dark side" of Enlightenment like Nietzsche and Sade, they knew the individual person had to be more complex than that, especially if he or she was to be the subject of creative culture. They also saw the individual as social in a way most ordinary theory did not, constituted by intersubjective relations with others, all the more important where they furthered a sense of non-identity, of the complexity of multiple involvements with others, that enabled a person to reach beyond narrow self-identity. They challenged the idea that works of art or literature should be interpreted in terms of seamless singularity of purpose or smooth fit with the patterns of an age, seeking instead tensions and projects that pushed beyond the immediately manifest. They challenged what they took to be the increasing and increasingly enforced sameness of modern society – both a conformism among its members and a difficulty in bringing underlying tensions, even contradictions, to public attention and action. They challenged recourse to ideas of human nature that were unmediated by understandings of what was specific to an era – above all the modern capitalist era – and to different pasts and social positions.

Most of the early key Frankfurt theorists were Jews. If this did not produce an acute enough interest in the politics of identity to start with – most of them coming from highly assimilated families and assimilating further themselves in the course of their studies – the rise of Nazism and broader anti-Semitic currents brought the issue home. Faced with the question why Jews were not just one minority group among many – for the Nazis certainly but also for most of modernity – Horkheimer and Adorno sought the answer in a characteristic way. Anti-Semitism represented the hatred of those who saw themselves as civilized, but could not fulfill the promises of civilization for all those who reminded them of the failures of civilization. "Those who spasmodically dominate nature see in a tormented nature a provocative image of powerless happiness. The thought of happiness without power is unbearable because it would then be true happiness."[31] Jews, like women, were at once "overcivilized" and recalled a closeness to nature that preceded civilization. The logical rules of noncontradiction did not apply because the image of the Jew was formed not in simple observation but in paranoid projection. And what distinguished Jews as a minority from women, blacks, aboriginals, gypsies and so on was the combination of the radical otherness of the Jewish God, unmediated by a son become human, with the pervasive images of Jewish intellectuality and Jewish involvement in the "dirty" work of capitalism. Jews were seen not only as personally weak and putatively close to nature, but as illegitimately socially strong, situated in the universities and banks, gifted in abstraction and in finance.[32] It was crucial that they be reduced to radical weakness, even destroyed, so that they would no longer bear implicit witness to the idea that the present civilization was both imperfect and impure.

The account was characteristic not only in its philosophical universality – the issue of anti-Semitism turns out to be the issue of the relationship between mind and nature – but in the extent to which a failure to conform becomes the source of persecution. This rang true existentially for the Frankfurt School founders, all of whom felt themselves to be in one way or another nonconformists and who remained deeply committed to ideas of individual distinctiveness, autonomy, and creativity. At the same time, this account of the Jews suggested to theorists who in the late 1930s and 1940s were still, in a sense, disappointed historical materialists, why "thinking from the standpoint of the Jews"

might offer the sort of radical insight into the totality of modern civilization Lukacs had earlier associated with thinking from the standpoint of
the proletariat.

This was by no means at odds with a materialist position. Human
nature meant the pursuit of happiness, the need for solidarity with
others, and natural sympathies. From human nature in this sense ema-
nated, according to Horkheimer, a form of reason implicitly critical of
civilization. Marcuse would perhaps extend this line of argument most
substantially by analyzing modern society in terms of the excess repression it required of its members. Capitalism and the instrumentally rational state posed demands against eros, against nature, that went
beyond what Freud had theorized as general.[33]

The existence of such tensions made possible a critical theory that
sought to expose them. But critical theory was (and is) more than that
effort at exposure. It is an effort to show that such tensions are present
not only between civilization and nature (human or external), but that
they appear also as contradictions internal to civilization and its specific
cultural products (e.g. philosophies). Indeed, basic to critical theory is the
argument that a kind of non-identity, a tension with itself, is built into
social organization and culture. One cannot have grasped the sources of
events and dynamism without grasping this underlying level of contradictions and differences.

Such a view was and is predictably anathema to those who demand a
straightforward empiricism or the kind of theory-testing envisaged by
logical positivism. As Horkheimer wrote in 1936:

> "The view that thought is a means of knowing more about the world than
> may be directly observed . . . seems to us entirely mysterious" is the convic-
> tion expressed in a work of the Vienna Circle. This principle is particularly
> significant in a world whose magnificent exterior radiates complete unity
> and order while panic and distress prevail beneath. Autocrats, cruel colo-
> nial governors, and sadistic prison wardens have always wished for visitors
> with this positivistic mentality.[34]

We are familiar with "traditional," non-critical theory not just from the
past but from most contemporary "positivist" and "empiricist" accounts
of the accumulation of knowledge and even from those hermeneutic
accounts that make a sharp fact/value distinction and maintain faith in
the notion that intellectuals can be set apart from or even above the
ordinary workings of society. What Horkheimer called traditional theory
was a broad category including much of the Kantian tradition as well as
more empiricist social science. What distinguished these many sorts of

work from critical theory was the conception that theory – and science generally – should somehow be understood as a thing apart from the rest of social practice, the province of a group of free-floating intellectuals as Mannheim saw it or simply the province of the individual knower in the tradition of Descartes and Kant.

"The traditional idea of theory," Horkheimer wrote, "is based on scientific activity as carried on within the division of labor at a particular stage in the latter's development. It corresponds to the activity of the scholar which takes place alongside all the other activities of a society but in no immediately clear connection with them. In this view of theory, therefore, the real social function of science is not made manifest; it speaks not of what theory means in human life, but only of what it means in the isolated sphere in which for historical reasons it comes into existence."[35] This view of theory is linked not only to social irresponsibility but to a misleading, if flattering, self-image for theorists. "The latter believe they are acting according to personal determinations, whereas in fact even in their most complicated calculations they but exemplify the working of an incalculable social mechanism."[36] The most important result of such a self-misunderstanding, a failure both of reflexivity and of accurate empirical analysis of the conditions of theorizing, is a tendency to treat the existing social conditions as the only conditions that could exist.

Because the theorist is unable to see his or her own activity as part of the social world, and because he or she simply accepts into theoretical self-awareness the social division of labor with its blinders, he or she loses the capacity to recognize the contingency and internal contradictions of the empirical world. "The whole perceptible world as present to a member of bourgeois society and as interpreted within a traditional world-view which is in continuous interaction with that given world, is seen by the perceiver as a sum-total of facts; it is there and must be accepted."[37] The theorist, like most individuals within society, thus, fails to see the underlying conditions of social order (or chaos), and exaggerates the illusory coherence offered by the standpoint of individual purposiveness. The theorist is also led mistakenly to affirm the treatment of those basic social conditions that cannot readily be understood through purposive rationality, especially those results of human activity that are alienated from the control of conscious human beings, as though they were forces of nature. Theory accepts the products of historical human action as unchanging and fixed conditions of human action, and thus cannot articulate the possibility of emancipation from these conditions.[38]

Even the sociology of knowledge, derived from the tradition of more critical theory, could fall into the habits of traditional theory, Horkheimer argued. Mannheim reconstructed the sociology of knowledge as a specialized, disciplinary field with its own narrower objects of study, cut off from analysis of the totality of social relations. While this sort of sociology might produce more or less interesting findings – e.g. regarding the relationship between intellectual positions and social positions – it lost its capacity critically to locate either the theorist him(her)self, or the conditions of the production of the facts under study.

The project of critical theory, thus, became for Horkheimer the recovery for human beings of the full capacities of humanity; it was in this regard a direct extension of marxism. Drawing both on the early Marx and the first chapter of *Capital*, and influenced by Lukacs' analysis of reification, critical theory aimed to show how human history had produced an alienation of human capacities such that social institutions and processes that were creatures of human action confronted people as beyond their scope of action. The mode of critique was thus "defetishizing"; it located the recovery of human capacities and thus the possibilities for social transformation in the restoration of truly human relationships in place of inhuman relationships in which people were just the mediations between things, commodities. External nature had to remain "other" to human beings, but this "second nature" did not. Theory could play a central role because the reified relationships of capital were constituted and maintained by a form of consciousness. Seeing them for what they were was already a step towards overcoming their dominion over human life.

The reification and alienation to be combated were grasped by Horkheimer and his early associates especially in the "opposition between the individual's purposiveness, spontaneity, and rationality, and those work-process relationships on which society is built."[39] This was linked to the critique of "positivism" which occupied Horkheimer and his colleagues through much of their careers.[40] Positivist social science accepted the world as it existed, indeed even precluded recognition of the possibilities for fundamental change, by reproducing rather than challenging the reification through which the human content – the original activity of human creation – was removed from the institutions and processes of the social world. This reification made it possible to treat these aspects of humanity as though they were merely aspects of nature, to treat social facts as things, in Durkheim's pithy phrase.[41]

The exaltation of the apparently isolated individual subject – the idealized knower – and the reification of the social world were linked. Moreover, this was not just an academic problem, it was a systematic elimination of the sort of consciousness that might recognize the tensions, conflicts, exploitation, and oppression built into existing social arrangements. Critical theory would be different. "Critical thinking is the function neither of the isolated individual nor of a sum-total of individuals. Its subject is rather a definite individual in his real relation to other individuals and groups, in his conflict with a particular class, and, finally, in the resultant web of relationships with the social totality and with nature."[42] To treat the individual as an asocial, ahistorical, objective starting point for knowledge, "an illusion about the thinking subject, under which idealism has lived since Descartes, is ideology in the strict sense."[43]

Writing in the 1930s, Horkheimer was still able to retain an optimism that this sort of critical theory would be linked to more or less marxist revolution. Narrowing the gap between intellectual understanding and concrete material practice was crucial to achieving the capacity for humanity to order its social relations in the new order that was about to emerge. Critical theory was not just an extension of proletarian thought, but a means of thinking about the social totality that would aid in the movement from the empirical proletariat's necessarily still partial view of society from its own class position to the achievement of a classless society, one not structured by injustice. Where fascists just expressed as ideology the underlying motives of certain segments of society, advocates of value-free science claimed to speak from an intellectual position outside all social conflicts. But, wrote Horkheimer, "critical theory is neither 'deeply rooted' like totalitarian propaganda nor 'detached' like the liberalist intelligentsia."[44] Critical theory took the starting point not of the proletariat in itself, or of any other specific social group, but of the kind of thinking – necessarily done by individuals – that addressed the most categorially basic structure of the whole society, that which made it whole, gave it its basic dynamism, and pointed to the possibilities for its transcendence. "The critical theory of society is, in its totality, the unfolding of a single existential judgment. To put it in broad terms, the theory says that the basic form of the historically given commodity economy on which modern history rests contains in itself the internal and external tensions of the modern era; it generates those tensions over and over again in an increasingly heightened form; and after a period of progress, development of human powers, and emancipation for the individual, after an enormous extension of human control over nature, it finally hinders further development and drives humanity into a new barbarism."[45]

Horkheimer's critical theory, in short, remained at this point clearly a species of marxism. But the seeds of its later crisis were already apparent. First, applied to the contemporary empirical situation, the theory pointed more directly towards a new barbarism than towards its transcendence (and indeed, in 1937 this was perhaps not surprising). Second, Horkheimer steered clear of establishing a clear account of the agents of potential revolution just as he steered clear of active political involvement on the side of the proletariat or any other group. His marxism remained abstract. Third, while Horkheimer was able to give a clear positive account of the contributions of critical theory in most intellectual regards, when it came to locating the theory socially, he was able mainly to offer negative comments on what it was not.

All these problems would return to produce a crisis in critical theory after the war. The fear of barbarism would remain acute even after Nazism was defeated. Critical theorists would search in vain for social agents with the capacity to succeed in projects of real transformation – and after considering not only the proletariat, but Jews, students, and the Third World poor would remain convinced that whatever the justice on the side of each, none had the capacity, and possibly none even had the inclination, for such revolutionary transformation. This was, indeed, part of the crucial, disturbing significance of the early Frankfurt studies on authority, especially the collective work *Studies in Authority and Family*.[46] Empirical research suggested that members of the German proletariat (and for that matter the supposedly free-floating intellectuals) were more prone to authoritarian attitudes than to opposition. Not least of all, the particular version of critical theory for which Horkheimer and Adorno were key figures retained a negative orientation that was only exacerbated as its leading figures gave up their early utopian ballast in the name of hard-headed self-discipline.

Part of the trouble was that Horkheimer and especially Adorno had largely abandoned the attempt to offer a historically and culturally specific account of the contradictions of modern capitalist society. In much (though not all) of their earlier work they had attempted to develop what Benjamin called "proto-histories," analyses of the present in terms of the historical dynamics producing it. These involved the location of crucial epochal changes, both at the large scale with the coming of capitalism and more specifically, as when both Adorno and Benjamin tried to work out the nineteenth-century origins of modernism. In his early work on bourgeois philosophy, as the term suggests, Horkheimer had sought to locate the specific relations of schools of philosophy to their social conditions and therefore to their periods – above all to the era of capitalism.[47] But Horkheimer and Adorno were ambivalent about historical specificity in *Dialectic of Enlightenment*, and in Horkheimer's *Eclipse of Reason*, the last vestiges of this historically specific approach gave way to a more transhistorical, weakly periodized critique of the depredations of instrumental reason.[48] Since instrumental reason in some form could be traced back intellectually to the Greeks, and in practice was presumably universal, it was hard to see from what historical groundings its progressive hyperdevelopment and growing dominion could be critically challenged.

> If one were to speak of a disease affecting reason, this disease should be understood not as having stricken reason at some historical moment, but as being inseparable from the nature of reason in civilization as we have known it so far. The disease of reason is that reason was born from man's urge to dominate nature, and the "recovery" depends on insight into the nature of the original disease, not on a cure of the latest symptoms.[49]

At the heart of critical theory lay the notion of "immanent critique," a critique that worked from within the categories of existing thought, radicalized them, and showed in varying degrees both their problems and their unrecognized possibilities.[50] "Philosophy confronts the existent, in its historical context," wrote Horkheimer, "with the claim of its conceptual principles, in order to criticize the relation between the two [ideas and reality] and thus transcend them.[51] Thus it was that Adorno spoke repeatedly of exploding bourgeois thought from inside and of bursting idealism open from within. As he praised Mahler's "symphonic reason," "Mahler leaves what exists in its place, but burns it out from within. The old barriers of form now stand as allegories not so much for what has been but for what is to come."[52]

Immanence by itself was not enough; one could not just trust to history to realize the possibilities embodied in the forms of culture or in material social relations. Critique was required as a tool for finding and heightening the tensions between the merely existent and its possibilities. For the first-generation Frankfurt theorists, this meant especially that critical theory depended on a dialectical analysis of the contradictions internal to every epoch, or social formation, or situation, or text. An immanent critique was particularly effective as a historically specific critique.

This is one reading of Horkheimer's and Adorno's famous exploration of the *Dialectic of Enlightenment*. Reason flourished in and through Enlightenment, but its development was contradictory. On the one hand, it brought the enormous progress of critical thought, including modern philosophy. On the other hand, it brought dehumanizing rationalization of society (more familiar to sociologists through Weber's image of the "iron cage") and the progress of technology that both enslaved human beings, stunting their creativity, and distanced humanity from both internal and external nature. "In the most general sense of progressive thought, the Enlightenment has always aimed at liberating men from fear and establishing their sovereignty. Yet the fully enlightened earth radiates disaster triumphant."[53] Simply to defend the Enlightenment meant to defend bureaucratization, out of control technology, and even the horrors of Nazi science. A critical engagement with the Enlightenment required recognizing how reason could be deployed, as it were, against itself and against the human subjects of reason. Yet this did not mean simply abandoning reason, both because the irrational contained as many horrors as the rational, and because reason alone offered an approach to the recovery of an opportunity for coherent practice. Social and cultural forces – science, capital, mechanisms of political power – had become autonomous, according to Horkheimer and Adorno; they had gained the capacity to dictate the course of social stability and change. Extending the argument Marx had offered in the first chapter of Volume 1 of *Capital*, they showed how human subjects were reduced to objects by the very forms of social relations they had created.[54]

This manner of reading *Dialectic of Enlightenment* suggests that Horkheimer and Adorno still thought that engaging capitalism (which they avoided naming out of political anxieties) and other specifically modern social conditions could offer some hope of transformation, even redemption. Neumann, Pollock, and other Frankfurt School associates who wrote directly on political economy were clearer in locating historically specific causes for current crises – the collapsing distinction between state and society, for example, and the erosion of the autonomy of the market under state capitalism. Although Horkheimer and Adorno would continue a more historically specific criticism of "the administered society" that emerged after World War Two, at its deepest their critical theory worked after the war at the level of transhistorical tendencies of reason in relation to nature. At best, *Dialectic of Enlightenment* was ambiguous on this point. Was it enlightenment (the progress of reason) in general that had led down the path to disaster, or was it the Enlightenment, with its historically specific institutionalization of bourgeois reason that had caused the trouble? Passages support each reading, but one offers more hope of a way out.

The *Dialectic of Enlightenment* was written in exile at the end of World War Two by two German Jews, onetime lovers of Enlightenment and German high culture. Perhaps it is not surprising that the authors were not able to seize with any conviction on sources of optimism. "Enlightenment," they wrote, "is totalitarian."[55] They meant not only the manifest political totalitarianism of Nazi Germany, but the reduction of human autonomy implied by a "culture industry" which mass produced what later thinkers would call the "simulacra" of art, music, and literature, reducing potentially creative human beings to passive consumers of entertainment. When Horkheimer and Adorno tried to find the basis for hope, the sources of a "better" enlightenment, a more positive concept of reason, they found themselves increasingly at a loss. They could not imagine a progress not guided by reason, yet rationality seemed to have betrayed its positive potential.

"When the idea of reason was conceived," wrote Horkheimer, "it was intended to achieve more than the mere regulation of the relation between means and ends; it was regarded as the instrument for understanding the ends, *for determining them*."[56] But reason seemed to have abdicated the realm of ends; by common agreement, decisions about basic values – about value itself – could not be the result of purely reasonable understanding.[57] Reason had been reduced to the merely instrumental; it – and even the specific institutions of science – could be placed at the service of the Nazi death industry as readily as turned to the task of eliminating poverty and suffering. As institutionalized, reproduced, and deployed not just by Nazi Germany but by modern society generally, reason seemed destined to nullify individual autonomy rather than to realize it. As Horkheimer remarked, the expression "to be reasonable" had taken on the meaning of adopting a conciliatory attitude rather than that of exercising one's capacity for rational judgment.[58]

The problem was not limited to politics. In religion, for example, an anti-theological spirit had challenged the value of reason as a source of basic insights (a view that continues today among many "fundamentalists"). This allowed religion to be compartmentalized away from the corrosive force of reason, the threats of science, because its truths were held to be based on sources other than those of reason. But this protection was achieved at the cost of radically reducing religion's capacity to engage critically with modern society let alone to apprehend its totality. The reduction of reason to a mechanism for subjective choice among means rather than objective determination of ends was no historical accident, Horkheimer argued; it reflected the material course of social change and accordingly could not be reversed simply by recognizing that it was a problem.

The existing state of society, Horkheimer and Adorno feared, allowed no truly transformative criticism, provided no bases for revolution or other practical action that would end the reproduction of a dehumanizing, repressive, and dangerous social order. The most they thought their theoretical work could do was to preserve critical thought – no longer in its strongly integrated form as critical theory, but as a "message in a bottle" for a future generation. This marked the onset of what has been

called the "pessimistic turn" of the Frankfurt theorists.[59] Both in America
– where McCarthyite anti-communism added to their gloom – and
especially in the repressive environment of a Federal Republic of Germany where ex-Nazis could return to power and present themselves as
mere realists while socialists and even left liberals were excluded – even
from universities – as ideological, it appeared to Horkheimer and Adorno
as though the most that could be done was to keep alive in purely
intellectual form the seeds of critical thought so that they might grow
anew if conditions ever became more favorable. Even this was not to be
easy, they thought. The subjectivization of reason and for that matter the
growth of "free enterprise" capitalism seemed to empower individuals,
but this was deceptive. "All the monads, isolated though they were by
moats of self-interest, nevertheless tended to become more and more
alike through the pursuit of this very self-interest."[60] Conformism as
ideology was thus matched by a genuinely increasing sameness among
people insofar as each responded strictly to the self-interests of a consumer in a world of corporate capitalism and mass culture. Similarly,
modern psychology built on a tradition stretching back to the Thomists
to declare "adjustment" the highest goal of an individual, rather than
seeing Truth and Goodness as critical values that might motivate discon-
tent and even social change, they were implicitly identified with existing
reality by those who held adapting to that reality to be the basis of
individual health.

No social group – proletariat, intellectuals, artists – seemed altogether
immune from this deadening of capacity to use reason to grasp the ends
of social processes. At first, Horkheimer and Adorno thought that some
crisis might be extreme enough to lay bare the antagonisms of modern
society (and between that society and the nature it attempted to dominate). Horkheimer spoke of "the possibility of a self-critique of reason"
when he could no longer believe in such a critique being carried out by
any specific agents. But even that possibility came to seem more and more
remote as instead of lurching into crisis the society of the 1950s and early
1960s marched forward in its combination of prosperity and repression.

V

When crisis came, in the 1960s, the aging critical theorists were generally
unprepared. Of the first-generation Frankfurt theorists, only Herbert
Marcuse was still able to think radical action possible when student
protests thrust open politics back onto center stage. Though the media
lionized Marcuse as a guru to the New Left, and though he did engage
with student activists directly and positively, he also disappointed them.

For Marcuse did not see the potential for real revolution as lying in the hands of European or American university students; he did not even agree that they were really an underprivileged class. Theirs was not the standpoint from which to grasp the crisis of the social totality, the successor to the proletariat. If any social group could claim that mantle, and also claim the social strength to wage real revolution, Marcuse (like Sartre) thought it was Fanon's "wretched of the earth," the oppressed masses of the Third World and their counterparts, the permanent unemployed of the First World.[61] He thought still within the Frankfurt paradigm that expected radical social change to emerge from radical negativity, from those most objectively disempowered by existing arrangements, those whose existence was most opposed to the established order. This had arguably been the proletariat at one time, and Horkheimer had argued it was the Jews in 1940; though students in 1968 might support the radically disenfranchised, they were not that group.

On the other hand, Marcuse had grasped as well as any contemporary theorist some of the sources of the student protest. He saw the ways in which certain forms of repression – including erotic repression – could become the basis for political action even amid affluence. Commodification, with its fetishizing reduction of human relationships to a single dimension, violated natural human potential in a way that necessarily occasioned resistance. Most centrally, perhaps, he expressed one of the key intuitions of the student protests in his more or less romantic argument that "to the denial of freedom, even of the possibility of freedom, corresponds the granting of liberties where they strengthen repression."[62] This anticipated his more radical argument about the repression inherent in a tolerance that refused to engage the genuine needs and demands of human subjects.[63]

Student critiques of postwar society were varied, of course, combining systemic analysis with pacifism and psychological and cultural concerns or personal politics. In their condemnation of an abstract, impersonal, and violent society, students indeed followed the path of the earlier Frankfurt School critical theory. But at the same time there was a much more substantial concern with facilitating directly interpersonal relationships and profound immediate experience. As Oscar Negt (an activist who had been Habermas's assistant in Frankfurt and later became a sociology professor) summed up, "The anti-institutional and anti-authoritarian element in the revival of critical theory fused with the attempt, via politicization of interests and needs, to accomplish three things: (1) to break through the compulsive and pervasive mediations of commodity exchange; (2) to break through the violence latent in the mechanisms of instrumental reason and structurally inherent in the sublimation and repression of basic instincts; (3) to establish meaningful immediacy, in which the split between communication and experience is in turn eliminated."[64] This critique drew on Wilhelm Reich and other radical inheritors of the psychoanalytic tradition in shifting the balance not only more towards the personal than the systemic, but also more towards an account of the virtues of immediacy itself. This was not without connection to critical theory's earlier account of abstract commodifed society, of course, but it also marked a shift in emphasis, anticipating the "new social movements" that grounded a personal politics in direct interpersonal relations and experience, with much less reference to high culture. This Habermas would come to analyze as the practice of resistance rooted in "the lifeworld" against impersonal, "delinguistified," systemic rationality.[65]

While Marcuse's willingness to join directly in the passionate politics of the 1960s shocked and worried Adorno and Horkheimer, who preferred to stay not just on the sidelines but secluded from the fray, it was also true that the theory of the earlier Frankfurt theorists had helped to make possible the students' political and cultural analyses in both Germany and America. Frankfurt theory once again became all but synonymous with critical theory.

The theorist who perhaps mattered most, however, was not a member of the first Frankfurt generation, but a sometime protégé of Adorno's named Jürgen Habermas. Deeply influenced by the early work of Horkheimer and Adorno, Habermas had moved to Frankfurt after his Ph.D. and begun to work in the Institute for Social Research. He initially sought to take his *Habilitation* (a higher doctorate or university teacher's qualification) under Adorno, but was blocked by opposition from Horkheimer (and Adorno's own caution). The objections were that he was too left wing, insufficiently critical of Enlightenment and excessively willing to take critical theory directly into open political debate.

In his early work, Habermas pursued two basic agendas, each designed to re-establish the possibility of politically significant critical theory. Each was oriented, in other words, by the problem of linking theory and practice. The first sought to recover the resources of previous theory and to show how conventional social science failed to develop their critical potential.[66] The second pursued an immanent critique of the actual historical institutions within which rational critical discourse achieved political significance.

Inspired by Hannah Arendt's *The Human Condition* and the transformations of the Aristotelian tradition, among other sources, Habermas sought to locate the possibility of a unity of theory and practice in the classical doctrine of politics. The issue was not just a use of theory in the service of political ends – a version of instrumental reason – but rather the development of a broader sense of political practice as the constitution of ways of living together that enabled the full realization of human potential. Critical theory, in this context, responded directly to political needs; it was "a theory of society conceived with a practical intention."[67]

All knowledge, Habermas argued, had to be understood in terms of the interests which led practical actors to create it.[68] This meant that when a critical theorist examined earlier theory, his task was to locate the relationship among the knowledge-forming interests that led to theoretical production, the historical conditions within which the theory was set, and the epistemic content of the theory. This was an elaboration, worked out in a series of studies of major modern philosophies, of Horkheimer's argument in "Traditional and Critical Theory" and "The State of Contemporary Social Philosophy and the Task of an Institute for Social Research." Like the earlier Frankfurt theorists, Habermas drew on Freud as well as Marx to develop a conception of theoretical critique as a way of establishing how "objective" knowledge – that which approached the world as a series of external *results*, could be reconnected with intersubjectively constituted meaning and capacity for action. A psychoanalytic patient cannot at first recognize the full meaning of his or her own life-history, and cannot take fully responsible and effective action in regard to it, precisely because of systematic repression of key aspects of that meaning and of the interpersonally effective interests that constituted those life experiences. Psychoanalysis itself provides an intersubjective relationship in which physician and patient work through the barriers to communication and make previously repressed motivations accessible to conscious understanding and control. Analogically, critical theory – itself an intersubjective, communicative enterprise – was to perform this function for a society that was similarly trapped in a systematic incapacity to recognize the true sources of its own history. Human capacities were repressed without recognition and could be liberated with movement towards fuller and freer communication.[69] Drawing on this image of psychoanalysis as a communicative process, Habermas envisaged "an organization of social relations according to the principle that the validity of every norm of political consequence be made dependent on a consensus arrived at in communication free from domination."[70] Moreover, "theories which in their structure can serve the clarification of practical questions are designed to enter into communicative action."[71]

In his second agenda, Habermas approached this same goal with a historically grounded, immanent critique of the institutions of the bour-

geois public sphere. The key work here was the very *Habilitationschrift*
that Horkheimer had resisted, seeing Habermas's orientation as entirely
too optimistic.[72] Indeed, one of the organizing features of Habermas's
work was a determination not to fall into the same incapacitating pessimism as Horkheimer and Adorno. In *The Structural Transformation of
the Public Sphere*, Habermas examined the origins, development, and
degeneration of the distinctive political institution that made bourgeois
democracy genuinely radical in its day.[73]

The public sphere of bourgeois, liberal society came into being on the
foundations of earlier literary public arenas, Habermas argued (somewhat surprisingly neglecting science and religion).[74] Both salon culture
and print media contributed. Discourse in the public sphere was, at least
in principle, based on rational–critical argumentation; the best argument
was decisive, rather than the identity of its proponents or opponents.
Only relative elites were admitted to the public sphere, but these elites
were of diverse statuses. Master craftsmen might rub shoulders with
landed gentry in coffee houses, nobility mixed with commoners in parliament and salons alike. The discourse of the public sphere did not so much
negate or challenge these differences as "bracket" them – Habermas
specifically used the phenomenological term – making them irrelevant for
the purpose of discourse itself. The public sphere addressed and could
influence affairs of state and of the society as a whole, although it was not
part of the state but of civil society. Citizens entered into the public
sphere on the basis of the autonomy afforded them both socio-psycho-
logically and economically by their private lives and non-state civil
relations.

The importance of the public sphere for Habermas was that it offered
a model of public communication which could potentially realize the
rational guidance of society. The potential of this communication had
not been fully realized, of course, but the categories of bourgeois democracy were not thereby made irrelevant as some marxists and more pessimistic critical theorists assumed. On the contrary, an immanent critique
could make the ideals of rational–critical discourse, like those of rights,
once again politically effective. These ideals had been reduced to ideology
by their incorporation in a discourse designed to affirm rather than
challenge existing institutions. But critical theory could make citizens
aware of their still unrealized potential and enable them to use these
ideals in struggle with those who nominally adhered to them but did not
in fact want to build on them.

That Habermas's account of the public sphere presented an eighteenth-century golden age followed by decline and degeneration was thus
not immediately incapacitating. Probing further, Habermas sought to

locate the social roots of the transformations that had deprived the public sphere of its initial strength of rational–critical discourse. The procedure of immanent critique could then presumably be combined with the identification of historical subjects capable of putting into practice the possibilities uncovered by theory.

Heavily influenced by the mass society theories of the 1950s, however, Habermas's account of the twentieth century undermined his own initial optimism.[75] He showed a public sphere that was not only deradicalized but fundamentally diminished by two major processes. The first was the progressive incorporation of ever larger numbers of citizens into the public. This followed the genuinely democratic logic of the early public sphere which could not sustain its own exclusiveness against recurrent demands that its democratic ideals be taken more seriously. But as the public sphere grew in scale, it degenerated in form. Even if the new participants had been as well prepared for its rational–critical discourse as their predecessors, which they were not on Habermas's view, their discourse would have been distorted by the necessity of reliance on mass media and the opportunities for manipulation of communication presented by advertising, public relations, and similar institutions. Secondly, the public sphere lost some of the basis it had once had in a civil society clearly distinct from the state. In the twentieth century, and especially after World War Two, the boundaries between state and society had been increasingly collapsed, Habermas thought, as government intervention in the economy increased, as welfare states were formed, as giant corporations took on political functions, and citizens were organized into (or represented by) interest groups. Social decisions were increasingly removed from the rational–critical discourse of citizens in the political public sphere and made the province of negotiation (rather than discourse proper) among bureaucrats, credentialed experts, and interest group elites.

Habermas followed directly in the footsteps of his Frankfurt predecessors in adducing the scale and mediated communication of mass society and the collapsed state/society distinction of "administered society" as the basic transformations in the structural foundations of the public sphere. Like his predecessors, this pushed him towards increasingly pessimistic conclusions, and the tone of the last part of his book differed markedly from that of the first. Though his immanent critique was able to locate unrealized emancipatory and rational potential in the forms of bourgeois democracy, he was unable to locate the material social bases for action to realize those potentials in the late twentieth-century public sphere.[76]

Accordingly, Habermas abandoned the project of an historically immanent foundation for critical theory. Instead of seeking critical purchase in the comparison of historically and culturally specific social formations, he sought it in the elaboration of universal conditions of human life. He grounded his critique not in historical developments as such, but in a broad idea of evolutionary progress in communication. During the years of the student movement he theorized potentials for concrete transformation, based especially on the idea that contemporary states were undergoing a legitimation crisis because they relied on cultural foundations that were undermined as more and more of social life fell under the sway of administrative planning.[77] Habermas retained his interest in seeing the public sphere reinhabited by genuinely political discourse, and it was on this basis that he welcomed the student movement (even while he decried its more extreme tendencies as "left fascism"). But at a deeper level, Habermas did not base his critical theory on actual or historical social institutions of discourse, but on the potential for unimpeded communication suggested by the rationality implicit in speech itself. His "universal pragmatics" started from a primordial split between communicative and instrumental reason, and even within communication between speech oriented to understanding itself and speech oriented to practical effects. Though the increasing "autonomization" of instrumental reason – the treatment of utilitarian, use-oriented reason as self-sufficient and adequate to a range of practical projects – was the source of social disasters and alienation, countervailing tendencies were inherent in the transcendental characteristics of speech itself. Thus every communication was based on the presumption of certain standards of validity – e.g. that speakers spoke not only the truth, but truthfully, without manipulative intent. Even where not articulated, these validity claims were always open to potential discursive redemption. Processes of social and cultural transformation could (and perhaps in evolutionary fashion would) move in the direction of making more and more communication live up to these immanent potentials.[78]

Habermas's later work on communicative action retained one crucial theme from his early work. He sought ways to realize the unfinished potential of the project of enlightenment or modernity.[79] With the shift to universal pragmatics, he found a more reliable basis for an optimistic orientation to critical theory than he had in his historically specific account of the public sphere. This was, indeed, a path that Horkheimer had anticipated, though not in published work. "To speak to someone basically means recognizing him as a possible member of the future association of free human beings. Speech establishes a shared relation towards truth, and is therefore the innermost affirmation of another existence, indeed of all forms of existence, according to their capacities.

When speech denies any possibilities, it necessarily contradicts itself."[80]
Adorno agreed with Horkheimer's insight, but faced with the manifest
contradictions of World War Two and Nazism they proved unable to
build on it and focused rather on the ways in which language had been
robbed of its very meaning.

Like Horkheimer and Adorno, Habermas started with an interest in
historically specific immanent critique and moved to a transhistorical
theory. Unlike his predecessors, he maintained a positive orientation to
action. Indeed, Habermas shifted away from history to recover a basis
for optimism while Horkheimer and Adorno moved away from history
in a kind of radicalization of their despair. Neither the first-generation
Frankfurt theorists nor Habermas has been altogether blind to the issue
of difference. Indeed, we have seen the centrality of the "dialectical"
themes of non-identity, resistance to a conforming, reconciled society,
and contestation of a social science reduced to affirming the existing
conditions without recognizing their contradictions. Adorno in particular was inspired by Hölderlin's aphorism, "what differs is good." Much
of Adorno's work was devoted to challenging the solipsism and absolut-
ism of "identitarian thinking," the implicit subjectivism and resistance to
difference of nondialectical thought.[81] Yet this universalized account of
non-identity and difference is a far cry from a capacity for making sense
of concrete particularities. Similarly, Habermas has insisted on the social
construction of individual identity: "socialized individuals are only sustained through group identity."[82] Yet he has not focused on basic differences among groups, nor on how groups affect their members differently;
he has pursued a theory of communicative action grounded in the universal presuppositions of language.

Habermas has sought to move away from Kant's grounding of knowledge and practical reason in individual reflection. Instead of such a
"monological" approach, Habermas favors a "dialogical" emphasis on
intersubjectivity. In this way, Habermas moves beyond a philosophy
rooted only in individual consciousness. It is language that demonstrates
our essential sociality. But this is the same for all human beings, and not
in itself definitive of the basic differences among us. Habermas's is,
moreover, a highly cognitive approach to human life and social practice,
one that assumes that all significant differences are ultimately resolvable
– at least in principle – on the basis of rational discourse.

VI

The Frankfurt School was – and remains – of extraordinary importance
for the specific studies its members undertook and perhaps even more for

helping to keep alive the project of uniting the best of the tradition of philosophical reflection and analysis with empirical social science. But it is not helpful to restrict the idea of critical theory to the Frankfurt School. The notion that the Frankfurters encompass rather than only exemplify critical theory has left their own preoccupations and limits too dominant and as a result left their pessimistic conclusions inadequately challenged. It has cut their version of critical theory off from other sources of intellectual creativity and potentially transformative critique. Identifying critical theory only with Horkheimer's friends and followers has even harmed the original project of the Frankfurt Institute for Social Research, insofar as that project called for the development of a new kind of integration of theory and research. Though members of the Frankfurt School did serious and significant empirical work, their legacy has been mainly a highly abstract form of theoretical work that has kept their critical tradition isolated from much of the mainstream of empirical social science.[83] At the same time, the contributions made by thinkers outside the Frankfurt lineage to the project of critical social theory often go unrecognized as such. Indeed, many of these other thinkers go to some lengths to distinguish themselves from the Frankfurt "theoretical theorists" (in the derisory phrase of Pierre Bourdieu) and to express their distaste for the abstract system-building which they identify today most of all with Habermas.

In the present book, I want to claim that thinkers as diverse as Pierre Bourdieu, Michel Foucault, Donna Haraway, Dorothy Smith, and Charles Taylor are all contributors to the common project of critical social theory along with Habermas and the other more direct heirs of Horkheimer and Adorno. Bourdieu, for example, is among the most important contemporary thinkers elaborating an account of embodied reason and attempting to push beyond the conventional academic division of labor; in both regards he echoes Adorno. Yet the border between France and Germany has often been a surprisingly strong filter in intellectual history, and the development of critical theory is no exception. Despite Walter Benjamin's obsession with nineteenth-century Paris as the capital of modernity, the original Frankfurt theorists drew overwhelmingly on German theoretical forebears. Their work related only glancingly to that of Sartre, Camus, or Merleau-Ponty, even though they were more or less of a generation and often explored similar problems. More recently, French thought in the eras of structuralism and poststructuralism, formulated significantly in response to influential French readings of Hegel, has often appeared as though it could be diametrically opposed to Frankfurt School critical theory. But though much is different, a number of themes and orientations are surprisingly similar. As Michel Foucault at one point said, "If I had known about the Frankfurt School in time, I would have been saved a great deal of work. I would not have said a certain amount of nonsense and would not have taken so many false trails trying not to get lost, when the Frankfurt School had already cleared the way."[84] Indeed, Foucault on occasion described his own work in terms remarkably reminiscent of Adorno (the Frankfurt thinker who most anticipated later "poststructuralist" themes), as "a rational critique of rationality."

Critical social theory, I shall suggest in short, should be seen not just as a "school," but as the interpenetrating body of work which demands and produces critique in four senses:

1   a critical engagement with the theorist's contemporary social world, recognizing that the existing state of affairs does not exhaust all possibilities, and offering positive implications for social action;
2   a critical account of the historical and cultural conditions (both social and personal) on which the theorist's own intellectual activity depends;
3   a continuous critical re-examination of the constitutive categories and conceptual frameworks of the theorist's understanding, including the historical construction of those frameworks; and
4   a critical confrontation with other works of social explanation that not only establishes their good and bad points but shows the reasons behind their blind spots and misunderstandings, and demonstrates the capacity to incorporate their insights on stronger foundations.

All four of these forms of critique, it seems to me, depend on some manner of historical understanding and analysis. The first calls for "de-naturalizing" the human world, recognizing it as a product of human action, and thus implicitly as the product of some actions among a larger range of possibilities. Beyond this, a theoretically serious critical engagement with one's social world calls for an account of that world in terms of its salient features for practical action, and an ability to place it in relation to other basic patterns of activity (e.g. other epochs as well as culturally or socially different contemporary settings).

The second calls for an account of the accomplishments and the particularities of history that make possible the vision of the contemporary theorist. This is not just a matter of the giants' shoulders on which one may stand, but of the entire social formation which grants one the opportunity for theoretical reflection and conditions, and shapes one's theoretical outlook.

The third calls for historical analyses of the ways in which ideas come to take on specific significances, to be embedded in different intellectual contexts and projects, and to be invested with certain sorts of references to the world of experience and practice. If we are to be seriously critical of the concepts we incorporate into our theories – such as the various "keywords" that Raymond Williams analyzed, like "individual" or "nation" – we need to see them in their historical creation, and to see that no attempt at operational specification will ever escape the impact of that history.

Finally, a truly critical confrontation with other efforts at explanation involves an attempt to grapple seriously with the historical embeddedness of all theory, approaching past theories not just as exemplars, partial successes or sources of decontextualized insights, but as works bounded by or based on different histories from our own. Even more basically, we need to see that confrontations between theories are seldom resolved by the victory or right over wrong, truth over falsehood. Theorists do not work in a world of right answers but of what Charles Taylor has called "epistemic gain," movement from a problematic position to a more adequate one within a field of available alternatives (rather than epistemology's mythical movement from falsity to truth).[85] This is not a movement well understood in atemporal, abstract terms. Individual theorists do not simply change their minds while they and the world remain otherwise unchanged. Rather, their environments and personal orientations to change; they change, and their minds (being indissolubly a part of them) change with them.

Notes

1   Davies, *Lyre of Orpheus*, p. 153.
2   Arendt, *Between Past and Future*, p. 201. See also Arendt's comments linking the modern idea of the philistine not only – or even primarily – to the Biblical root of the term, but to the Greek notion of a "banaustic spirit," an orientation to life common to mere fabricators; p. 215.
3   "In this fight for social position," Arendt wrote twenty years before Bourdieu's *Distinction*, "culture began to play an enormous role as one of the weapons, if not the best-suited one, to advance oneself socially, and to 'educate oneself' out of the lower regions, where supposedly reality was located, up into the higher, non-real regions, where beauty and spirit supposedly were at home. . . . Culture, more even than other realities, had become what only then people began to call 'value,' i.e. a social commodity which could be circulated and cashed in exchange for all kinds of other values, social and individual" (Arendt, *Between Past and Future*, pp. 202, 204).

4 Though not with the same emphases, this is one of the morals to Bourdieu's story in *Homo Academicus*. Bourdieu presents this aspect of academic culture as more universal and unavoidable, less a matter of degree, than I would choose to do.

5 Rorty comes close to this sort of dualism in positing an analogy to Kuhn's account of normal vs. revolutionary science; see *Consequences of Pragmatism*. Taken too strongly (as by a number of postmodernists and, for purposes of critique, in Habermas's somewhat tendentious reading in *Philosophical Discourse*, p. 206) this would be a hindrance rather than a help in achieving an adequate openness to the world.

6 Arendt, *Human Condition*, pp. 179–80.

7 This is by no means useless. The world changes in innumerable small ways and for the reproduction of a host of daily activities we require new descriptive knowledge of the variations in social patterns. At the same time, each of us comes into the world ignorant and must learn anew – and sometimes more than once – basic insights that shed great light on our familiar world, though they do not challenge it. So I do not mean to suggest either that only the production of knowledge capable of transforming world views is to be valued, or that only radically new knowledge can be transformative in human life.

8 Attention to narratives is also important because narratives of various sorts exercise a more basic grip on the imaginations and decisions of most sorts of actors throughout the world. See Ricoeur, *Time and Narrative*, and the sociological discussions of narrative in Somers, "Narrativity," Somers and Gibson, "Epistemological Other," and Abbott "From Causes to Events," and "Conceptions of Time and Events."

9 This is something Stinchcombe, *Theoretical Methods*, demonstrated pointedly, though he limited the term "theory" to universal, propositional formulations and treated analogies as something other than theory.

10 See Adorno, et al., *Positivist Dispute*. The confusion of empiricism and positivism was all the easier, perhaps, because the most important empirical researcher in the direct experience of the first generation of the Frankfurt School was Paul Lazarsfeld, who had been influenced by the Vienna School before his emigration to America. The meaning of positivism had, in fact, shifted toward empiricism – away from Comte and toward Mach – in the course of the nineteenth century.

11 Popper, *Conjectures and Refutations*.

12 Merton, *Social Theory and Social Structure*; Merton did not distinguish the first two senses altogether adequately from each other.

13 That is, science which seeks to solve explanatory problems within established paradigms but not to change the paradigms. See Kuhn, *Structure of Scientific Revolutions*.

14 This line of argument has been developed most importantly by Gadamer (esp. *Truth and Method*) and Taylor (*Sources of the Self* and *Selected Essays*).

15 Foucault is commonly taken to have posed a radical assault on truth by arguing that "effects of truth are produced within discourses which in themselves are neither true nor false" ("Truth and Power," p. 118). Whether or not Foucault posed such a radical challenge, however, we can also read in this comment a recognition that specific truth claims can only be offered within broader discourses that cannot be reduced to structures of truth claims. Thus both Weber and Durkheim offer broad theoretical discourses – and serve sociology by helping to ground broad theoretical discourses – within which "truth effects" may be produced and more specific propositional truth claims offered. But it is meaningless to assert in general that Weberian sociology or Durkheimian sociology as a whole is either true or false. Similarly, as we shall see in the last chapter, the discourse of nationalism helps to make possible a variety of truths or truth effects, and ways of posing possibly true propositions and arguments, without itself being either true or false.

16 Heisenberg quoted from Arendt's (*Between Past and Future*, p. 44) interesting discussion of the concept of history.

17 The struggle over methods made famous by the late nineteenth-century German *Methodenstreit* continues, of course, but it is no longer grasped by the categories that came to the fore when history still had realistic pretensions to be an encompassing, identity-providing discipline of predominant public importance.

18 Quoted from Arendt (*Between Past and Future*, p. 7); see also Bernstein's discussion of Arendt's work including her use of this metaphor in *The New Constellation*, pp. 15–30.

19 I draw this image from Gadamer, *Truth and Method*.

20 Megill (*Prophets of Extremity*) also reminds us that Kant was the point of departure for the tradition running from Nietzsche through Heidegger to Foucault and Derrida. In particular, the tension introduced by Kant's sharp division of the realms of understanding (pure reason), moral action (practical reason), and aesthetics (judgment) was deeply troubling, especially insofar as the disjuncture between Kant's first two critiques could not be seen as adequately mediated by the third. This was of course also Hegel's basic concern with regard to Kant. See both *The Phenomenology of Spirit* and *The Difference Between the Fichtean and Schellingian Systems of Philosophy* for ways in which this reflection of Kant as the paradigmatic modern philosopher shaped Hegel's early work.

21 Kant, *Critique of Judgment*, p. 161.

22 Ibid., p. 162.

23 See Arendt, *Lectures on Kant's Political Philosophy* and compare Habermas, *Communicative Action* and *Justification and Application*.

24 Horkheimer, "Traditional and Critical Theory."

25 Habermas, *Philosophical Discourse*, p. 4. This book is perhaps the best guide to the place of Hegel in the tradition of critical theory, as well as to the more general theme of its title. I am indebted to it, and to Taylor's reading of Hegel (in *Hegel*) in the following paragraphs.

26 This is one reason for the attraction felt for the young Hegel by Lukacs (see *The Young Hegel*), himself in turn a crucial influence on the Frankfurt School.

27 Perhaps the most sustained argument for the historical specificity of Marx's categories appears in Postone's *Time, Labor and Social Domination*.

28 The crucial text is "Reification and the Consciousness of the Proletariat," the central chapter in Lukacs, *History and Class Consciousness*, though the themes weave in and out of Lukacs' work as a whole. Marx had drawn on similar ideas of aesthetic unity and especially of the unity of the craft producer's thought, labor, and productivity, but he did so more consistently in his early work. In his mature work his increasing recognition of the systematicity of capitalism makes him (apparently) more doubtful of the continuing validity of this critique rooted in pre- or early capitalist production; though the critique of alienation does not quite disappear, it ceases to be the organizing principle of the later work. This paves the way for critical theorists and others to greet the delayed publication of Marx's early texts (recovered to scholarship in the 1930s though not immediately widely known) as both the occasion for an extraordinary reorientation in marxist thought and as the occasion for a marxist critique of actually existing socialism (that is to say, of Stalinist communism – and later, after 1976 of Maoist communism as well.

29 Horkheimer and Adorno, *Dialectic of Enlightenment*, p. 134.

30 Ibid., pp. 145–6.

31 Ibid., p. 172.

32 This account appears in Horkheimer and Adorno, *Dialectic of Enlightenment*; see also Wiggershaus, *The Frankfurt School*, pp. 338–44.

33 Marcuse's *Eros and Civilization* is thus in a sense a recasting of Freud's *Civilization and its Discontents* as an historically specific critique of capitalist modernity.

34 Horkheimer, "Der neueste Angriff auf die Metaphysik," quoted in Wiggershaus, *The Frankfurt School*, p. 184.

35 Horkheimer, "Traditional and Critical Theory," p. 197.

36 Ibid.

37 Ibid., p. 199.

38 A particularly compelling instance of this is the analysis of nationalist violence (such as that in Bosnia in the early 1990s) as simply the unavoidable, if regrettable, result of primordial ethnicity and ancient conflicts rather than (1) seeing ethnic identities and tensions as themselves created, and (2) seeing pre-existing ethnicities as subject to very recent and ongoing manipulations. The "traditional" view, when articulated by prominent political leaders (like US Secretary of State Warren Christopher) becomes a rationalization for inaction, an affirmation of the world as it is – no matter how regrettable – rather than a basis for seeing how it could be otherwise. See chapter 8 below.

39 Horkheimer, "Traditional and Critical Theory," p. 210.

40 As we saw above, Horkheimer, Adorno, and later Habermas would persist

in using "positivism" as a convenient catch-all term for those approaches to social science which affirmed the simple positive facticity of the social world, those that failed to uncover its creation by human beings and its related internal contradictions. They did not mean more narrowly the Vienna Circle of logical positivists, and still less dissidents like Karl Popper whom they recognized as having a more critical stance at least with regard to the nature of theory and its categorial distinction from empirical generalization.

41   The Durkheimian version of this positivism was not the immediate object of Horkheimer's critique, as it happens, and it is relevant that the Weberian emphasis on interpretative understanding, *Verstehen*, which is typically counterposed to Durkheim's approach in sociology courses, was no guarantee of a challenge to reification. On the contrary, as Horkheimer made clear in his critique of Mannheim, an interpretative approach could remain focused at the level of individual subjectivity in such a way that the social world remained opaque to it and while the meaning to contemporary individuals of historically created institutions was assessed, the seeming autonomy of the individual and the reification of the social realm could go on unchallenged.

42   Horkheimer, "Traditional and Critical Theory," pp. 210–11.

43   Ibid.

44   Ibid., pp. 223–4.

45   Ibid., p. 227.

46   This was the most important early work in which the Frankfurt theorists – the associates of the Institute for Social Research – attempted to put into practice their vision of the interdisciplinary unity of theory and empirical research. In addition to Horkheimer, others involved included Erich Fromm, Herbert Marcuse, and Karl Wittfogel. The more famous *The Authoritarian Personality*, in which Adorno played the central role, was in many ways an extension of this early project, reshaped by a more central focus on anti-semitism.

47   English language readers can now see this better with the publication of Horkheimer, *Between Philosophy and Social Science: Selected Early Writings*.

48   Indeed, Horkheimer and Adorno had long been ambiguous about the question of historical specificity. They had treated Marx's idea of labor generally as a transhistorical category of work, for example, rather than as a specifically constitutive category of modern capitalism. See Postone, *Time, Labor and Social Domination*.

49   *Eclipse of Reason*, p. 176. Similarities to much of today's "deep ecology" are apparent; in the latter case, a transhistorical account equally undermines historically concrete purchase on the dynamics of the depredations of nature.

50   On the different ideas of critique and their relationship to Frankfurt School critical theory, see Seyla Benhabib, *Critique, Norm and Utopia*.

51   Horkheimer, *Eclipse of Reason*, p. 182.

52   Quoted in Wiggershaus, *Frankfurt School*, p. 187; see also pp. 188 and 531 among many.

53 Horkheimer and Adorno, *Dialectic of Enlightenment*, p. 1.

54 This is a theme that comes up recurrently in work of the Frankfurt School; in addition to *Dialectic of Enlightenment*, see especially Adorno's *Negative Dialectics* which seeks to elucidate a positive concept of enlightenment – reflective enlightenment – to counter the negative one developed in *Dialectic of Enlightenment*.

55 Horkheimer and Adorno, *Dialectic of Enlightenment*, p. 6.

56 Horkheimer, *Eclipse of Reason*, p. 10; emphasis in original.

57 See also Arendt's nearly contemporary analyses of the same issue in *The Origins of Totalitarianism* and *Between Past and Future*.

58 Horkheimer, *Eclipse of Reason*, p. 13.

59 In addition to the works of Jay and Wiggershaus already cited, see Postone and Brick, "Critical Pessimism." It should be noted that this pessimistic turn affected Horkheimer and Adorno more deeply than some other members of the senior generation of the Frankfurt School (though in a sense a version of this pessimism had already taken the life of their associate Walter Benjamin who so resisted the need to leave Europe that he waited too late, and thinking he had failed in his attempt to escape occupied France committed suicide). Most notably, Herbert Marcuse never surrendered to it and continued to seek the possibilities for radical social transformation and to support social movements in a way Horkheimer and Adorno were afraid to do, seeing the likely end of all such movements as either repression or new terrors.

60 Horkheimer, *Eclipse of Reason*, p. 139.

61 See Fanon, *The Wretched of the Earth*, and the introduction written by Jean-Paul Sartre.

62 Marcuse, *One-Dimensional Man*, p. 244.

63 Marcuse, *Critique of Pure Tolerance* (with R. P. Wolff and B. Moore).

64 Negt, "Mass Media," p. 65. Negt's collaboration with Alexander Kluge, *The Public Sphere and Experience*, was a major attempt to work out this multifaceted development of critical theory in the context of the student movement.

65 Something of the same issue – addressed in a radically different way – informs Derrida's criticism of philosophies and artistic practices that pursue presence, and thinking that presumes speech to offer a ground of immediacy from which we are distanced by writing. In treating writing – with its nonimmediacy and differences – as primary, Derrida responds directly to what he seems to see as the illusions and dangers in the pursuit of immediacy. As I suggest further in chapter 4, reaction to this feature of the politics of the 1960s (as of existentialism and phenomenology – and for that matter of Romanticism) is an important source of the postmodern sensibility and structuralist/poststructuralist theory.

66 In addition to work directly on the relationship of theory to practice, thus, in this first agenda Habermas also took on debates about the methodology of the social sciences, trying to establish both the importance of going beyond a mere hermeneutics and the fallacy of positivist beliefs in a sharp separation of objective knowledge from interested human action. See

Habermas, *On the Logic of the Social Sciences* and his contribution to Adorno, et al., *The Positivist Dispute*.

67 Habermas, *Theory and Practice*, p. 1.

68 See Habermas, *Knowledge and Human Interests*. As Habermas summed up in *Theory and Practice*, p. 9, "the technical and practical interests of knowledge are not regulators of cognition which have to be eliminated for the sake of the objectivity of knowledge; instead, they themselves determine the aspect under which reality is objectified, and can thus be made accessible to experience to begin with."

69 See also Habermas, *Towards a Rational Society*.

70 Habermas, *Knowledge and Human Interests*, p. 284.

71 Habermas, *Theory and Practice*, p. 3.

72 Habermas took his *Habilitation* at Marburg under Wolfgang Abendroth, perhaps the only publicly active socialist professor in Germany at the time.

73 In addition to Habermas's *Structural Transformation* itself, see the essays in Calhoun, ed., *Habermas and the Public Sphere*, including the exposition and contextualization of Habermas's book in the introduction.

74 On the neglect of science and religion, see Zaret, in Calhoun, ed., *Habermas and the Public Sphere*. On the way in which scientific discourse has remained intertwined with the political public sphere, see Ezrahi, *The Descent of Icarus*.

75 Mass society theory itself grew partly out of the work of the earlier Frankfurt School, though the idea was broad and its roots older.

76 I have summarized Habermas's argument, and theoretical predicament, in more detail in the introduction to *Habermas and the Public Sphere*.

77 Habermas, *Legitimation Crisis*.

78 The key source here is Habermas's *Theory of Communicative Action*; a variety of later works have refined the basic theory presented there. The field of ethics has been a particularly important focus of attention; see Benhabib and Dallmayr, eds: *The Communicative Ethics Controversy*.

79 See Bernstein, ed., *Habermas and Modernity*; Honneth et al. (eds), *Philosophical Interventions in the Unfinished Project of Modernity*.

80 Letter from Horkheimer to Adorno, 1941, quoted in Wiggershaus, *The Frankfurt School*, p. 505. In *Philosophical Discourse of Modernity*, Habermas traces this theme back to a path of seeking the communicative redemption of free subjects broached, but abandoned, by the young Hegel.

81 See Adorno, *Negative Dialectics*, esp. p. 183.

82 Habermas, "A Positivistically Bisected Rationalism," p. 222.

83 It is now a joke to recall that on his return to Germany after the war, Adorno was invited to speak on the subject of empirical social research methods (largely because of his association with Lazarsfeld and the Princeton radio research project). Hubris being what it is, Adorno of course accepted.

84 Quoted in Wiggershaus, *Frankfurt School*, p. 4.

85 Taylor has helpfully discussed this idea (which has provenance in Gadamer among other sources) in his "Excursus on Historical Explanation" in *Sources of the Self*. I discuss this issue more fully in chapter 2 below.

2

Interpretation, Comparison, and Critique

I

Histories of sociology commonly tell us how the discipline was formed in the nineteenth-century struggle to understand the combined upheavals of the great political revolutions and the industrial revolution. These overturned the established order and posed a variety of questions that remain with us still: questions about class, community, the nature of social integration and processes of social change. This version of disciplinary history is true enough, but most tellings leave out important causal factors: the impact of voyages of discovery, of long-distance trade and colonization, of slavery, of nationalism, and of easier travel and communications on the transformation of European consciousness. Sociology, in other words, was born partly as comparative sociology, seeking to understand the ways in which societies (or cultures or peoples) differed from one another. A variety of dimensions were of interest, but perhaps none more so than differences in political system. Partly because Europeans were in the process of challenging absolutist authority and the divine rights of kings, they were particularly interested in contrasts that pointed up the extent to which certain countries enjoyed liberty, rule of law, and government in the interest of the people that were denied to others. The contrasts could be between France and Britain, between the Old World and the New, historically between the *ancien régime* and its successors, and perhaps most tellingly between Western Europe and "the East." Montesquieu and Tocqueville stand as the great "founding fathers" in this tradition.

It is easy to forget how powerful the East/West contrast was in constituting early modern social thought. Its *locus classicus* lay in accounts of Persia, such as Montesquieu's *Persian Letters*. But the East could also be Ottoman Turkey, India, China, and even Russia and on occasion Eastern or Central Europe. These views were generally "orientalist," as Edward Said has argued,[1] but the most crucial point for present purposes is not the prejudiced view early social thinkers had of the "East," but that they looked at other countries and epochs not only to learn about those places and peoples for their own sakes but to draw lessons for the contemporary West. As so many of us do all the time and at all levels of analysis, the founders of sociology looked at others to learn about themselves. When they looked at the "others," thus, scholars often took as obvious what it meant that some people were cannibals, or ruled by sultans, or married to multiple partners at once. This was as true of early anthropologists like James Fraser and Edward Tylor, with their vast apparatuses of classifications and interpretations of practices and myths divorced from their cultural contexts. It was in its revolt against this sort of thinking that anthropology (led perhaps above all by Bronislaw Malinowski) made itself into the discipline that argued that the meaning of such things was not obvious but had to be explained in the context of an account of a whole "indigenous" society or culture. But sociology (not altogether a separate discipline at the outset) was not entirely ethnocentric, and also developed traditions that problematized the cross-cultural constitution of meaningful interpretations.

If sociologists, and modern social theorists more generally, started with a concern for difference, however, they also projected it outward in "them/us" contrasts. From very early on, European thinkers approached human diversity with a vision of differences among types, not a ubiquity of cross-cutting differentiations.[2] This affected not only their views of others, but their views of themselves. Especially under the influence of nationalist ideas, they developed notions of societies as singular, bounded, and internally integrated, and as realms in which people were more or less the same. On this basis, a great deal of modern social theory came to incorporate prereflectively the notion that human beings naturally inhabit only a single social world or culture at a time.[3] People on borders, children of mixed marriages, those rising through social mobility, and those migrating from one society to another were all constituted for social theory as people with problems by contrast to the presumed ideal of people who inhabited a single social world and could therefore unambiguously place themselves in their social environments. The implicit phenomenological presumption was that human life would be easier if individuals did not have to manage a heterogeneity of social worlds or modes of cultural understanding. An ideal of clarity and consistency prevailed. This ideal of course reflected broadly rationalist thinking, but it should not be interpreted as limited to rationalistic (or

Enlightenment) views. Much of the jargon of authenticity in Romantic and later anti-rationalist thought shares the same idealization of the notion of inhabiting a single self-consistent life world.[4] This notion of the external world mirrored a preFreudian (not to mention preBakhtinian) notion of the potential self-consistent internal life of the individual – one represented in the very term "individual" with its implication that the person cannot be internally divided.

This notion of inhabiting singular social contexts or lifeworlds as integral beings reflected both assumptions about how actual social life was organized and ideals about how social life ought to be organized. It invoked, in other words, an idea of normality. But the early theorists did not for the most part see their contemporary world as unproblematic on this dimension. Rather, they recognized that people around them faced challenges in trying to come to terms with differences, border crossings, and interstitial positions. This led to an understanding of the past as one in which singular social worlds more completely enveloped people; in which society was less differentiated and less complicated. This was for some a golden age, but most social scientists emphasized that for better or worse modernity meant parting with such visions. One powerful version of this argument has been Weber's notion of the differentiation of value spheres, itself an elaboration of a Kantian distinction.[5] In modern societies, Weber suggested, the realms of truth (theory), morality (practice), and aesthetics (judgment) must be differentiated; dedifferentiation is a pathology. This view carried forward directly into the work of the early Frankfurt theorists and continues to shape that of Habermas (among many others).

Durkheim took a partially similar tack when he contrasted mechanical to organic social solidarity.[6] He stressed that the older, mechanical form of social solidarity was one rooted in sameness and consensus. The modern organic form was rooted in the division of labor and presupposed functional interdependence based on difference. But, actually existing modern societies were pathological on Durkheim's account, for they lacked the necessary means of reconciling individuals to these differentiated societies. Durkheim conceptualized these means first in social terms – the need for strong groups of intermediate scale, like occupational associations – and second in cultural terms – the need for some overarching ideology or collective representations that would reveal the nature of the singular whole of their social world to individual members.

There are obviously senses in which the view that modern social life is distinctively characterized by differentiation makes sense. Social life is organized on an extremely large scale and subgroups that have a high level of autonomy in some respects are at the same time closely interdependent with each other. Whether because it is necessary or simply because it has been historically produced, the distinction among truth, goodness, and beauty (and/or its analogs) does indeed structure a great deal of contemporary discourse.

Yet there is problematic baggage packed into this way of understanding epochal change. Along with an appreciation of the scale, differentiation, and intensification of modern social life these accounts present us with the presumption that earlier modes of life were basically organized in terms of internal sameness or dedifferentiation. This is what gives Weber's account its special pathos, for example, because Weber sees the differentiation of value spheres as essential to maintaining rationality and a fragile arrangement constantly vulnerable to collapse and as yet simultaneously part of what produces the iron cage. His successors who lived through the Nazi era were even more impressed with the threat of dedifferentiation. Durkheim too saw the pathologies of modern people as stemming significantly from the difficulties of coping with this internally differentiated world. And both Durkheim and Weber saw differentiation producing these challenges even without seriously questioning the notion that people would live inside one social world, one society (or subculture) at a time.

Both Durkheim and Weber in this way reflected emerging features of modern thought that were closely associated with nationalism. They saw human life as "naturally" involving social worlds of internal sameness and only contingently and with difficulty adapting to worlds of high differentiation. Within worlds of high differentiation they saw people managing by locating themselves firmly within one or another sphere of social relationships and orientations to action. They developed nothing like DuBois's concept of "double consciousness."[7] In Weber's most classic contrast, thus, one opted for science or politics as a vocation, not for both.

But of course Weber's own life suggested otherwise.[8] He wrote purely academic treatises and entered directly into public life and practical action. He revealed that it was indeed possible to inhabit multiple social worlds and to manage their conjunctures and disjunctures (if not always happily). Modernity may present a number of distinctive challenges of this kind, but we should also be careful not to follow the many classical social theorists whose examination of "other cultures" was conducted in a way that hypostatized both the otherness and the integral unity of cultures. People have long inhabited multiple social worlds at the same time. Multilinguality is as "natural" as monolinguality. Trade has established linkages across political and cultural frontiers. The great religions have spread across divergent local cultures and maintained connections among them. Even in the relatively small-scale, low-technology societies that most informed Durkheim's notion of mechanical solidarity, people inhabited multiple horizons of experience, for example as members simultaneously of local lineages and far-flung clans. In great civilizations like India that were not organized as singular political units, this was all the more true.

It is important, thus, both that we recover from the traditional histories of sociology the extent to which the discipline was formed in the challenge of confronting difference and that we recognize the way in which difference was constituted for most sociologists as a problem when it came to be manifest inside putatively singular social worlds. Comparative sociology for the most part reinforced the presumption of internal integrity by taking presumptively "whole" societies as its units. From its beginning, in short, sociology posed basic questions about how to interpret the meaning of different ways of life, but it tended not to grasp how much and how often those different ways of life could be inhabited simultaneously by the same persons.

It is important today to recover the sociological tradition of addressing the challenges of cultural and historical difference, but to do so in ways that do not render observed differences the bases for hypostatizing contrasting "whole" societies or cultures as though they were internally integral. It is in something of this spirit that Sorokin generations ago criticized those who studied cultures with the presumption that these were necessarily cognitively or logically integrated units, rather than seeing such integration as an empirical variable.[9] We need to see not only that empirical variable, however, but the practical activity by which ordinary people manage cultural complexity and the interfaces among social worlds.[10] The issue is not just to avoid "essentialist" invocations of integral identity, but to see that just pointing to "social construction" offers little if any analytic purchase.[11] It is not just that collective identities and ways of life are created, but that they are internally contested, that their boundaries are porous and overlapping, and that people live in more than one at the same time.

II

None of this, of course, makes the more straightforward issues of how to undertake interpretation and comparison across lines of difference any less important. It is a serious deficiency that contemporary sociologists (especially in the US) recognize the deep relation of their discipline to the historical challenge of interpretation and difference mainly in terms of vague references to Weber's notion of *Verstehen* and his involvement in the *Methodenstreit*, the turn-of-the-century German struggle over the nature of historical knowledge, science, and the claims of social science. Still, even if stopping the story at this point is a problem, this is not a bad place to begin. It was in this context, arguing against Schleiermacher's notions of historical recovery, that Weber claimed "one does not need to be Caesar to understand Caesar."[12]

In the rest of this chapter, I want to discuss something of the ways in which sociologists have struggled with the challenge of understanding Caesar – or others different from themselves. I will first explore further some of the conditions that initially both made this problematic and opened certain particular intellectual approaches to it. I will then turn to the different theoretical nexuses in which the problem of interpretation has been posed for sociologists, and finally to the ways in which this issue is addressed – or more often avoided – in the contemporary sociology of culture. I will suggest that grappling successfully with the set of issues thus posed is crucial not only for comparative or cross-cultural sociology as a general pursuit of knowledge, but specifically and vitally for the development of critical sociology able to break with the received categories of social understanding, to engage not simply in an endless production of different interpretations but in dialogue across lines of difference, and thus to inform normative discourse. Taking interpretation seriously, in short, is essential to developing sociology as part of our human capacity for practical reason. Later chapters will press further both the issue of "cross-cultural" interpretation and the issue of "internal" contest over culture.

Discourse that takes interpretation seriously is typically called "hermeneutics." The term "hermeneutic," in this discussion, is both a general term for the study of interpretation, and therefore for sociology's struggle with interpretation, and the label for one particular historical tradition of tackling the problems posed by interpretation – that expanded from roots in Biblical scholarship, Schleiermacher, Dilthey, Heidegger, and Gadamer. At the present time, a variety of different analytic traditions are bringing forward serious accounts of interpretation, and of the effects of different ways of framing and presenting social analysis: Hans-Georg Gadamer is by far the most important figure, but in addition to hermeneutics narrowly conceived there are rhetoric, which is enjoying a resurgent influence (exemplified in the social sciences by Donald McCloskey's work in economics and more generally by that of Wayne Booth), new understandings of legal argument and change such as that of Ronald Dworkin, new trends in the philosophy of science from Kuhn through Feyerabend, the poststructuralist movement in cultural theory, and the revitalized interest in the American tradition of pragmatism.

Hermeneutic problems are of significance for social theory primarily because of historical distance and cultural difference. We are especially apt to become aware of difficulties and uncertainties in the interpretation of meaning, in other words, when we attempt to understand social actions whose meaning is embedded in contexts very different from our own. The relevant differences of context may stem from either material conditions or differences in the symbolic production of meaning. By material conditions I mean those various concrete pressures and possibilities that shape action and meaning in different settings whether or not they are recognized by actors or exert their influence through discourse. We face a hurdle, thus, in understanding those whose lives and actions never involved printed texts, widespread literacy, or electronic communications technologies, for example, since these are ubiquitous in our own lives and constitutive of our own understanding of social life. Variance in population density also shapes communication and other meaningful aspects of social life, even when it is not made into an object of discourse or cultural meaning. Differences of context may also stem from the internal cultural construction of meaning. Such differences arise in language, in schemes of identification and valuation, and in orientations to social practice. They bear on the fact that understanding human beings is not just a matter of interpreting their action, but also of understanding the ways in which their own interpretations and constructions of meaning shaped their action. This is what Anthony Giddens famously dubbed the "double hermeneutic."[13]

In both these senses, then, we face difficulties in interpreting social life that is differently constituted from our own. In a nutshell, our resources for making sense of it, for giving meaning to what we can observe of it, derive from our own culture (including intellectual traditions) and from previous experience. These are the only resources we have, but in applying them we necessarily run the risk of failing to grasp meanings operative in other contexts while constituting for ourselves meanings that were not at work there.

In a very general sense, the problem of interpretation across lines of difference is at work in any conversation; it is implied by the philosophical problem of how we know other minds. It is, therefore, no accident that many approaches to this problem focus on a model of conversation. Hans-Georg Gadamer, for example, presents a hermeneutics built around the notion of dialogue, the reciprocal process of questioning and learning from each other by which two or more parties move towards consensus at least on certain aspects of what they have discussed. This dialogical model is rooted in Gadamer's appreciation of the earlier Socratic dialogues in which all parties participate actively and each learns from the others (by contrast to Socrates' domination of the later dialogues). Jürgen Habermas, by contrast, worries that Gadamer's conversational model does not distinguish adequately between consensus based on persuasion and that based on truth. In an account of the "ideal speech situation" and similar regulative ideals he attempts to ground an account of discourse on validity claims implicit in all speech. These claims – to truthfulness, sincerity, and rightness – propel discourse forward in a cumulative development towards truth and certainly, even if these are only approached asymptotically.[14]

But there are problems with this whole approach to interpretation and dialogicality through the model of conversation. It grasps a good deal, to be sure, and we can learn from both Gadamer's and Habermas's analyses. But both, and especially Habermas, tend to focus so completely on interpersonal conversation that they do not recognize the full significance of intrapersonal dialogue. One of the key resources we have for communication with others (it is more or less redundant to say "others who are different from ourselves" since this is always a matter of degree, however radical) is that we are not entirely "self-same." Freud and Bakhtin in different ways stressed the internal complexity of the person. Whether in object-relations or ego-analytic terms, thus, psychoanalysis points out the extent to which being a person means coping with a variety of different identities, identifications, and objects; balancing impulses, self-criticism, and sense of reality. Much of what Bakhtin saw in the modern novel was a reflection of a human capacity to carry on an interior dialogue, indeed the constitution of the human being through this dialogicality.[15] Because we already engage ourselves through interior dialogue, we are better placed to come to understandings of others and to bridge significant differences than if we were only monological speakers of self-sameness.[16]

Habermas approaches internal complexity mainly through recognition of the importance of intersubjectivity. That is, he sees that people are not self-identical in any simple sense because each is constituted as a person both through relations to others and through participation in more or less impersonal but social processes such as language. Our very capacity to speak of ourselves thus draws on resources partially outside ourselves. This is a crucial insight linked to recognition of the centrality of internal dialogue, but also significantly different.

Habermas remains within an approach that presumes consensus as its goal. If one takes the notion of interior dialogicality seriously – if one grants that people are constituted by tensions within themselves, as well as by their definitely held views or propensities – then one cannot quite imagine perfect consensus as a desirable social goal. Certainly we do seek consensus about various matters of truth and practical action. We hold more or less rational and in any case discursively available values and understandings of the world that we wish to be confident that others share. But creatures who had only such discursively available and definite understandings and values, and who were altogether or even basically self-consistent about them, would not be recognizable as humans.

Part of the problem is that Habermas has adopted a strong version of the widespread assumption (noted at the beginning of the chapter) that human beings naturally inhabit a single horizon of experience, a single social world, at a time. This informs a view in which establishing consensus is the program both for living within that social world and for building bridges to other social worlds. But if we start from the view that human beings can and indeed very commonly do inhabit multiple and internally differentiated social worlds – for example, if we take seriously the idea of double consciousness – then we are led less to see consensus as the orientation of all communication. For one thing, we are led less to rely on sender-receiver models that presume the issue is one of adequate translation between "thoughts" that start out in one head and are transmitted to the other.[17] Beyond this, we can recognize that each of us develops various practical skills for managing our lives in multiple social worlds, and for constituting ourselves against multiple horizons of experience. These practical skills are basic to meeting the challenge of communicating across lines of difference. What we seek – and indeed often achieve – is not consensus as such, but adequate mutual understanding for the pursuit of various practical tasks in which we are jointly engaged. Just as we do not come to complete self-understanding or complete "consensus" among the voices in our interior dialogues, so we do not do so in exterior, interpersonal or societal dialogues. Indeed, we cannot and it does not altogether make sense even to conceptualize this as the central goal or ideal for our efforts. This does not mean that consensus is not important, but (1) that it is an account of the nature of mutual understanding appropriate to certain domains of rational critical discourse and not to all of social life, and (2) even those restricted domains (e.g. law courts) in which the rational critical pursuit of consensus is what we would want rest on foundations not just in language but in less discursive and less consensual practical agreements.

The conversation model for interpretation and mutual understanding also has other limits. Notably, accounts like Habermas's and Gadamer's tend to posit participation in conversation as a given and recognize inequalities and power only as distortions and intrusions. It is hard to relate such model discourses to those settings in actual social life where conversation itself is imposed by force and maintained by unequal power. Perhaps the most obvious of these are slavery and colonialism.

Even more generally, the whole modern problem of interpretation across lines of differences has been constituted by the processes of state-building and capitalist expansion. Both within Europe and throughout the world, the challenges of cross-cultural relations did not arise and still do not arise either as mere intellectual pursuits or as results of the unconstrained choices of free and equal partners to engage in conversation. They are produced in large part by the exercise of power, whether that power appears in the form of a centralizing state suppressing subordinate ethnicities, of a colonial state backed by an army, of a multinational corporation, or of the dominance of Western communications media. Power is not simply a distortion of the conversation, it is its occasion. Yanomamo in the Amazon basin and Papuans in New Guinea generally have not simply sought out Europeans for dialogue aimed at mutual understanding.

Now of course Habermas and Gadamer can both answer to the effect that they were not analyzing actual conversations (and still less cross-cultural relations) but proposing accounts of how we might understand conversation to be able to move towards mutual understanding and truth. Nonetheless, the problem is a serious one. In the first place, it simply poses an unrealistic notion that meaning can be separated from distorting influences rather than appearing always and only in relations constituted in part by power (as well as by other determinations not reducible to meaning, such as social structure). Approaches such as Gadamer's and Habermas's are superior to the idea of a pure semiotics; at least they locate the pursuit of meaning in dialogue rather than in the external point of view of a semiotician. They do not advocate the kind of science of pure meaning suggested by semiotics (and attacked for example by Bourdieu[18]). Their views are plausible accounts of the pursuit of understanding – and thus can represent viable contending positions in the philosophy of science, or inform accounts of legal processes. The catch is that cross-cultural relations are not occasioned primarily by the pursuit of understanding. The efforts of social scientists to interpret other cultures are never free from the larger structures that bring the different cultures into relationship. Much the same could be said of many interpersonal relations – they are crucially constituted by power. This is, for example, the crux of Nancy Fraser's criticism of Habermas's tendency to ground his notion of a lifeworld free from systemic distortions of communication in appeals to idealizations of family life. Families are hardly realms of free and uncoerced mutual pursuit of understanding.[19] Habermas's appeals to the model of psychoanalysis are similarly problematic.[20] It is not clear how one could establish a collective analog to the roles occupied by analyst and analysand. We can learn from the importance of intersubjectivity to achieving self-understanding, from ideas about systematically motivated blockage and distortion, and from how a mixture of strategic and pure communicative action is required, but it is hard to figure out what sort of collective *project* is strictly analogous to psychoanalysis, and especially what sort of project *between different cultures*.

Not least of all, the very notion of difference with which social scientists work is constituted by the way in which the modern world has developed. "Cultures" and "societies" are not simply given as units in the nature of things, nor is this an arbitrary construct of social scientists, a sort of unmotivated mistake. Cultures and societies have been constituted as putatively bounded units in a world-system that is presumed to divide into an exhaustive and more or less mutually exclusive set of such units. Conditioned by state-building and the global expansion occasioned above all by capitalism, moderns have come to see the world through the lenses of nationalist discourse – that is, in terms of the kinds of collective identities and divisions defined paradigmatically by the notion of nation. "Nation" is a particular construct informed by power relations; it shapes not just the specific interpretations of those who use the concept but the very idea of difference between discrete cultures that is implicit in all our discussions of cross-cultural relations.

Similarly, the social scientist's standpoint of observation is constituted as the synoptic view of a representative of an international culture. Institutionalizing this notion of an international culture was one of the achievements of the Enlightenment; at the same time, the Enlightenment itself depended on an infrastructure of networks across lines of cultural difference to provide the social organizational basis for its discourse. It is only from the vantage point of "international culture" that seemingly disinterested accounts of particular cultures or of the general problem of cultural difference can be posed. International culture constitutes the ground of a specifically social scientific equivalent to the Cartesian "view from nowhere" that informs the modern notion of science and epistemology generally. But of course it is a view from somewhere, even if not precisely spatially located. And it is a view that preforms the supposedly brute facts of social science observation – for example, by constituting nations as appropriate units of comparative research.

This construction of "cultures," "societies," and "nations" as basic units of modern collective identity and of comparative social science research has significant implications. In the first place, it implies that each one is somehow discrete and subsists as an entity unto itself rather than only as part of a world system or some other broader social organization or discourse that defines it as a constituent unit or part. This boundedness is suggested, in large part, by the sharp boundedness of modern states; the ideology of nationalism promotes the notion that each state has or should have its own singular culture (and vice versa). We extrapolate from archetypal examples. French culture is claimed as something clearly distinct from German (never mind the Alsace); Norwegian culture is something clearly distinct from Danish (no matter how much they have been joined historically, how mutually intelligible their languages, or how similar they seem by comparison with Borneo). This way of constructing cultures as objects of our study, however, obscures interconnections. It implies, for example, that neither the Scandinavian language family nor the Nordic group of societies is more than an aggregate term; Norwegian, Danish, Swedish, Finnish, and Icelandic cultures are implied to be the only primary units. Or to take an example of more practical moment, it makes it hard for us to figure out the relationship between the term Europe and the various putative nations that also have claims on the identities of Europeans. This idea of discreteness is also a key factor in constituting the modern problem of ethnicity, minorities, or subcultures. In a nutshell, these are terms we apply when we want to deny that some collection of people constitute a fully autonomous and/or modern culture because this would imply that they constituted a nation which would imply that they had a legitimate claim on a state. We do not leap to list Sami (Lapps) as one of the constituent Nordic cultures, I think, largely because Sami have played little role in the history of contentions over the proper constitution of nation-states in the region.[21]

The Sami not only confound our notion of a discrete Norway, secondly, they confound the notion that Norway has a completely unified, integrated culture. Yet referring to "cultures" and "nations" as integral is a second key implication of our typical usage. We refer to each as though it constitutes a single thing to which determinate reference can be made, rather than a cluster of tensions, contradictions, and agonisms. Thus we assume that with an appropriate sample, we can compare Japanese culture to Norwegian culture. We take it as given in such studies that the "culture" can be an object of unitary reference rather than a term needing to be deconstructed. We assume that it is something "out there" to be revealed to us by the responses of a set of individuals, and that the main issue before us is the methodological problem of accurately constituting a "representative" set of individuals. This reflects, in part, our characteristic understanding of the nation as comprising a set of individuals rather than subordinate powers or communities; national identity is understood as inscribed directly into individual identity, the relation between the two terms is unmediated.[22] At the same time, thinking of cultures as integral, we tend both to hypostatize them and to direct attention away from the ways in which they are internally complex and continually reshaped by struggle.

Thirdly, in speaking of "cultures" and "nations" as units, we tend to imply that they are equivalent. This is sometimes a practical, political issue – as for example San Marino with its 24,000 citizens enjoys the same formal status in organizations like the United Nations as do Germany, the United States, and Brazil. It is also a prejudgment that shapes our understanding of ways of life different from our own. We attempt to understand their putatively discrete, integral cultures on analogy to our own, assuming that they must be functional equivalents. This sort of assumption – along with those of discreteness and integrity – has been challenged in a good deal of recent anthropology. Famously, for example, Jack Goody challenged attempts to define a set of discrete, equivalent, and internally unitary cultures in Northern Ghana. He pointed out the ways in which language, religious observance, mythology, and kinship patterns varied along a continuum in certain locales. Previous British observers, thus, had developed a categorization of "Lo" and "Dagaa" as separate and distinct cultures. This was a misunderstanding, Goody argued, for Lo and Dagaa are really more like poles to a continuum. Those in the middle were not marginal to each of two different cultures, or representative of some confusion between them. They were full participants in a way of life defined in varying degree by different forms of practice – not unlike the children of Norwegian immigrant mothers and Irish Catholic fathers who in the US are just as American as anybody else.[23]

The point here is not that we must abandon the notions of culture or nation, assuming that such a thing would be possible. It is that we need to recognize the ways in which such units (1) preform our empirical observations of the world, (2) constitute central dimensions of the modern idea of difference that informs our problems of cross-cultural understanding, and (3) constitute the premise of our own putatively synoptic understanding of the world of such differences on the basis of our position in an international culture. This last, for better or worse, does not remove us from the play of practical concerns and allow us the universal view of free-floating intellectuals. It positions us within a sociohistorical process (or set of processes) that by virtue of expanding throughout the globe pose us certain problems and open certain paths for solving them.[24]

III

Obviously both differences and interrelationships among people – and peoples – existed long before what we call the modern epoch. Ancient Greeks commented on the differences among their city states and between Greeks generally and various other people with whom they came in contact. The great empires of world history all involved long-distance trade, tributary legations, and military recruitment that established contact among diverse people; many created cosmopolitan cities in which cross-cultural relations were a matter of daily contact. What then made the problem of difference and consequent problems of interpretation distinctively modern? The philosopher Wilhelm Dilthey gave one important answer when he described the birth of modern hermeneutics as the "liberation of interpretation from dogma."[25] Dilthey referred to the Protestant Reformation with its attack on the authority of the ecclesiastical hierarchy to dictate proper interpretation of the Bible. The Roman Catholic Church had attempted to impose theological uniformity; Protestants were inherently schismatic. Martin Luther was not the first heretic, of course; indeed, the Catholic Church had only achieved its capacity to enforce a certain orthodoxy in the late patristic era – fighting a host of heretical sects – and it was never complete. But Luther and the Protestant Reformation generally helped to expose orthodoxy as an imposition of force and so – contrary to the intentions of many – to encourage a basic presumption of heterodoxy.

Pierre Bourdieu has usefully discussed the movement of doxai – opinions or beliefs – from being simply the taken-for-granted background conditions of life – what he calls *doxa* – through *orthodoxy* with its recognition but implicit condemnation of otherness and *heterodoxy* with its sense of the unavoidability of multiple views. The Protestant Reformation figured prominently in this story. This is not because Protestants were necessarily tolerant; many were as quick to discover heretics or witches as their Catholic brethren. What Protestants did was (1) to create conditions in which Catholic orthodoxy could not appear as taken-for-granted and was likely to be seen as imposed, (2) to offer a series of competing orthodoxies which predisposed their followers (and other observers) to some acceptance of the heterodox nature of the world (even despite their leaders' best intentions), and (3) to make religious faith a matter of active choice, bringing forward disputes over a variety of particulars from the proper mode of communion to the status of the Trinity and the legitimacy of priestly marriage. In this context, the interpretation of Biblical texts took on a new significance – and a new excitement and danger. At the same time, once people began to inquire in this way into the significance of Biblical teachings, they were led to note certain distances between the historical conditions portrayed in the Bible and their own lives. For the first time, Christians faced on a large scale the challenge that had long been posed to Jews, and which had helped to occasion the Talmud – that of adapting a manifestly historically specific set of sacred texts to serve as guides to lives lived under historically different conditions.

Similar issues have shaped relationships to classical or sacred texts in other traditions – to Vedic lore in India and to Confucian texts in China, for example. Once the distance between the texts and present-day life was established, once they could not be fitted immediately into the same unproblematic background *doxa*, then interpretation became problematic. Attempts could be made to impose orthodoxy, but social change always brought the prospect of heterodox challenges.[26]

Protestants of course lapsed back into dogma and orthodoxy of their own, but they established a basic principle of hermeneutics – the idea that sacred texts are to be understood, at least in part, on their own terms and for themselves even though they come to us across a basic gulf of historical change. It was this idea that posed problems of interpretation. It suggested the need for direct access to the sacred texts, of course, thus occasioning a pressure for printing, for widespread literacy, and for refusal of priestly restrictions on reading the Bible. But it also suggested the need for some rules of interpretation to help in the reading. For example, efforts to understand the Bible could be guided by the principle of trying to achieve consistency among its many diverse parts and seemingly conflicting statements.[27]

The Reformation was but one moment or phase in a long series of transformations that helped to inaugurate the modern era as one crucially constituted by the interplay of orthodoxy and heterodoxy, sameness and difference. As Gadamer has written:

> When the remoteness of the lofty and the remoteness of the recondite needed to be overcome not simply in specialized domains such as religious documents, texts of law, or the classics in their foreign languages, but when the historical tradition in its entirety up to the present moment moved into a position of similar remoteness, the problem of hermeneutics entered intrinsically into the philosophic awareness of problems. This took place in virtue of the great breach in tradition brought about by the French Revolution and as a result of which European civilization splintered into national cultures.[28]

It is perhaps best to think of the French Revolution as a symbol for a cluster of decisive events, including not least of all the Protestant Reformation, rather than the sole and sufficient cause of this momentous transformation. Nonetheless, Gadamer's point is strong. The problem of radical otherness is constituted as a problem of the universality of interpretation across lines of difference because modernity appears (1) as a break with tradition, turning tradition into history, and (2) as a breaking-up of the broad social and civilizational commonality within which (at least European) ways of life were loosely differentiated, replacing Western Christendom with bounded nations (and reified cultures). Of course, modernity is not the first occasion of a break in tradition. Once more or less unitary Islam has been divided into theologically and ethnically distinct variants since very early in its history – the introduction of nationalism and secular states into the *umma Islam* has exacerbated the problem, which provides the occasion for a project of reunification which helps to inform contemporary Islamic fundamentalism. In another vital sense, the literate, orthodox "big traditions" of religious and cultural transmission already constituted major breaks with the "little traditions" of every passing on of information and reproduction of the social world in all its immediate identities and relationships.[29] The unity of Christendom broke the grip of numerous local cultures and traditions, both religious and secular. Indeed, in the hermeneutic tradition and in modern Western thought more generally, "tradition" is too easily identified with Catholic orthodoxy and other aspects of medieval Europe rather than with the more radically traditional social organization characteristic of many ways of life around the world. Like other literate "big traditions," Christianity was always subject to hermeneutic problems and self-conscious interventions in reflected understandings not typical of traditions passed on locally, face-to-face, without the mediation of textual experts – whether in acephalous African societies, village India before Mughal rule, or elsewhere (including alongside or beneath the very gaze of "big traditions").

In very much the same sense that Dilthey thought the Protestant Reformation liberated Biblical interpretation from dogma, the development of the social sciences – especially sociology and anthropology – might be taken as liberating cross-cultural comparison from established European accounts of the heathen world. This does not mean that sociologists or anthropologists were free from prejudices, any more than Protestants were. Many reproduced the attitudes of colonists towards colonized, for example. More generally, as I have hinted and Gadamer has argued at length, there is no such thing as an understanding free from prejudices: we are always shaped by our origins, our thought is always situated, we are unable to think without taking some things for granted. What we take for granted is determined by our own cultural backgrounds, and more specifically by our academic training. Nonetheless, whether biased or not, sociologists and anthropologists set about attempting to make sense of other ways of life, other forms of social organization or culture, in terms of the way they worked internally. Functionalist analysis obviously reflected this, but so in a different way did Weber's adoption of the notion of *Verstehen*. What this meant was that in a central way, especially insofar as it was necessarily comparative, sociology took on the task of interpreting contrasting ways of life. This was fundamentally different from the practical understanding of other ways of life occasioned, for example, by living in the same imperial city. In Istanbul, for example, Jews might be in daily contact with Muslims and Christians, but have no reason to develop a sociology of the gentile world. Neither, in this example, would it have been necessary to choose between absolutizing the difference between Jews and others as "nations," or reducing their differences to mere ethnic variation among the citizens of a single nation. Among other reasons, though they would have needed to interact, they would not have been called upon to deliberate or to confer legitimacy on a government.[30]

Confronted with other cultures, sociologists could find no access to these contrasting ways of life through "brute facts" not needing some manner of interpretation. This was perhaps equally true of sociology's domestic analyses, but more easily ignored.[31] At the very least, looking abroad, it was necessary to translate from one language to another in order to make study possible. Generally, translation depended on some level of more general interpretation. Usually, this more general level operated at least partially in its own terms and understandings; it was, in the currently fashionable term, a "metadiscourse." How could one make sense of the kin relations, for example, without situating a variety of indigenous terms in relation to one another in order to construct analogies between the set of relationships being studied and those described in the analyst's language? Translation adequate to comparative analysis requires an interpretation of a whole organization of activity, not just the matching of vocabulary. Indeed, as the next chapter will explore in more detail, the very metaphor of translation may be of limited value in explaining how cross-cultural understanding is achieved. Even within a single cultural setting, interpretation of practical activity faces significant inherent problems, since most practical activity is not directly amenable to discursive rendering. It is difficult, that is, to put into words the embodied understandings and practical skills by which a host of everyday activities are made possible. To think all human action reducible to rules, and therefore to potentially decontextualized explication, is one of the fallacies Pierre Bourdieu criticizes as characteristic of "objectivism." "The logicism inherent in the objectivist standpoint leads those who adopt it to forget that scientific construction cannot grasp the principles of practical logic without changing the nature of those principles: when made explicit for objective study, a practical succession becomes a represented succession."[32] A large part of the role of theory in sociology is providing the guidelines for these efforts of interpretation. This is one reason why so much of the most influential "classical" theory is hard to reduce to testable propositions; it is rich with empirical description and offers frameworks for interpretation.

Neither theories nor specific interpretations can be proved or checked for correctness solely by reference to a set of methodological principles. They must be constructed and evaluated in relation to a range of empirical knowledge through a process of judgment and practical reason. They are judged by whether they are persuasive, whether they seem to make sense, whether they seem adequate to various practical projects. The criteria for this include systematicity, parsimony, scope, intuitive insight, and the like. But these are never conclusive. They do not establish which theory is right when two theories clash, or which of two conflicting interpretations we should believe. The same problems arise in deciding which of the criteria to prefer when they themselves clash. Above all, we evaluate complex empirical interpretations in relationship to the range of other such interpretations we have accepted and in general what we know of the world. One of the best examples of this as an aspect of academic training is the way in which anthropologists master (or at least used to master) a variety of ethnographies from all over the world. These formed the context for their evaluation of new studies.

Despite what I have argued is the centrality of the interpretative task to the history and role of sociology, we do not try to teach it or thematize it very directly as a problem in sociology. The discipline has long been characterized by efforts to repress it or reduce it to a minor and seemingly unproblematic preliminary stage of research. These efforts have been occasioned largely by attempts to make sociology more "scientific." Indeed, a good deal of the relationship of hermeneutics to sociology in recent years has been focused on the philosophy of science question of how similar to the natural sciences sociology is or should be. Unfortunately, regardless of the merits of the arguments, they have often cast hermeneutics (and similar lines of argument) in a negative role. That is, arguments about the centrality of interpretation to sociology have appeared largely as critiques of prevailing scientism and empiricism. The point has been made over and again that positivist sociology fails to attend to the essentially meaningful, preinterpreted character of human life, and by attempting to reduce human beings to mere objects misses something fundamental to their nature. I will not repeat such arguments now. The problem is not to make this negative point better, or more often, but to focus attention on how better to do the actual interpretative work of sociology.

IV

Rather than simply expostulating on my ideas of what a good sociology would look like, let me turn for a moment to the soicology of culture as it already exists. A great deal of sociology has been conducted as though culture were a separate field of study that could unproblematically be left to anthropologists, literary critics, and others. Recently, however, culture has returned to sociology, sometimes with a vengeance. Where sociology has seemed to have little to say about culture, moreover, it has often been excluded from or devalued in exciting and influential interdisciplinary discourses (to the loss of both sociology and those other discourses). To a surprisingly large degree, however, the sociological subfield of cultural analysis is not a particularly good place to look for serious hermeneutical engagement. One could say the glass is half full, that after years of repressing culture sociologists are studying it in increasing numbers. But those who see the glass as half empty will have to retort that too many sociologists of culture are doing so in ways that avoid serious hermeneutical (and socio-historical or theoretical) questions in order to maximize their newfound legitimacy.

There are several senses in which attention to culture has been urged on sociologists. First, and with fewest transformative implications, it has been argued that as a set of more or less objective social products – books, films, paintings – culture deserves more sociological attention than it has received. Culture, in this sense, is understood as a special domain of objects, social actions, and institutions. Studies aim to understand who produces these objects and how, who gets access to them and why, what processes determine the fate of different producers and products, how formal organizations shape, select, or disseminate cultural products and so forth. Though some of these studies are more creative, it is quite possible to contribute to this literature by applying conventional sociological research techniques, conceptualizations, and theories to this specific domain. Thus one might ask about the socio-economic status of those who go to museums, or the structural position of those who make decisions about arts programming, or the ways in which artistic producers forge a community or subculture. Two common threads unite work in this approach: (1) culture is treated in terms of more or less objectified indicators; and (2) attention to culture is compartmentalized within sociology as the study of a specific domain of social life, analogous to law or medicine. These two characteristics remain distinctive and in force even when this approach is expanded beyond the study of the arts in which it originated and includes studies of popular culture.

A second claim about the importance of culture has more central sociological significance. This turns on the argument that social research in general requires paying attention to culture as a sort of methodological propaedeutic. In constructing surveys, thus, sociologists must be concerned to avoid or control for cultural bias. In developing categories of analysis, sociologists must be clear that they are often working with culture-specific categories that they have induced as though they were obvious in their meaning and nonproblematic. Thus sociologists using the term race need to worry about the "cultural baggage" that comes with the use of this term, the extent to which it represents a historically specific and possibly prejudicial understanding of certain social phenomena, the number of different meanings that it bundles together (though analysis might fruitfully unpack them and make them several separate dimensions or variables), and the extent to which its meaning is inherently contestable. This series of arguments can be presented narrowly as a critique of specific terms and part of a project of finding better, less problematic terms, or more broadly as an argument for the necessarily unstable and multivocal character of sociological concepts and the need for them to be analyzed as parts of broader cultural contexts.[33]

Recognition of this led to a new wave of cross-cultural research, still designed largely as part of an effort to uncover universal processes or laws; researchers assumed accordingly that cross-cultural variation, while possibly interesting at a surface level, was not deeply problematic; it was in some combination (1) a matter of residual variance, (2) a matter of extraneous factors to be controlled for, or (3) a "black box" standing in for proper structural or other variables that had not yet been discovered. Culture became the object of somewhat more serious study within this tradition, perhaps ironically, as the result of methodological problems rather than substantive interest. Researchers found that translating survey instruments was more than merely technically difficult, more than simply a matter of finding the right words, since people in different cultures apparently thought differently about various issues, used different schemes of evaluation, and categorized their experiences in different ways.

Attention to this cluster of issues is valuable for all sorts of sociological work, of course, but it has been brought forward because of sociologists' increasing awareness of cultural diversity. This constitutes a third program of increasing sociological attention to culture. One could call it the "culture as a variable" approach. Many sociologists have attempted to expand operationalizations of their conventional sociological problematics by asking whether cultural difference is a significant intervening variable changing the relationship between, say, fathers' class positions and sons' educational attainment, or between environmental complexity and span of control in organizations.[34] Many of these new studies involve cross-national comparisons, though they are logically similar to others comparing subcultures or ethnic groups. Such studies generally do not begin with the idea that cultural differences might prove internally very problematic. Culture is a label for social groups or categories that become units in the analysis; to the extent that culture becomes significant in explanations it is generally as a kind of residual category putatively accounting for variance that cannot be explained by other, more clearly identified and better understood, variables.

In trying to deal with these methodological problems, some of these "culture as a variable" researchers have begun to touch on the most basic and potentially transformative of the ways in which culture has demanded the attention of sociologists. This fourth agenda starts with the recognition that social life is inherently cultural, that is, inherently shaped and even constituted in part by differences in the ways in which people generate or recognize meaning in social action and its products. It is fitting that methodological concerns should drive one sociological effort to connect with culture as both basic to sociology and basically a matter of meaning. This is so because positivist methodological concerns to stick to an "objective" way of studying social life have been responsible for much of the repression and/or marginalization of interpretative methods and concerns in postwar sociology. Interpretive, culturally oriented sociology has of course existed since the beginning of the discipline. It appears in every lineage of classical theory from Marx to Durkheim to Weber and Mead. It has maintained a continuous tradition in symbolic interactionism, in the sociology of knowledge and cultural sociology of scholars like Mannheim and Elias, and in variants of Marxist sociology, especially in the Frankfurt tradition and the new Gramscian currents in and after the 1960s. Yet though culture never quite disappeared from sociological attention, it was banished to the margins of the field wherever positivist methodological concerns reigned, especially in America.

Even in the course of reviving the subfield of sociology of culture since the late 1970s, for example, many researchers have felt constrained to make sure that their work did not focus on the problem of interpreting meaning, lest it appear to be unscientific.[35] The result, of course, was that they were obliged to interpret the social world as one in which meaning was not problematic. It is precisely in taking meaning as problematic, often under the pressure of trying to cope with manifest differences in interpretations of texts or of actions, that some strands of empirical sociology opened the possibility of a more fruitful relationship with hermeneutics.[36]

In a sense, the split between positivist, empiricist sociology and more interpretative, cultural sociology mirrors the divide between Anglo-American philosophy and its Continental counterparts. This offers only cold comfort for positivists, since the last several years have seen even analytic philosophers (like Quine and Popper) demolishing empiricism and related conventional views of science for the natural sciences (even if they weren't as radical as Feyerabend and Lakatos); Kuhn's and others' historical studies carried similar import. It is no longer just that there are doubts as to whether the social sciences can be more like the natural sciences; it is widely recognized that the natural sciences as practiced are much more deeply culturally (and theoretically) constructed – more dialogical and multi-perspectival – and therefore much less positive, than textbook accounts of science have suggested. It is not just the alleged relativism of Gadamer or Derrida that positivist sociologists have to fear, in other words, it is Einstein with his idea of relativity.[37]

Neither Gadamer nor Derrida holds all the answers. On the contrary, each brings the deep problems of difference and interpretation forward in a problematic form. In the first place, both intellectualize, both treat as essentially cognitive a field of knowledge that owes more than they recognize to embodied practice and structures of social relations. Secondly, while Gadamer is inattentive to power and the difference between the sway of ideology and the more general fact of prejudice or situatedness, Derrida universalizes power and ideology, making it hard to distinguish whether any specific intellectual claims can be said more to warrant acceptance on their intellectual merits than others. Even more for the crasser followers of Derrida and other poststructuralists, because there is no absolute foundation for judging truth, there is no relative basis for judging "epistemic gain" or partial improvement either (as there is in Gadamer and Taylor). If Gadamer is insufficiently critical, as Habermas suggests, then deconstructionism is critical in so undifferentiated a manner as to lose practical, especially constructive, purchase. Both Gadamer and Derrida leave us with the knowledge that we can never entirely escape from our interpretative traditions or communities. Yet this has less force than at first appears. All knowledge, justifications, and interpretations may indeed be internal to traditions or interpretative communities, but there is never *a* singular and unitary tradition or interpretative community. Membership must always overlap, such traditions or communities must be internally differentiated and at odds at least on some significant issues, and will be the more so as there is a break between "big" and "little" traditions.

V

As I stressed at the outset, it is important to recognize how much of our approach to problems of difference, and therefore interpretation, is contingent on the way in which we have tacitly accepted the notions that cultures (and even intellectual traditions and interpretative communities) are discrete, integral, and equivalent. But this is a construct we can reexamine. As we work to develop a more complex cultural sociology, it will be only one of many cases in which the meaning of the basic objects we study is reconstituted by critical, theoretically informed reflection, historical and cultural analysis, and the effort to make better sense of as broad a range of empirical observation as we can.

The role of theoretically informed interpretation is basic to this project. The first of the sociologist's tasks – and perhaps the most important and problematic – is the constitution of the object of study. As Bourdieu and his colleagues have written, social facts do not just appear, they must be won.[38] When taken seriously, this effort always situates objects within broader contexts, generally theories of social life, interpretations of specific ways of life (including epochs or socio-geographic and cultural settings), and their comparison. There is always room for variation in approaches to constitution of objects of study, for tradeoffs between more local detail and wider comparison, for example, or for emphasizing different aspects of social life – structure, action, culture, power, function, etc. The point is to see the process as basic and never ending, and to subject it to our continuing critical attention, rather than to imagine that it is somehow settled once and for all, or merely a matter of operational definition.

The objects of sociological study do not present themselves in nature any more than farmland presents itself. Farmers may look at plains that have never been tilled, as some Scandinavian immigrants to the American Middle West did a century ago, and see rich fields. But this vision is one shaped by their tradition and one rooted in their practical orientation. Just as the farmers must win the fields from nature (or from previous inhabitants who are sometimes dismissed by assimilating them to the category of nature), so too sociologists must win the objects of their research. In this struggle, interpretation is always central. It can be informed by theory, and guided by wise precepts, but it can never be settled by method in such a way as to guarantee the fertility of the fields or to make sure in advance that they grow the scientifically correct crops.

Taking interpretation seriously in research, recognizing how deep its problems run, restores the connection of even the most methodologically sophisticated social science to the grounding of judgment and practical reason, and saves it from worshipping the illusions of scientific self-sufficiency that offer the future to the putative certainty of those experts who would be social engineers.[39] Precisely because problems of interpretation cannot be solved in advance but only lived through in history, science does not preclude choice. It is up to us to create a discourse in which choices are made on the basis of knowledge, practical reason, and judgment, challenged by criticism, and open not just to the range of social interests but to the novelty of contending understandings.

Notes

1   Said, *Orientalism*.
2   See Todorov, *On Human Diversity*, for an evocation of how exoticism in portrayals of nonWestern peoples dovetailed with racism and nationalism; also Gilman, *Difference and Pathology*.
3   On the idea of "social world" see Strauss, "A Social World Perspective," and for the phenomenological notion of lifeworld that informs Strauss's account, but also puts the notion of social world on a somewhat different theoretical basis, see Schutz and Luckmann, *Structures of the Lifeworld*.
4   See Adorno, *The Jargon of Authenticity*.
5   See "Science as a Vocation," and "Politics as a Vocation," among a number of Weber's works; Kant's three critiques are distinguished on just these lines.
6   See Durkheim, *The Division of Labor in Society*.
7   DuBois, *Souls of Black Folk*. DuBois referred to the tensions – and possibilities – raised by being, for example, both black and American. See Gilroy, *The Black Atlantic*, for a powerful expansion of this idea in a diasporic and internationally mediated context.
8   This is evident immediately from recognition of the substantial public and political work he did (e.g. helping to draft the Weimar constitution) alongside his scientific or scholarly production. For a deeper sense of the extent to which Weber did not in fact choose sharply between these vocations see Marianne Weber's wonderful (and very sociological) biography, *Max Weber*.
9   Sorokin, *Social and Cultural Dynamics*.
10   See Hannerz, *Cultural Complexity*, for a nice contemporary suggestion of this issue. Also, Hannerz, "The World in Creolisation."
11   See chapter 7 below.
12   Compare Arendt's contemptuous formulation of a central theme in pragmatism (which she understands more broadly than just the American philosophical school, and which she charges with deeply pernicious effects on modern education): "that you can know and understand only what you have done yourself" (*Between Past and Future*, p. 182).

13 See Giddens, *Studies in Social and Political Theory*, following Taylor, "Interpretation and the Sciences of Man," and Gadamer, *Truth and Method*.

14 Gadamer, *Truth and Method, Philosophical Hermeneutics, Reason in the Age of Science*; Habermas, *Logic of the Social Sciences, Theory of Communicative Action*.

15 I will not attempt to lay out the enormous range of appropriate references to Freud and psychoanalysis. The most accessible of Bakhtin's texts is probably *The Dialogical Imagination*. The work of Vygotsky (also published under the pseudonym Voloshinov) helps to open up related themes. See Holquist and Clark, *Bakhtin*; Wertsch, *Vygotsky*.

16 This insight is partially suggested in Mead's notion of taking the role of the other (*Mind, Self, and Society*), but not really developed in the same way.

17 See the further discussion in the next chapter of translation as a problematic metaphor for the pursuit of understanding across lines of difference.

18 Bourdieu, "Lecture on the Lecture," in *In Other Words*.

19 Fraser, "What's Critical about Critical Theory." Part of the problem is that Habermas does not see the need for a specifically gendered analysis but tries to achieve universality by transcending gender (which keeps it from being thematized but not from being relevant).

20 Habermas is certainly aware that there are problems with applying the model of doctor and patient to large-scale subjects such as classes; he indicates in *Theory and Practice*, p. 30, that the key is to distinguish strategic confrontations, to which the psychoanalytic model does not apply, from normative reflection and communication, to which it does, though this still seems both to strip psychoanalytic therapy of its strategic dimension and to imagine an improbable sort of social encounter.

21 The recent formation of a Sami Parliament does appropriate nationalist rhetoric and (like other mobilizations of subordinate nationalities and regional identities) pose a question about distributions of power among the constituent identities of a potentially unified Europe.

22 See Calhoun, "Nationalism and Ethnicity," "Nationalism and Civil Society," and chapter 8 below.

23 Goody, *The Social Organization of the Lo Wiili*.

24 The international intellectual discourse thus does not attain objectivity, though it attains salutary diversity, from the inclusion of the voices of postcolonial intellectuals. It is important also to remember that, for example, South Asian participants in this international discourse are not simply representatives of the anthropological other but elites empowered by education and/or class to enter into this realm. Though diasporic writings contest much in international culture, they also reproduce much of its peculiar subject positioning.

25 Quoted in Warnke, *Gadamer*, p. 5.

26 Such attempts are often understandable from the point of view of priestly power as well as theology, cf. Bourdieu, "Genesis and Structure."

27 Earlier Biblical redactors and copyists seem sometimes to have responded to internal inconsistencies by assuming them to be the result of previous

transcription errors – and often trying to resolve them by altering texts to achieve consistency and to accord with prevailing doctrine. See Ehrman, *The Orthodox Corruption of Scripture*.

28   Gadamer, *Reason in the Age of Science*, p. 97.

29   Redfield, *The Little Tradition*.

30   See discussion in Weintraub, "Introduction"; Eisenstadt, *Political System of Empires* and *Decline of Empires*; and in the concluding chapter below.

31   Bourdieu, Chamboredon and Passeron, *Craft of Sociology*, offer a strong, though not explicitly cross-cultural, analysis of this in their discussion of "winning the social fact."

32   Bourdieu, *Outline*, p. 117.

33   It also reveals the limits of the idea of a 'pure structuralism" in sociology, such as that advocated by Peter Blau. Blau's sociological structuralism involves studying interaction rates between various categories of persons – e.g. rich and poor, black and white. Inescapably, though, Blau must begin with inductions of such categories from some cultural framework. If they are objectified in data sources (such as census items) it is easy to treat them as though they were objective and forget that they were not only chosen by individuals but constituted by culture. Whether or not this is the case, Blau's reliance on these categories implicitly calls not just for tests of their salience (i.e. their ability to predict interaction rates), which is his own main concern, but for an account of how they are derived and why they are the most appropriate representations of the cultural factors that make the variance in interaction rates meaningful (which Blau does not offer). Blau, *Inequality and Heterogeneity*; see also discussion in Calhoun and Scott, "Introduction."

34   A somewhat similar style of research introduces gender as a variable into analytic models that had previously ignored it – but without undertaking a more general rethinking of the importance of gender as a category constitutive of both the social world and sociological problems. See further consideration of this issue and the "feminist standpoint" response to it in chapter 6 below.

35   See, e.g., Wuthnow's attempts to move "beyond the problem of meaning"; *Meaning and Moral Order* and *Communities of Discourse*; and my response in "Beyond the Problem of Meaning."

36   It is also, by the way, in taking meaning as infinite and lacking any intrinsic relation to "truth" or application that "poststructuralist" and "postmodernist" lines of thought have differed most decisively from hermeneutics. See chapter 4 below.

37   Or even more, with his understanding of the transformative implications of Planck's work. See the quotation from Heisenberg in the Introduction above on the ways in which different questions, not just different answers are opened to us by different theories, and the necessary multidimensionality of scientific knowledge. But the implications of this should not be overstated. In particular, social scientists should not collapse the issue of interpretation completely into the contrast between quantitative and qualitative methods –

equating quantitative techniques with analysis and viewing interpretation as either an imprecise version of analysis or somehow its opposite. First, quantitative sociology also depends on interpretation and this is sometimes done with great sensitivity. Second, much quantitative sociology is essentially descriptive; the use of numbers does not guarantee causal or other forms of analysis, let alone relation to theory. Third, while some qualitative sociology is overwhelmingly descriptive in aim, much focuses on analyses aimed at clarifying the conceptual constitution of phenomena under study. Finally, a good deal of qualitative sociology is in fact model-building and shares both the use of abstraction and the goal of precision with quantitative analysis – or even more, with mathematical model-building. If there is a real issue in this sociological debate, it is the question of whether meaning is constituted by a rich relation of the specific objects of study to a broad socio-cultural context, or narrowed and even violated by wrenching variables from their contexts.

38 Bourdieu, Chamboredon, and Passeron, *Craft of Sociology*, ch 1.
39 In Kantian language, the social sciences depend largely on judgment, for the social world is not accessible to pure reason. But since social scientists are not passive, external observers but engaged social actors, their work is necessarily guided by the ethical imperatives of practical reason as well.

3

Cultural Difference and Historical Specificity

I

Two different ideas have been involved in the project of developing "general" theory in sociology. The first of these is breadth, richness, or reach of application. The theories of Marx, Weber, and Durkheim, for example, are said to be general because they can be applied to so many areas or dimensions of social life. They are thus contrasted both with theories of the middle range (*pace* Merton) and with the very local theories which are proposed and tested in most sociological research (e.g. the "theory" of the demographic transition, or even more the basic building blocks in Stinchcombe's conception of sociological theory).[1] Alternatively, theory is held to be general on more positivist grounds, because of its relative success in producing universally applicable, preferably law-like statements.

The first of these understandings points to a virtue of the classical tradition of sociological theory, the attempt to build theories adequate to the understanding of social life in its rich fullness. It accepts rather too easily, however, the claims of the classical theorists – or at least of most of them, most of the time – to be able to grasp with a single theory the sum total of instances of "society" or "social life." Even more, this understanding follows Parsons in exaggerating the extent to which the classical theorists were developing theory which was independent of specific historical and cultural contexts, and which was about a similarly abstracted notion of social life. In fact, Marx especially and in many ways Weber were quite attentive to the historical (if not always the cultural) specificity of social theory. This is one reason why their conceptual frameworks, although very broad in reach, were always developed in close relationship to specific empirical historical accounts;

their abstractions were not free-floating but historically specific and determinate.

The second understanding of general theory derives from a widespread modern notion of science as discovery of universal truths. Durkheim was its main expositor among classical social theorists.[2] This second understanding of generality does not have to do with reach so much as with universal validity, certainty, positivity. It shapes not only debates over general theory but sociologists' folk imaginings of what physical scientists do: (1) theorizing about universal phenomena; (2) making universally valid statements about restricted scopes of phenomena; (3) attempting to make specific empirical or abstract propositions add up to maximally general ones; and (4) attempting to deduce specific subsidiary theories as special cases of more general ones.

This project has been challenged in a variety of ways. It has been shown for example that putatively universal laws were either false or applicable only within a very narrow empirical scope. Thus innumerable claims about "human nature" have been shown to apply only or primarily to the American college students of the 1950s or 1960s who formed the population from which research subjects were drawn. This challenge, of course, strikes only at particular theories; although it complicates the inductive dimension of positivist theory-building, it does not in itself invalidate it. Similarly, the argument that sociology shows few, if any, cases of either the deduction of successful local theories from more general ones, or of the combination of tested propositions and/or local theories into more general ones does not demonstrate that the discipline cannot in principle do better in the future. In some ways, epistemological critiques are more damaging. The hermeneutic argument against the easy assumption of the pure facticity of observations (let alone survey or interview responses) suggests the fundamental impossibility of a theory pure in its empirical as well as its logical positivism. This challenge is often presented in such a radical way, however, as to make all research seem pointless because no secure grounds can be given for comparative evaluation of results. Paradoxically, perhaps, this encourages researchers to feel justified in ignoring the critique. In any case, theory of the sort challenged thrives, even where the challenges would seem on philosophical grounds to have been fatal. At least the beginning of an explanation for why lies in the very separation of "abstracted empiricism" from "grand theory" which C. Wright Mills critiqued two generations ago.[3]

I want to turn my attention in this chapter not towards further epistemological critique, but to the question of what sort of work should be offered as an alternative to both abstracted empiricism and positivist grand theory. One of the problems of many epistemological critiques is that they have seemed to endorse or entail a relativism so thoroughgoing as to make empirical research – and most scholarly discourse – meaningless. I want to argue not only for the importance of empirical work, but for the necessary mutual implication of theoretical and empirical work. Specifically, my claim is that most good sociological theories – especially those which attempt to grasp social life in something of its fullness – need to be attentive to cultural difference and historical specificity. My argument is not just for the virtues of history and ethnography or cultural interpretation, but for the virtues of a theory which can take each of them seriously. Yet, let me stress in advance, this is an argument for theory – including both empirical and normative theory, and theory of very broad reach – and against extreme relativism. It offers two cheers for particularism, but suggests that though theoretical groundings are always by nature incomplete, they are nonetheless achievable in some proportion and worth pursuing. The kind of theory I advocate would be continuous with cross-cultural and historical description, but not identical to them because the explanations the theory proposes would purport to anticipate or account for cases beyond those for which they were developed.[4] The theory would recognize that actual cases are always an incomplete sample of possible cases, and seek to understand the production of cases, not just generalize from them.

Four sections follow. In the first, I shall elaborate on what it means to take cultural difference seriously. In the second I shall similarly explore the notion of historical specificity. The third section will take as given my claim that social theory should be culturally sensitive and historically specific, and ask just what such theories should look like. The final section will discuss briefly the relationship of the project suggested here to relativism, especially as raised by debates over postmodernism.

II

We need to be attentive to problems of cultural difference in a way social theorists seldom have been. I do not mean simply seeing theories as embedded within cultural traditions and lacking resources for extending communication across cultural divisions. Likewise, I do not mean simply learning various supposedly basic information about those different from ourselves, and I do not mean indulging in an easy relativism that may amount in practice to refusing to take difference seriously. Such an easy relativism fails to recognize that some differences among social actors amount to conflicting or at least incompatible claims on our attention or action, while others involve claims to a kind of recognition that is only meaningful if it is based on seriously applied standards of judgment.[5]

Taking difference seriously is therefore a difficult and challenging proposition, and implies a never-ending task. The challenge of difference cannot be met by opposing any variety of relativism to an ideology of science based on decontextualized truth claims. Relativism of some sort seems a necessary starting point in the project of taking difference seriously – an opening to new knowledge and understanding – but it is not a satisfactory endpoint. Similarly, Enlightenment universalism has certain normative virtues, grounding aspects of liberalism which have not outlived their usefulness, but it also poses serious problems.

The very scientistic attempt to sever empirical theory from normative theory has contributed to normative theory's problematic over-commitment to a culturally insensitive Enlightenment universalism. Normative theory has continued to adopt an eighteenth-century view of human beings as essentially interchangeable individuals. Both the individualism and its usual corollary that individuals are or should be essentially similar are problematic and ethnocentric. This is somewhat ironic, since critiques of Western ethnocentrism are often couched in the language of liberal individualism; they are in essence arguments that the underlying similarities of individuals are more important than the apparent cultural (and other) differences among them. There are even cases where extreme relativism and strong universalism actually meet in a shared individualism. On the one hand, assertions that there are no generally defensible grounds for normative judgment make this individualism into a declaration of the inevitability of arbitrary subjectivity. On the other hand assertions that certain moral injunctions (like the Kantian categorical imperative) must apply to all individuals because all are intrinsically equivalent make an alternative individualism the basis for claiming to discover implicitly universal grounds for morality. In this sense, both that branch of modernity which has lately traveled under the name of postmodernism and the explicit Enlightenment modernism proclaimed for example by Habermas suffer from weaknesses of cross-cultural sensibility. The former strain of thought is apt to make cultural difference out to be an insuperable barrier to both general discourse and normative critique (ironically enough, since it thrives in such eminently cross-cultural discursive fields as the post-colonial diasporas). The latter is apt to reduce cultural difference to mere positions in a developmental scheme, or grant it no theoretical significance whatsoever.[6]

Enlightenment universalism with its impoverishment of cross-cultural outlook informs not only the normative theories directly in its lineage but the bulk of universalizing empirical theoretical discourse. The idea that we can make significant general statements true of all human action, or human beings, or society at large is its heir. Such a notion is not false, I hasten to add, for I believe there are some such statements to be made. Rather, problems arise when theorists try to make such statements beyond a very narrow range of minimal and generally highly formal and highly qualified propositions. There is a long-standing critique of this sort of ethnocentric positivism, which is not worth reproducing here.

The recent struggles between self-proclaimed postmodernists, poststructuralists and similar thinkers, on the one hand, and adherents of the Enlightenment project of modernity as rationalization on the other, however, suggest that the normative dimension requires more comment. One of the virtues of the work of Foucault, Derrida, and a number of other fellow-travelers has been to thematize the importance of difference. Here I will only point schematically to two lessons to be learned, drawing them out by discussion of Habermas's more universalistic theory.

The first lesson I would call the importance of fundamental differences of value. Universalist thought tends towards the position that there can only be one set of fundamental values; others can be justified to the extent that they are derivative from these. These need not be concrete norms, as they might be in Aristotelian thought, but are commonly categorical or procedural injunctions. For Habermas, famously, these are held to be implicit in the validity claims of all speech (to intelligibility, truthfulness, rightness or appropriateness, and sincerity).[7] Since any responsible participation in communicative action must be open to redemption of these implicit validity claims, Habermas can claim an empirical basis for his normative theory, and indeed for expecting its developmental advancement. The relevant catch, for present purposes, comes with his decontextualized treatment of the giving of reasons.

Habermas seeks to combine a neo-Kantian philosophical approach with various sources of universal norms. Two of his most prominent approaches involve (1) reasoning from the norms implicit in all speech (hence, a communicative ethics), an approach rooted in the speech act theory of Austin and others, and (2) seeing progressively more universalistic norms as implicit in human psychological development, an approach rooted in Kohlberg's account of moral reasoning as a hierarchical sequence of stages in which justice is conceptualized in progressively more abstract and general ways. As the now famous Kohlberg–Gilligan debate makes clear with regard to the latter case, however, this understanding of moral reasoning privileges one mode over others.[8] *A priori*, it grants greater validity and rationality to "postconventional" moral reasoning (that which is maximally universalistic and in which the giving of reasons for moral judgments is oriented to a decontextualized discussion of formal, general "rights" or other principles of decision). So, generally, do the courts and most philosophers and other arbiters of

moral judgment in the West. But do Kohlberg or Habermas offer an
adequate basis for denying that a partially particularistic, situated moral
reasoning based on ideas of care rather than abstract justice should not
be considered comparably "advanced"? I think not. Though Habermas
does stress the importance of conceiving human beings intersubjectively
rather than individualistically, he does not advance this approach to a
fully social understanding of morality. Rather, he returns moral judgment to a Kantian realm of decontextualized individuals. He does not
consider whether the best moral judgment might not begin with relationships rather than individual persons, for example. Indeed, if (as seems
true) the very notion of individual is culturally and historically specific,
this affects normative statements incorporating it. And human individuals may be nonequivalent in varying ways internal to cultural formations
or historical epochs. The nonequivalence, noninterchangeability of men
and women in our own and nearly every other culture is of major import
for moral theory.[9] More to the point of the present discussion, Habermas
never questions that moral theory requires that all moral questions be
rationally decidable, at least in principle, and that rational decision
requires both that there be a clear and singular hierarchy of procedures
and reasons for moral judgments and that the framework for decision be
complete so that alternatives are exhaustively eliminated. In other words,
within the scope of Habermas's theory (and not just where he bases his
work on Kohlberg) there is not much room for recognition of a plurality
of equally meritorious orientations to reason or action. Habermas's
scheme can recognize conflicts between principles – between equality and
freedom, say, or justice and nonviolence – though it presumes these
principles to be ultimately commensurable. It cannot recognize basic
conflicts over what counts as a moral decision.[10]

The second lesson is that we should appreciate not only differences of
value but the positive value of difference. In other words, contrary again
to Habermas's vision, cultural difference among human societies and
differences among people within societies or communicative communities are in themselves desirable. In Hölderlin's words, quoted recurrently
by Adorno and others of the first generation of Frankfurt theorists, "the
differences are good." Like the multiplicity of species in the biological
world, and like the plurality of individual human existence extolled by
Hannah Arendt, there is an intrinsic advantage to the production of
cultural variation; it is a source of possibility including the possibility of
reflective self-awareness. This is, of course, not an unlimited advantage;
like most others it can reach points of diminishing return and must be
hemmed in by other fundamental values. Nonetheless, difference is good.
It is the necessary concomitant of creativity, and as Arendt stressed, it is

basic to the action that distinguishes human life from nature. Freedom entails difference, it seems to me, and creativity may well depend on diversity. Moreover, social integration and reproduction both depend on at least some sorts of difference.[11] Empirical social theory that does not fully address cultural and interpersonal difference at the most fundamental levels reinforces the tendency of normative theory to devalue difference. Here we confront the complicity of theory in the normalizing process to which Foucault has drawn our attention.[12]

Related to these two points is the need for social theory to recognize the cultural construction (rather than natural autonomy) of putatively general categories. Race and gender, for example, need to be seen as socio-cultural organizations of roles and identities, not simple derivations from the alleged facts of biology. This much has been a staple of sociological wisdom for generations. The step that many sociologists do not take is to recognize the fundamental significance of such categories. Even many self-declared feminist sociologists, for example, address issues of gender only by adding the variable of sex to established research paradigms like status attainment. They do not consider how the cultural construction of a categorical opposition between male and female shapes the very way in which we conceptualize society and social hierarchies. Nor do they reflexively evaluate the place of gender in scientific practice as more than a problem of material opportunities for female graduate students and scientists. A genuinely culturally sensitive social theory has to analyze and ask about the implications of the fact that we live in a deeply gendered world. Similarly, such a theory must go beyond the opposition between seeing race as a biologically given category and, by deconstructing its biological foundation, acceding to a claim that it exists only in the eyes of the biased observer. The latter sort of liberal critique of racism returns to the Enlightenment notion of essentially similar individuals. Just as a really serious feminism includes rethinking the categories of gender, not just getting women to wear business suits, so a really serious approach to race must begin with the cultural production and reproduction of race as a socially salient category and involve basic categorial rethinking not merely reduction in objective consequences of racial sorting.[13] We must recognize the assimilationist bias built into the liberal critique of racism.

One of the implications of trying to take difference seriously is that theory must be contentful, not purely and exclusively formal. There is certainly room for purely formal theory, but it must be recognized that it cannot and does not stand alone as an enterprise.[14] Social theory can only be constructed on the basis of some explicitly or implicitly induced knowledge of the world. The categories used in declaredly purely formal theory – categories like gender, race, class, individual – are always at some level culturally specific inductions. This is not simply a flaw which is to be avoided or minimized by maximally abstract and artificial definitions of the phenomena under study, but rather the occasion for making clear the immanent relationship of any theory to its own empirical context and history. Making this relationship clear is not simply a prolegomenon to theory construction, but the primary means of establishing connection between the most fundamental categories of a theory and the empirical world on which they purport to have purchase.[15] The place of empirical content in theory, and especially the assertion that basic categories are always linked to such content, raises the problem of theoretical generality in a particularly provocative way. We can approach this by looking at the problem of translation and evaluation across cultural boundaries.

Peter Winch's *The Idea of a Social Science* set off a controversy about cross-cultural imputations of rationality which poses fundamental questions for the notion of general social theory.[16] Drawing on Wittgenstein's notions of differences between forms of life and language games, Winch argued that it was irrevocably the case that different cultures had different standards of judgment, and that it was therefore necessary to admit of a plurality of standards of rationality. To judge beliefs or understandings internal to one form of life or statements internal to one language game directly by the terms of another was a "category error" much like mixing terms from two languages. This much I think has to be granted. Winch also argued, however, that it was impossible to translate among and compare these standards of rationality in a way that did justice to the internal meaning of each, or justified treating any one of them as superior to the others. Our preference for our own must be seen as purely arbitrary and accidental. It is primarily around these latter points that debate has raged, foreshadowing in some ways aspects of "postmodernism."[17] Most claims that there is a single universal standard of rationality are really claims for the absolute superiority of one standard, and are compatible with recognition that other people may act on other standards though arguers may wish to deny the label of rationality to those standards.[18] The fundamental questions are: can we translate among very different cultures (or, at the extreme, among any differing discourses), and on what grounds can we claim superiority for one standard of judgment? These are very hard questions and I do not propose to attempt a full answer here. Rather, I want simply to raise certain implications of the debate for the practice of social theory.

The problem of translation arises at two levels. The first is the difficulty of rendering observations, interpretations, or propositions in language which is neutral and equivalent across cultural contexts. In other words, to take a simple example, sociologists are apt to use a single term like "person," "family," or "monastery" to refer to a range of concrete instances which are designated by varying and not entirely synonymous terms in different languages. This may be inevitable and even necessary, but we need continually to remind ourselves of its problematic nature. There is no self-evident warrant for treating a Buddhist "monastery" as a token of the same type as a Catholic monastery. Rather, our use of a single term to refer to both is an assertion about their commonality. The type is our construct; it does not inhere in some external reality, and like any construct it is language as well as referent dependent. We modern Western (and especially English-language) sociologists are remarkably prone to treat extensions of terms defined within our linguistic and institutional universes as though they were transparent, neutral, and able to fit precisely to referents in culturally variant contexts. But the problems which arise from the fact that "monastery" may not mean precisely the same thing as the terms from other languages which we gloss with it, or indeed that "class" and its putative synonyms may not refer to the same categorical constructs in all Western (let alone nonWestern) settings are ultimately the easier of the two sorts of problems of translation. The problems of translation in this sense begin with the potential looseness of fit in any linguistic exchange, even in conversation between competent speakers of the same language. Each speaker may refer to slightly different things by the same term, fix the term slightly differently in the web of intra-linguistic associations, and intend or experience slightly different emotional feelings or perlocutionary effects. Ordinary conversation allows a good deal of redundancy, as well as opportunities for checking and exploring understandings, as ways of dealing with this. The problem is similar, though much more complex, when cross-linguistic understanding is sought.

The second level of problem of translation arises when we seek to understand linguistic meanings that are not simply different from our own, but involve what have come to be called "incommensurable" practices. It is one thing, for example, to learn that dozens of shades and hues of blue have different names, and that recognition of the phenomenal differences may depend in part on learning the categories by which they are labeled. The misunderstanding that might have come from translating terms for azure, indigo, and turquoise all simply as blue can be remedied fairly straightforwardly. Indeed English has a great many color terms that are familiar to artists and not common in ordinary discourse; these may allow for progressively better translation. The situation is made simple by the fact that the English speaker and the speaker of the other language are usually engaged in similar practices when using names for colors. It becomes a great deal more complicated when translation is attempted among practices that are fundamentally different, and especially so when those different practices are "incommensurable" with our own.[19]

Practices are incommensurable when they are incompatible in principle, when they cannot be carried on simultaneously. One cannot play rugby and American football simultaneously, for example; the rules are not just different but in fundamental conflict such that actions would be understood quite differently in each framework. Each is organized according to a different set of rules, and the rules conflict in fundamental ways (e.g. with regard to whether a forward pass is a legitimate tactic or a foul). As this example suggests, we may know about and have the capacity to participate in a multitude of incommensurable activities within our own daily lives and cultural contexts. This does not mean, however, that we can easily translate among them. How would we make rugby understandable in terms of American football (literally, in terms of, not simply in relation to or to a player of American football)?

Arguably, one could construct a metadiscourse of games such that both rugby football and American football could be understood simultaneously. This is, however, an intellectualistic solution at best.[20] Much would be lost in any attempt to reduce either system of embodied practice to mere discourse, "the mistake of enclosing in concepts a logic made to dispense with concepts," as Bourdieu puts it.[21] The challenge becomes more complex and more theoretically salient when we take up the issue of translating between incommensurable practices in very different cultures – say, comparing traditional Chinese and modern Western medicine.[22] One cannot simply translate from Chinese medical terminology into Western without missing the point of one or the other of these systems of practice, and no one has produced a metalanguage that does not do violence to one system (although it is one of the myths of Western science that it is such a metalanguage). The two medical systems not only include competing practices but offer competing and contradictory accounts of their practical concerns. Any claim to understand one from the point of view of the other must be evaluative – as a rugby player must understand a forward pass to be an invalid tactic so long as he is playing rugby. The Western physician cannot approach Chinese medicine solely with the attitude of learning from the other; she must see some prescriptions as mistaken and even potentially dangerous. The ideal of a full understanding of each discourse from within the other, thus, is impossible. If, in the medical example, the respective groups of practitioners were to achieve a full understanding of each other, it could only be by creating some new form of medical practice which incorporated elements of each tradition but was not reducible to either. Then, of course, the groups would have changed. They can only be fully and simultaneously understood if there is some transformation of the knower. In other words, translation is too static a model for the process of coming to an understanding across lines of deep difference. We must grasp how actors – even cultures, if I may be permitted that shorthand – change in becoming capable of understanding various others.

To the mere incompatibility among practices, thus, we must add a third level of difficulty. This comes when two sorts of practices are not only different in form and content, in mode of reasoning and material prescription, but also make competing claims to something of the same practical efficacy. When they are brought into relationship with each other, they are naturally apt to become competitors. It is, moreover, nearly unavoidable that some judgments of their relative efficacy will be made (at the very least by practitioners or consumers, if not by "disinterested observers"). Chinese traditional medicine is also at least as much different from Western architectural practices as from Western medicine, but it is not incommensurable with the former in the same strong sense, and indeed Chinese traditional medicine is happily practiced in Western-style buildings.

The point of all this is to suggest that overcoming ethnocentrism in social theory involves not just appreciating differences but coming to terms with incommensurable practices. The implications of this are somewhat surprising. It is commonly assumed that the appropriate approach to cross-cultural understanding, the antidote to ethnocentrism, is simply to suspend critical judgment. This is sometimes made into a ground for thoroughgoing relativism. The very task of understanding incommensurable practices, however, challenges this relativism.

To be sure, a first principle for understanding the practices of people very different from oneself is to suspend the sort of critical judgment one might apply to apparently similar practices in one's own culture. One should first attempt to understand just what the practice is, not categorize it immediately on the basis of its surface similarity to practices with which one is familiar. Unfortunately, too many sociologists do not take seriously the difficulty of this first step. As Taylor says:

> The very nature of human action requires that we understand it, at least initially, in its own terms; that means that we understand the descriptions that it bears for the agents. It is only because we have failed to do that that we can fall into the fatal error of assimilating foreign practices to our own familiar ones.[23]

Because he saw this category error as nearly inevitable, Winch suggested that cross-cultural translation was so problematic that full understanding of a very different society was impossible. A variety of other thinkers have described principles of "charity" or "benefit of the doubt" by which would-be interpreters should approach strange customs. The attempt to grasp them in their own terms and/or in the meaning they have for those who practice them is one such principle. Another is Hilary Putnam's idea that we should always prefer those interpretations that encourage us to regard others as maximally human.[24] This does not mean that we must justify all such customs or adopt the beliefs linked to them. "Interpretative success does not require that the translatee's beliefs come out the *same* as our own but it does require that they come out *intelligible* to us."[25]

Generally, however, at least as researchers and social theorists, we do not wish to stop with this effort to understand an action in its own terms. Indeed, where investigators claim that such an understanding is the sole object of their investigation, they are generally disingenuous. They are engaged in an investigation that is itself outside of the practice they are investigating; they try to render practical knowledge discursive; they write articles and books aimed at audiences not composed of participants in the practice (or else urging participants to take a somewhat distanced stance towards their own practice). More generally, researchers usually are quite explicit in their intention to achieve, minimally, a translation of the practice into a form understandable in some discourse outside of that practice – usually that of the researcher's scholarly associates. Anthropologists do not go to New Guinea simply to become Papuans, or Ilongat or what-have-you; they go in order to return and reveal something of what it means to be Papuan, or Ilongat, or what-have-you. Translation is thus a vital part of achieving social knowledge. We are able to begin this process because incommensurability and cultural incompatibility or difference are seldom complete. There is always some overlap in the practical problems of life, in the conditions of social structure, and in the understanding of each of these that provides a starting point for cross-cultural discourse.

But is translation *per se* a good description of how the anthropologist or other investigator first achieves understanding? Largely, especially for the best fieldwork, I think not. In the first place, the knowledge of a practice is in many cases itself a largely practical, intuitive, even embodied sense not objectified in discourse. "Performing a rite presupposes something quite different from the conscious mastery of the sort of catalogue of oppositions that is drawn up by academic commentators striving for symbolic mastery of a dead or dying tradition (e.g. the

Chinese mandarins' tables of equivalences) and also by anthropologists in the first stages of their work."[26] It is for this reason that Bourdieu suggests, contrary to structuralism, that "understanding ritual practice is not a question of decoding the internal logic of a symbolism but of restoring its practical necessity by relating it to the real conditions of its genesis."[27]

Even for purely discursive knowledge, however, the process of achieving understanding across lines of cultural difference does not seem to be one of translation as such but of a richer, more complex discourse and potential process of change. Interlocutors – anthropologist and informant, say – engage each other in a process of gradually improving understanding that must be conceived in dynamic terms. It involves dialogue, not merely one-way communication. Both the anthropologist and the informant are changed by it. They achieve the understanding precisely because they change into people who can understand each other, not because one translates the static, fully formed knowledge of the other into a form which he or she can appropriate without becoming a significantly different person. Since knowing is an activity constitutive of the person, not a mechanical storing up of data, gaining in knowledge always means changing somewhat. But specifically where there are basic incompatibilities in practices (and accordingly in practical knowledge and sensibilities) achieving understanding involves becoming a person who in principle can play two different games which cannot be played simultaneously and which cannot be translated directly into the terms of each other. The anthropologist may thus construct an ethnography of the Azande, revealing a good deal of what it means to be Zande, but doing so is not simply translating Zande life into Western anthropological (or ordinary) language.[28] Moreover, the anthropologist is doing something which stands not only outside of but in a hierarchical relationship to what Azande generally do (since, for example, Azande do not send anthropologists to Britain).[29] The transformations that are entailed by mutual understanding need not be symmetrical.

I chose the example above of Chinese traditional medicine confronting Western "scientific" medicine (and vice versa) precisely because this is not as starkly hierarchical a contrast as the one commonly used in the literature on cross-cultural translation and evaluation of rationality: that of witchcraft vs. modern science.[30] While we do not imagine that the participants in Zande discourse on witchcraft attempt to comprehend Western science in Zande terms (though something of this might in principle be imaginable), there clearly is some such effort on the part of traditional Chinese medical practitioners. These not only attempt to understand Western medicine, they have appropriated aspects of it –

both specific treatments and especially a quasi-experimental mode of research into and discussion of traditional medicine.[31] Nonetheless, the existence of incommensurable practices forces on us the necessity of evaluation. Where two activities are simply different, we may (disregarding opportunity and resource costs) say "let a hundred flowers bloom" and enjoy the diversity without pretending to evaluation. Indeed, where difference is complete, comparative evaluation may be either impossible or a purely subjective, rationally arbitrary matter. But incommensurable activities are precisely linked by certain similarities; though they may be radically different, they pose related claims on the attention of observers – and, in the case of medicine, of potential clients. Possibly neither Chinese nor Western medicine is "better" in some overall way, but within certain domains where both claim efficacy, they are bound to be the subject of comparative evaluations. Moreover, it is not the case that such evaluations are merely arbitrary exercises of subjectivity or the will to power (as post-Foucauldian discourse might lead one to believe). Western medicine reveals sufficient technical effectiveness that it demands some combination of acceptance, explanation, or suppression (as, indeed, did Western science when it first began to achieve notable technical success in the West). In China itself, practitioners of Chinese medicine are, in fact, forced onto the defensive whenever they are put into direct competition with Western-style medicine on one of the latter's strong points. But of course the latter has weak points as well, and there is at least room for Chinese specialists to advance compelling practical claims of their own in these areas. Thus acupuncture and certain herbal remedies travel Westward where an attempt is made to appropriate them – an attempt which will continue to make Western specialists uneasy until their efficacy is fully explained on grounds internal to the Western scientific medical discourse.

Such an explanation – even if favorable to acupuncture – would not be produced from within Chinese traditional medicine. Neither would it be a neutral metalanguage for bridging incommensurability. It would be a new form of practice, perhaps more capacious than its predecessors, but surely with limits of its own. If it developed out of Chinese traditional medicine and Western "scientific" medicine, its very existence would mean that both those practices (and groupings of practitioners) had changed. The same, I would contend, is true of all the sorts of cross-cultural discourses in which we engage and on which our theories' claims to generality rest.

Similarly, in the realm of science that first led Kuhn to formulate the notion of incommensurability of paradigms, it is generally not neutral metadiscourse but historical change that produces new cognitive capacities and orientations that enable scientists to grasp – perhaps distortedly – each of two incommensurable paradigms. We need not agree with Foucault that structures of knowledge – epistemes or large-scale paradigms – simply change, succeeding each other without gradual transitions or possibility of comparative evaluation.[32] Practical activities bring such structures into simultaneous use and under some circumstances force comparative evaluations.[33] But there is no guarantee that the historical changes that enable understanding across previously incommensurable paradigmatic divides are the only ones that could have taken place. Even if we agree that they brought epistemic gain – an advance of knowledge in some sense – this does not imply that they are the only transformations of thought that could have done so. Relatedly, we must be careful to avoid the presumption that cultures (or discourses) are inherently unitary. A practice from another culture may be subject to competing interpretations or evaluations within that culture. This can help the would-be interpreter, as Tambiah points out: "if there are internal criticisms and evaluations within a society, then its agents have to exercise some choice between alternatives and engage in debate about the 'rationality' of their rules and conventions. These internal critiques help sensitize the anthropologist and orient him for his own task of intelligible translation and structural evaluation."[34]

The doing of theory is itself a form of discourse which grows as it is transformed in changing historical circumstances and cultural contexts. It cannot achieve true generality simply by subsuming or being tested against data from a wide range of cultural settings and historical periods. Nor can it be translated transparently across cultures in a way which does not in some combination change the original, impose the original as an alien, dominating form, or simply fail to communicate. As a result, it will always be incumbent on social theorists – the more so the more they attempt to grasp fundamental social categories – both to situate their work in its cultural context, and to open themselves to reformation by confrontation with other cultural contexts.

At the same time, the would-be objects of understanding can hardly be presumed to remain unchanged. Both sides to any dialogue are affected. The relevant changes, moreover, are historical as well as biographical. The anthropological or sociological effort at understanding cannot be disengaged from the long historical process that created the occasion for cross-cultural contact and will continue to transform each party to it, however asymmetrically. This historical process includes that which formed the individual researcher and shaped her tools of analysis, but it is not summed up by that. It also made wars and colonialism and mass media, all of which helped to make the conditions for any cross-cultural understanding as well as to present historically specific obstacles to such understanding.

III

I have already introduced the issue of historical specificity by talking about processes of cultural and theoretical change. Indeed, many of the issues posed by historical change are similar to those posed by cross-cultural variation – with the added difficulty of the impossibility of engaging in a proper dialogue to achieve mutual understanding. Cultural and historical specificity are thus inextricably linked, but there are some specific points to be made about the latter.

In advocating "historically specific" theory, I mean not merely "taking history into account," and still less claiming to explain all of history. Rather, I mean recognizing that (1) the production of theories is a historical phenomenon, (2) the categories used in theoretical discourse are often adequate only to specific historical epochs (partly because they are inevitably contentful as suggested above), and (3) theories exist in discursive fields, in relation to other theories, and are not self-sufficient statements of their meaning. Dialogue and historical change allow a bridging of cultural difference that has no equivalents for historical epochs.

That the production of theories is itself a historical problem is now widely, though hardly universally, recognized. At least within the discourse of critical theory, the need to ground a theoretical statement with an account of its own production (or the potential for such an account without performative contradiction) is generally accepted. This idea of grounding is more or less distinctive to critical theory, however; it does not figure significantly at all in "mainstream" social theory.[35] Most self-proclaimed positivist theory is constructed without any attempt to make the act of theory construction itself intelligible within the theory.

The historical specificity of theoretical categories themselves is much less widely accepted. This is somewhat surprising inasmuch as both Weber and Marx worked in large part through historically specific conceptualization. Even devout followers of each, however, have often tended to ignore their (admittedly sometimes ambiguous) historical specifications and treat their concepts and theories as transhistorical timeless truths. Consider the use of the term "labor" in marxist theory. Most readings of Marx take labor to be a transhistorical category applying to all epochs and cultures. Others argue – correctly, in my view – that as a category in Marx's fully developed theory, "labor" should be treated as specific to capitalism. To be sure, work – in some general sense – may be understood to occur more broadly, but this is precisely because it is an untheorized term. The notion of labor is central to the mature Marx because labor as a form of abstract value – commodified and quantitatively measurable – is theoretically constitutive of capitalism, and it is a concept adequate and specific to a society in which capitalism as a set of cultural categories as well as material relationships can be said to exist.[36]

The historical specificity and contentfulness of all complex theoretical categories cannot be eliminated by analytic reformulation. It constitutes a reason why theoretical work cannot be strictly cumulative, in the positivist sense, and why deductive formulations are always limited and parasitic on inductive accounts. The hope for a theoretical millennium of deductive and cumulative theory is misleading at best.[37] Among the effects of pursuing this chimera, I would contend, is a necessary impoverishment of theoretical categories and consequently theories. No effort to specify the "scope statements" for a theory solves (or even really addresses) this problem, for it presumes the adequacy of the accounts of the basic categories across the lines of contexts in which the theory's propositions are found to hold or not to hold.[38]

The need for historical specificity does not derive simply from the difficulty an omniscient author has of indicating which of his equally true statements apply at what moment in a narrative of dramatic changes. Rather, it is the need to recognize (1) the limited vantage points provided by the historical perspective of each and every theorist, and (2) the immanence of theoretical categories in the world of practice. With regard to the latter, I mean first off and quite simply that it is not imaginable that Marx would have developed his theory of capitalism had he lived in the ninth and not the nineteenth century. More specifically, even theoretical concerns which run through the whole history of social thought – the attempt to understand and specify what a person is, for example – are always only thinkable in ways which are inextricably tied to the nature of society (and hence of persons) within the realm of experience and learning of a given thinker. Scholarship may help to overcome the limits imposed by the reach of one's own experience; it may make one less ethnocentric and less historically naive. Nonetheless, personal experience must be assigned a central role in accounting for the understandability (and particular reference) of theoretical categories and concepts, and of the theories into which they are woven.

The issue of historical specificity arises at all levels of analysis. It also concerns all time periods. Thus, there are historical changes that distinguish the context of theory production from one generation to the next. But the most important application of this point comes in the demarcation of epochs in human history, and the construction of conceptual frameworks adequate to epochal changes. Thus historical specificity comes to be of special significance for debates about whether modernity is giving way to postmodernity, whether theories based on the economic strategies of individual capitalists explain much about contemporary capitalism, or whether normalization of power is a social process of distinctive significance to modern societies or more general application. To reiterate, the issue is not simply one of scope statements. It is more fundamentally a matter of how the conceptual construction of these basic historical demarcations determines what sorts of categories will be appropriate to the analysis of phenomena internal to them. This is particularly important for a theory which proposes to take a critical stance towards existing social arrangements. It is essential that such a theory be able to show that it stands in an immanent relationship to such social arrangements in order for its critique to avoid being merely an arbitrary subjective expression on the one hand, or an only slightly less arbitrary imposition of external, possibly universalistic values.

The importance of the fact that theories exist in historically and culturally limited discursive fields has partly to do with the impossibility of separating the evaluation of any theory from the range of possible alternatives to it. Choices are made with regard to epistemic gain, not absolute truth; political advantage, not political certainty, and so forth.[39] Such choices are always part of a process of projection and examination of possible future paths, thus, and inevitably of communication concerning the range of options. Such theoretical communication presents itself as being able to rise above the ordinary problems of communication, to offer not only greater clarity and precision, but in Habermas's terms to offer readier redemption of validity claims. There is, I think, some truth to this self-presentation of theory. Among discourses about society, theoretical ones have some particular advantages in enabling communication across lines of cultural difference. They have these advantages generally, because even where theory does not thematize reflexivity it nonetheless involves it. But the advantages are greatest where the theory can be clear about its historical grounding and application.

Under the best of circumstances, however, communication is never perfect. As Derrida in particular has stressed, language itself produces and makes inevitable the potential for infinitely ramifying interpretations and plays of difference.[40] Because theory sets up an especially high standard for its own internal discourse, it makes an easy target for critique. In particular, it is easy to show that theory presenting itself as politically and otherwise neutral is strongly biased, and that theory claiming objective clarity and certainty can do so only by presupposing a foundation in the habitus of its practitioners and the tacit assumptions of their culture – "that which can be left unsaid." The answer to this, I am suggesting, lies in increasing the grounding of theories in the self-reflexivity of theorists, in cultural sensitivity and historical specificity, not in suggesting that because theoretical discourse cannot live up to its own ideals we must forfeit those ideals as regulative constructs. We must make choices among available theoretical options or abandon a great deal of contemporary scholarly, political, and ethical discourse. The path of avoiding such choices, of letting the inadequacy of all available theories be a license for dismissing them all, is far more radical and problematic than many of its seeming advocates suppose.

IV

If theory is truly historically grounded and sensitive to cultural variation, then the project of developing maximally general social theory cannot take some of the forms which have been proposed for it, or in which it has been proposed. To begin with, theory must be a polyphonic discourse, not a monological statement.[41] That is, for the most part theory will not be a matter of simple right answers. It will not be cumulative in any simple sense and it will not be possible for it to be "completed." More specifically, the achievements of theory will appear in the form of a discourse in which many voices shed light on a problem from different vantage points.[42] Indeed, internal to the best theories, there will be some play of different voices, a dialectic which does not attempt to reduce the world to a set of surface descriptions.[43] In this sense, the notion of polyphony shares much with the structuralist insight that aggregation of empirical instances of a phenomenon may be misleading as to the underlying structures generating a range of objective possibilities, and with the dialectical understanding that what exists at any one point in time is not necessarily the most fundamentally real and certainly not the limit of the real. A good theory of the more "general" sort must not pretend to closure, but open itself internally to the play of contending tendencies and possibilities.[44] Even more, it must be recognized that individual theories derive their meaning largely from the field of theoretical discourse in which they are developed and presented; they are not self-sufficient.

Relatedly, we need to recognize that the strong versions of claims for deductive theorizing and aggregation of tested hypotheses into theories are unreachable (claims 3 and 4 of the list of claims about theoretical generality presented in the introduction to this chapter). Local theories do not add up to middle-range ones; these do not add up to general theory. Each level of theory may encompass lower levels, or receive guidance from more general ones. It is not, however, possible to produce or understand a middle-range theory, say, simply by enumerating a series of local theories – still less a series of successfully tested propositions – in its domain. There is separate theoretical work which must be done, not least of all in establishing the historical grounding of the theory and in clarifying the cultural context of its concepts, as well as in relating different more local theories to each other. Local theories in any case cannot altogether escape implication in cultural outlooks and historical processes which cannot be grasped internally to them. Such cultural and historical dimensions can, of course, be left naively unspecified. This may mask an implicit reliance on a more general theory – as much local theory in sociology today relies on a loose mixture of functionalism and positivism without serious intellectual attention to either. And nonspecification of cultural and historical situation removes the grounding for a critical relationship between a theory and the social context of its production.

Local theory thus cannot escape dependence on more general theory. Either it will be directly dependent on a specific line of more general theory or it will be dependent on an untheorized set of cultural factors which could only be theorized at a more general level. Conversely, however, complete deduction of local and middle-range theories from more general ones is no more plausible an ideal.[45] It is certainly possible to construct a deductive theory, and such efforts have some value in restricted areas, but they do not point a plausible path for theoretical development overall. An entirely (or even mainly) deductive theory cannot be very culturally sensitive or very well historically grounded. It must be overwhelmingly formal and minimally contentful.[46]

Such deductive theories (e.g. rational choice theory, Blau's macrosocial structuralism) are often taken as models for general theory. In the sense of this chapter, however, this "generality" is highly restricted. Universal (or nearly universal) application is bought at the expense of cultural sensitivity and historical specificity such that the theory cannot ground itself in any rich way in concrete social life. Putatively universal propositions or structures of propositions about relatively narrow ranges of phenomena, or higly abstract aspects of phenomena are in this sense not "general theory" but variants of local theory. Rational choice theory, for example, consists of a highly general set of procedures or guidelines for constructing highly local theories; it does not offer much of a general theory *per se*.[47] Whether we call it "general" or something else, the best social theory (in the sense of most adequate to accounting for social life in all its multidimensionality and cultural and historical variation) is empirically rich. It combines comparative and historical substantive (empirical) discourse with reflection on and development of categories. Marx, Weber, and to a large extent Durkheim thus remain exemplars in ways which Parsons and Habermas (especially after his abandonment of the more empirically rich strategy of *Structural Transformation of the Public Sphere*) do not quite achieve.

The best of the "general" theories (in the sense of universalizing, especially deductive theories) are not strictly speaking theories of social life. Rather, they theorize certain of the conditions of social life. This is true of a good part of Simmel's work, and in this it has a modern heir in Peter Blau's macrostructural theory of inequality and heterogeneity and, with more complexity, in Harrison White's theory of identity and control.[48] Theories of social life must always be historical because social life is always a historical process, and contentful because social life is always culturally particular. While a formal theory like Blau's can be very wide in its application, perhaps even universal (and in that sense general), it cannot be concretized or become in any way empirical without becoming to some extent particular, in both historical and cultural terms.[49] This is something Simmel recognized rather more, or at least more explicitly, than Blau.[50] As we saw in chapter 2, even the simplest or most "obvious" concrete categories with which Blau illustrates his formal theory – e.g. those of race and class – must be at least implicit and *ad hoc* introductions of the historically and culturally particular into the theory.[51] The importance of cultural and historical particularity within good theories, however, does not preclude cross-cultural and cross-time generalization or comparison. One of the illusions of recent debates between self-styled postmodernists and self-styled defenders of reason is the notion that we face a sharp choice between attention to the multifaceted and particular and the search for generalizable knowledge.

The pursuit of cultural and historical specificity challenges universalism but can give only two cheers to particularism. The postmodernist decontextualization of referents is held to mirror various contemporary social and cultural processes: mediatization, internalization, mobility, etc. I think there is a great deal to this, but the question is how to respond. Seeing only a choice between totalizing power and free play of thought at the expense of relativism, postmodernists have generally opted for the latter. But I have tried to show in this chapter that other paths are open – particularly a culturally sensitive and historically specific sort of theory which must be highly contentful and aim at epistemic gain, not final truth.

Postmodernist approaches, as we shall see in the next chapter, do allow for, even encourage, the recognition of a multitude of voices in history. This, for example, is perhaps the most important critical counterweight which they offer to Habermas's highly universalistic theory. They sharpen our awareness of difference, but they provide no basis for comparison and in some cases make it seem impossible from within the approach. The reasons are somewhat similar to those producing normative relativism. Ironically, in this way postmodernists are often the mirror image of the Enlightenment universalists they challenge, making of difference – especially Derrida's *différance* – an absolute as rigid as unitary identity or universalism is to their enemies. And if positive, unitary identity is a form of violence against difference, so absolutized difference is a form of violence against intersubjectivity, or more specifically, the human will to bridge the gap between people, traditions, cultures.

What is called for must be a *processual* approach to understanding. It will require a form of communicative action (*pace* Habermas[52]) which allows for discourse in which intersubjectivity grows. It will expect that mutual understanding itself will be achieved not simply by translation but by a historical process of change on both sides. It will situate comparative scholarship within such a historical process, seeking epistemic gain through highly contentful theories which must be subject to a continual play of reinterpretation. It will attempt to make clear the historical and cultural frames of reference which make it possible, not losing sight of the finitude and limited generalizability of those frames.

In short, doing social and political theory and doing historical and cross-cultural comparison must be continuous, mutually involved enterprises.

Notes

1 Merton, *Social Theory and Social Structure*; Stinchcombe, *Constructing Sociological Theories.*
2 Though not without some ambivalence, as Alexander, *Theoretical Logic*, vol. 2, has shown. Parsons, *Structure of Social Action*, attempted to overcome the division between this positivist notion of science and the approach of Weber and the other classical theorists whom he accepted into the sociological canon. Sica, *Max Weber*, has recently shown how far Parsons' reading was from the hermeneutic dimension of Weber's theory.
3 Mills, *Sociological Imagination*.
4 On this desideratum for theories, see Lakatos, "Falsification."
5 See Taylor, *Multiculturalism* and *Ethics of Authenticity*, and chapter 7 below on some of the reasons why "soft relativism" frequently implies a refusal to engage others in ways that either take them as seriously as they ask or submit ourselves to real challenge from them.

6   "Orientalism" of the sort epitomized by Montesquieu and prominently critiqued by Said, *Orientalism*, is a variant of this problematic treatment of cross-cultural variation. While difference is made theoretically salient by this sort of orientalist, his or her project is not the understanding of the other but rather the use of accounts of the other to inform ethnocentric self-understanding. Such accounts may be positive ("see what we can learn even from the noble savage or the heathen Chinese") or negative ("we may lack full democracy but thank God we don't live under Kadi, pasha or some other form of oriental despot") in their view of the other. The other may be given a more schematic or more richly detailed description. Nonetheless, in such accounts, the other is understood only externally and as a marked rather than primary or independent category.

7   Habermas, *Theory of Communicative Action*, vol. 1.

8   Gilligan challenged Kohlberg's notion of fixed, universal stages of moral reasoning as being a reflection of male patterns with no greater intrinsic validity than contrasting predominantly female ones. In addition to the original contributions of Kohlberg (*Essays on Moral Development*) and Gilligan (*In a Different Voice*) see Benhabib's insightful commentary and theorization of the controversy ("The Generalized and the Concrete Other").

9   See Young, "Impartiality and Civic Virtue," on the problems built into the assumption that justice must rest on impartiality; also her *Justice and the Politics of Difference*.

10   As McCarthy ("Legitimacy and Diversity") has recently argued, Habermas assumes that ethical–political discourses are similar to discourses about truth claims in that it must be possible in principle for all to result in rational consensus, even if compromise and accommodation are required in the short run. But it is not clear why we should not expect debates on, for example, abortion, to continue indefinitely and not to be resolvable by rational consensus among social actors as they are currently constituted.

11   Habermas does grant solidarity a place alongside justice in his account of basic social goods, and recognizes Durkheim's arguments for the possibility of solidarity based directly on reciprocal need (and hence difference). But Habermas does not treat difference as good or productive in and of itself, rather than as inevitable and deserving of tolerance. This means that even in considering social integration based on communication, he does not attempt to theorize cultural difference or the problems of mutually empowering discourse across lines of basic difference. See Calhoun, "Populist Politics."

12   Foucault, *Madness and Civilization, Discipline and Punish*.

13   See Taguieff, *La force du préjugé* on the way in which liberal anti-racism has incorporated and built – usually without reflective awareness – on the categories of race.

14   For a sympathetic methodological critique of Blau's formal theory of social structure following this same direction, see Calhoun and Scott, "Introduction."

15 We shall see something more of what this means in considering the historical specificity of theoretical categories in the next section.

16 Winch, *Idea of a Social Science*.

17 See Wilson, ed., *Rationality*, and Hollis and Lukes, eds, *Rationality and Relativism*. Winch was first challenged importantly by Alasdair MacIntyre and eventually a range of different thinkers took positions in these debates.

18 Theories of economizing or utilitarian rational choice may constitute partial exceptions to this. To the extent that they involve empirical claims rather than hypothetical constructs, they do seem to claim that actors do in fact always or almost always behave according to a single universal standard of rationality.

19 Kuhn borrowed the notion of incommensurability from mathematics; see *Structure of Scientific Revolutions*; see discussion in Taylor, "Interpretation and the Sciences of Man"; Bernstein, *Beyond Objectivism and Relativism*; and Tambiah, *Magic, Science, Religion, and the Scope of Rationality*, among many.

20 One of the ironies of the postmodernist critique of "modernist" or Enlightenment theory is that it often retains the extremely intellectualist assumptions of the parent discourse. Thus when Lyotard challenges the idea of resolving differences among language games by metadiscourse, he simply points to the impossibility of achieving a neutral metadiscursive representation of truly incommensurable language games. He does not consider the inaptness of the metadiscourse model as such. See Lyotard, *The Postmodern Condition*. At the same time, some languages of widespread international use – like English – are shaped by being called into frequent service as metalanguages (however nonneutral).

21 Bourdieu, *Outline*, p. 116.

22 Culture is not, it should perhaps be stressed, the static collection of norms, values, and beliefs that introductory sociology textbooks present it as. It is a dynamic dimension of social practice and even our use of a singular notion of *a* culture must be provisional shorthand, for cultures are seldom sharply bounded, and never completely internally homogenous. In the present context, to be a member of a culture is to be engaged in a variety of practices that are incommensurable with those of other cultures, from ways of eating to religion and family life. To be both an American (of any specific sort) and a Nuer, say, is to be engaged in many incommensurable practices; in a sense, to be American and to be Nuer *are* incommensurable practices. This is the source of the fundamental challenge in reporting anthropological fieldwork.

23 Taylor, "Rationality," p. 93.

24 Putnam, *Reason, Truth and History*, p. 117.

25 Ibid.

26 Bourdieu, *Outline*, p. 118; see also discussion in chapter 4 below.

27 Ibid., p. 114.

28 Indeed, as Steiner, *After Babel*, has famously argued and modern semiotics

generally would suggest, all translation is in some part construction, not mere rendering of equivalences.

29 Of course, Third World anthropologists have worked (albeit rarely) in Western settings, but this is not quite as reciprocal as it sounds. Such anthropologists are still participants in a discourse which had its origins not in their traditional culture, and not in the national cultural or international Third World culture to which that traditional culture may have partially given way, but in the West and in the international culture to which it gave rise (however colored that may be by the growing inclusion of Third World voices). By becoming anthropologists, these people, even if of Nuer or other traditional ancestry, and even if highly committed to an alternative Third World view, nonetheless leave the realm of practices internal to traditional culture. This does not mean that such practices are not internal to their own current culture – anthropology is now an internal part of Sudanese culture, say, and much more so of Indian. But though internal, it is not altogether indigenous and is not the product primarily of traditional practices.

30 See Winch, "Unerstanding a Primitive Society," and the essays in Wilson, ed., *Rationality*, and Hollis and Lukes, eds, *Rationality*. There is an excellent discussion in Tambiah, *Magic, Science, Religion*.

31 I first learned something of this in observation of and discussions with traditional medical practitioners and instructors in a college of tradional medicine in Chengdu in 1984. I say "quasi-experimental" both because the experiments most commonly conducted involve "tests" of the remedies prescribed in the classical texts which always result in their confirmation, and because the link between causal reasoning and experimentation in the Western scientific sense is commonly absent.

32 Foucault, *The Order of Things*.

33 It is worth recalling that a central part of Evans-Pritchard's famous argument about Azande witchcraft concerned the fact that they generally do not make comparative evaluations of the efficacy of their practices; see *Witchcraft, Magic and Oracles*. And of course it is not only the Azande who try to employ all possibly effective techniques in many practical situations, thus making comparative evaluation of their respective efficacy difficult.

34 Tambiah, *Magic, Science, Religion*, p. 122.

35 In fact, this notion of grounding is one of the key distinguishing features of critical theory. Bourdieu's explorations and development of a self-reflexive social science are a central example outside the Frankfurt School. See Bourdieu and Wacquant, *An Invitation*.

36 See Postone, *Time, Labor*, for an excellent statement of the view that labor should be treated as a historically specific category.

37 See Turner, "The Strange Life."

38 Compare the optimism of Walker and Cohen, "Scope Statements," with regard to scope statements.

39 On the notion of epistemic gain as an alternative to complete relativism and absolute truth claims, see Taylor, *Human Agency and Language*, *Philosophy and the Human Sciences*. See also Gadamer, *Truth and Method* (esp.

280ff) on the intrinsic orientation to action that is a part of the knowledge of the human sciences, and which limits both absolute truth claims and relativistic failure to decide on approximate truths.

40 See especially Derrida, *Writing and Difference*.

41 Taylor, *Human Agency and Language*, ch 10.

42 The writings of Pierre Bourdieu and Jacques Derrida have gone further in this direction than those of any other major contemporary theorists, continuously playing perspectives against each other and thereby sometimes frustrating those who wish to read them monologically. Both, but especially Derrida, have experimented with novel presentations of text on the page. Foucault and Lyotard, by contrast, tend to write more or less monologically even when their writings are meant to critique the monological normalization imposed by modern society and culture. So do most of the "American deconstructionists" who half-follow and half-distort Derrida (see discussion in Norris, *Derrida*) and other postmodernists who declare but often fail to evidence commitment to a plurality of voices.

43 Though current academically fashionable usage extends the term "polyphonic" very widely, it was introduced by Bakhtin specifically to refer to the internal play of voices within a certain sort of novel. The same novels of Dostoevsky were seized upon by Freud as exemplifications of psychoanalytic insight before the invention of psychoanalysis. This connection warrants the observation that polyphonic discourse ought not to refer simply to a toleration for the voices of many individuals each speaking monologically, but rather to a capacity for internal speech, a tolerance for the internal complexity which suggests that the singular human being is not altogether monological, and accordingly is not strictly speaking individual – an irreducible whole – at least not in all senses.

44 This is an advantage of many of the uses of the textual metaphor for society (advocated for example by Brown, "Social Science"). It is crucial that such a metaphor always be used in a clearly polyphonic or dialogical way, to describe a "text" of many contending voices, and not allowed to encourage a notion of monologically "reading" society. At the same time, the textual metaphor does have serious drawbacks, not least a tendency to treat society only or mainly as a symbol system and not as a material historical process.

45 See also Turner (*Search for a Methodology*, "The Strange Life") for other reasons bearing on the same point.

46 More specifically, this is true of deductive theories which claim considerable autonomy from induction. It does not apply equally to the place of deductive, formal reasoning as a moment in a more contentful theory. Formalization may serve a useful role of codification, rigorous self-checking, and suggestion of new hypotheses in the latter sort of case.

47 See also critical discussion in Wacquant and Calhoun, "Intérêt, rationalité, et histoire."

48 Blau, *Inequality and Heterogeneity* and Blau and Schwartz, *Cross-Cutting Social Circles*; White, *Identity and Control*.

49 See Calhoun and Scott, "Introduction."

50 This is also a point recognized more clearly by White, *Identity and Control*.

51 In this theory, Blau never addresses gender in any very substantial way. Ironically, his main exemplification of how groups can be defined by the prevalence of in-group over out-group association is intermarriage rates. Needless to say, he does not show homosexual marriages outnumbering heterosexual, yet gender remains a salient category. This suggests some problems for his contention that there is no significance to culturally defined membership categories which are not characterized by such prevalence of in-group association on all or most important dimensions.

52 Habermas, *Theory of Communicative Action*, vols 1, 2.

4

Postmodernism as Pseudohistory: The Trivialization of Epochal Change

I

The challenge of difference does not arise only between cultures, or only between genders, ethnic groups, classes, or other social and cultural categories or organized groups. Difference is basic and comes along infinite dimensions. By the same token, this means that differences are often cross-cutting and we cannot understand all problems of difference from the presumption that each raises the challenge of radical alterity, total otherness.[1]

In this connection, self-styled "postmodernists" are misleading to claim that the presence of ambiguity and ethnocentrism in all previous means proposed for overcoming breakdowns in communication constitutes grounds for their dismissal or radical relativization.[2] Some postmodernists are happy relativists – perfectly prepared to acknowledge that there are no certain truths and perhaps even no ways to be sure of meaningful communication across intellectual traditions or cultures, untroubled by the lack of grounding this leaves them for normative judgments and either scholarly or practical disputes. They eschew the gloom which the prospect of radical relativism suggests to Enlightenment thinkers and adopt instead a Rabelaisian carnival attitude, playful before the intellectual abyss.[3] Others adopt an apocalyptic tone but offer no more way out. Though taken all too commonly in English-language discourse as an unambiguous partisan of postmodernism, Derrida has been as sharply critical of these attitudes as anyone. The necessary critique of the logocentricism of traditional philosophy, Derrida suggests, by no means demands – nor for that matter makes possible – escape from the necessity to proceed by means of serious critical thought, working through the possibilities for and limits to knowledge in a fashion not altogether distant from Kant, and insisting also on recognition that human life demands ethics as well as epistemology of our thought.[4]

It is not always realized that while the widespread postmodernist attitude avoids a tendency to intellectual domination characteristic of many Enlightenment theories, the way in which it recognizes otherness borders on the trivializing. The "other" may be omnipresent, difference intrinsic to the very possibility of knowledge, but if this is construed in a relativist direction, no other in particular gains strong intellectual or normative claims on us.

Relativism is not the only problem with this manner of thinking. Ironically, while extolling difference, much postmodernist thought actually fails sharply to make sense of real cultural or historical specificity. It is presented above all as though it is grounded in a historical claim, but in the first part of this chapter I will suggest that this is a pseudohistory. A kind of pseudo-specificity is introduced by the use of the prefix "post" and the proliferation of contrasts to putative modernity or modernism. Such contrasts sometimes point to significant variables differentiating social practices. They are seldom developed as very precise categories, however, or concretized in serious historical or cross-cultural analyses. Rather, the Enlightenment is evoked as though it were the archetype of a unidimensional and uncontested modernity. Or the nonWestern world or Third World is posed as a critical vantage point on the West in an ironic new Orientalism, without consideration of the enormous internal heterogeneity of those constructs. In each case, a crucial question is how a social change has shifted the conditions and capacities for human action. The broad postmodernist discourse obscures this issue, however, by positing an end to subjectivity or rendering it universally problematic rather than addressing the ways in which agency and subjectivity are constructed in specific historical and cultural situations.

In the present chapter, I want to question how much the genuinely dramatic social and cultural changes that are going on around us are a real departure from previous trends, and to the extent that they are, whether this is part of a social transformation sufficiently basic to warrant an argument that modernity is dead or dying. I will argue generally against the postmodernist view. Though changes are real and major, they do not yet amount to an epochal break. Indeed, many of them reflect continuing tensions and pressures which have characterized the whole modern era.[5] Two counter-claims inform my account of problems with the claim that postmodernity is upon us: First, the two basic organizing forces in modernity – capitalism and bureaucratic power – have hardly begun to dissolve. Second, the problems of self and agency are neither new to a postmodern era nor obsolete because superseded either historically or theoretically; these problems continue to shape our lives and thought as they have shaped them throughout modernity. Rather than narrowing our notion of the modern in order to justify the use of the prefix "post," I will argue that we need to incorporate the insights of postmodernist thinkers into a richer sociological approach to the entire modern era.

In the second part of the chapter, I will argue briefly for reading poststructuralist theory, and especially Derrida and Foucault, apart from any argument about postmodernism. Derrida and Foucault are claimed as part of the movement though they never proclaimed themselves postmodernists. Moreover, too much English language appropriation constructs an illusory unity to the intellectual positions of Parisians commonly at odds with each other. Likewise, the structuralist background to poststructuralist theory is widely forgotten or misunderstood.[6] While I will not rehearse this history, I will argue that we need to avoid exaggerating any emphasis on the prefix "post" and recognize the extent to which Derrida and especially Foucault write as inheritors of structuralism.

The third part of the chapter will address the difficulty postmodernism, and to some extent poststructuralism more generally, confronts in finding a vantage point for comparative analysis (as distinct from mere celebration of difference and/or syncretism). Closely linked to the last is the difficulty of reconciling the normative positions of postmodernism (e.g. extolling the virtues of difference and condemning the vice of repressive normalization) with its generally relativist theoretical orientation. Performative contradictions abound as postmodernists issue authoritative pronouncements on the basis of theoretical positions that deny any non-arbitrary basis to authority.

II

What then are we to make of the frequent declarations that we have entered a postmodern age? Is this something that has happened to architecture, but not to society? Or have cultural analysts noticed something that has eluded the attention of sociologists?[7]

Postmodernism is a confluence of several partially distinct trends:

1 Perhaps with clearest meaning, postmodernism is a rejection of artistic modernism (e.g. the international style in architecture) in favor of freeing the aesthetic from the functional, putting signification, intertextual reference, and self-reflexivity forward as independent goods. While architects like Venturi and Jencks have played a pri-

mary role in promoting the conceptualization of postmodernism, related changes are current and self-identified throughout at least the visual and dramatic arts (including cinema) and literature.

2   Postmodernism as a theoretical and/or critical position derives substantially from poststructuralism. This is a largely retrospective label for a series of French-led shifts in cultural (and psychological and social) theory, notably the critique of subject-centered reason, monological texts or readings, grand narratives, general truth claims, and the normalization of Enlightenment rationality. Central players include Derrida, Foucault (a little ambiguously), Lyotard, Baudrillard, and various British, American, and Antipodean epigones.

3   Closely related to poststructuralism in many accounts is the postmodernist critique of "foundationalism" in philosophy and theory. At a minimum, this is an extension of the Nietzschean and Heideggerian critique of metaphysics into an attack on all claims to an external standpoint for judging truth. In the work of Rorty, for example, a level of necessary theoretical indeterminacy is made the basis for a call to abandon repressive demands for certainty in favor of a "liberal" toleration of diversity on even the most basic epistemological and ethical points. In other hands, antifoundationalism becomes an attack on theoretical systematicity itself.[8]

4   Finally, postmodernism includes sociological and political economic claims to identify a basic transition from "modernity" to a new stage of (or beyond) history. These variously emphasize postindustrial, information or knowledge society as the new societal formation. A new centrality is posited for media, information technology, and the production of signification (e.g. culture industry) as an end in itself. Key figures in this line of argument (notably Bell and Touraine, and popularizers like Toffler and Naisbitt) are not directly a part of the postmodernist movement, but their arguments have influenced it substantially.

The four lines of influence are not strictly commensurate. In particular, the "post" prefix may oppose modernism as an artistic movement of the late nineteenth and early twentieth centuries, foundationalism as a feature of early modern science and Enlightenment discourse, modernity as an epoch of much longer duration, or the very construction of a progressive historical narrative such as those used to identify "modernity" in the first place (primarily during the eighteenth and nineteenth centuries). Nonetheless, the various strands of the phenomenon draw strength and significance from being intertwined.[9]

Postmodernism is a recognizable artistic and more generally cultural trend that can be distinguished from and indeed reacts against modernism. But this is not the same as saying that modernity has given way to postmodernity. Even in the cultural realm, it is hard to place postmodernism. Surely we can recognize it in recent video and performance art, in the architecture of pastiche, and in novels whose weight cannot be borne by the narrative of any subject. But are these extensions of early trends or something dramatically new? The period from the 1890s to the 1920s must be reckoned the glory days of high modernism. Bauhaus architecture, Russian formalist painters, the French and German novelists, and English poets of the day seem unquestionably modern. Brecht and Simmel, Joyce and Woolf are paradigmatically modern. Yet they also seem very close to the so-called postmodern. Baudelaire only coined the term modernism in the late nineteenth century, though drawing on the older figure of the struggle between ancients and moderns. Postmodernism in a sense issues almost immediately thereafter from the (more recently accelerated) effort to claim an autonomy for art, free from any justification in terms of its moral significance. The themes of fragmentation of consciousness, the distance between the intentions and ends of action, the severing of symbol from referent are all felt in the art and social thought of the high modernist era. Robert Musil's *The Man Without Qualities*, written mainly in the 1920s, is strikingly "postmodern," an anticipation of Kundera, in its account of the insufficiency of the self as bearer of the weight of "modernist" subjectivity.[10] If these are all to be embraced as part of the postmodern, then (1) the postmodern must be understood as part and parcel of the modern, and (2) the label must be seen as essentially misleading, perhaps willfully so, perhaps simply conditioned by the general modern sensibility that the new is always better than the established.[11]

It is hard, in this connection, to distinguish the postmodern from the merely antimodern – that is, from the various sorts of oppositions to dominant themes in modernity which have accompanied modernization from its beginning. In this sense what is new is only the highly modernist stylization of conservatism, on the one hand, and the production of sometimes very unconservative antimodernisms on the other. But the issue goes one step deeper. Not just the antimodernism of Catholic conservatives and country squires, or of the scholastic defenders of artistic classicism and traditional iconic languages of representation, accompanied modernism from its inception. So did very modern, but in many ways antimodernist, figures like Nietzsche. Modernism, and modernity, have always been internally complex.

The postmodernist critique (and the defense of modernity mounted by figures like Habermas) tends to equate modernity with the rationalist Enlightenment.[12] But the Romantics were as modern and as new as the rationalists. Characters crucial to modernity – most notably Rousseau but also Goethe and some of the English Romantic poets – combined elements of both rationalism and romanticism in their writing and their lives. The individualism we identify as so central to the modern experience and modern society and culture was shaped by both romantic and rationalist notions, by Enlightenment modernism and the other side of modernism represented paradigmatically by Rousseau, Goethe, and Nietzsche, but also, only somewhat more ambiguously, by Freud and Simmel.[13] The complexity of interplay across rationalist and romantic lines is important to grasp. Shelley is certainly a paradigmatic Romantic, yet we might recall that Shelley was drawn to Godwin for the very rationalism of his anarchist political theory even before he eloped with his daughter. The late eighteenth century in many parts of Europe and America saw versions of the circle of connections which knit the Godwins, Wolstonecraft, Shelley, and Byron together. A not dissimilar confluence of influences – rationalist German idealism, Romanticism, Nietzsche and the dark side of Enlightenment (even Sade) shaped the thought of Horkheimer and Adorno. There may be an important battle between rationalist universalism and attention to the irrational, between the value of the particular and the repressive, disempowering, and deceptive side of individualism. But to equate that with a battle between modernity and its putative successor is to fail to recognize how deeply a part of modernity that whole battle, that whole frame of reference is. And this is only to speak of Western modernity.

Another sort of argument has been incorporated into the postmodernist position, however, which stems much more from claims about changes in the empirical world. This is the claim that we need a postmodernist theory because we live in a postmodern age. The proliferation of such labels was a particular feature of the 1970s and 1980s. Daniel Bell's and Alain Touraine's different accounts of postindustrial society marked early versions. The postmodernists posed much more radical claims about the implications of computerization, new communications media, and related socio-technical changes. Bell had already joined Habermas and other thinkers in suggesting that the advance of information processing and automating technologies meant that labor should no longer be privileged (in the marxist sense) as the basic source of value.[14] Jean Baudrillard, among others, has argued that the whole form of social organization based on production relations and power has given way to a society and economy organized on the bases of consumption and seduction, for example by advertising.[15] In such a postmodern society, the sign becomes the autonomous source and form of value, the signifier is detached from the signified. The structure of relations which now matters is not that by which capital dominates labor, or centers of power grow and eliminate the territorial organization of power. Rather, the structure of relations which now matters is among signs. The representations are more real than the things represented. People are "exteriorized" into a techno-culture of "hyperreality" where significance replaces reification and we know only the simulacra of mass existence. Or as Guy Debord put it in *Society of the Spectacle*, the alienation of the commodity form is experienced to such a degree of abstraction that the commodity becomes a mere image detached from its previous ground in human labor or concrete use value. As a result, the critiques based on use value and concrete labor are rendered impotent.[16]

But the positing of an epochal change is problematic. There has undoubtedly been an increase in the role of advertising and the media generally (and not only in the economic sphere, but also in politics and efforts to influence personal decisions – e.g. about abortion, cigarette smoking, or drug use). Consumption has indeed been thrust to the foreground of practical concerns, both for those who attempt to manage it in the business world and for everyone in the organization of everyday life. These genuine changes, however, and others like them, do not add up to a very conclusive case either that production has lost its basic importance or that signification has gained the status of self-production free from any need for creative subjects or material referents.[17]

This postmodernist argument against Marx depends on a rather rigid reading of *Capital* in which, among other things, Marx is treated as having underappreciated his own argument as to the importance of abstraction in the commodity form through which labor is rendered into capital, in favor of a naturalistic (and therefore transhistorical) understanding of labor.[18] This issue, however, goes beyond a fight about marxism. The claim that material production is no longer central to the organization of economic and social life is meant to reveal the postmodern age to be free from a whole series of constraints discussed in nearly every version of economic theory; it is meant to have liberated culture from material social determinations. Yet even on the face of things it appears false, mistaking the rising importance of information technology within capitalism for a basic transformation of capitalism, not just into a new phase but into something altogether different. No evidence is presented that capital accumulation is not basic to economic activity and social power today (though it may never have been as exclusively fundamental as some marxists have claimed). And though industry employs a declining percentage of the population, this does

not mean a decline in all measures of its importance. The very implemen-
tation of labor-saving technology requires an increasing capital investment, and the distributive (consumption, financial, etc.) orientation of
business (which has been widely criticized in recent years by supply-
siders and more conventional economists and business analysts alike) can
still be understood as a response to the problem of utilizing productive
capacity.

Our cultural orientation, moreover, seems still to be very productivist
and very much focused on the acquisition of material goods. What are we
to make of claims, like this from Frederick Jameson? "Henceforth,"
writes Jameson comparing the 1920s and 1930s in which Surrealism
flourished with what he sees as the impoverished material world of the
late twentieth century, "in what we may call post-industrial capitalism,
the products with which we are furnished are utterly without depth: their
plastic content is totally incapable of serving as a conductor of psychic
energy. All libidinal investment in such objects is precluded from the
outset."[19] Who is the "we" here? Has Jameson never met someone who
named their notebook computer or their car? Who wore a favorite shirt
until it disintegrated? Who treasured the records they bought with a
now-departed lover? Or does he mean to exclude the realm of ordinary
life for a claim to aesthetic transformation evidenced only in the relation
of artists to manufactured objects (and then dubiously)? Last but not
least, the insight gained from focusing on movement away from productive industry – whether basic or minor – seems hardly able to make sense
of any entire economy; at most it may have purchase on that portion of
the international economy which is located in the rich – e.g., OECD –
countries. And even there, the rush to generalize about the movement
away from material goods and industry seems riskily to ignore the
possibility that its observations are keyed to cycles both in economic
activity (was "postmaterialism" dependent on the long growth wave that
broke with the early 1970s recession?) and in consumer predilections
(our interests in consumer durables are not consistent, but ebb and flow
with saturation of desires and recognition of the burdens those durables
impose on us).[20]

Lyotard has more plausibly suggested that postmodernity "is undoubtedly a part of the modern."[21] Postmodernism in this view is a phase
in modernism's constant push to negate the existent and produce the
new. This makes sense (though it makes the label misleading). Indeed, in
more recent work, Lyotard had more sharply challenged the utility of the
label postmodern with which he is so inextricably linked. The phrase
"rewriting modernity," he says (and I agree):

seems far preferable to the usual headings, like "postmodernity," "postmodernism," "postmodern," under which this sort of reflection is usually placed. The advantage of "rewriting modernity" depends on two displacements: the transformation of the prefix "post-" into "re-" from the lexical point of view, and the syntactical application of this modified prefix to the verb "writing," rather than to the substantive "modernity."[22]

But of course the lexical and syntactical horses are already out of the barn. Lyotard's early work did offer, albeit not altogether consistently, the suggestion of a different sort of basic historical change which provides a grounding for postmodernism's currency.

On this account, postmodernity suffers from a loss of meaning, or a meaningfulness that can only be repressively imposed, because the great legitimating narratives of modernity have been exploded. Lyotard is hardly the only figure to stress this sort of argument. He gives it one of its most prominent expositions, however, suggesting that this is not just a possible intellectual stance but a basic social transformation:

> the old poles of attraction represented by nation-states, parties, profes-
> sions, institutions, and historical traditions are losing their attraction. And
> it does not look as though they will be replaced, at least not on their former
> scale.[23]

I think it is somewhat dubious whether the key modern collective identities and "poles of attraction" have been quite so completely displaced. On this point too, the very fragmentation claimed as distinctive of postmodernity has often been claimed as equally distinctive of modernity. Giddens has suggested, thus, that the sort of changes claimed in the quote from Lyotard's *The Postmodern Condition* are more plausibly read as the completion or radicalization of modernity than as the coming of postmodernity.[24] The discourse does not, in any case, provide any but the most ambiguous of answers to the question of what constitutes an epochal historical transformation.

The distinction between modernity and postmodernity has the surface appearance of being a historically specific claim about the end of one epoch and the beginning of another. But in fact postmodernists split into two groups: those who seek to identify concrete changes in social history – e.g. the end of Fordism – and those who evoke Heiddegger's more primordial sense of crisis.[25] As an intellectual project (or style), postmodernism is an internal product of modernity, not its true opponent. It is a counterpoint to the modernist project, but one generated from within modernity, a recurrent modern form of challenge to Enlightenment universalism and foundationalism (and thus not simply a sort of throwback to the premodern resistance to modernity). Though he is inconsistent, and sometimes reverts to treating postmodernity as a period, Lyotard is distinctive in recognizing at least at times that "postmodernity is undoubtedly a part of the modern.[26] Postmodernists are quite modern, for example, in style, not least of all in constantly searching for the new, suspecting that which has been received. "A work [of art] can become modern only if it is first postmodern. Postmodernism thus understood is not modernism at its end but in the nascent state, and this state is constant."[27] In nearly all material ways the modern tendencies continue: centralization of power, demand for economic productivity. Even the exploding and fragmenting of once more integrated cultural systems or communities is not "after" modern. It is, rather, something modernity has done throughout its existence.[28]

Elsewhere, unfortunately, Lyotard does tend to treat postmodernity as a historical period and postmodernism as a separable project.[29] Thinner studies and popularizations exaggerate this tendency, and are replete with diagrams opposing the tenets of supposed modernity and postmodernity in the most modernist of dichotomous fashions.[30] Nearly all accounts are vague as to postmodernism's beginnings (an aspect of their pseudohistorical character). Yet such treatments force us to ask when the postmodern era began if we are to be able to figure out whether the theory traveling under the name postmodernist is historically specific or transhistorical. There are a number of possible answers implied by various writings within the postmodern tradition (this very vagueness is testimony to the nonspecificity of the theories):

- With "poststructuralism" in the late 1960s. Derrida might be taken as marking this break most strikingly with his publication of three books in 1967.[31] Poststructuralism itself is a move visible only retrospectively in the careers of former structuralists who decided they could decenter the subject and still reflect critically on the categories of thought, and thus could give up structuralism's denial of epistemology which was based on the belief that it could only be pursued in terms of a philosophy of the subject.
- With "postindustrial society," computerization, and/or other sociotechnical changes taken to undermine the privileging of labor as the source of value. This is an idea put forward by Lyotard especially.
- With the ascendancy of consumption/seduction over production/power, an argument launched by Baudrillard.
- With nontraditional critics of modernity from Nietzsche (emphasizing the will to power) to Heidegger (who described Nietzsche's

time and implicitly also his own as "the epoch in which the completion of the modern age begins") to Simmel (the fragmentation of
society) to Musil (who in *The Man without Qualities* put forward a
notion of the self as insufficient to bear the weight of "modernist"
subjectivity).[32]

Underlying this concern is the problem of how to relate the intellectual
current of "postmodernism" to change in social life. Identification of a
new age "postmodernity" is postmodernism's main possibility for claiming a historical grounding.

The great pioneer of poststructuralist analyses of historical transformation was Michel Foucault. Unlike most of the self-declared
postmodernists (many of whom claim him for their camp despite the fact
that he did not explicitly join it), Foucault was, first and foremost, an
analyst of modernity, indeed early modernity. He helped, however, to set
the stage for postmodernism with his discussion of historical ruptures
and his thematic stresses on the repressive character of modernity, its
arbitrary construction of the subject as a disciplinary ploy, and the
inescapable mutual imbrication of power and knowledge.[33] Especially in
his earlier work, Foucault lays great stress on the ways in which internally coherent modes of understanding lost their grip and were superseded, and by showing these breaks both situated modernity and implied
criteria for judging what might constitute a fundamental intellectual
transformation.[34] At the heart of his most influential account was the
distinctively modern production of knowledge from the standpoint of the
individual knower, a standpoint constituted in turn through a fundamentally new play of power. If this marks modernity, then it is apparent that
a loss of capacity for coherent subjectivity – and with it a certain
production of meaning – would spell modernity's end.

Both Lyotard and Baudrillard want to go further. Baudrillard suggests
forgetting Foucault as an account still caught in modernity's grasp, just
as Marx was (on his view) caught in capitalism's.[35] Elsewhere, he declares
the death of the social, the end of true social relations and their replace-
ments by the simulacra of hyperreality.[36] What is for Derrida the absence
of an approach to the social becomes for Baudrillard an explicit devaluation of the social.[37] Modernity has been ruptured, he asserts, by the
collapse of normalizing power, expanding material productivity, and
the possibility of grasping social life as a relation among subjects. The
modern sense of the social had been dominated by the centralization and
deterritorialization of power (by implication the effect of the growth of
the state), and the production of commodities which gained their value
from abstract human labor and the pattern of circulation of which could

be criticized from the standpoint of concrete use value and concrete labor. In other words, modernity was the era of power and the production of commodities. Postmodernity is the era of the sign and the seduction of consumers. The structure of relations which now matters is among signs. People are "exteriorized" into a techno-culture of "hyperreality" where significant replaces reification and we know only the simulacra of mass existence. Baudrillard's vision is basically a tragic account of the completion of the abstraction of power suggested by the Weberian notion of rationalization, and of production (reconstituted as seduction) by the marxian commodity-based system of capitalism. But it takes him far from those masters theoretically. And it leaves him facing nihilism squarely and advocating an attitude simply of "ironic detachment" – an attitude at least as lacking in capacity for positive critical engagement with the contemporary world as Horkheimer's and Adorno's belief that all they could hope to do was to leave "a message in a bottle" for a future era. Baudrillard almost celebrates the fear of mass culture which helped make Adorno and Horkheimer into such pessimists. As he asks:

> Are the mass media on the side of power in the manipulation of the masses, or are they on the side of the masses in the liquidation of meaning, and in the fascination which results? Is it the media which induce fascination in the masses, or is it the masses which divert the media into spectacles?[38]

At one level, Baudrillard retains within his tragic vision some sense of historical specificity: we face the abyss; our ancestors did not. A key reason is because he ties his vision of postmodernist culture to a more general view of postmodern society; he does not make postmodernism something free floating, purely within the realm of ideas. But his theses of the implosion of meaning and the out-of-control production of signification suggest the impossibility of any theoretical grounding, and of cross-cultural evaluation. And Baudrillard radicalizes Barthes' vision of the destruction of cultural difference by the media.[39] His theory thus has an enormous amount in common with the views of mass society, mass culture, or the revolt of the masses which have been endemic to the twentieth century – if not all modernity. We might question, however, whether there is not a great deal of internal differentiation among "the masses" which might be addressed by an empirical theory more focused on cultural variation, and which might be valorized by a normative theory more respectful of differences.

On the other hand, there is in much postmodernist thought an interesting resistance to the very narrative bases for discussing historical specificity. In this sense (though not in its arguments for the importance of difference) such postmodernist thought is directly opposed to the program put forward here. Lyotard, for example, suggests that the core difference between modernist and postmodernist thought be seen in the tendency of the former to impose suprahistorical narratives on the concrete and ultimately directionless flux of history: Modern science relies on metadiscourses that appeal to grand narratives of history. Lyotard at one point defines *"postmodern* as incredulity toward metanarratives."[40] But there is an enormous difference that Lyotard does not consider between such grand metanarratives – the Hegelian dialectical realization of spirit, for example – and actual historical arguments – say, about the transition from feudalism to capitalism. In more contemporary terms, one can meaningfully speak about the hoped for end to the cold war and enormous post-1989 realignment of world politics without resorting to the Hegelian fantasies of Francis Fukuyama's *The End of History and the Last Man*. Lyotard's idea of postmodernity is not far distant. Unlike Heidegger and Derrida, thus, who almost completely refuse to provide sociological grounds for their accounts of crisis, Lyotard at least hints schematically at one. If he is right, sociological analysis focused on these institutions or "poles of attraction" can no longer grasp the social condition very well.[41] Instead we must look at the flow of communication through a social grid in the form of endless language games.

For Lyotard, not only the claim that society is a functional, systemic unity is a spurious modern view, so is its main opposite, the view that society is a conflictual field of struggles held together by power. Both of these accounts, on his view, represent unacceptable "metanarratives":

> I will use the term modern to designate any science that legitimates itself with reference to a metadiscourse of this kind making an explicit appeal to some grand narrative, such as the dialectics of Spirit, the hermeneutics of meaning, the emancipation of the rational or working subject, or the creation of wealth. . . . Simplifying to the extreme, I define postmodern as incredulity toward metanarratives.[42]

Historically, grand narratives pursued (and to some extent achieved) legitimation of the social order, as the metanarrative either of a reflective subject (spirit, knowledge actualizing itself) or of a practical subject (humanity liberating itself).[43] But in postmodern culture, such grand narratives have lost their credibility. Science seeks its own internal and external legitimation, sometimes in terms of old narratives of knowledge and emancipation. Other times it offers up simply its "performativity" – achieving the best input/output equation for its sponsors.[44] But increasingly, science appears simply as playing its own language game, and therefore incapable of legitimating itself or other language games.[45] It is first and foremost science which has challenged the hegemony of narrative, Lyotard suggests, because the pragmatics, the criteria of acceptance, are different for scientific and narrative knowledge.[46] Yet, for a time it appeared that one might appeal to science itself to save a great legitimating narrative of modernity. But this is not so: since "science plays its own game it is incapable of legitimating the other language games"; in fact, "it is incapable of legitimating itself."[47] So, though it is powerful, science is ultimately just one more game in a world in which "all we can do is gaze in wonderment at the diversity of discursive species, just as we do at the diversity of plant or animal species. Lamenting the 'loss of meaning' in postmodernity boils down to mourning the fact that knowledge is no longer principally narrative."[48] The postmodernist is called upon to "wage a war on totality" because totality breeds terror.[49] This much is reminiscent of Foucault. But where Foucault offered a historical account of this as a dimension of modernity, Lyotard's account is severed from any specific (let alone consistent) historical contextualization. Lyotard, moreover, tends to reduce the social almost entirely to the linguistic – "the observable social bond is composed of language 'moves'," but then fails to introduce any account of how participants in different discourses can ever be expected to reach agreements or even mutual understandings.[50] Because these are competitive moves in language games, they cannot be grasped by a purely cybernetic theory, but must be seen in terms of their agonistic aspect. Society, then, has become "atomized" into flexible networks of language games; Lyotard claims that the prominence of bureaucratic and other institutional constraints or control mechanisms does not seriously challenge this view; these limits are merely the stakes and provisional results of language strategies.[51]

III

The greatest gain offered by postmodernism is not the analysis of any epochal historical change, but a refocusing of our understanding of modernity. There are some qualitative novelties in recent history, but so far these have not been sufficient to overturn basic organizational features of the epoch. Capital accumulation and centralization of power, thus, both continue on a world scale. Efforts to gain effective agency through collective action (including the reformulation of claims to identity and loyalty) must still confront the constraints imposed by the greater power of corporate and state organizations, for example. In the early nineteenth century the attempt of workers to reach beyond community to class organizations at the level of the nation-state and its domestic market was in part an attempt to catch up to the level at which economic and political power were already coordinated against them.[52] By the late twentieth century capital was becoming increasingly globalized, and while the state remained both powerful and the crucial arena in which social movements could mobilize to pursue their collective agency, the internationalization of capital and new political forms like the European Community were putting a great deal of power once again out of the grasp of popular agency mediated through social movements. At the same time, Lyotard notwithstanding, large-scale collective identities like nation – with their metanarratives of both primordiality and development – continue to provide emotional weight to social movements and to offer individuals senses of location within the world-system even when they appeared out of synch with states and other organizations of power. Global flows of communication continue to produce both cross-cultural influences and challenges to cross-cultural understanding.

To reverse the trends towards capital accumulation, globalization of culture and social relations, and centralization of power would indeed be to bring on a postmodern condition. But we need to be careful not to mistake more superficial, if still important, changes for these basic ones. Consider for example the claim that information technology has fundamentally altered or even brought an end to the modern era. One argument for this claim is the evident dispersal of production relations and other important activities which coordination through telecommunications and computers makes possible. But note the importance of coordination; dispersal of activities serves centralization of power in many cases. When capital flows across borders this demonstrates rather than reverses centralization of power; it hardly puts an end to the basic drive of capital accumulation. Information technology facilitates further changes of other sorts as well, many of them momentous. But we need to recognize that power was based substantially on knowledge long before microelectronics, and the capacity to control others through organizations run through regularized information flows hardly waited for computers or constitutes a break with modernity.[53]

All this is not to say that nothing has changed, but that changes have been overstated and poorly conceptualized. The expansion of an organizational and technological infrastructure throughout the modern era has, for example, both enhanced state power and transformed it. Revolutionary potential, for example, is diminished in the West, largely because of the spatial deconcentration of power. Whether one wants to call the recent transformations of communist societies revolutions or not, it is important to see the extent to which they depended on the concentration of the institutions of power in capital cities and the underdevelopment of the infrastructures which have dispersed its application in "more modern" societies. But the displacement of power from readily visible individuals into market systems and bureaucratic organizations does not mean that there cease to be social relations of domination, that they no longer involve active subjects, or that power is not centralized.

Habermas's conceptualization of a split between system and lifeworld suggests something of why these problems are hard to recognize and disempowering of collective agency.[54] Social organization is undertaken simultaneously through directly interpersonal relationships, impersonal or systemic steering media, and large-scale (generally corporate) social organizations which appear from the point of view of everyday social life as autonomous and distant.[55] Both impersonal, notably market systems and corporate organizations have grown in importance throughout the modern era. While they organize more of social life – exerting more causal influence over the lives of individuals – they remain inaccessible to most forms of everyday (lifeworld) social knowledge. Large-scale markets can only be understood on the basis of statistical reasoning foreign to the conduct of everyday interpersonal relationships.

The omnipresence of "system" – that is of large-scale market and bureaucratic-corporate influences on our immediate lives – shapes some of the cultural responses problematically identified as postmodern. In relation to problems of collective agency specifically, it encourages two equally disempowering visions. One is of a world out of control, one which doesn't make sense. The other is of a world all too controlled, but only by distant, hidden actors. Modern consciousness vacillates, I think, between the first, a schizoid chaos of radical and widespread incommensurability; and the second, a paranoid world view in which understandability is won only by belief in omnipresent conspiracy.[56] Both have roots in the basic split between the lifeworld experiences which give life its basic meaning and the systemic steering and bureaucratic-corporate power which upset the order of the lifeworld but are poorly grasped – indeed necessarily obscured – by the conceptual framework of the lifeworld. It is in this context, for example, that we can see the source of postmodernist critiques of "intentionalist illusions" – putatively spurious belief in the capacity of human subjects to organize significant aspects of their own lives in response to conscious decision. Given the anti-universalism of postmodernism, however, it is ironic that instead of locating the source of commonly exaggerated faith in intention, and its problems, many postmodernists universalize a critique of intention as fundamentally illusory.

The vision that reality does not make sense, indeed intrinsically cannot make sense, or else only makes sense when remythologized on the basis of illusion and/or power struggles, is a widespread postmodernist theme. Those who pose claims to demonstrate an order to life and culture must either be paranoid or repressive, or both. Our only legitimate options are to simply accept disorder and uninterpretability or to make highly contingent, local, and ultimately only weakly defensible efforts to bring order to a small part of the world.

This vision of the chaotic, fragmented world is often traced to the break-up of a (implicitly once unified) modern economic and/or political structure. Yet even here, we should be cautious about seeing this as totally new rather than newly prominent. David Harvey thus has provocatively analyzed the culture of postmodernism as a response to a systemic crisis (but not supercession) of capitalism.[57] Fordist production methods have brought on a crisis of overaccumulation; this has called forth a search for new regimes of accumulation (as well as new, post-Fordist production relations). This search fosters new aesthetic movements. Harvey's argument is schematic and somewhat reductionist on the relationship of aesthetics to economics, but powerful in its account of a variety of recent phenomena not as evidence of the end of the modern era but as aspects of a shift – not the first – in the internal organization of capitalism.[58]

The broad themes of postmodernism, then, are not new and do not mark any sharp break with modernity or modernism. What of the more specific claims postmodernism, most notably poststructuralism, makes within the realm of social theory? The poststructuralist turn, we need to remind ourselves, was much broader than deconstructionism or any other single approach, and includes a number of figures – including Pierre Bourdieu – who are not amenable to the label postmodernist. This poststructuralism was not really announced at its birth; it appears only retrospectively and most clearly as refracted through the appropriation of French thought in the English-speaking world. Structuralism had in a sense denied epistemology on the grounds that it could only be pursued in terms of a philosophy of the subject. The poststructuralists (who were all structuralists at some point) sought ways to do a sort of epistemology, an inquiry into knowledge, without basing themselves on such a theory of subjectivity.

The contributions of the poststructuralist tributary into the postmodernist current were first and foremost (1) the absorption of structuralism's critique of subject-centered thought, and (2) the argument that monological statements of truth – originary speech, in Derrida's term – were in some combination misleading, false, and/or repressive. In varying ways, then, the poststructuralists showed the tensions within seeming truths, the difficulties involved even in seemingly ordinary understandings, the constant effort of construction involved in accepted truths, as well as the constant tendency of those truths to break down and reveal their internal inconsistencies and aporias.[59] Some, like Bourdieu, made this crucially a social argument; the tensions involved in understanding derived not simply from textuality, but from interpersonal struggles and fields of power. For many others, materiality, physical embodiment, and social relations were lost in treating all aspects of culture and human action as texts. In all versions, the poststructuralist move was for the most part an essentially theoretical shift, not a claim that anything in the external world had changed to necessitate a new theory.

The theoretical roots to the special stress on difference in Derrida's work, thus, have nothing to do with claims about epochal transformations. Indeed, as Norris has suggested, Derrida's exploration can be seen in this regard as an extension of Kant's despite their different substantive arguments and conclusions.

> Foucault's extreme epistemological scepticism leads him to equate knowledge with power, and hence to regard all forms of "enlightened" progress (in psychiatry, sexual attitudes or penal reform) as signs of an increasing sophistication in the applied technology of social control. Derrida, by contrast, insists that there is no opting out of the post-Kantian enlightenment tradition, and certainly no question of our now having emerged into a post-modern era where its concepts and categories lack all critical force. On the contrary: it is only by working persistently *within* that tradition, but *against* some of its ruling ideas, that thought can muster the resistance required for an effective critique of existing institutions.[60]

Derrida's work is particularly difficult to relate to sociology because he is among the most text-centered and least explicitly social of the poststructuralists.[61] Derrida's stress is on the ways in which the basic phenomena of distinction and contraposition produce identity, as opposed to essentialist attempts to locate identity in the inherent attributes of any entity – either a subject or an object. Derrida positions his argument for the importance of difference (or *différance*) mainly within a dialogue with a Western philosophical tradition that approaches truth monologically, even often as substance.[62] These assertions Derrida deconstructively shows to conceal the play of hidden dialogicality. In doing so he offers a defense of the very complexity of thought itself such that truth or knowledge becomes something much more difficult than we have thought, though not therefore something to be dismissed.[63] *Différance*, for Derrida, is really a property of discourse, not subjects, and indeed (following on the structuralist tradition) subjects appear in his work mainly as creatures of discourse rather than speakers able to claim some primacy over it. It is important, though, that Derrida's approach draws attention to difference among subjects not just as multiplications of the same sort of identity, differently situated, but as radically singular.[64]

Difference is also crucial to Foucault. In the first place, he offers an account of the way modern subjects are constituted and disciplined as individuals who experience a simultaneous production of desire and its repressive normalization.[65] This suggests a certain special priority to human difference. Foucault is ambiguous, for on the one hand he can be read as asserting only that certain kinds of difference among people were subjected to normalizing discipline in the historically specific production of modernity. On the other hand, however, particularly in his later work on sexuality, Foucault appears to ascribe to all humans a kind of natural propensity for resistance to the normalizing tendencies of social life (which also appear as increasingly general rather than historically specific, present in ancient Greece and in China as well in modern France).[66] Throughout, though it is never clearly articulated in his major works (as distinct from interviews), Foucault implies a normative defense of difference against normalization. Foucault is ambiguous as to the grounding of this evaluation and thus as to the way large-scale collective processes can inform politics and personal struggles. At least in his early work, however, he is clear about the centrality of the radical epistemological ruptures that separate the understandings of different ages.[67] Though he links these epistemic breaks somewhat to changes in social life, this is not his major theme and his argument does not rest on shifts in any underlying causal factors such as economy, military power or demography but rather on the transmutation of systems of knowledge such that they become incommensurable. In offering one of the most profound articulations of what it means for systems of knowledge to be radically different, and particularly of how such difference can occur historically within a "civilization," rather than only cross-culturally, Foucault augments an important discussion of incommensurability with roots in philosophy of science and hermeneutics.

This emphasis on difference is the most valuable and defensible of postmodernist arguments, though it is not defensible on postmodernist terms. Both Derrida and Foucault (and many postmodernist followers) mobilize their arguments about difference as bases for rejection of all grand narratives without any search for a substitute ground for normative discourse. In doing so, they introduce a particularism so extreme that it ultimately, ironically, results in a decontextualization, an incapacity to place the particular in relation to other phenomena.[68] A particularism so extreme – which is not, I think, what most postmodernists want but what a hastily espoused theory offers – cannot justify even the very value on difference with which it starts.

Faced with this, one might become pessimistic, become nostalgic for the old narratives, or – if one is a good postmodernist – simply accept that legitimation can only spring from people's own linguistic practice and communicative interaction.[69] For Lyotard the most important result of such acceptance is rejection of the "transcendental illusion" – the fantasy of putting all the heterogeneous language games of the world together in a single whole.[70] Totalization of this sort breeds terror (especially, we might add, the historically specific sorts of terrors of the nineteenth and twentieth centuries, like genocide). Such material terrors are the counterparts of intellectual and aesthetic violence done by attempts to impose a single vision of reality or set of standards on the diverse experimenters of art, thought, and life. Lyotard thus joins Derrida and Foucault in wishing to show the agonistic element in all culture, but is left with a more or less arbitrary assertion. But even Foucault and Derrida, let alone Lyotard, are left with a program of pure critique, showing the dragons which lie the way of modernism but offering no real analytic purchase on the problem of analyzing the transformation of power and social structure as it bears on practical action in the modern world.

IV

Treating variations and disputes in artistic style, social consciousness, and theory within the frame of epochal historical transformation produces a misunderstanding, even where the changes are of some significance. Postmodernism is a continuation of modernism in at least aspects of its style (e.g. the claim to be the latest avant-garde, the self-legitimation of mere novelty). More basically, the crucial dimensions of variation are mostly long standing, and postmodernism carries on basic themes of all modernity – which indeed produced an internal anti-modernity from the beginning, as well as splits of rationalists from romantics, realists from figuralists, etc.

Perhaps the most distinctive feature of postmodernist *theory* is the denial of any basis for critical judgment and moral responsibility that is not the arbitrary reflection of a tradition. This poses basic problems for the attempt (otherwise furthered by much postmodern theory) to take cultural difference seriously, since it precludes genuine learning from the Other. It opens postmodernist theorists (and political activists) who attempt to persuade others to the charge that either they are committing a performative contradiction or they are simply exercising a will to power no more legitimate than any other.

In relation to both critical judgment and historical transformation, postmodernist theory at the very least crucially overstates its case. As suggested in the previous chapter, accounts are needed of epistemic gain which does not imply a sharp opposition of truth and falsehood, and of historical change that does not mean epochal rupture.

Part of the problem comes from a tendency to focus on the evils of potentially authoritarian claims to adjudicate universal truths rather than on more moderate approaches to epistemic gain that do not claim perfection. As Habermas has remarked in a footnote to his critique of Derrida's and Rorty's contentions that the genre distinction between philosophy and literature cannot be maintained:

> They are still battling against the "strong" concepts of theory, truth, and system that have actually belonged to the past for over a century and a half. . . . If reason were bound, under penalty of demise, to hold onto these goals of metaphysics classically pursued from Parmenides to Hegel, if reason as such (even after Hegel) stood before the alternative of either maintaining the strong concepts of theory, truth, and system that were common in the great tradition or of throwing in the sponge, then an *adequate* critique of reason would really have to grasp the roots at such a depth that it could scarcely avoid the paradoxes of self-referentiality.[71]

Where there is recognition of something like epistemic gain in many postmodernist and cognate traditions (including, e.g., Rorty's adaptation of pragmatism) it is commonly held to be radically internal to intellectual traditions. In Nicholson's words:

> the postmodernist need not abandon the distinction between legitimate and illegitimate claims to power as she or he need not abandon the more encompassing idea of criteria of truth. The difference between the postmodernist and the modernist on these issues is rather that the former and not the latter denies the possibility of such criteria external to any specific historical tradition.[72]

Presumably these claims can be seen as general in their proposed scope of application, though not in their openness to communication across traditions. Indeed, Nicholson suggests relativism is not so much an intellectual position as a "life-possibility," reflecting the prior breakdown of communication.

By implication, since communicative conflicts are to be solved by finding a common belief or value, the more "historical tradition" people share the better, and the less the worse. If this is so, then any grounding of theory only in cultural traditions (*pace* Rorty) confronts serious problems. Such an account recognizes difference, but it makes evaluating it positively an arbitrary choice outside the range of theoretical justification. With attention thus deflected from the search for practical ways in which to achieve communication, the path is open for the view that all ways of knowing are exercises of power. Rorty espouses liberal values, asserts that adherents of incommensurable ways of knowing should live together in mutual tolerance, but (1) this remains an arbitrary proposal, however attractive, one his theory cannot ground, and (2) this reduces the meaning of "together" in the phrase "living together" to mere spatial proximity or sharing a state but not the joint activity of citizens.

Of course, this is not to say that a theory offering genuine epistemic gain could not be elaborated, drawing on insights from so-called postmodernist thinkers, but generally speaking this has not occurred; indeed Foucault spoke prominently against the impulse to theorize.[73] The effort to develop a postmodernist social theory (and in fact much of the postmodernist empirical literature) is prone to performative contradictions: asserting claims to rhetorical persuasiveness as more true or more adequate while denying the meaningfulness, legitimacy, utility, or interpersonal adjudicability of the notions of truth or adequacy.

It was Foucault, above all, who taught both the mutuality of knowledge and power and the extent to which all ways of knowing are exercises of power. "Truth is a thing of this world; it is produced only by virtue of multiple forms of constraint."[74] This power is not reducible to interpersonal domination, but is constitutive of social life and culture generally.

> If power were never anything but repressive, if it never did anything but to say no, do you really think one would be brought to obey it? What makes power hold good, what makes it accepted, is simply the fact that it doesn't only weigh on us as a force that says no, but that it traverses and produces things, it induces pleasure, forms knowledge, produces discourse.[75]

Power is, in this sense, "decentered," not the property of any subject. Power is normalized, rendered into discipline, practiced routinely by subjects upon themselves insofar as they reenact the premises of their culture. This seems to grasp a dimension of the modern experience of power, but at the same time it obscures the specifically modern increase in occasions and resources for people to distinguish between what power is and ought to be. As Habermas points out, Foucault shares with Horkheimer and Adorno failure "to do justice to the rational content of cultural modernity that was captured in bourgeois ideals."[76] One of the central problematics of power disappears in this formulation: there are no criteria for distinguishing legitimate from illegitimate power. Foucault's theory, indeed, may actually make such criteria internally impossible.

A fundamental challenge for most postmodernist theories is to offer bases for making critical judgments. I have argued above that such bases need ideally to be grounded in strong recognition of their cultural and historical specificity, and preferably to stand in an immanent relationship to the context of their development. Nonetheless, to be meaningful – both politically and theoretically – such bases need to allow for critical judgments to be arguable, defensible, in discourse across lines of cultural, ideological, or other differences. A position which cannot give reasons for why it should be persuasive to those who are not already a part of its "tradition" is a severely problematic political as well as scientific tool. Agreement must then be arbitrary, or imposed; if people are moved, there is no internal account of why. At the same time as discourse among people different from each other is vital to democracy and public life, so it is crucial that people within any one tradition (and for that matter individuals within their own lives) be able to give accounts simultaneously of how they have come to be who they are and how they want to become better in the future. That is, a critical historical consciousness implies an ability to express and defend not only one's interests but the project of developing better interests, wanting to have better desires.[77] Foucault does offer social criticism, pervasively through his tone and choices of descriptive content, but also sometimes explicitly. It is not clear, however, that he – any more than Derrida or Lyotard – could ground such criticism without performative contradiction. The potential for doing so within his theory is weakened especially when it loses its historical specificity.

In his early and middle works (up through *Discipline and Punish*; originally published in 1975), Foucault emphasizes deep ruptures between historical epochs and focuses his attention on the birth of modern power in the reformation of institutions of carceral control in the seventeenth and eighteenth centuries. But in his later work on sexuality and some interviews and essays, he implies that the mutuality of power and knowledge is universal, not distinctive to modernity, and that similar analyses can be developed for all cultures and historical periods. Foucault does enunciate something of the distinctiveness of the power/knowledge implication in modernity, even as late as the 1970s:

> It's not a matter of emancipating truth from every system of power (which would be a chimera, for truth is already power), but of detaching the power

of truth from the forms of hegemony, social, economic, and cultural, within which it operates at the present time.[78]

Foucault holds out the option of specific criticisms of the modern forms of hegemony, but he does not suggest any specific direction in which criticism should move. Like most of the "postmodernists" who claim him (though he did not explicitly identify with that label), he can advocate only resistance not emancipation. At extremes, he seems to imply that anything would be better than what obtains now. But this sort of account is in an odd tension with the historical approach he developed earlier. There he argued for recognizing the centrality of epochal transformations which made sense of many small changes (but made historically specific sense, within the context of a specific epochal transformation, not the sense which comes from imposing a single transhistorical narrative or set of categories on historically specific events):

> In order to analyse such events [e.g. the introduction of a new form of positivity or other epochal shifts in consciousness], it is not enough simply to indicate changes, and to relate them immediately to the theological, aesthetic model of creation . . . or to the psychological model of the act of consciousness . . . or to the biological model of evolution. We must define precisely what these changes consist of: that is, substitute for an undifferentiated reference to change – which is both a general container for all events and the abstract principle of their succession – the analysis of *transformations*.[79]

It is curious that the advice informing the history and genealogy (though less so, perhaps, Foucault's earlier formulation, the archaeology) of forms of power/knowledge should not provide a different outlook, one with a normative direction, for the analysis of contemporary questions. Indeed, it is arguable that Foucault's whole enterprise was undertaken "to make politics possible."[80] It may be that its politics is obscure because what had seemed before to block politics were great and rigid teleologies of history – Hegel's or Stalin's. But such a normative direction need not involve a "metanarrative" of history, a single moral to all stories. It could consist, rather, of suggestions of the direction which we should move from where we are, recognizing that new considerations will inform decisions about the appropriate directions to be followed thereafter. It seems to me that the nature of practical involvement in the world, especially political involvement, calls necessarily for confronting such questions of directionality. Our knowledge is always situated, but also framed in relation to action – starting even with projects of understanding – that orient us beyond our initial situations. Moreover, seeking understanding across lines of important cultural differences necessarily involves confronting contrasting normative directions because these produce incommensurable practices of the sort (discussed in chapter 3 above) that cannot coexist without posing competing claims for adherence. Foucault's approach to incommensurability did not confront such problems of action. Influenced by Bachelard and Canguilheim, Foucault sought to eliminate "humanistic" emphases on the subject in favor of studying abstract structures of knowledge. The famous "epistemological break" that, according to Bachelard, enabled the physical sciences to achieve true objectivity or scientificity was rooted in a similar overcoming of subject-centered thought. Foucault's emphasis remained epistemological, though his understanding of the breaks in knowledge-producing structures of thought no longer was linked to the notion of a historical progress towards scientificity as was Bachelard's (or Althusser's).[81]

At this point, where it cannot achieve historical specificity or confront the incommensurable practices of different cultures, Foucault's analytics of power loses its potential critical edge. Ironically enough, fashionable anthropologists have followed the lead of the later Foucault and begun to unravel ubiquitous subjectless power in all settings, while combining this with a self-declared critical orientation and affirmation of cultural difference.[82] It seems to me that the postmodernist claim to historical grounding – indeed, even to historicity – is in important aspects spurious. The history which is introduced is often remarkably unsystematic.[83] Like postmodernist architecture, its historical side consists of incomplete and decontextualized borrowings. Even in the hands of an extraordinary historical scholar like Foucault, this sort of (allegedly postmodernist) historical writing is often a bit like an Orientalism of the past – an appropriation of history for purposes of debating the contemporary condition directly, not an inquiry into the fullest possible understanding of another way of life which might indirectly or in later comparison shed light on our own. It is partly for this reason that Foucault, the great theorist of historical ruptures, in his later work began to find the same mechanisms of power/knowledge at work in ancient Greece, China, and modern France, and everywhere else he looked. Most importantly of all, the postmodernist position is not historically or culturally *specific*, either in grounding or in analytic purchase.

Foucault, of course, did emphasize the poststructuralist, postmodernist theme of difference: "What is found at the historical beginning of things is not the inviolable identity of their origin; it is the dissension of other things. It is disparity."[84] This is the meaning of the "death of the author," an explicit echo of Nietzsche's death of god sounded by both Foucault and Derrida, but without a faith comparable to Nietzsche's in salvation through will. This theme, however, is especially associated with Derrida, for whom it has remained enduringly central. Derrida's *différance* is a "primordial nonself-presence."[85] It is transcendental, even prior to presence and the transcendental reduction; it is "not something which occurs to a transcendental subject. It is what produces it."[86] The structuralist and poststructuralist displacement of the subject from modernity's and philosophy's center is thus basic to Derrida; it is not the self that we presuppose in all thought and action, but *différance*. In Dew's words, "in the majority of his work, Derrida bases his analyses on the concept of absolute difference: of an essential *logical priority* of non-identity over identity."[87] It is this which orients the deconstructionist project to the discovery of internal incoherencies within texts, rather than reading them more conventionally by "constructing" from them a meaningful whole.[88]

Not only the unity of a text, but subjectivity itself, the originating unity of consciousness, is for Derrida merely a thought, a fiction.[89] This is the basis for viewing the world as a textual or discursive structure to be deconstructed, its incoherencies exposed. Derrida's opposition is to the notion of speech as transparent, self-sufficient presentation of truth. Knowledge starts with writing, with the attempt to fix the transitory; its textuality always embodies tensions and hence makes deconstruction possible (or perhaps even inevitable). Thus Derrida challenges the "logocentrism" of Western thought. But left to itself this offers only a critical moment. It is a very problematic basis for social or political analysis. Even Derrida is unwilling to regard social institutions as merely textual or discursive structures (though some of his followers have not balked at this). Derrida insists on retaining the option of social and political criticism, but falls back on Heideggerian grounds for it. He is, in other words, forced to make ontological statements about the nature of life and what the world is "really" like. His own theory cannot ground a critical account of political antagonisms insofar as these cannot be reduced to logical antagonisms. Deconstruction can offer a certain sort of constant vigilance and attempt to escape mere positivity, but as theory or method it cannot in itself offer a political or ethical program, or a properly explanatory analysis.

Similarly, though Derrida attempts to avoid the radical relativism some of his followers embrace, he does not succeed in explaining theoretically why he should do so. His very attempt to absolutize *différance* produces incoherencies in his theory. Moreover, the theory offers no openings to sociality or to material factors in history and social relations. It severs cultural from social and political-economic analysis. The deconstruction of a text plays infinitely on its internal capacities for dissemination; it neither needs nor addresses other sources of meaning. Unlike some other approaches influenced by phenomenology (or hermeneutics) and despite (or perhaps because of) its idealization of *différance*, deconstruction offers no approach to historical or even cultural specificity. All texts have a life free from specific contexts; they cannot be grounded within them. There is, thus, no satisfactory basis for comparison. This, by the way, is part of the attraction of Derrida for those who regard all canons as *mere* exercises of power, rather combinations of power with more satisfactorily grounded judgments.

V

Postmodernist reasoning makes it hard to justify any collective response, any attempt at agency, in the face of centralization of power and global capital accumulation accomplished through exploitation. Most postmodernist discourse is normatively incapacitating, even where it is profoundly normative in tone or motivation. Because processes of power and exploitation are increasingly systemic and removed from the everyday discursive grasp of the lifeworld, however, it is all the more important that a critical *theory* be developed through which to understand them. It is not enough to rely on play, intuition, and ordinary experience.

Postmodernist thought has generally been presented in a radical, challenging mode and rhetoric, as though it were a critical theory with clear implications for collective struggle. Indeed, the postmodernist movement has without question informed and in some cases invigorated popular struggles. But it is not equally clear that postmodernist thought can stand very clearly the tests which must be demanded of a critical theory.

Ideally, a critical theory ought to provide for an account of the historical and cultural conditions of its own production, to offer an address to competing theories which explains (not just identifies) their weaknesses and appropriates their achievements, to engage in a continuing critical reflection on the categories used in its own construction, and to develop a critical account of existing social conditions with positive implications for social action. Postmodernism contributes to some of these desiderata, but also falls short of them in varying degree. Most notably, the vagueness with which many postmodernists conceptualize what it might mean to transcend the modern epoch trivializes a basic concern. How, we want to know, can existing social and cultural conditions be critically engaged and transformed? Postmodernism doesn't tell us.

The postmodernist attention to difference raises the issue of cultural particularity, but difference is often made so absolutely prior to commonality that no basis for mutual engagement or even respect is provided. By overstatement, the theory thus undercuts one of its own greatest contributions.

Likewise, the postmodernist "decentering" of the subject poses a challenge for a theory desiring to address agency and moral responsibility. Though postmodernist accounts here offer a needed counterpoint to typical individualism, they too often become nearly as much its mirror image as Durkheim. If a critical theory is to hold meaningful implications for action, it must grant actors and action a more significant place. The next chapter explores a nonpostmodernist poststructuralist theory – Pierre Bourdieu's – in search of a stronger approach to practical action, but without giving up the concern for historical specificity and cultural difference.

Notes

1 This is a view associated with Emmanuel Levinas; see especially *Totality and Infinity*. Derrida's notion of *différance* does not turn on this same notion of radical alterity so much as on the play of difference, deferral, and displacement in language. But though Derrida has challenged Levinas fruitfully on many points, as well as learned much from him, he seems to accept this totalizing sense of alterity and even to argue that Levinas should have located it phenomenologically: "To make the other an alter ego, Levinas says frequently, is to neutralize its absolute alterity. [But] . . . One could neither speak, nor have any sense of the totally other, if there was not a *phenomenon* of the totally other, or evidence of the totally other as such" (*Writing and Difference*, p. 123). It is not clear, among other things, why the existence of the phenomenon should be essential to the "sense" or idea in this case more than that of unicorns.

2 In the immediately following discussion I shall accept the premise that there is some scholarly position of sufficient coherence to warrant the single label "postmodernism." In fact, it is not at all clear that this is so. In France, Foucault, Derrida, Lacan, and other thinkers commonly grouped together in American discourse appear largely as rivals; their differences are much more strongly accented. "Postmodernism" is associated less with them than with its self-declared apostles like Lyotard and Baudrillard.

3 This is at least as reasonable as gloom, of course. There was no rational reason why Weber's Calvinists, believing in predestination, faced with the prospect of likely damnation and a distant God unwilling to reveal the elect, chose to seek the simulacra of salvation through hard work and worldly asceticism; an attitude of "eat, drink and be merry" would have followed just as logically from their predicament.

4   This was already Derrida's stance in *Writing and Difference*, but this engagement with trends widely labeled postmodernist is clearer in "Of an Apocalyptic Tone," pp. 3–37. Norris's discussion in the last chapter of his *Derrida* is helpful on this.

5   See Calhoun, "Infrastructure of Modernity." In this respect, my argument resembles those of Jameson (*Postmodernism*) and Harvey (*Condition of Postmodernity*) to the effect that so-called postmodern is really a new phase of the modern, a reflection of late capitalism. Their accounts, however, seem to me to border on the reductionist, making the stages and logic of capital too directly determining of cultural forms. Moreover, they neglect many of the similarities of the current era to earlier periods which I want to point up.

6   See Dosse, *L'histoire du structuralisme*, for a helpful review.

7   That is, at least of most sociologists writing in English. Jean Baudrillard, one of the central French postmodernists is, of course, a sociologist (though as he has become more postmodernist and postmarxist, his work has become less oriented to social relations as such). A little belatedly, a self-declared postmodernist sociology is being forged in Britain, North America, and Australia, absorbing previous arguments – e.g. about new social movements, postindustrial society, and claims to the autonomy of cultural change (see, e.g., Lash, *Postmodernist Sociology*; Rosenau, *Post-Modernism*).

8   Rorty, *Philosophy and the Mirror of Nature, Consequences of Pragmatism*, and *Contingency, Irony, Solidarity*. Especially in his more recent works, Rorty's pragmatism is extended beyond a critique of foundationalist philosophy to a series of claims about the virtues of bourgeois, liberal democracy, which are found to adhere not so much in universalistic rationality as in liberal-pluralist openness. Valuable critical discussions of Rorty's extension of his philosophical position to social practice (each of them questioning whether it can be so free of "universalism" as Rorty implies) are offered by McCarthy (*Ideals and Illusions*, ch 1) and Bernstein (*The New Constellation*, chs 1 and 9).

9   See discussion in Harvey, *Condition of Postmodernity*; Kellner, "The Postmodern Turn"; and Rosenau, *Post-Modernism*.

10 Other texts that have more recently become a part of English-language scholarship, and that bring to the fore some of the themes associated with postmodernist arguments, also date from or have their roots in the early twentieth century version of modernism. Vygotsky's psychology and Bakhtin's literary theory, for example, both challenge the supposedly unitary modernist notion of self – as indeed did Freud. Bakhtin's account of dialogicality and polyphonic discourse – rooted significantly in analysis of Dostoevsky's novels – shares much with the sensibility of the late twentieth-century challenge to simpler notions of narrative and truth.

11 On modernity's time-consciousness, see Kosseleck, *Futures Past*.

12 See, e.g., Habermas, *Philosophical Discourse of Modernity*. Conversely, much postmodernist and antipostmodernist discourse also overstates the conservatism of hermeneutic thinkers like Gadamer, and accepts too much at face value the claims of Derrida, Rorty, and others not to be children of

the Enlightenment. In fact, Gadamer (*Truth and Method*) is not hostile to reason or a discourse about truth; as Bernstein (*Beyond Objectivism*) has suggested, his hermeneutic arguments operate against claims to ahistorical, methodological certainty (and thus coincide with postKuhnian philosophy of science and a theme raised in a very different way by some post-structuralist thinkers like Derrida). Conversely, despite their attacks on "logocentrism," foundationalism, and universalism, both Derrida and Rorty pose arguments that depend on capacities for generalization and appeal to reason that they share with much Enlightenment discourse and for which they are largely unable to provide alternative theoretical grounds.

13   Frisby's account of Simmel, Kracauer, and Benjamin brings out this aspect of Simmel rather well (*Fragments of Modernity*).

14   Bell, *The Coming of Post-Industrial Society*. I have criticized such a view in Calhoun, "Infrastructure of Modernity." It is particularly disturbing coming from Habermas, where it marks a willingness to accept systems-theoretical accounts of economic activity without attempting to dereify them to see the role of human action behind production even where self-regulating systems coordinate it, and to see the production of knowledge as itself a form of creativity activity – labor, if you will, though perhaps in a way posing problems for many orthodox marxist accounts of the labor theory of value.

15   Baudrillard, *The Mirror of Production*, *Oublier Foucault*, *For a Critique*.

16   Baudrillard's early work (cited above), like that of Debord, is written as part of a critical social analysis that attempts to theorize the standpoint and conditions of its critique. Baudrillard's later work (e.g. *America*) increasingly abandons this attempt at critical theory, though he never entirely joins that part of the postmodern current that adopts a fully celebratory style. Many of the most striking aspects of Baudrillard's work were anticipated by Debord, whose work is helpfully discussed and situated both in relation to the "Situationalist International" and postmodernism by Plant, *The Most Radical Gesture*.

17   In addition, it is not clear that attention to consumption and efforts to influence it through advertising have undergone qualitative change more than a quantitative expansion in the postwar years. It may be that a better theoretical revision would focus more of our attention on the prominence of consumption issues from the beginning of the capitalist (or modern) era.

18   See not only Baudrillard, but also, following his lead, Kroker and Cook, *The Postmodern Scene*, p. 185. For a sophisticated reading of *Capital* treating labor as a historically specific category and properly stressing the role of the dialectic of abstract and concrete labor and time, see Postone, *Time, Labor*.

19   Jameson, *Marxism and Form*, p. 105. Jameson remains given to this kind of image for epochal transition in his later work, as when he considers whether we will have to grow new sense organs to appreciate Portman's hotel architecture (which, by the way, strikes me more as simply extravagant and bad than postmodern).

20   On the latter point, see Scitovsky, *The Joyless Economy*, and Hirschman's discussion of it in *Shifting Involvements*.

21 Lyotard, "Answering the Question," p. 79.

22 Lyotard, *The Inhuman*, p. 24.

23 Lyotard, *Postmodern Condition*, p. 14. I have elsewhere tried to show the simple empirical falsity of this argument (Calhoun, "Infrastructure of Modernity"), evident especially when one looks momentarily outside of the North Atlantic axis. The continuing importance of nationalism and nation-state is discussed further in chapter 8. Here it is enough to see that Lyotard is claiming that the world has changed such that a sociological analysis focused on these institutions or "poles of attraction" can no longer adequately grasp the state of social life.

24 Giddens, *Modernity and Its Discontents*. This is a view close to that of Horkheimer and Adorno, and precisely the conclusion Habermas resists (though within the same frame of reference) in pointing to the "unfinished project of modernity"; see "Modernity and Postmodernity," "Questions and Counterquestions," and *Philosophical Discourse of Modernity*.

25 See Harvey, *The Condition of Postmodernity*, for a strong, but critical, summary of the arguments about political economic change as the source of historical rupture. Megill, *Prophets of Extremity* (pp. 125–41) is very good on Heidegger's ambiguity about whether his account of crisis is or is not rooted in specific features of the modern epoch.

26 Lyotard, *Postmodern Condition*, p. 79.

27 Ibid.

28 Thus Simmel raises a number of the themes characteristic of today's postmodernists, including especially that of the fragmentation of culture, yet he emphatically must be considered a theorist of modernity (Frisby, *Fragments of Modernity*, "Georg Simmel"). Of course, both Simmel and Weber share with many of the postmodernists the stamp of Nietzsche's influence.

29 Lyotard, *Postmodern Condition*.

30 See, e.g. Rosenau, *Post-Modernism*.

31 Those of us in the English-speaking world, especially in sociology, have been a bit behind the Parisian fashions in this regard. Just as we were assimilating structuralism, especially beyond the dominant influence of Lévi-Strauss in anthropology, and therefore including Althusser, Poulantzas, etc. – there was a new turn in dominant intellectual fashion. This was the move beyond structuralism by some of its leading, mostly younger, figures. Lacan and Derrida are perhaps the most paradigmatic thinkers; in different ways both Foucault and Bourdieu made the same sort of move in relation to structuralism.

32 The quotation is from Heidegger, "Plato's Doctrine of Truth," and is cited from Megill, *Prophets of Extremity*, p. 127.

33 Foucault, *Madness and Civilization*, *Discipline and Punish*, *Power/Knowledge*, *History of Sexuality*.

34 See especially Foucault, *Order of Things*. Foucault's earlier studies distinguish the modern era sharply from its predecessors. One version of this distinction stresses the transformation of a system of knowledge rooted in resemblances into one drawn from a new form of analysis of relations such

as cause and effect (*Order of Things*). Another – more influential – located the fundamental transformation in the constitution of both the subject and knowledge itself as products of a radically new form of power (*Discipline and Punish*, *Power/Knowledge*). But by his last series of works, *History of Sexuality*, vols 1–4, Foucault began to abandon the theme of historical specificity and see the workings of power/knowledge nearly everywhere.

35 Baudrillard, *Oublier Foucault*.

36 See especially, Baudrillard, *For a Critique*, *In the Shadow*.

37 Baudrillard, *Mirror of Production*, *Oublier Foucault*, *For a Critique*; Kellner's, *Jean Baudrillard* is helpful.

38 Baudrillard, *In the Shadow*, p. 105.

39 Barthes, *Empire of Signs*.

40 Lyotard, *Postmodern Condition*, xxiii–xxiv.

41 Chapter 7 will attempt to shed some light on whether he is right in this regard.

42 Lyotard, *Postmodern Condition*, xxiii–xxiv. In *The Inhuman*, as noted above, Lyotard changes his stance significantly and I think in the direction of greater clarity. Emphasizing the sense in which "the postmodern is always implied in the modern because of the fact that modernity, modern temporality, comprises in itself an impulsion to exceed itself into a state other than itself," he also suggests (echoing Foucault) that "what would be properly opposed to modernity here would be the classical age" (p. 25).

43 Ibid., p. 35. Compare Habermas, *Philosophical Discourse of Modernity*, esp. chapter 3. The transcendental practical subject could also be conceived within a production paradigm, as in traditional marxism.

44 Lyotard, *Postmodern Condition*, p. 40.

45 Ibid.

46 Ibid., pp. 25–6.

47 Ibid., p. 40.

48 Ibid., p. 26. It is striking that Lyotard's claim comes so precisely at the same time as a major positive reevaluation reversal of narrative in history and the social sciences; see Ricoeur, *Time and Narrative* and the review and discussion in Somers, "Narrativity" and Somers and Gibson, "Reclaiming." In much history-writing (e.g. Schama's very successful *Citizens*) narratives are still constructed without much manifest self-critical reflection or invitation to readers to see the narratives as problematic or constructed. At the same time some philosophers of history have opened significant new awareness of how historical narratives do their rhetorical work; see White, *Metahistories* and *Tropics of Discourse*. Despite the alleged end of grand narratives, traditional narratives like Schama's have attracted widespread popularity and seem to remain politically persuasive in many arenas (including in the still active metanarrative worlds of nationalism and ethnicity, from Serbia to versions of Afrocentrism). At the same time, while the "disrupted narratives" of postmodernist styles may not have penetrated Harlequin romances or replaced conventional history, they too have their artistic and mass cultural champions and their popular, especially video, audiences. At one

level, talk of "loss of meaning" echoes rather obviously a key theme of earlier modernists including, rather strikingly, Horkheimer and Adorno. In the terms of my argument below, however, it does perhaps reflect extensions in the severing of the world of practical knowledge and tradition in direct relationships from the coordination of large-scale systems of action through indirect relationships. Science is the principal antagonist of narrative and thus of the sort of language game which combines to form the social bond. But note here that the postmodern condition seems to describe a "loss of meaning" which has been lamented for at least a century in very similar terms, and that science as the antagonist of narrative must be seen to have played a role in nearly the whole history of *modern* culture. In other words, the "postmodern" critique grasps something of contemporary life because it grasps something of a modernity which continues, not because it calls attention to something new.

49 Lyotard, "Answering the Question," p. 82. Horkheimer and Adorno agreed about totality and terror, but thought (in their maturity at least) that waging war on them was futile. The most they thought they could do was to pass the spirit of critical thinking – not even precisely critical theory – on to the future.

50 Lyotard, *Postmodern Condition*, p. 11; see also discussion in the previous chapter.

51 Ibid., p. 17. Like many other postmodernist theorists, Lyotard here turns the social almost entirely into the linguistic – a radical reduction of even social relations in which communication plays a part, let alone of material factors in social life. Where for structuralists like Lévi-Strauss linguistic phenomena provided an instructive heuristic example of social phenomena, perhaps even a privileged and pre-eminent one, for many postmodernists – Derrida more extremely than Lyotard, for example – the linguistic becomes the only form of the social to which their theory gives them access.

52 Calhoun, "Class, Place and Industrial Revolution."

53 Compare Calhoun, "Infrastructure of Modernity" with Melucci, "Social Movements" (p. 249); Keane, *Civil Society and the State* (p. 8, n. 6).

54 Habermas, *Theory of Communicative Action*, vols 1, 2.

55 Neither Habermas nor Parsons (on whom he draws) makes clear why power should be considered an impersonal systemic steering medium comparable to money; I accordingly treat corporate bureaucracies as distinct from markets. I would also suggest that it is important to see system and lifeworld as different analytic aspects of social life, not as different realms since it is virtually impossible to give a meaningful account of a lifeworld in modern society that is not deeply influenced by systemic factors. What we can see are directly interpersonal social relations that are understandable on bases distinct from the impersonal conceptualizations required by markets and corporations.

56 The extreme of schizoid incommensurability is evoked, for example, by Deleuze and Guattari, *Anti-Oedipus*.

57 Harvey, *Condition of Postmodernity*.

58 Jameson (*Postmodernism*) reaches somewhat similar conclusions. Of course, to see capitalism as still a powerful causal factor – and thus a basis for making the world interpretable – need not be to suggest that capitalism explains every aspect of modern social and cultural transformations.

59 In this, the poststructuralist work resonates very closely with the substantially contemporary work of the ethnomethodologists in English-language sociology.

60 Norris, *Derrida*, p. 217 (as a frustrated Kantian, Lyotard attempts precisely to opt out of the enlightenment tradition).

61 See, e.g., Derrida, *Writing and Difference*; *Margins of Philosophy*, esp. 1–27. The unsociological character of most poststructuralism makes Bourdieu's work all the more important as we shall see in the next chapter. It shows that what is usually claimed as poststructuralist warrant for ignoring social matters in favor of a free-floating culture is based on a thin version of structuralist and poststructuralist theory.

62 See esp. Derrida, *Of Grammatology*, *Dissemination*.

63 Here again, the similarities between Derrida and Gadamer are worth noting, despite their very different overall approaches; they are due in part, it appears, to their common indebtedness to Heidegger.

64 Derrida does tend to absolutize the notion of difference, and thus to remove the human actor and the concrete social relationship from the discourse. Nonetheless, unlike many other approaches to "alterity" and "other-centered" or "dialogical" understanding, such as that of Levinas, Derrida rejects the idea that this radical otherness precludes treatment of the other as *alter ego*. While it may not be possible in strong senses to have real knowledge of the other, it is nonetheless crucial for Derrida – and in his view the starting point of all ethics – to approach interaction and discourse with "*respect* for the other *as what it is*" (Derrida, *Writing and Difference*, p. 138). There is a good discussion of this in Bernstein, *The New Constellation*, ch 3.

65 See esp. Foucault, *Discipline and Punish*.

66 Foucault, *History of Sexuality*.

67 Foucault, *Archaeology of Knowledge*, and *The Order of Things*.

68 This is related to deconstructionism's arguments against attempts to discipline the reading of texts by imposition of contextualizing explanations. Yet surely the issue must be not simply to free text from context, but to understand processes of entextualization and especially to establish and understand the variable extent to which different discourses attain independence of the contexts of their initial production or of any later deployment.

69 Lyotard, *Postmodern Condition*, p. 41.

70 Lyotard, "Answering the Question." pp. 81–2.

71 Habermas, *Philosophical Discourse of Modernity*, p. 408; see also Habermas, *Moral Consciousness and Communicative Action*. As Turner ("The Strange Life") has suggested, the proponents of critical "post-positiv-

ist" programs often employ notions of fundamental proof which have all too much similarity to those found in positivism. This tends rhetorically to elimnate the possibility of a middle position between foundationalism and extreme relativism.

72 Nicholson, "On the Postmodern Barricades," p. 87.

73 Foucault, *Power/Knowledge*.

74 Ibid., p. 73.

75 Ibid., p. 61 (in Rabinow, ed.).

76 Habermas, *Philosophical Discourse of Modernity*, p. 113; more generally see chapters 9, 10.

77 Taylor, *Human Agency*, chs 1 and 2; *Philosophy and the Human Sciences*, ch 3.

78 Foucault, *Power/Knowledge*, p. 75.

79 Foucault, *Archaeology of Knowledge*, p. 172.

80 For biographical perspectives, see Eribon, *Michel Foucault* and Miller, *Foucault*.

81 A curiosity of the appropriation of Foucault in translation is that he is identified overwhelmingly with "poststructuralism," not structuralism, and is read as though he were a successor to Althusser, not a contemporary and indeed a crucial influence on Althusser's move to structuralism. Similar oddities inflect the whole construction of "postmodernism" on the Western side of the Atlantic; structuralism appears not as a movement with a history of its own but as a reference to the bad guys who came before. For a corrective, see Dosse, *L'Histoire du structuralisme*.

82 It seems a widespread anthropological neurosis at present to combine, despite their logical incompatibility, a highly critical stance towards "First World" depredations and often towards the play of power in all settings with a radical relativism and a cultural survivalism.

83 It is worth noting, however (since sociologists are often confused on this issue), that though Foucault was firmly anti-positivist, he was very much an empiricist, and one able to command a masterful range of sources, even if his deployment of data was disturbingly decontextualized, his willingness to generalize on the basis of highly particular evidence sometimes misleading, and his manner of citing sources sometimes cavalier.

84 Foucault, *Nietzsche, Genealogy, History*, p. 79.

85 Derrida, *Speech and Phenomena*, p. 81.

86 Ibid., p. 86.

87 Dews, *Logics of Disintegration*, p. 27; Dews in fact argues that "despite all appearances, *différance* is itself a powerful principle of unity," an absolute (p. 43). The similarities to Adorno should be noted.

88 Derrida, *Writing and Difference*; see also the challenge to Hegelian semiotics in Derrida, *Margins of Philosophy*.

89 Dews, *Logics of Disintegration*, p. 31.

5

Habitus, Field, and Capital: Historical Specificity in the Theory of Practice

I

The most visible debates over difference and universalism have pitted postmodernists like Lyotard and Derrida against defenders of modernity like Habermas. Most of these debates have remained remarkably abstract; they have been played out at some distance from concrete social analysis. In different ways, both sides demand a strong separation of form from content and thus lose touch with the concreteness of actual human social life. Both sides argue largely from the history of philosophy, not social or cultural history, or the study of concrete social relations. If Habermas has focused heavily on the possibilities of pure communication, Derrida has as resolutely focused his attention on texts and Lyotard remained a speculative thinker.

Pierre Bourdieu has tried in the strongest terms to distinguish his work from these more abstract modes of analysis, seeking to do theory primarily in concrete, empirical analyses and to oppose the antinomy of form and content (among many other antinomies).[1] He has decried the "theoretical theory" of the Frankfurt critical theorists. Yet, he is equally hard to place among the postmodernists (though he seems as clearly a "poststructuralist" as most theorists more commonly placed under that label). Most importantly, he has resisted the tendency common to much poststructuralist and critical theory to approach social life only through intellectual life, while at the same time retaining attention to both culture and action. Largely through his development of the notion of "habitus," he also brought to center stage the physical embodiment of human knowledge and practical action. Bourdieu's quest for another path is, thus, extremely valuable for efforts to overcome the increasingly sterile opposition of modernism and postmodernism. In this chapter I will explore some of its possibilities, but I will also argue that because of a lack of clarity on one issue dividing so-called modernists and postmodernists – universalism vs. historical specificity – Bourdieu's position is more ambiguous than it at first appears, and thereby more problematic.

Overall, the debate between self-declared modernists and post-modernists seems to echo the inconclusive debate on rationality and cross-cultural analysis that was sparked off by Winch's Wittgensteinian argument for a contextualization of knowledge so radical that it seemed to make cross-cultural understanding an impossible goal.[2] That debate generated a variety of interesting arguments, but ultimately was carried out at such a remove from the empirical work of most social scientists (and the practical concerns of most political activists) that it was unable to effect much reform of our understanding. In the postmodernist/modernist debate as well, sensible third paths seem hard to identify, the positions rhetorically overdrawn, partly because they tend to be presented in great abstraction from actual analysis and social practice. The apparent exceptions, like Foucault and Bourdieu, are in fact not protagonists of the debate. Though Foucault's work is now central to it, this was not his main frame of discourse. He offered a critique of modernity, to be sure, but no argument for postmodernism as cultural form or social reality.

In the present chapter, which I am afraid is fairly abstract itself, I want to pose the question of whether Pierre Bourdieu's work might offer some suggestions as to such a sensible third path between universalism and particularism, rationalism and relativism, modernism and postmodernism – the whole linked series of problematic dichotomies. I do not want to set it up as an argument of the same sort, partly because I think Bourdieu has admirably stayed away from such absolute claims as are made on both sides of those divides; his call for heterodoxy in social science strikes me as eminently sound.[3] But Bourdieu's work has substantial similarities to both sides of the current discourse, even while it is sharply distinct. It shares with "poststructuralism" or "postmodernism" both structuralist roots and a recognition that structuralists were wrong to reject all critical inquiry into basic categories of knowledge as necessarily based on a philosophy of the subject.[4] Like Derrida and Foucault, Bourdieu has carried out significant critical, epistemological inquiries without embracing traditional philosophy of consciousness or subjectivity. Yet Bourdieu is unlike these other "poststructuralists" in a different, more agonistic (though still important) relationship to Heidegger, in a determination to develop a genuinely critical theory, and in an emphasis on the material practicality of social concerns, even in the realm of culture.[5] He has also sharply rejected the substitution of quasi-poetic discourse "which becomes its own end [and] opens the door to a form of thinly-veiled nihilistic relativism . . . that stands as the polar opposite to a truly reflexive social science."[6]

This sort of argument places Bourdieu somewhat closer to Habermas.[7] Both, I would suggest, are heirs to the tradition of critical theory, not just in the Frankfurt School but extending back to Marx, and both propose projects which substantially reformulate the foundations for critical theory. It may be somewhat surprising to place Bourdieu in the camp of critical theorists, so let me defend that for a moment. It is true that Bourdieu follows the lead of the older generation of Frankfurt School theorists – Adorno, Horkheimer, Marcuse – much less closely than does Habermas (indeed, Adorno's substantive themes are echoed more by Foucault and Lyotard). He is, moreover, greatly indebted to other traditions which had little resonance in Frankfurt School thought – notably the phenomenology of Merleau-Ponty, Lévi-Straussian structuralism, and, despite great ambivalence and even occasional hostility, Sartrean existentialism. Nonetheless, as I argued in the Introduction, to restrict the label critical theory to followers of the Frankfurt School is to make it unreasonably into a kind of proprietorial claim, and to lose sight of core features that give it meaning and significance today. Following chapter 1, we may understand as critical theory those projects that undertake simultaneously (1) critique of received categories, (2) critique of theoretical practice, (3) critical exploration of the reasons for aporia or contradictions in other lines of social explanation, and (4) critical substantive analysis of social life in terms of the possible, not just the actual. Bourdieu shares all four moments with Horkheimer and Adorno – and Habermas – even while his theoretical style and substantive analyses differ.

There are other important similarities between Bourdieu and Habermas. Both strive to maintain an analytic focus on agents or agency even while avoiding the philosophy of the subject.[8] Both are engaged in projects intended to overcome, or enable one to overcome, the traditional opposition of theory to practice. Both derive significant insights from Weber's account of Western rationalization as well as from marxism (though they do quite different things with these insights in their respective theories).

The differences from Habermas are many also. They start, perhaps, with Bourdieu's opposition to theoretical system building, to what he has called "theoretical theory," the development of conceptual schemes divorced from concrete analytic objects or projects.[9] One may evaluate this negatively, pointing out that Bourdieu engages in a good deal of generalization even while he declines to work out a full theoretical basis for it, or positively, noting how he avoids the charge of arbitrary formalism which has been leveled at Habermas. In any case, the difference is significant. So is that which stems from Bourdieu's focus on the relationships of power that constitute and shape social fields.[10] Power is always fundamental to Bourdieu, and involves domination and/or differential distribution. For Bourdieu, in other words, power is always used, if sometimes unconsciously, not simply and impersonally systemic.[11] Habermas's theory, like Parsons', allows both relational and distributive understandings of power to take a back seat to power understood as a steering mechanism and a general social capacity.

In short, there is reason to think (1) that Bourdieu is engaged in a project of critical theory partially similar to Habermas's, but (2) that his work is much more open to the kind of positive insights that have been offered by the so-called postmodernists (some of which, like the imbrication of knowledge in relations of power, he put forward at least as early as those poststructuralists who became famously associated with them). His work is essentially contemporary with these others (e.g. Foucault and Derrida), and of comparable scope, though until recently it has been less widely read in the English-language world. I want here to explore the idea that it might suggest ways out of what seems increasingly to be becoming a sterile and boring impasse between Habermas and the postmodernists. I will take up only one thread of the dispute here. This is the issue of difference. As the previous chapter argued, some postmodernists make such a fetish of attention to difference that they are prepared to embrace a thoroughgoing relativism. This Bourdieu has sharply opposed. Habermas, on the other hand, is sufficiently rigid in his universalism (even though he distinguishes his own as "small 'u'" compared to Kant's "capital 'U'") and his separation of form from content, that he seems unable to offer much more than lip service to the importance of difference, to the idea that social and cultural differences might be positively desirable and not merely tolerable on liberal grounds.[12]

Difference as such is not a central theme of Bourdieu's. I am not sure it is even a peripheral theme. In at least one sense, his theory is weakened by inattention to this issue: he offers an inadequate account of how to address the most basic categorial differences among epochs, societies, or cultures, and corresponding differences in how his analytic tools fit or work in historically or culturally distinct instances. Despite this, I will argue that Bourdieu's work does give us extremely useful ways of approaching parts of this issue, and that it thereby contributes importantly to getting contemporary theoretical discourse out of the rut of postmodernist vs. modernist.

II

The issue of how to understand differences in societal types, epochs, civilizations, or cultures is a central one for social theory. It figures at least implicitly in the modernist/postmodernist debate as the question of whether the contemporary era is, or is about to become distinct in some basic categorial way from that of the last three hundred or more years. The very idea of modernity, of course, posits a break with the premodern (usually conceived of as the medieval European, and/or as a category which collapses and obscures the wide range of variation in non-Western societies). Some such idea of the distinctiveness of the modern West has informed anthropology and sociology from their inception, despite recurrent criticism of various specific formulations: *Gemeinschaft/ Gesellschaft*, traditional/modern, folk/urban, etc.

The dual messages of anthropology (to which I alluded at the beginning of this book) have in part to do with efforts on the one hand to show that "primitive" people are rational, despite the manifest conflicts between their beliefs and practices and what we "know" to be true, and on the other hand an effort to maintain the otherness of the people studied either out of respect for their concrete way of life or as a mirror for our own. The post-Winch rationality debates were about just these issues, for example about how we can determine whether or not the people of a different culture are "rational." It seems to me that Bourdieu's work both reflects the general ambivalence about this issue and suggests a way to grapple with part of it. I will try to demonstrate the latter by developing an account of the transformation of the workings of the habitus involved in movement from a minimally codified "traditional" social organization towards on the one hand more complex civilizations outside the modern Western ambit, and on the other capitalist states in the modern West. More briefly, and with more attention to problems, I will look at Bourdieu's later argument about multiform and convertible capital. At stake is whether we should understand Bourdieu's analytic apparatus – his conceptual tools like habitus, field, and capital – as applying universally without modification or as situationally specific. Moreover, in either case, we want to know whether they help us to make sense of differences among situations, not just their commonalties. Bourdieu is concerned with both sides of this:

> There are general *laws of fields*: even such different fields as the field of politics, the field of philosophy, and the field of religion have functionally invariant laws (it's because of this fact that the project of a general theory is not senseless, and that, therefore, one can make use of what one under-

stands of the functioning of each particular field to interrogate and interpret other fields, thereby getting past the mortal antinomy between
idiographic monographs and formal and empty theory).[13]

The issue is not, as critics have sometimes charged, whether Bourdieu
neglects change or struggle; he does not, but rather pays attention to
both.[14] The issue is how to describe a change sufficiently basic that it calls
for different categories of analysis. In his early work, Bourdieu contrasted Kabylia with France, the traditional with the modern. Starting in
the 1960s, he embarked on a long-range trajectory of studies of France
which used the categories he had developed in studying Kabylia and
argued substantially for the similarity of the basic social issues across
cases.[15] Bourdieu does not conclusively decide between the two general
stances, the emphases on similarity and difference. He has described his
project as "uncovering some of the universal laws that tendentially
regulate the functioning of all fields." But in the same interview, he also
uses more qualified expressions: "one of the purposes of the analysis is to
uncover *transhistorical invariants*, or sets of relations between structures
that persist within a clearly circumscribed but relatively long historical
period".[16]

Bourdieu is simply unclear as to how historically and comparatively
specific his conceptual frameworks and analytic strategies are meant to
be. He has not done much systematic comparative or historical analysis
which would indicate how – or whether – he would make critical distinctions among epochs, or types of societies or cultures. His conceptual
development is generally couched in the context of concrete analysis –
part of his opposition to "theoretical theory"; this makes for an element
of contextual specificity to his terms. On the other hand, it leaves the
historical and comparative frame for such specificity relatively
unexamined. Bourdieu's predominant presentation tends towards a
transhistorical conceptual framework and analytic approach which partially obscures the specificity of epochs and types of society or culture. At
the same time, much of Bourdieu's conceptual apparatus can be employed in an analytic approach which does a better job of achieving
historical and cultural and social organizational specificity. In other
words, we can use Bourdieu's conceptual apparatus to develop an account of breaks that distinguish social arrangements and cultures such
that different issues arise and different analytic categories and strategies
are appropriate to them.

Some of Bourdieu's categories may readily fit all social settings; for
example, I would think that no one could be without a habitus. Others
are trickier. Is the notion of capital altogether transhistorical? The issue

is muddied by divergent readings of Marx and some ambiguity about how closely related to Marx Bourdieu means his conception to be. This is worth exploring in some detail.

III

Bourdieu appears to begin his analyses of capital with Marx very much in mind. In one major essay, for example, he introduces this definition in the first paragraph. "Capital is accumulated labor (in its materialized form or its 'incorporated,' embodied form) which, when appropriated on a private, i.e., exclusive, basis by agents or groups of agents, enables them to appropriate social energy in the form of reified or living labor."[17] Bourdieu intends to take quite seriously this version of a labor theory of capital, describing the social world as "accumulated history," and going on to argue that we can analyze the various forms of capital through the different means by which they are accumulated and transmitted to succeeding generations. "The universal equivalent, the measure of all equivalences, is nothing other than labor-time (in the widest sense); and the conservation of social energy through all its conversions is verified if, in each case, one takes into account both the labor-time accumulated in the form of capital and the labor-time needed to transform it from one type into another."[18] Bourdieu's qualifier about the widest sense of labor-time is appropriate, for unlike Marx, Bourdieu does not examine the historically specific conditions under which labor is abstracted into temporal units of measurement. As this passage makes clear, Bourdieu means by labor-time simply the amount of work. For a universal equivalent, this is somewhat problematic. We must wonder how the various concrete forms of work involved in the reproduction or production of capital are in fact made equivalent to each other where a process of abstraction (e.g. into commodified labor) is lacking. Bourdieu's account works well to show us how qualitatively different forms of work may contribute to the putatively common project of achieving or reproducing hierarchical distinction. It does not show us any way in which these qualitatively different forms of work are transformed into a quantitative equivalent. In certain ways, thus, Bourdieu adds to the account one can derive from Marx – for example by arguing that a much wider range of labor is productive of capital than Marx suggested, including the labor of familial reproduction of the embodied sensibilities which distinguish classes. On the other hand, by treating capital simply as wealth or power he sacrifices one of the linchpins of marxist theory, and despite his use of terms like universal equivalent loses the capacity to clarify the nature of a social system which produces universal equivalents.

What is of interest in this is not an argument over Bourdieu's choice among the many possible readings of Marx. Rather, it is the implications of this sort of account of capital for the analysis of a range of historical epochs or culturally different contemporary social arrangements. Certainly one could apply the idea of different forms of capital anywhere, so long as one simply meant to point out descriptively the existence of different resources of power, differently reproduced. But if the convertibility of capital is something more than a postulate, or a restatement of the definition of capital as power (and hence cultural or social attributes as capital only to the extent they yield power), then it would seem to be historically variable. At the very least, the extent and ease of convertibility must be quite different in different contexts. A high level of convertibility is, I think, characteristic especially of relatively complex, market-based, and above all capitalist societies. Capitalism, moreover, seems to have a logic of increasing convertibility. Where capitalist relations enter, traditional barriers to conversion of forms of capital are undermined. Bourdieu himself showed this accurately in his accounts of the behavior and relationships of Algerian peasants who had earned substantial amounts of cash outside the traditional village field of production.[19] Their attempts to convert their economic capital to cultural and social capital were thwarted and made difficult by the traditional normative structure and habitus. At the same time, as their introduction of cash gained a foothold, it proved insidious, undermining customary patterns of practice. Paying for services in money rather than in accumulated social debt undermines a pattern of more or less stable reproduction and helps to bring about basic changes.

What Bourdieu's approach to convertible and multiform capital lacks is an idea of capitalism. That is, he is not in a position to give an account of what is distinctive to those societies that operate with a compulsion to expand their reach, and whose patterns of practice have a corrosive power over others. Bourdieu uses a number of shorthand expressions for the societies in which fields proliferate and are sharply divided and in which the convertibility among forms of capital is most central to social organization. Like the rest of us, he calls them variously "relatively complex," "differentiated," "highly codified," etc. A marxian understanding of capitalism would be one way to clarify this opposition – or at least aspects of it – theoretically. I will want to suggest that Bourdieu's theoretical framework offers us additional ways potentially to make these sorts of terms much more precise and useful. First, though, we must examine the significance of the fact that he stays away from describing any of these complex societies as capitalist, and addressing the special role capital accumulation plays in their constitution.[20] Where Marx stressed that capital was not simply wealth but a moment in the complex relations of production called capitalism, that it entailed a compulsion to intensify and expand the processes of exploitation by which it was produced, and that it turned crucially on the distinction of its constitutive category abstract labor power from mere work, Marx was laying the foundations for a historically specific theory of capitalism.[21] Bourdieu, on the other hand, consistently sees capital simply as a resource (i.e. a form of wealth) which yields power.[22] The link to Marx suggested by the common emphasis on capital and labor, a suggestion reinforced by aspects of Bourdieu's rhetoric, is misleading.

Bourdieu's considerable achievements in his work on cultural capital are linked to this difference from Marx. Bourdieu's key original insights are that there are immaterial forms of capital – cultural, symbolic and social – as well as a material or economic one, and that with varying levels of difficulty it is possible to convert one of these forms into the other. It is this notion of multiform, convertible capital that underpins his richly nuanced account of class relations in France:[23]

> The social world can be conceived as a multi-dimensional space that can be constructed empirically by discovering the main factors of differentiation which account for the differences observed in a given social universe, or, in other words, by discovering the powers or forms *of capital* which are or can become efficient, like aces in a game of cards, in this particular universe, that is, in the struggle (or competition) for the appropriation of scarce goods of which this universe is the site. It follows that the structure of this space is given by the distribution of the various forms of capital, that is, by the distribution of the properties which are active within the universe under study – those properties capable of conferring strength, power and consequently profit on their holder. . . . These fundamental social powers are, according to my empirical investigations, firstly *economic* capital, in its various kinds; secondly *cultural* capital or better, informational capital, again in its different kinds; and thirdly two forms of capital that are very strongly correlated, social capital, which consists of resources based on connections and group membership, and *symbolic* capital, which is the form the different types of capital take once they are perceived and recognized as legitimate.[24]

Economic capital is essentially that which is "immediately and directly convertible into money,"[25] unlike educational credentials (cultural capital) or social connections (social capital). The most interesting parts of Bourdieu's work in this area are his treatments of cultural capital. He has made particular strides by recognizing how much of cultural capital presupposes embodiment of distinctive and distinguishing sensibilities and characteristic modes of action. Thus it is that he is able to show how the labor of parents is translatable into the "status attainment" of their children in ways not directly dependent on financial inheritance or even better schools. Such parental labor depends on the availability of time free from paid employment, however, which shows the dependence of the other forms of capital on economic capital.[26] The importance of this sort of cultural capital is greatest, moreover, where for some reason it is advantageous to deny or disguise the inheritability of position.[27] Bourdieu does not directly explore the social conditions and histories which make such "strategies of reproduction" particularly advantageous.

The issue is an important one. Bourdieu repeatedly urges us to see history and sociology as inseparably linked, but his sociology does not offer purchase on the transformation of social systems.[28] It is geared towards accounts of their internal operation. The issue is not simply whether Bourdieu offers a "motor of history" in the crude marxist sense. Rather it is that his accounts of the general system of social and cultural organization always render it as essentially conservative; they suggest no reasons why a logic of reproduction would not work. There is nothing in his theory like the notion of contradictions in Marx's work (or Hegel's or that of the early Frankfurt School).[29] Bourdieu's theory does imply dynamism, but crucially it does so at the level of the strategic actor (individual or collective, or, in those writings where he is more attentive to the problems of rooting his analysis in any positing of actors as fundamental, at the level of the strategy itself). That is, the motive force of social life is the pursuit of distinction, profit, power, wealth, etc. Bourdieu's account of capital is an account of the resources people use in such pursuit. In this sense, despite his disclaimers, Bourdieu does share a good deal with Gary Becker and other rational choice theorists. Bourdieu sharply and probably rightly rejects the charge of economism; he is not assuming that the "interests" which are fundamental are basically "economic." He deals less with the charge that he fails to consider action which is not consciously or unconsciously strategic. He accepts the notion of interest, albeit as part of a "deliberate and provisional reductionism," in order to be able to show that cultural activity is not "disinterested" as Western thought has often implied since the development of the modern ideology of artistic production.[30] He is quick and forceful in pointing out that:

> the concept of interest as I construe it has nothing in common with the naturalistic, trans-historical, and universal interest of utilitarian theory. . . . Far from being an anthropological invariant, interest is a historical *arbitrary*, a historical construction that can be known only through

historical analysis, *ex post*, through empirical observation, and not de-
duced a priori from some fictitious – and so naively Eurocentric – conception of "Man."[31]

Quite so, but then we must ask why this particular concept of interest
arose historically and gained special power in both lay and academic
analyses of human action in the present epoch. In any case, this recourse
to empiricism rather than naturalism is not so problematic for economic
or rational choice theorists as Bourdieu believes. "Revealed preference,"
they can reply. There are certainly important differences between
Bourdieu's theory of practice and rational choice theory.[32] But though
Bourdieu points out the historical particularity of all interests, he does
not deny the universality of interested action. Implicitly, at least, he goes
further, beyond treating all action simply as interested – which is little
more than saying "motivated." He treats all interests, historically particular though their contents may be, as formally similar in their implication of strategies designed to advance some manner of acquisition of
power or wealth. Bourdieu is saying something more transhistorical and
anthropologically invariant about human actors than he lets on, especially in his accounts of capital.

  Bourdieu's theory is social in a powerful sense in which rational choice
theory is not. His conception of strategy in the idea of an intersubjective
habitus conditioned by "objective" situations gives a much less
reductionistic and more useful sense of human action. Bourdieu's sociology provides for effective accounts of the influences which objective
circumstances, historical patterns of distribution of various resources,
and the trajectories of different actors through social fields all have on
power relations. It relies little on any notion of creativity. Most centrally,
it gives an account of the various socially determined interests people
may pursue, and the ways in which social structures constrain such
action, but not of any internal tendencies of those structures to change in
particular directions. Bourdieu's theory is at its best, therefore, as a
theory of reproduction, and at its weakest as a theory of transformation.
In this it shows its structuralist roots.

IV

Bourdieu has rightly protested that his work is by no means bracketable
as a theory of reproduction *tout court*.[33] But he is centrally concerned
with how the various practical projects of different people, the struggles
in which they engage and the relations of power which push and pull on
them, nonetheless reproduce the field of relations of which they are a

part. "The source resides in the actions and reactions of agents who, unless they exclude themselves from the game, have no other choice than to struggle to maintain or improve their position in the field, thus helping to bring to bear on all the others the weight of the constraints, often experienced as intolerable, which stem from antagonistic coexistence."[34] In *Homo Academicus* and *La noblesse d'Etat*, Bourdieu reports that he is impressed by the stability of the basic field of relations even while incumbents change and struggles continue. In his work on Kabylia (e.g. *Outline, Logic*), ruptures in traditional practices always appear as the result of exogenous influences.

When Bourdieu approached the idea of reproduction, a key underlying concern was overcoming the antinomy between structure and action.[35] He wanted to show how patterns of social life could be maintained over time without this either being specifically willed by agents or the result of external factors beyond the reach of agents' wills. That is, he wanted to show that reproduction was the result of what people did, intentionally and rationally, even when reproduction was not itself their intention: "each agent, wittingly or unwittingly, willy nilly, is a producer and reproducer of objective meaning. Because his actions and works are the product of a *modus operandi* of which he is not the producer and has no conscious mastery, they contain an 'objective intention,' as the Scholastics put it, which always outruns his conscious intentions."[36] The practice which the habitus makes possible is not merely a determined result of the antecedent conditions; neither is it the sort of intentional action which many theories conceive of as action following a rule:

> Talk of rules, a euphemized form of legalism, is never more fallacious than when applied to the most homogenous societies (or the least codified areas of differentiated societies) where most practices, including those seemingly most ritualized, can be abandoned to the orchestrated improvisation of common dispositions: the rule is never, in this case, more than a second-best intended to make good the occasional misfirings of the collective enterprise of inculcation tending to produce habitus that are capable of generating practices regulated without express regulation or any institutionalized call to order.[37]

The last part of this quotation poses an essential issue: how is the coordination of actions to be achieved without either external determination (or what amounts to almost the same thing, reference to the unconscious as an equally unwilled internal determination) or the issuance of some formal rule or communication involving a decision process (and hence the self-imposition of a rule)?[38] Objectivists either simply record regularities without explaining them, or reify various analytic notions

such as "culture," "structures" or "modes of production" and imagine
that they exist as such in the world, external to actors, and constraining
them towards regularity. Bourdieu's attack on this objectivism is powerful, but it is worth noting that it does not involve systematic attention to
differences among societies in the extent to which formal rules are issued,
or to which action appears to actors as reified external determination.[39]

In *Outline*, Bourdieu's argument is aimed particularly at French structuralists, and he adopts the language of economizing strategies (from a
mainly Anglo-Saxon discourse) largely to challenge the structuralist
elimination of agents, of practices. But even here, he is careful to show
that the economizing is not that of individuals understood discretely, but
inheres in the habitus as a social creation. Bourdieu is careful to distinguish his position also from a subjectivism which imagines that agents
are not overwhelmingly products of their backgrounds and situations, or
that their actions simply originate with their choices among abstractly
conceived possibilities. Sartre is the particular subjectivist Bourdieu has
most in mind, and he points precisely to the problem Sartre created for
himself by refusing to recognize anything resembling durable dispositions. He thereby made each action into "a sort of unprecedented confrontation between the subject and the world."[40] In so doing, he made
social reality inexplicably voluntary and ultimately, therefore, arbitrary.
Against this view, Bourdieu argues that agents act within socially constructed ranges of possibilities, durably inscribed within them (even in
their bodies) as well as within the social world in which they move.
Moreover, the relation between agent and social world is a relation
between two dimensions of the social, not two separate sorts of being:

> The source of historical action, that of the artist, the scientist, or the
> member of government just as much as that of the worker or the petty civil
> servant, is not an active subject confronting society as if that society were
> an object constituted externally. The source resides neither in conscious-
> ness nor in things but in the relationship between two stages of the social,
> that is, between the history objectified in things, in the form of institutions,
> and the history incarnated in bodies, in the form of that system of enduring
> dispositions which I call habitus.[41]

Against some of the cruder forms of economistic choice theory, Bourdieu
holds that agents' use of the possibilities available to them, while strategic in a sense, is often not strictly speaking calculating because not
discursive. The economizing or calculation is built into the practical play
of the game. The habitus constitutes a regulated form of improvisation,
necessary because choice among the available "moves" is never fully
specifiable in terms of rules.[42] An analyst might, thus, see how a course of

behavior effectively achieves some instrumental end, while the actor engaged in the behavior understands her action in relatively altruistic terms of being a good friend, or wife, or daughter. "The objectivist reduction which brings to light the so-called objective functions of myths and rites (for Durkheim, functions of moral integration; for Lévi-Strauss, functions of logical integration) makes it impossible to understand how these functions are fulfilled, because it brackets the agents' own representation of the world and of their practice."[43] It is essential to some strategies that they can only be played by people who misrecognize them. But this is not a simple matter of an analyst claiming that social actors have false consciousness. It is a claim about the culturally specific mode of grasping the nature of actions, the "conditions of existence and the dispositions of agents" and the available cultural vocabularies.

> The Kabyle woman setting up her loom is not performing an act of cosmogony; she is simply setting up her loom to weave cloth intended to serve a technical function. It so happens that, given the symbolic equipment available to her for thinking her own activity – and in particular her language, which constantly refers her back to the logic of ploughing – she can only think what she is doing in the enchanted, that is to say, mystified, form which spiritualism, thirsty for eternal mysteries, finds so enchanting.[44]

Above all else, it is crucial to grasp, Bourdieu argues, that agents do not generally adopt the theoretical attitude of seeing action as a choice among all objective possibilities; they usually see only one or a few possibilities. "The habitus is the source of these series of moves which are objectively organized as strategies without being the product of a genuine strategic intention – which would presuppose at least that they are perceived as one strategy among other possible strategies."[45]

Bourdieu's concern is with how the coordination of social activities is achieved. His riposte to both objectivism and subjectivism is to stress practical mastery, a sense of playing the game which is at once active and nondiscursive. "We shall escape from the ritual either/or choice between objectivism and subjectivism in which the social sciences have so far allowed themselves to be trapped only if we are prepared to inquire into the mode of production and functioning of the practical mastery which makes possible both an objectively intelligible practice and also an objectively enchanted experience of that practice."[46] Bourdieu stresses that this is not simply a matter of phenomenologically reconstructing lived experience. It is necessary that a theory of practice give a good account of the limits of awareness which are involved in lived experience, including both misrecognition and nonrecognition, as well as show the kind of genuine knowledge which is involved, often nondiscursively, in practice. Moreover, there is struggle over knowledge including even prelinguistic knowledge:

> The individual or collective classification struggles aimed at transforming the categories of perception and appreciation of the social world and, through this, the social world itself, are indeed a forgotten dimension of the class struggle. But one only has to realize that the classificatory schemes which underlie agents' practical relationship to their condition and the representation they have of it are themselves the product of that condition, in order to see the limits of this autonomy.[47]

Thus critics have overstated the extent to which Bourdieu's account focuses on reproduction at the expense of openings to the possibilities for action to create a new and different world – for example to revolutionary struggle.[48] Bourdieu's emphasis on reproduction does not foreclose contrary action, though it also does not introduce any notion of systematic pressures for such action. Bourdieu addresses the issue of revolutionary collective actions directly, although very briefly, and argues that they are imbricated within conjunctures, and still crucially dependent on the same habitus that had hitherto organized reproduction. In other words, revolution does not mark a break with the habitus, but is based on it, even though it breaks the pattern of stable reproduction:

> It is just as true and just as untrue to say that collective actions produce the event or that they are its product. The conjuncture capable of transforming practices objectively coordinated, because subordinated to partially or wholly identical objective necessities, into *collective action* (e.g. revolutionary action) is constituted in the dialectical relationship between, on the one hand, a *habitus*, understood as a system of lasting, transposable dispositions which, integrating past experiences, functions at every moment as a matrix *of perceptions, and actions* and makes possible the achievement of infinitely diversified tasks . . . and an objective *event* which exerts its action of conditional stimulation calling for or demanding a determinate response, only on those who are disposed to constitute it as such because they are endowed with a determinate type of dispositions.[49]

This, Bourdieu suggests, is the source of "the frequently observed incapacity to think historical crises in categories of perception and thought other than those of the past, albeit a revolutionary past."[50] Bourdieu recognizes also the role of the modern market and related economic changes – capitalism, I would say, though at this specific point he does not – in freeing "agents from the endless work of creating or restoring social relations" and providing the occasion for the break with the idea that society was held together by will and the recognition of the more or less impersonal, self-regulating mechanisms which play a central role in social integration.[51]

In this line of argument, we can see something of an analogue in Bourdieu's account to Habermas's story of the uncoupling of the system and the lifeworld (discussed further in the next chapter). In Bourdieu's account in *Outline*, the creation of self-regulating systematicity marks a crucial epochal break distinguishing kinds of societies and implicitly modes of analysis appropriate to them:

> The greater the extent to which the task of reproducing the relations of domination is taken over by objective mechanisms, which serve the interests of the dominant group without any conscious effort on the latter's part, the more indirect and, in a sense, impersonal, become the strategies objectively oriented towards reproduction: it is not by lavishing generosity, kindness or politeness on his charwoman (or on any other "socially inferior" agent) but by choosing the best investment for his money, or the best school for his son, that the possessor of economic or cultural capital perpetuates the relationship of domination which objectively links him with his charwoman and even her descendants. Once a system of mechanisms has been constituted capable of objectively ensuring the reproduction of the established order by its own motion (. . .), the dominant class have only to *let the system they dominate take its own course* in order to exercise their domination; but until such a system exists, they have to work directly, daily, personally, to produce and reproduce conditions of domination which are even then never entirely trustworthy.[52]

Bourdieu implies a distinction very close to that which I would describe as between direct and indirect social relationships.[53] And at this point, without particularly stressing it, or even labeling it, Bourdieu has given us not just an account of a distinctive mode of domination, but of the break between two modes of societal integration. In the first, the coordination of actions in society is achieved primarily through a web of personal relationships, each of which must be played like a highly nuanced game. This game is hardly ended in modern societies, I might add; the key difference is that it is no longer the central, constitutive way of organizing social relationships at large. Rather, the various apparently self-regulating systems perform that function most centrally. It is at this point, moreover, that it becomes particularly necessary for Bourdieu to introduce his concept of field.[54]

There is no intrinsic reason why "less differentiated" societies should not be described in terms of fields, though this is not done in *Outline* and at points Bourdieu does suggest that "complex or differentiated" socie-ties are precisely those which are characterized by having a number of fields. In any case, once attention is turned to "more complex" societies, something like the field concept is needed. Why? The reason has to do, I think, with an uncoupling of fields.[55] This uncoupling manifests itself first of all as a reduction in the extent to which the same agents are linked to each other in a variety of fields – say kinship, religion, economic produc-tion, etc. – in other words a reduction in "multiplexity" of relationships, to use Max Gluckman's concept.[56] But the uncoupling also manifests itself in a growing heterogeneity among fields, a reduction in the extent to which each is homologous with the others. This latter – if I am right about it – presents somewhat more of a problem for Bourdieu, given his general argument (e.g. in *Distinction*) that the various fields are homolo-gous. This does not necessarily preclude Bourdieu's pursuit of a "general theory of fields," though it may limit it. The extent of homology can readily be made into an empirical variable, but the issue is important.

To see why, let us turn to a schematized notion of macrohistorical social change. The change we are interested in lies in the means by which coordination of social action is achieved. At one level, what we are doing is adding some needed complexity to the Weberian notion of movement from tradition to modernity.[57]

V

Max Weber sought to theorize above all else the distinctive Western process of rationalization.[58] His analysis of this had a variety of moments and influences, but crucially it involved a neoKantian theme of the differentiation of value spheres. In developing his three separate critical analyses of pure reason, practical reason, and judgment, Kant presented truth, ethics, and aesthetics as distinct realms of cognition and reality. Though he did not explicitly present this as a historical break, it helped to constitute a distinctive vision of modernity. Weber developed this theme in terms of the differentiation of social action, social relations, and social institutions, as well as cognitive forms. It lies for example behind his famous distinction of the vocations of science and politics. And, it helps to make sense of how he thought reason had been emancipated from tradition and emotion and come into its own. That his ultimate analysis, especially after the completion of his studies of world religions, turned this at least partially into a tragic story of the iron cage within which an increasingly soulless reason (and modern humanity) was trapped did not change the logic of the story (though it did set the stage for the pessimistic turn of Horkheimer and Adorno).

Weber conceived of tradition simply as respect for "that which has always been,"[59] and conceived of traditional social organization primarily as simple continuity rather than the more complex project of reproduction. But let us not think of tradition in Bagehot's sense of the hard cake of culture; starting closer to its etymology, let us reconsider tradition also as an active verb, as *traditio*, referring to the passing on or handing down of information.[60] Tradition, then, is a mode of transmission of information, particularly, for present purposes, that crucial to the coordination of action. Following Bourdieu's account of the habitus, we may note that the information need not be rendered discursive; it may be tacit knowledge, even embodied in modes of action that agents are unable to bring to linguistic consciousness, like basketball players able to perform hook shots better than describe them. The habitus, on Bourdieu's account, works to shape this process even while it provides the regulated source of improvisations, and indeed precisely because it does.

One of the crucial features of Bourdieu's account of the habitus is that it allows for a process of continual correction and adjustment: "the habitus . . . makes possible the achievement of infinitely diversified tasks, thanks to analogical transfers of schemes permitting the solution of similarly shaped problems, and thanks to the unceasing corrections of the results obtained."[61] Most tradition is not passed down in ritual performances, schools, or other situations where that passing down is itself the main manifest project. On the contrary, most passing on and subsequent affirmations of culture take place in the course of interested actions in which people pursue a variety of ends, both conscious and unconscious. As people succeed or fail, meet with approval or disapproval, in trying to carry out their manifold projects of daily life, they may adjust slightly the traditional information they have received from various others in the course of previous interactions. A basketball player, to continue that example, may imitate – or be explicitly taught – another's shot technique, but learns to adjust the velocity to compensate for his own height, or to add spin because it makes a favorable bounce more likely; the adjustments may be unconscious or conscious, and in either case mandated by the recurrent evaluation of each shot as a success or a failure. Each shot is embedded in strategy – the game – but not a product of conscious calculation. But the example is imperfect; the basketball player, we may assume, at least knows that he is playing basketball. Or does he? Might this be a limited perception of what is in fact a more complex strategy – achieving success in one field which seems relatively open while minimizing investment in another – say school – which seems closed, while half-consciously or even unconsciously engaging in strategies for achieving a sense of personal autonomy or perhaps escaping a ghetto and gaining a better standard of living?

In any case, the basketball player illustrates the possibility for continued correction or adjustment in the passing on of tradition. This may be a crucial element of traditionality, of the extent to which tradition can actually serve to coordinate social activity, in many settings. If tradition were rigid, it would soon meet with disastrous consequences and prove itself an extremely inefficient means of coordinating action. It is precisely because it can be adjusted with (often unconscious) regard to the success or failure of various practical projects that the tradition embodied in the habitus can be supple enough to change with other aspects of a society.

More complex societies never lose this element of tradition, but it organizes proportionately less of what goes on, and is often compartmentalized within specific spheres or at least at the local level. In classical India or China, thus, tradition of this kind took place constantly, resulting in a variety of local adaptations and idiosyncrasies. But at the same time, the passing on of information – still tradition and still with an attitude of preservation not innovation – took place through other, especially textual means. These other means introduced a new institutional dimension – the role of authorized arbiters of correctness. This, I take it, is what Bourdieu refers to when he speaks of the "codification" of culture:

> The extent to which the schemes of the *habitus* are objectified in codified knowledge, transmitted as such, varies greatly between one area of practice and another. The relative frequency of sayings, prohibitions, proverbs and strongly regulated rites declines as one moves from practices linked to or directly associated with agricultural activity, such as weaving, pottery and cuisine, towards the divisions of the day or the moments of human life, not to mention areas apparently abandoned to arbitrariness, such as the internal organization of the house, the parts of the body, colours or animals. Although they are among the most codified aspects of the cultural tradition, the precepts of custom which govern the temporal distribution of activities vary greatly from place to place and, in the same place, from one official informant to another. We find here again the opposition between official knowledge . . . and all kinds of unofficial or secret, even clandestine, knowledge and practices which, though they are the product of the same generative schemes, obey a different logic.[62]

In China, India, much of Islamic civilization, and, indeed, medieval Europe at least for a time, the operation of these more codified modes of transmission did not imperialistically challenge the simultaneous operation of more informal tradition within personal interaction. One of the distinctive features of the modern West may be the extent to which the transmission of "official" information through authoritative channels has in fact been destructive of the transmission of information through direct interpersonal relationships or challenged the predominance of such "direct relations" in the realms of information previously local or considered private.[63]

Linked to this is the problematization of the informal tradition (1) through differentiation of fields, (2) through increasing contact with people of different cultures, and (3) through increasing exercise of individual choice. The first, I think, is clear enough to need little comment. As various fields become differentiated, the information that can be passed on informally as part of the ordinary round of daily life becomes segmented. If there is more general information called for, it is increasingly likely to be passed on through codified, authoritative means. And it is likely that at the very least, those in power will find it necessary that some such information – say about the virtues of their rule – be passed on. Information of this sort may still be traditional in the colloquial and/or Weberian sense that it embodies an attitude of deference for "what has always been" (whether or not it is in fact ancient being a matter quite secondary to whether it is believed to be). But the shifts from directly interpersonal to large-scale, mediated transmission, and from "tacit" to codified form change its social implications dramatically.

The presumptive faith in "that which has always been" is more likely to be ruptured when people are brought into routine contact with others quite different from themselves (especially under a common authority, which – as all participatory republican regimes do – prevents them from treating their fellow-subjects as quite radically other).[64] This does not by any means imply that people necessarily become tolerant of those different from themselves or embrace liberal pluralism. It is more accurate to follow Bourdieu in seeing this transition as a passage from the "doxic" attitude of not considering another form of existence or belief to the "orthodox" attitude of demanding correctness with regard to authoritative standards of belief.[65] It is still a further step when an increase in apparently independent decision-making (either by individuals or groups) poses the challenge of heterodoxy. Like the Protestant Reformation, this may involve an objective proliferation of power regimes and schemes of belief and action, without producing a tolerant attitude on the part of the orthodox. Recognition that any orthodoxy is one among many nonetheless fundamentally changes the consciousness of devotees and the extent to which society is open to and productive of new courses of thought and action.[66] What apparent independence means is not just not following traditional rules, but acting in a habitus which is not highly congruent with those of others in one's fields.[67]

Bourdieu does not address this increase of independent decision making very directly in either *Outline* or *Logic of Practice*. It is linked to his borrowing of economizing language to describe the strategies built into the play of the habitus. We need, however, to unpack the several dimensions of the notion of rationality. A notion of maximization is in fact only one possible meaning or aspect of rationality. Bourdieu suggests that at least some sort of maximizing is universal, because there is always scarcity. Of course, there may also be scarcity which is specific to various social fields and maximizing may be in part a historically specific orientation to action. Just as maximizing is variable, so are the other dimensions of rationality. There is, for example, the question of how far a strategizer extends her horizons of calculation, how many of the objectively possible courses of action and their potential effects she actually analyzes. One of the crucial characteristics of the configuration of habitus and field in "traditional" societies was that they radically limited the range of options considered by rational actors. Whether actors were maximizing or not, this gave a much greater chance to traditionality as a means of coordinating action. For every increase in the range of options a decision-maker considers not only increases the complexity of her own decision-making, it makes her less predictable to others. This loss of predictability is apt to be part of a vicious circle, as others in a decision-maker's field are led to plan on shorter and shorter time horizons in order to allow themselves the opportunity to adjust to the unpredictability. This sort of attitude, this vicious circle, is antithetical to maintenance of stable traditional patterns of social relations. When coupled with increasing scale or reach of social relations, it leads to the necessity of adopting statistical measures of the probability of various courses of action, preferably averaged not only over time but across a range of other members of a field. At that point, we have left the coordination of action through tradition and entered the world of at least putatively self-regulating systems.

These self-regulating systems call for a more theoretical form of understanding; the practical attitude of the habitus is less likely to be able to attain practical mastery of relationships with them. This is not to say that there is no reason to talk of the habitus as governing the generation of improvisational strategies for dealing with such systems. On the contrary, there is no conceivable point at which human beings could be perfect rational actors; since they will always work within various forms of bounded rationality it will always be necessary to consider the socially produced means of generating strategies which are open to them, and which reflect the organization of the fields in which they act and their own trajectories through them. And in this sense, a theoretical attitude should not be too sharply opposed to the notion of habitus (as Bourdieu, e.g. *Outline*, has sometimes implied). Rather, a theoretical attitude should be seen as a variety of habitus, itself reflecting a certain social placement and participation in specific socially constructed projects. Thus it is not simply that "moderns" adopt theoretical attitudes, but that certain members of modern societies do so with regard to certain of their practices. An economist employed by the ministry of finance may rely on a theoretically informed habitus in conceptualizing the stock market and developing his own practical dealings with it (or its consequences). At the same time, a "pit trader" may work on the floor of a stock exchange, executing buy and sell orders with a supreme practical mastery minimally informed by any theoretical understanding of the overall market (though it is true that her habitus would be unlikely to resemble the doxic complete investment of a member of a highly homogenous and relatively self-contained society, for the floor trader would almost certainly be aware of the availability of other ways of understanding stock markets).

In a modern society, apparently self-regulating systems like large scale markets are crucial links in the reproduction of patterns of social relations. Both they and the relatively high levels of distinction among fields encourage an attitude of a high level of rationality (understood as selecting among a wide range of options on the basis of maximal information about likely outcomes in order efficiently to pursue some goal). Therefore, even in the absence of internal contradictions which hamper their capacity to reproduce stably, the self-regulating systems nonetheless are apt to give rise to social relational patterns which do undermine stable reproduction. Of course, such systems – e.g. capitalism – may have basic internal contradictions, in which case stability is even more doubtful.

This conclusion need not be seen as problematic for Bourdieu's work (indeed it is produced through thinking along with parts of Bourdieu's work) *except* insofar as he *assumes* rather than empirically demonstrates a high level of homology among fields, an absence of systemic contradictions, and therefore a tendency towards social integration and stable reproduction of the encompassing field of power. I think he tends towards assuming this in *Distinction*, *Homo Academicus* and *La noblesse d'Etat*. I do not think that this assumption is necessary to his analysis.

VI

My argument in this chapter has led to the conclusion that there are important, basic differences among kinds of societies. I believe that thinking through Bourdieu's own arguments suggests this, although he has not made it entirely clear what sorts of categories should be taken as historically specific and which as transhistorical. There are, of course, many possible kinds of difference and issues about difference which might be raised; I have only introduced, not exhausted that subject. Indeed, there is a certain ambiguity about just what is to be generalized and what not in Bourdieu's empirical studies of various fields. Obviously the answers turn on further empirical investigations, but there is an implication of greater formal comparability than seems immediately warranted. It is one thing to ask how much the conceptual apparatus and analytic strategy of *Homo Academicus* would have to change to address the American case. It is a deeper matter to ask the reasons (not merely the "amorphous anecdotes of factual history") for the transformation of the medieval university through various stages into its modern namesake and successor.[68] As Bourdieu recognizes, "it is necessary to write a structural history which finds in each state of the structure both the product of previous struggles to transform or conserve the structure, and, through the contradictions, tensions and power relations that constitute that structure, the source of its subsequent transformations."[69]

Be that as it may, the specific sort of difference in transmission of culture addressed above is very important. It establishes, first of all, the basic grounding for addressing the question of what societies or modes of organizing social life are comparable for purposes of comparative research. And not least of all, it brings us back to the "modernity-postmodernity" debate.

On the one hand, Bourdieu's analyses of the relationship between habitus and field can be seen as adding crucial dimensions to Habermas's argument concerning the centrality of an uncoupling of system and lifeworld to the history of rationalization in the West.[70] At the same time, Bourdieu's analysis shows a weakness in Habermas's theory which results from Habermas's thoroughgoing rationalism and inattention to both the importance of practical mastery in any account of social action, and especially to the role of tradition transmitted informally as part of everyday strategic activity in accomplishing the coordination of social action and therefore in some cases societal integration.[71] My examination of Bourdieu's account also suggests that in order to mount more than a superficial claim to a "postmodern condition" (*pace* Lyotard),[72] one would need to show a basic change in the mode of coordinating action, and/or in the basic relational organization of fields, and the relation of habitus to fields.

This is a dimension precisely missing from most postmodernist accounts. That is, they address various changes in media, style, the shift from production-oriented capitalism to an advertising- and seduction-based consumerism, etc., but they do not address the empirical question of whether in fact social relations, most basically relations of power, are undergoing fundamental transformations – and whether these transformations affect more the systemic character of indirect relations or the quality and cognitive content of directly interpersonal relations. I read Bourdieu as arguing that they are in fact remarkably stable, but this is not the key point. Rather, the point is what would have to be shown in order to make a good case for a postmodernist transformation of society.

At the same time that Bourdieu's work points to these gaps in the modernist/postmodernist debate – and thus potentially to a more interesting direction for theoretical and empirical exploration – it can be seen to suffer from a weakness or gap of its own. This is (to condense a cluster of related matters) a very minimal level of attention to the actual workings of the self-regulating systems of modern, large-scale societies, and more generally what I have called indirect social relations – those mediated by information technology (communications, especially, but also other computer applications and surveillance) and complex administrative organizations as well as by markets and other self regulating systems. Bourdieu has made profound contributions to our understanding of the relationship of embodied, prelinguistic, or nondiscursive knowledge to social action. His concepts of habitus and field direct our attention to crucial phenomena. But his other most distinctive notion, that of capital as multiform – social, cultural, economic, and symbolic – grasps only an aspect of capitalism. It grasps primarily that which is distributive and/or central to relations of power. It does not grasp equally the sense in which capital itself – on an alternative reading of Marx (such as that of Lukacs or Postone)[73] – is a form of mediation. Bourdieu tends to reduce capital to power, or a complex notion of wealth defined as resources for power, quite in contradiction to Marx's argument.[74] More generally, Bourdieu's work so far includes an insufficient attention to the nature of mediation, the constitution of actors – and their complexly varying identities – and the modes of coordinating action in contemporary large and complex societies. This is not a severe criticism, for Bourdieu's theory is not closed to this; rather, it seems to me simply an important direction for our attention to turn. The roles of information technology, very large-scale administrative organizations, and impersonal markets all are important both in their own rights, and as factors militating for basic changes in habitus and fields. Such basic changes can have an enormous impact on the capacity for linking critical discourse to radical political action, as the next chapter explores, without amounting to a transcendence of modernity. Bourdieu's theory gives us a basis for linking the constitution of social relations on very large and relatively small scales, and for seeing both as produced and reproduced in practical action rather than only seen by distanced analysts from abstracted standpoints. This offers a possibility of escaping from the duality of critique founded solely on quasi-universal or essentialized standpoints and a radically relativizing politics of identity, the themes of the following chapters.

Notes

1   In this connection, Foucault is closer to Bourdieu than to Derrida, Lyotard, or Habermas.
2   See chapter 3 above.
3   "Vive la crise!," and, in a similar vein, Bourdieu and Passeron, "Sociology and Philosophy."
4   One important difference is that Bourdieu's involvement with structuralism came primarily through the work and teaching of Claude Lévi-Strauss, had little to do with Lacan, and never drew him into the once popular camp of Althusserian marxism.
5   Bourdieu, *Political Ontology of Martin Heidegger*.
6   In Wacquant, "Toward a Reflexive Sociology," p. 35. Bourdieu here is specifically criticizing recent trends in anthropology (e.g. Clifford and Marcus, *Writing Culture*) and the sociology of science (e.g. Latour, *Science in Action*).
7   My account of Habermas's theory here applies primarily to his work from the mid-1960s to the present, and especially to his theory of communicative action and his discourse ethics (Habermas, *Theory of Communicative Action, Philosophical Discourse of Modernity*).
8   See Habermas, *Philosophical Discourse of Modernity*, for a suggestion of how central a goal this is for his project even though his approach to it remains very abstract. See also Wacquant, "Toward a Reflexive Sociology" (p. 37), and, more generally, Bourdieu and Wacquant, *Invitation*.
9   In Wacquant, "Toward a Reflexive Sociology," p. 50. More generally, Bourdieu has sharply rejected the intellectual totalism he associates with the Frankfurt School, with Sartre, and to some extent with marxism generally. "Never before, perhaps, has there been so complete a manifestation of the logic peculiar to the French intellectual field that requires every intellectual to pronouce himself totally on each and every problem" ("Sociology and Philosophy in France," p. 174; see also the preface to *Logic*; "Vive la Crise!"; Bourdieu and Wacquant, *Invitation*). Bourdieu sees this as a feature not only of marxism but of an intellectual field in which marxism occupies a central place, obliging every intellectual to declare and explain his or her adherence or nonadherence.
10 On fields see Bourdieu, *Logic*; *Distinction*, pp. 113–20; *Homo Academicus*; "Force of Law."

11 Even capital becomes, for Bourdieu, a matter primarily of power ("Forms of Capital," p. 252).

12 Habermas, "Morality and Ethical Life." Habermas's treatment of difference remains thin even in recent works that try to explore it more seriously in relation to the politics of immigration and European integration and to Taylor's development of a politics of recognition; see "Citizenship and National Identity" and "Struggles for Recognition."

13 Bourdieu, *Distinction*, p. 113; all emphases in quotations are original.

14 "It follows that the form taken by the structure of systems of religious practices and beliefs at a given moment in time (historical religion) can be far from the original content of the message and it can be completely understood only in reference to the complete structure of the relations of production, reproduction, circulation, and appropriation of the message and to the history of this structure" (Bourdieu, "Genesis and Structure," p. 18). Bourdieu goes on to stress the centrality of struggles for the monopoly of religious capital, including both struggles between clergy and laity, and those between priestly authorities and heretical, quasi-religious or other challengers. "Genesis and Structure of the Religious Field" has not been widely enough recognized as Bourdieu's key, seminal text on fields. There he shows clearly what he means by going beyond the "pure" study of meaning and interaction to study the underlying relations of struggle which produce and shape meanings and interactions and constitute their frame. The approach to religion expounded there anticipates that he has more recently begun to develop towards the state (cf. Bourdieu, "La noblesse d'Etat").

15 As, e.g., in his study of kinship and matrimonial strategies in his own village in Béarne (Bourdieu, *Logic*, pp. 249–70). Bourdieu's account revealed many commonalities with what he had seen in Kabylia and in general showed that his approach could yield insights as readily into either setting. On the other hand, it did not address certain basic issues of difference between the settings – e.g. the fact that kinship is more central to the constitution of Kabyle society than to France, where it is central primarily to a compartmentalized local field, but not to the state or economy in general.

16 Wacquant, "Toward a Reflexive Sociology," p. 36.

17 Bourdieu, "Forms of Capital," p. 241.

18 Ibid., p. 253.

19 Bourdieu, *Outline*.

20 The issue is somewhat clouded because Bourdieu developed his tools as part of his continuing engagement with concrete analytic problems, and so we cannot be sure when to treat a conceptual or analytic shift as having to do with a change in case (from his earlier work in Kabylia to his more recent work in France) and when with an intention to reformulate more generally. Thus, for example, the concept of field plays little role in the *Outline of a Theory of Practice*, a substantial role in the *Logic of Practice*, and a central role in Bourdieu's recent writings on French academic institutions and professions (*Distinction*, "Force of Law," *La noblesse*). Is this simply theoretical advance, or a result of reflection on a different sort of society?

21 This is evident not only in *Capital*, but especially in the *Grundrisse*, where the direction of Marx's thinking is sometimes clearer because its processes are more transparently laid out. See the forceful argument for this reading of Marx in Postone, *Time, Labor*.

22 Bourdieu, "Forms of Capital," p. 252; "What Makes a Social Class?," p. 4.

23 Bourdieu, *Distinction*.

24 Bourdieu, "What Makes a Social Class?", pp. 3–4.

25 Bourdieu, "Forms of Capital," p. 243.

26 Ibid., p. 253. Bourdieu's argument is that children gain from the added nurturance they receive from mothers who stay at home with them, something that only mothers in relatively well off families can do. This illustrates the point well, though it is both empirically uncertain and arguably reflects sexist assumptions in not considering other relationships of parental gender to nurturance.

27 Ibid., p. 246.

28 Bourdieu, *In Other Words*, p. 42, and in Wacquant, "Toward a Reflexive Sociology," p. 37.

29 This is largely true of Habermas as well, at least in his mature, largely evolutionary, theory of communicative action.

30 See Wacquant, "Toward a Reflexive Sociology," p. 4. Bourdieu's arguments on the genesis of this notion of a pure aesthetics and its consequences for the analysis of culture are themselves important; see Bourdieu, "The Production of Belief," "The Historical Genesis."

31 Wacquant, "Toward a Reflexive Sociology," pp. 41–2.

32 Bourdieu suggests, indeed, that "far from being the founding model, economic theory (and rational action theory which is its sociological derivative) is probably best seen as a particular instance, historically dated and situated, of field theory" (in Wacquant, "Toward a Reflexive Sociology," p. 42). See also discussion in Wacquant and Calhoun, "Intérêt."

33 Bourdieu, *In Other Words*, p. 46, and Bourdieu and Wacquant, *Invitation to Reflexive Sociology*.

34 Bourdieu, *In Other Words*, p. 193.

35 Ibid., pp. 9–17, 34, 46.

36 Bourdieu, *Outline*, p. 79.

37 Ibid., p. 17.

38 On the relationship of Bourdieu's account of the workings of the habitus to Wittgenstein's consideration of what it means to follow a rule, see Taylor, "To Follow a Rule."

39 Bourdieu "Genesis and Structure of the Religious Field" is a partial exception to this, making a point of historically different levels of codification or systematization of religion. The promulgation of increasingly codified religious systems is a product of specific groups – generally priests or clergy – struggling to institutionalize their dominance in the religious field. Simultaneously, such systematization furthers the autonomy of the religious field.

40 Bourdieu, *Outline*, p. 73.

41 Bourdieu, *In Other Words*, p. 190.

42 "Habitus" is a term of art for Bourdieu, but we should not exaggerate its idiosyncrasies. There is some danger that, as happened with Freud's concepts of the "it" and the "I" – rendered impressive and theoretically esoteric and loaded in English translation as the "id" and the "ego" – Bourdieu's notion of the habitus will be disconnected by its nontranslation into English from its prior usages in Latin, French, and German. Weber spoke of the *"aussren habitus"* to describe the physical comportment treated as a signal of ethnicity; Norbert Elias used the term in ways broadly similar to Bourdieu.

43 Bourdieu, *Outline*, p. 115.

44 Ibid.

45 Ibid., p. 73.

46 Ibid., p. 4.

47 Bourdieu, *Distinction*, pp. 483–4. Note, by contrast, Lyotard's unwillingness to see the issue of knowledge as a matter of socially organized, individual and collective *struggles*. Instead, they are so many moves in a potentially infinite series of language games, shaped to be sure by the will to power but not systematically by social life.

48 See e.g. Garnham and Williams, "Pierre Bourdieu and the Sociology of Culture."

49 Bourdieu, *Outline*, pp. 82–3.

50 Ibid. See Calhoun, "The Radicalism of Tradition," for an attempt to develop a systematic empirical approach to the role of this grounding of radicalism in a pre-existing habitus.

51 Bourdieu, *Outline*, p. 189.

52 Ibid., pp. 189–90.

53 Calhoun, "Indirect Relationships and Imagined Communities."

54 And alongside the concept of field, that of multiform (social, symbolic, and cultural as well as economic) and convertible capital. "The structure of a field is a *state* of balanced forces (*rapport de force*) between agents and institutions engaged in a war, or, if one prefers, it is a distribution of the specific capital which, accumulated in the course of previous wars, orients future strategies" (Bourdieu, *Distinction*, p. 114; see also "Forms of Capital").

55 In discussion at the conference where this chapter was first presented, Bourdieu accepted and reiterated the importance of proliferation of fields for describing "complex" societies, by contrast to societies in which the division into fields is minimal.

56 Gluckman, "Les rites de passage."

57 This is the sort of "long-term history" which Bourdieu derides as "one of the privileged places of social philosophy" (Bourdieu, *In Other Words*, p. 42). But, in the same paragraph, Bourdieu sets himself "the problem of the modern artist or intellectual," a problem intrinsically framed by reference to long-term history. So it is hard to escape broad historical schemas, like Weber's, even when one correctly notes the weakness of their empirical foundations, or their susceptibility to overgeneralization.

58   Among the many sources on this, see sepecially Schluchter, *The Rise of Western Rationalism*.

59   Weber, *Economy and Society*, p. 36.

60   See Shils, *Tradition*, and Arendt, *Between Past and Future*, ch 3.

61   Bourdieu, *Outline*, p. 83.

62   Bourdieu, *Logic*, pp. 333–4. Bourdieu suggests that codification renders things simple, clear, and communicable (Bourdieu, *In other Words*, p. 101). This seems sound, although he does not consider (at least to my knowledge) the possible counterbalancing aspect, the extent to which codification (alongside writing) allows for a dramatic increase in information flow and accordingly in overall complexity, even if the bits are simple.

63   This is another way of conceptualizing what Habermas gets at through the notion of colonization of the lifeworld. It is also a recurrent theme for Lasch (e.g. *True and Only Heaven*) and other socio-cultural critics.

64   See chapter 8 below.

65   Bourdieu, *Outline, Logic*.

66   This follows on Durkheim's suggestion (in *The Division of Labor in Society*) that once people begin to think of their religion as one among many, it can never have quite the same hold on them. This suggestion would seem to pertain, however, only with regard to religions that are to some extent detached from the immediate "primordial" traditions of a people. It is not problematic in the same way for Tallensi in Northern Ghana to know that their neighbors do not share in worship of the Namoos or Talis shrines, or for Nuer to know that the *kwoth* they revere is a specifically Nuer concept. Durkheim made an unwarranted leap, moreover, to assume that the recognition of heterodoxy within social fields would produce a linear trend of secularization.

67   The notion is much like that of Simmel's ("The Metropolis and Mental Life," *Conflict and the Web of Group Affiliations*) account of individuality as deriving from distinctiveness in social networks, specific intersections of social circles.

68   Bourdieu, *In Other Words*, p. 46.

69   Ibid., p. 42.

70   I have argued elsewhere (Calhoun, "Classical Social Theory" and "Infrastructure") that Habermas's is a flawed conceptualization of a fundamentally important change.

71   I think Bourdieu would also have a good deal of trouble with Habermas's discourse ethics. In the first place, there is Habermas's attempt to work through a notion of communication devoid of interested action. Bourdieu would presumably reject this, even as a regulative ideal. "Every exchange contains a more or less dissimulated challenge, and the logic of challenge and riposte is but the limit towards which every act of communication tends. . . . To reduce to the function of communication . . . phenomena such as the dialectic of challenge and riposte and, more generally, the exchange of gifts, words, or women, is to ignore the structural ambivalence which predisposes them to fulfill a political function of domination in and through

performance of the communication function" (Bourdieu, *Outline*, p. 14). Even in the realm of "universal norms," Bourdieu wants to ask "who has an interest in the universal," and to see the history of reason as inescapably interested, like all other history (Bourdieu, *In Other Words*, pp. 31–2). See also discussion in Wacquant, "Toward a Reflexive Sociology," e.g. p. 50.

72 Lyotard, *Postmodern Condition*.
73 Lukacs, *History and Class Consciousness*; Postone, *Time, Labor*.
74 E.g. Bourdieu, "The Field of Cultural Production," "Social Space and the Genesis of Groups," "Forms of Capital."

6

The Standpoint of Critique?
Feminist Theory, Social Structure,
and Learning from Experience

I

The great Enlightenment thinkers, including French philosophes, German professors, and British and American political essayists, praised universalism as one of the premier intellectual virtues. The apparent alternatives, partiality and inconsistency, seemed to have relatively little to commend them. But the enlighteners did not claim to have achieved perfect universalism; they claimed, rather, to move in that direction. This was the direction of progress.

Progress towards a more universal truth, or a more universalistic ethics or political practice or artistic judgment, meant the continual overcoming of partiality. The universalistic project was, accordingly, an inherently critical project. It not only offered warrant to innumerable charges of partiality against less enlightened intellectual or political positions, it made partiality seem inherently wrong, or at least less noble. Within this logic of increasing universality, how could one say with pride that one was partial? Similarly, the pursuit of universality was linked closely to the critique of inconsistency. One of the problems with failing to take a universal view of any practical problem was that one was likely to be caught in an inconsistency, like a thief who wants to use the right of property to claim what he has stolen.

Much critical thought has simply assumed universalist values as part of its background, and focused on ferreting out partiality and inconsistency. That is, it did not seek to find the universal in a positive sense, but to bring progress by challenging the blatantly nonuniversal. Those who did try to think through more deeply what the universal meant commonly distinguished (not always using these words) between generality and universality.[1] This is what is at stake in Rousseau's distinction of the general will – singular, indivisible and universally right – from even the will of all with its contingency, let alone the greater or lesser consensus of mere majorities.[2] Kant saw generality, likewise, primarily in terms of empirical and thus contingent phenomena – as for example agreement about the beauty of a particular painting or flower might be more or less general. But the actual beauty of either painting or flower did not inhere in that agreement; those who praised them by saying "this is a beautiful painting" or "what a beautiful flower" did not mean that many others asserted similar tastes or experienced agreeable sensations in the museum or the garden. They meant that the painting or the flower *was* beautiful, that this judgment was universal.[3] Even more sharply, there could be no confusing the universal truths of transcendental deductions with mere empirical observations, and so understanding was more than just knowledge, precisely because its basis was more universal. The famous categorical imperative was an injunction to act in the most completely universalizable way possible.

It is in this line of more confident attempts to discern the universal as a positive location that what we now know as "standpoint theory" has its origins. It has developed in two lineages that we can recount fairly simply (though in fact they are so complexly intertwined that probing deeply into their intellectual histories would not be so simple). At the apex of both lineages stands the critique rooted, as for Kant and much of the humanistic enlightenment, in a conception of universal man, who has "a *broadened way of thinking* if he overrides the private subjective conditions of his judgment, into which so many others are locked, as it were, and reflects on his own judgment from a *universal standpoint* (which he can determine only by transferring himself to the standpoint of others)."[4] Following Kant, there was a series of demonstrations that different versions of this claimed standpoint were in fact false universals.

One direction of critique developed the standpoint emphasis by focusing on the hidden privilege accorded certain socially constructed identities in forming the relevant conception of universal man. Thus Marx sought to show that the man taken as universal by the philosophers of individual rights was only bourgeois man, man as citizen, but not man as worker.[5] It was with this in mind that Marx began to articulate the standpoint of the proletariat which he thought offered a kind of scientific and political universality – and thus certainty – that had been lacking in earlier theory. The echoes of Rousseau and Kant are clear when Marx writes that "it is not a question of what this or that proletarian, or even the whole proletariat, at the moment regards as its aim. It is a question of what the proletariat is, and what, in accordance with this being, it will historically be compelled to do."[6] Lukacs was even more Kantian when he developed his analysis of the history of modern philosophy and science as a history of partial knowledge that would be completed only by taking the truly universal standpoint of the proletariat as the origin point of knowledge.[7]

One feature of Marx's and Lukacs' proletariat was that though it was putatively all-encompassing it seemed in fact to be primarily male. Like the category of citizen before it, it was a false universal, in this case a putatively genderless term that in fact hid the gender bias of its construction. An important part of the early socialist-feminist project was to overcome this partiality in order that a truer universal standpoint might be discovered (or produced). In this sense, the path from Enlightenment humanism through marxism to at least one strand of feminism retained the critical focus on the universal. Indeed, in each instance what was sought was a universal, transhistorical, self-moving subject-object: man, class, or gender-neutral person.[8] The idea of standpoint was the epistemological counterpart to this search for the self-moving subject-object, for only from the standpoint of such a subject-object could there be truly universal knowledge.

The second lineage of standpoint theory descended from Kant through Hegel. Marx is as much a part of this lineage as the first. Hegel challenged the ahistorical character of Kant's position, suggesting that it was not in human nature or any other such transhistorical notion of humanity that a universal standpoint could be found but rather in the culmination of dialectical human development, the perspective of realized potential, standing at the edge of history. The course of history, moreover, was not for Hegel one of simple linear progress in knowledge any more than in anything else. The key text is his famous dialogue of master and slave.[9] To oversimplify, Hegel suggested that while the master's standpoint offered an illusory autonomy, it was in fact both distorted and dependent on the recognition of the slave. Hegel sought the standpoint of history and social totality. In pursuit of the same value of universality, the Left Young Hegelians argued that a greater perspicacity – though not quite an objectivity – was offered by the standpoint of the oppressed subordinate. Thus the proletariat was not just more inclusive a class than the bourgeoisie, it was given a special claim to universality by the very nature of its chains, especially in the context of Marx's expected class polarization. Since Marx, a variety of other theories have taken up Hegel's dialectic of master and slave in a similar radical spirit (though not always with equally confident expectations of revolutionary resolution). The prominent wave of "subaltern" studies shows the influence of both other ideas rooted in Indian experience and tradition and a broader marxist influence, but is also a theory that places the Hegelian version of standpoint at its center.[10] It is in feminist theory that this version of standpoint theory has become most developed.

Along the way, however, especially in the course of the development of feminist theory, the search for a universal standpoint began to be challenged. First, a variety of thinkers began to wonder if particularism was always so bad as it was assumed to be when viewed as the alternative to universalism. In some sorts of public activities, thus, like voting, one might want a high level of universalism as in rules of equal enfranchisement. But what about other realms of life. Would society really work very well if we loved all others equally? What if parents loved all children equally and drew from that the conclusion that they had no special responsibility for or to their own? This is, in a sense, a consequentialist argument that while universalism might have a place, it ought not to be a trump card in all social decisions. This argument has, I think, considerable force against certain varieties of popular liberal thought which invoke universalism in such a way as to reflect commodification and the market in a logic of universal equivalences. But it may not be a terribly deep problem for Kantian theory – one can follow the (universalistic) categorical imperative quite nicely in willing that all parents should feel a special responsibility towards their children – and thus may not point at the most basic reasons why universalism has become a term of abuse in so many theoretical circles after being a term of obvious approbation for centuries.

The second and more basic argument had to do with the relationship of epistemological standpoint to experience. Perhaps, suggested some feminists, the gulf between male and female standpoints was simply unbridgeable, the difference incommensurable.[11] Increasingly, the term standpoint came to denote not the search for a standpoint capable of offering universal understanding, knowledge, or guidance for action, but recognition of the divergence of standpoints rooted in different experiences. The Kantian approach to knowledge attempted to abstract from what was different in the particularities of human experience. Many post- and/or anti-Kantian philosophies have tried to ground themselves in experience. Among other things, they seek to overcome what they regard as a distancing from life and an excessive rationalism in the Kantian position (and many others). And one of the crucial features of the life that is affirmed is its plurality, its intractable difference.

There is a catch. To claim a standpoint is not the same as simply to celebrate difference. In particular, where the standpoint is putatively that of a collectivity, the claim involves a strong assertion that the members of the collectivity are as one – like the members of Marx's or Lukacs' proletariat or the participants in Rousseau's general will. To base this claim on what is shared in experience is to court refutation from an infinitely ramifying range of experiences. It is also to focus attention on what is held to be the source of the common experience constructive of the new epistemic standpoint – shared oppression, for example, or the same kinds of bodies. In the next chapter, I shall turn to the opposition of essentialism and constructivism in which arguments about such similarities and the differences that cross-cut them are played out. Is the claimed standpoint of women really the standpoint of middle-class white women, for example? This is a critique that directly extends the first lineage of standpoint critiques of false universals.

Somewhat more novel, however, is the further branching in the standpoint family tree that produces the argument that it is meaningless (or at least problematic) to give priority to any particular standpoint. Does not human life admit of – indeed necessarily produce – innumerable standpoints? Here there is a sort of culmination – and dialectical transformation – of the second, Hegelian, standpoint lineage. "Perhaps 'reality' can have 'a' structure only from the falsely universalizing perspective of the master. That is, only to the extent that one person or group can dominate the whole, can 'reality' appear to be governed by one set of rules or be constituted by one privileged set of social relations."[12] To avoid the domination, suggests this postmodernist-influenced line of argument, it is necessary to forego the attempt at universalization. And this strikes, moreover, even at such partial universalizations as *the* standpoint of women (or of African-Americans, or gay men, or lesbians).

II

The starting point of feminist standpoint theory is the observation that "women's different lives have been erroneously devalued and neglected as starting points for scientific research and as the generators of evidence for and against knowledge claims."[13] A number of feminist researchers have drawn attention to the extent to which both natural and social science were not only predominantly male ventures but also failed to see that which became evident when women's lives were taken as a starting point and nonetheless presented themselves as gender-neutral. The idea of a feminist or women's standpoint theory has been a vehicle for both theorizing and overcoming this situation. Perhaps its most important pioneer has been the Canadian sociologist Dorothy Smith.

Smith has argued for and worked to develop a sociology "from the standpoint of women" and a "sociology for women." Women's standpoint offers Smith a starting point mainly because there is "a disjunction between how women experience the world and the concepts and theoretical schemes by which society's self-consciousness is inscribed."[14] From such a starting point, feminist sociology can not only add new information – e.g. making gender a variable in research designs that previously studied only men – but also reveal aspects of social organization that tended to remain hidden by the reproduction of the standpoint of men as though it were gender-free and universal. Women's experience could challenge such reifications both when women became sociologists and when sociologists studied women's lives (and of course these two conditions were generally met simultaneously).

The constitution of public life and the discourses of power and economic systems as male in both their predominant membership and their operational character was won at the expense of (1) alienating men and therefore the discourse to which they were central from the realm of immediate, local, embodied experience, and (2) constituting as women's work not only the maintenance of this predominantly "domestic" realm but its articulation with the ruling apparatus. As Smith puts it, "In the social division of labor the work of articulating the local and particular existence of actors to the abstracted conceptual mode of ruling is done typically by women. The abstracted conceptual mode of ruling exists in and depends upon a world known immediately and directly in the bodily mode."[15] A sociology from the standpoint of women thus brought into play a bifurcated consciousness that could fully recognize the split between the impersonal discourse of power and the personal realm of concrete relations. The tensions in women's lives became the basis for recognizing an aspect of social ontology obscured by the privileged but still alienated constitution of men's lives and discourse.

One problem, of course, is how to build on this recognition of historically constituted differences in typical male and female social positions without either introducing an ontological essentialism into gender identities or reproducing a troubling public/private dichotomy within feminist thought. It seems, for example, more accurate to suggest that rather than simply women and men there are a host of cross-cutting differentiations that make it hard to grasp gender categories in anything like a pure form. It is far from obvious that female gender has similar meanings for African-Americans and white Americans, thus, let alone for members of various different classes, ethnic groups, nations, or religions within Africa, say, or Asia. Likewise, there are a number of only partially overlapping regimes of power, a number of partially overlapping publics, and no single realm of directly "local and particular existence" or inter-personal relations but rather many.[16] In fact, in order to grasp the distinctive place of women in making it possible for men to undertake their labors of abstraction and domination (by caring for them and their children), we have to abstract from the particularities of women's specific, immediate situations and experiences not simply have recourse to them. The very construction of a women's standpoint, thus, not only relies on the distinctive experience of women but on the creation of an abstract category of women that is not given by that experience but by theory.

Indeed, Smith saw that in order to establish and develop a feminist standpoint, she needed to go beyond mere reference to particular women or even women as a class; it was not enough that more and more women spoke or that some women spoke on behalf of all women. Smith's insight – along with several others – was that a feminist sociology needed women's speech not just to be the voice of the "other," but of the other speaking from within the immediacy of social life, from the center, rather than from some Archimedian point outside social life and not in the voice characteristic of archetypally male omniscient narrators. In order to achieve this insight, however, Smith had to develop a substantive analysis of the bifurcation of discourse and experience, ruling apparatus, and everyday life. This appears in her work largely as a necessary precondi-tion to the feminist sociology of knowledge; it is accordingly not devel-oped in as much detail as it might be. What is developed in detail is Smith's methodological argument about conducting research in which the researcher does not operate as authority or agent of bureaucratic power, but rather as participant in a dialogue of equals with those who possess from the experience of their own lives knowledge to which the sociologist wants access. I will return to this methodological argument later, because I think it holds the seeds of a different and more satisfac-tory theory of how all sorts of voices might inform our understanding than that of substantive standpoint theory. I want to focus first on this substantive theoretical project, however, as I think the questions it raises are not only of intrinsic interest, but of particular importance for criti-cal theory insofar as it aims to establish a place for potentially transformative human agency.

III

Although Smith sees her account of a women's standpoint as grounded in ontology, hers is not a simple biological essentialism, a recourse to the notion that "woman" is a transparently given category. At least in principle, Smith seeks a historically specific account of the construction of gender and the exclusion of women from many discourses of power in the modern world. The historical construction of gender is more Smith's premise than her project, and is addressed more by others and still with much debate, but since gender essentialisms still proliferate it is worth keeping in mind.[17] Much feminist theory has relied on a relatively transhistorical account of male power, sexist practices, and androcentric thought.

Smith's historical account draws on Marx to identify the historically specific production of putatively neutral, impersonal, autonomous, and systemic realms that in fact exclude women and obscure the role of powerful agents in their own creation and continued operation. She is concerned to develop a critique of the "gender organization of the apparently neutral and impersonal rationality of the ruling apparatus."[18] This sort of understanding is most easily illustrated, perhaps, in the case of the economy.

It is not simply a general pattern of male bias that leads to the devaluation of women's work in modern society. Rather, it is also (1) the constitution of "the economy" as though it were not a realm of human action but of abstract systematicity, and (2) specifically the reliance on a universalized category of labor tied to the capitalist commodity form. It is this distinctively modern construction that defines most of women's lives out of public realms and the attention of sociologists, as for example it defines women's work in the home as not really labor. Many versions of marxism have had a hard time recognizing this adequately because they are based on taking a transhistorical concept of labor as the basis for the marxist critique of capitalism. But as Moishe Postone has shown, and as Smith herself hints, this is not necessarily the best reading of Marx's position.[19]

In his mature work, Marx can be seen as using the category of labor to denote the historically specific process by which the products of human productive activity come to appear as external forces acting on humans. On this view, labor is a kind of social mediation; it is a process whereby indirect social relations are formed that are not and cannot be recognized from within the system as social relations, and that involve agency. Since labor in capitalism takes the form not of work in general but of incorporation into this system of abstract mediation, the sequestering of much work of social reproduction – such as child rearing – in the home and in the realm of women excludes it from the economy as an apparently self-moving, impersonal phenomenon. A partially, but not completely similar, process is at work in realms of administrative organization. This helps to explain why women and issues of reproduction have so commonly been invisible to social (including economic) theories developed to attend to the "important," public realms of life.

The counterpart to the invisibility of women and certain practices associated with women within much social theory and much public life is a bifurcated consciousness among women. That is, women both learn the established culture and develop a consciousness that problematizes it on the basis of their own experiences (recall DuBois and "double consciousness"). Men's experiences are more likely to be congruent with the dominant story (or theories) and so less likely to be the source of problematization. Of course these tendencies are not perfect correlations. One important line of critique starts by asking "which women?" and "which men?" noting that some women's lives are relatively privileged and some men's lives are very much at odds with the dominant order and theories. I want to put this aside for the time being (it receives more attention in the next chapter) in order to focus on the question of just what is involved in grounding understanding in experience and/or standpoint.

The awkward "and/or" in the previous sentence should be a clue that a conceptual ambiguity is involved. This is particularly clear in the work of Sandra Harding (and results among other things in shifts in her account of Dorothy Smith's work). Here is Harding in 1986 summarizing Smith (with approval): "we should regard women's subjugated experience as starting and ending points for inquiry that are epistemologically preferable to men's experience."[20] Here is Harding in 1990 (with Smith again explicitly included as an exemplary standpoint theorist):

> standpoint theorists are not claiming some kind of transhistorical privilege for research that begins in women's lives. Nor, it is worth recollecting, are they arguing that women's biology, women's intuition, what women say, or women's experiences provide grounds for knowledge. What women say and what women experience do provide important clues for research designs and results, but it is the objective perspective *from women's lives* that gives legitimacy to feminist knowledge, according to standpoint theorists.[21]

Now to be sure, Harding knows that there is some tension between her 1986 and 1990 books. She describes this as due to the recognition that in her earlier work she shared with many standpoint theorists a tendency to essentialism that she contests in the later book.[22] In the later book, Harding sets out to demonstrate a "rapprochement" between standpoint and postmodernist theories, and to respond to various perceived problems with her own and others' articulations of standpoint theories. But by attempting to preserve the notion of standpoint theories while abandoning experience, she reflects rather than resolves a tension in the discourse.

The core idea of standpoint theory is that a determinate social structural position will create conditions for learning from experience that will be epistemologically privileged in producing certain sorts of knowledge. Standpoint theory is thus not equivalent to the general claim that certain orientations to knowledge are privileged. Many religious beliefs, for example, privilege knowledge based on personal revelation, sacred texts, or clerical authority. None of these is the same as a standpoint theory because none is based on the link between social structural position and learning from a determinate sort of experience.

On the one hand the idea of standpoint is rooted in the notion of concrete, experiencing subjects. On the other hand, the idea of standpoint employs a categorial logic to analyze positions in social structure. These are both crucial moments, for standpoint theories suggest a partial overcoming of the materialist/idealist antinomy. Thus Marx in the "Theses on Feuerbach" remarks on the "this-sidedness" of all knowledge. The social and material position of every knower (and by extension every culture, every generation, every class, and even every sort of scientifically trained researcher) makes some knowledge possible even while it inhibits or precludes other knowledge. We see what we see only from where we stand. But Marx also seeks escape from the limits of his immediate historical and social position by means of theory. Drawing especially on Hegel, he historicizes the Kantian problem of knowledge, and locates the standpoint of a more universal knowledge in a universal class which only appears in that dusk at which the owl of Minerva famously flies. What makes the proletariat universal is its categorial place in history, and in the totality formed by capitalist commodification of labor. But what leads the members of the proletariat to knowledge and practice reflecting this universality is their concrete and simultaneous experience of both exploitation and the social organization of production.

So too with feminist standpoint(s). Dorothy Smith seeks to bring out two themes. First, there is the idea of women as the (or a) category excluded by the way in which the apparatus of rule and the dominant discourse are constituted (in invisibly gendered terms). The female gender (women as a class but not so clearly as concrete individuals) takes on an epistemologically privileged status by virtue of its position within the societal organization constituted by a particular apparatus of rule. Second, there is the notion of women as concrete actors. This is a standpoint distinctively available to women because of their accustomed involvement with "everyday lifeworlds" of social relationships, childrearing, etc. and because of their distinctive importance in the work of cementing social relationships in such a way that they can be taken as given by the mostly male participants in the ruling apparatus. In this second sense, it is the experience of these concretely situated women that can be expected to lead them to deeper knowledge (perhaps with the aid of vanguard feminist sociologists).

In Smith's work as in Marx's, then, the question becomes one of how to reconcile the categorial claims with the notion of learning from experience. What leads the class in itself to adopt the standpoint of the class for itself? Smith rejects, rightly I think, the notion that we can get a good sense of the standpoint of women as the perspective of all women; it is no more a simple summation of women's experience than is the general will equivalent to the will of all for Rousseau. But at least implicitly Smith is nonetheless interested in appeal to a standpoint of concrete actors, not only to a category of the excluded. What Harding sees in her second book, then, is the difficulty of moving from unmediated experience to anything that counts as an objective or universal standpoint:

> Some thinkers have assumed that standpoint theories and other kinds of justifications of feminist knowledge claims must be grounded in women's *experiences*. The terms "women's standpoint" and "women's perspective" are often used interchangeably, and "women's perspective" suggests the actual perspective of actual women – what they can in fact see. But it cannot be that women's experiences in themselves or the things women say provide reliable grounds for knowledge claims about nature and social relations. After all, experience itself is shaped by social relations: for example, women have had to *learn* to define as rape those sexual assaults that occur within marriage. . . .
>
> For a position to count as a standpoint, rather than as a claim – equally valuable but for different reasons – for the importance of listening to women tell us about their lives and experiences, we must insist on an objective location – women's lives – as the place from which feminist research should begin.[23]

It is easy to see why, drawing from a more developed reading of postmodernist writings, Flax suggests that "the notion that there is *a* feminist viewpoint that is more true and not just different from previous male ones seems to rest upon many assumptions uncritically appropriated from and dependent upon Enlightenment thinking."[24] But I am not interested simply in Harding's unacknowledged reliance on now unfashionable Enlightenment thinking. The real point is the tension left unresolved between the immediacy and critical potential of experiences that are discordant with hegemonic cultures and the need for some source of shared understanding.

IV

The issue of shared understanding has been loaded with double freight in most modern discourse. It reflects both the search for certainty and the search for commonality. For the most part, the early modern approach was to try to establish the truth with maximal certainty, and then to expect rational people to acknowledge it and therefore share it. The emphasis at the outset, therefore, was on establishing the right understanding; sharing itself was not seen as deeply problematic. Indeed, sharing might easily occur for the wrong reasons (the mere persuasion that gave the word rhetoric a bad name) without the necessary foundation in truth.[25] As various problems developed for the pursuit of certainty and objectivity, the issue of sharing moved to center stage. Both political contests and social movements within seemingly common cultures, and difficulties of achieving cross-cultural understanding made sharing understanding seem increasingly difficult in and of itself. Indeed, so did a host of problems of "interpersonal communication" that arose especially in the spheres of intimate relations that proliferated and grew more emotionally loaded in the modern era.

Moderns tried in various ways to grasp how communication across lines of difference could work to restore confidence in mutual understanding and shared truth. In chapters 2 and 3, however, I argued that the most common metaphor, translation, is a problematic way to grasp cross-cultural understanding. The same goes for the notion that although simple translation cannot overcome deep differences the construction of metalanguages or metadiscourses can. Lyotard, for example, describes the "modernist" approach to incommensurable language games – e.g. deep cultural differences – as one of constructing a metadiscourse which appears as universal and neutral within which the competing claims can be adjudicated. The most powerful of these are the "master narratives" of philosophy and history. And his "postmodernist" argument is that this procedure is either specious or does violence to the contending "games" or both.[26] Indeed, both the translation and metadiscourse models are too static, too inattentive to the extent to which our mutual understandings are in fact constructed through processes of historical change, and too exclusively intellectualistic. But Lyotard's critical account in a sense shares all these faults; he does not have a grasp of the historical and practical processes by which people come to shared understandings without translations or metadiscourses; he simply reaches a different conclusion about the possibility of neutral metadiscourses.[27]

Looking at the character of practices rather than the character of subjects might help us address the linked problems of figuring out why we should have confidence in and share any particular "knowledge." Most standpoint theories share with Descartes and Kant an emphasis on the exploration of what it is possible or impossible for various sorts of subjects to know. They remain caught within foundational projects that seek to ground the accomplishments of modern scientific knowledge in some combination of empirical observation and rational deduction. These operations appear to depend on individual observers and deducers, and indeed on universal characteristics of generic observers and deducers who are relevantly distinguished perhaps by the level of their acuity but not the modality of their knowledge.

But let us ask whether this is an accurate representation even of the scientific revolution itself. Certainly the replacement of authority and tradition by reason and empirical observation as modes of validation of knowledge is a central part of the story of modern science and the Enlightenment more generally. In a sense, postmodernist critics contest this account from within when they argue that authority and tradition retain far greater roles than scientists' usual narratives about themselves allow. Even without postmodernists, we know from the history and sociology of science the extent to which various traditions (call them paradigms in some cases, but note also the influence of disciplines and national scientific cultures) shape the understanding scientists have of the problems before them and the possible ways of dealing with these. Science has ramified into so many branches that it is no longer conceivable (even if it was always a fantasy) for a single scientist to know everything relevant to his or her work on the basis of observation or rational deduction. Much is necessarily accepted on the authority of others and out of tradition. Contests over paradigms turn on power relations and the socially constructed relations of authority and communication among scientists.[28] But the contest in these accounts has to do with the extent to which the subject's (the scientist's) new capacities for observation and deduction supplanted "unenlightened" reliance on authority and tradition.[29] It underestimates another, crucial, aspect of modern science and the Enlightenment which perhaps can help us in the current problem.

The conventional narrative about science puts the experiment on center stage, but leaves in the wings the crucial matter of dialogue among scientists. That is, it conceptualizes the validation of knowledge in terms of the procedures of reason and observation that a paradigmatically individual scientist might use to produce knowledge. This knowledge is foundational because of the procedures by which it is produced and the characteristics of the subject who knows it. But wouldn't we grasp better the nature of the scientific revolution (and of the practice, though perhaps not the rhetoric, of contemporary science) by focusing on the nature of the public discourse among scientists by which putative new knowledge is subjected to the critical examination of a range of interrogations? Isn't the obligation to publish one's results honestly for peer analysis as fundamental as any methodological guideline for a scientist? What of the relations among teachers and students, collaborators in research projects, and colleagues in broader research programs? We need to refocus our attention away from the reification and hero-worship of the individual knower to recognize to collective practice by which knowledge is constituted and continually modified.

Obviously a variety of thinkers – not least of all Kant – have recognized that communicability is a key aspect of knowledge. One does not have to stretch Kant too far in a Habermasian direction to see the notion of universal communicability as an indication that knowledge would only be complete when all different (but clearly commensurable) standpoints were included in the conversation of knowledge.[30] Kant explicitly saw taking the standpoints of others – and ideally of everyone else – as the way to "escape the illusion that arises from the ease of mistaking subjective and private conditions for objective ones."[31] Equally, the example of the Socratic dialogues as well as the early modern proliferation of scientific societies, correspondences, and publications has alerted scholars to the importance of discourse among scientists. What is not so clearly recognized is that this dialogue – and I choose the term to emphasize that this is not just any sort of discourse but a specific sort which helped also to pioneer standards and practices for the political public sphere – has a bearing on the validity of scientific knowledge rather than just its encouragement, spread, or after-the-fact verification. We should not conceptualize the dialogue among scientists as simply an error-correction mechanism, or as a means of sharing that which is already known, but as one of the actual bases for knowledge.

This is not the place for me to pursue this as a general line of argument in either epistemology or the study of science. Rather, I want to draw three related implications of this "dialogical" view of science for the notion of standpoint.

The first implication is that the importance of the gendered production of knowledge need not be conceptualized primarily in terms of the foundational practices of observation and reason. Standpoint theorists get caught unnecessarily in a problematic foundationalism when they pursue arguments that a feminist standpoint must be legitimated as an objective source of universal truth. This makes claims hard to demonstrate both within typical rhetorics and understandings of science where the neutral (and perhaps neuter) observer and thinker is hypostatized *and* within the postmodernist debate over Enlightenment thinking where the feminist standpoint is prone to immediate deconstruction.

In order to understand the distinctive insights brought by women scientists (and male scientists taking nontraditional views of gender) it is important to recognize that they saw different things (e.g. in the study of reproduction and the relations between males and females in primate biology) without seeing them on a fundamentally different foundation of reason and observation. If the work of such researchers had depended completely on the alternative foundation of a women's standpoint, it is hard to see how it could have had the impact it has had in biology. But if there was enough shared basis in observation and reason for a meaningful conversation to ensue, then the epistemic gains of the new insights could be recognized even if the conversation was stilted and biased by male dominated hierarchies and hegemonic consciousnesses. This is, in fact, what Donna Haraway has shown.[32]

Recognizing the extent to which science is a collective enterprise pursued largely through discourse allows one to make sense of the extent to which women scientists have had their views shaped by male teachers and male-dominated understandings as well as the ways in which their work sometimes challenged or modified these. It allows one to see the importance not just of different foci (or even modes) of observation or reason, but of different situations in the conversation. At the same time, science is not just discourse, nor just empirical observation and rational deduction. It is a much more complex congeries of practices that make possible not only "epistemic activities" but the creation and alternation of institutions and concrete interpersonal relationships. These are not only sources of bias (whether to be eliminated in the conventional account or analyzed in the recent critical views); they are sources of common understandings. It is sometimes in the not altogether discursive practices of working together in the field or at the paradigmatic bench that scientists come to common understandings that only later they are able to express articulately.

A similar argument can be made for grounding feminist theory not in concrete women or the category of women but in dialogical feminist practices. Thus Mary Dietz, for example, argues that seeing the experience of women as the source of a categorically different feminist subjectivity introduces a problematic essentialism.[33] On the other hand, the feminist movement has developed a cluster of practices attentive to difference (and, we might add, to concrete experience). These may provide the setting for development of distinctively feminist knowledge, and it may be that dialogical setting that is crucial, not the standpoint of any singular subject position. On such a view, feminism could mark a more substantial break with the traditional understanding of science that locates the basis of knowledge in the characteristics or location of certain idealized subjects. We could extend this approach, without need for a specific standpoint theory, to include attention not only to the dialogic context of the women's movement but the whole range of practical projects which create interests in knowledge-formation for women (and for others).

In this connection, the crucial insights offered by Dorothy Smith's work lie not in the notion of a women's standpoint but in the methodological argument that researcher and research subject need to be seen as equals and enter into mutually informing dialogue. This conception of research (rather than the paradigmatic experiment with its ideal of control) is inherently intersubjective and also reflects the dialogical practices of the women's movement.[34] Its implications include, as Smith suggests, recognition of how the fact that observation constitutes a social relationship introduces change into what is observed (a phenomenon noted famously in other sciences but resisted in "positivistic" social science) and shapes what we learn from it.[35] This sort of feminist research actually challenges the notion of a singular objective standpoint that can be discovered "out there" by subjects constructed as ideal observers and reasoners.[36]

The second implication of the dialogical view of science for standpoint theory is that there is not necessarily a sharp and mutually exclusive opposition between taking seriously the notion of science as conversation and recognizing that reason and observation have a role to play in knowledge. The postmodernist "discovery" of discourse is often presented as though it proves the notion of truth based on foundational observation and deduction to be false, rather than as a qualification and relativization of such truth claims. To a large extent, the postmodernists (including in this case not only the French poststructuralists but Richard Rorty) see conversation as essentially arbitrary. Unlike his predecessors among American pragmatists, thus, Rorty suggests that we can only judge conversations to be more or less interesting, not claim practical consensus as a validation of knowledge. In the postmodern era, philosophers (and scientists) will be able only to "compare and contrast cultural traditions," not to claim epistemic gains.[37] Somewhat surprisingly for a self-declared pragmatist, however, such a view assumes that either knowledge-claims are grounded in the perspectiveless universal truth of reason and observation or they must be fundamentally incommensurable; it recognizes no history of concrete social practices that encourage mutual understanding and even epistemic gain.

Standpoint theorists are prone to accept the same sort of either/or opposition, and thus to feel a need to claim an implausible fixity (and even universality) for certain standpoints in order to avoid the trivialization of all standpoints in a postmodern welter of incommensurable points of view.[38] Yet this is at odds with one of the attractive features of many feminist standpoint theories, the attempt to introduce a critical self-reflexivity and historical self-consciousness into all scientific knowledge. As Harding puts it, "the sciences need to legitimate *within scientific research*, as part of practicing science, critical examination of historical values and interests that may be so shared within the scientific community, so invested in by the very constitution of this or that field of study, that they will not show up as a cultural bias between experimenters or between research communities."[39] And as Harding goes on to argue, this means identifying the social sources of good as well as bad beliefs, of knowledge as well as error.[40] A dialogic approach reminds us that these social conditions of scientific knowledge are built into the very project of science, they do not just come to it from outside. A feminist voice that reminds us of these social conditions is itself an interested voice within science, not a reversal of the interestedness of male-dominated science, and yet this does not imply that science must thereby cease seeking better knowledge because it admits to partiality and interest.

It is important for theorists who would help scientists to think from women's lives to see the stark opposition of subjective and objective as a trap (whichever side one favors). Consider, for example, how Harding incorporates the subjective/objective dichotomy into her own account, imagining that to accept a feminist standpoint as in any way subjective must be to admit wholesale relativism:

> The leading feminist theorists do not try to substitute one set of gender loyalties for the other – "women-centered" for "man-centered" hypotheses. They try instead, to arrive at hypotheses that are free of gender loyalties.[41]

Harding seems to be describing exactly the gender neutrality claimed (speciously) by conventional scientific mythology. Feminism must correct for androcentrism, but knowledge need not be gendered:

> It is true that first we often have to formulate a "woman-centered" hypothesis in order even to comprehend a gender-free one. But the goal of feminist knowledge-seeking is to achieve theories that accurately represent women's activities as fully social, and social relations between the genders as a real

– an explanatorily important – component in human history. There is nothing "subjective" about such a project, unless one thinks only visions distorted by gendered desires could imagine women to be fully social and gender relations to be real explanatory variables. From the perspective of feminist theory and research, it is *traditional* thought that is subjective in its distortion by androcentrism – a claim that feminists are willing to defend on traditional objectivist grounds.[42]

In order to maintain connections to "the real world," Harding feels she must defend objectivism and argue against the contention that knowledge is in significant part conditioned by the social situation of the subjective knower (and by implication, even the social organization of the scientific dialogue). In her subsequent book, she straightforwardly reverses this view, without abandoning the implied antinomy; her focus shifts to "the subject of feminist knowledge."[43] Yet if we take the dialogical view seriously, we need not face this stark choice, but should be able to see that our subjective situation in the dialogue is not incompatible with epistemic gain based on intersubjective understanding and verifiable research procedures. This is, I think, close to what Haraway suggests with the language of "situated knowledge" – which includes situation within both history generally and the specific history of science – rather than women's standpoint.[44]

The third implication of a dialogical view of science is that it is not necessary to resort to an ontological account of a women's standpoint to ground a critique of the exclusion from the scientific conversation of either women as concrete actors, or the knowledge-generating concerns raised by women's lives. Smith, in her opposition to postmodernist approaches, unfortunately reaffirms her reliance on ontology as the ground for truth claims.[45] This is of more than passing interest because it has, I think, an intellectual connection to her reliance on the notion of the standpoint of concrete experience, a reliance she shares with other feminists including those who would be hesitant to follow her attempt to ground it in ontology.[46] Smith proceeds in a way quite analogous to the marxian discovery of the "proletarian standpoint" that Lukacs saw as crucial to marxism's capacity to challenge the reification of ordinary social consciousness and theory.[47]

This very similarity suggests one of the reasons why some feminists closer to the postmodernist project have rejected Smith's approach as too close to the Enlightenment and marxist desires for a "true" theory; they prefer a rejection of all such claims to general truth in favor of the acknowledgment of an inescapable multiplicity of partial knowledges, contradictory discourses, and conflicting perspectives.[48] Some of these others, like Dietz, have tried to preserve the notion of a theoretical standpoint by locating it not in the ontological category of women, but in feminism as theoretical orientation or set of political practices.[49] In Harding's words, "having women's experiences – being a woman – clearly is not sufficient to generate feminist knowledge; all women have women's experiences, but only at certain historical moments do any of us ever produce feminist knowledge."[50] Rather than just women, the subjects who produce feminist knowledge are indefinitely many and varied. "The issue here is about the possibility of *feminist*, not female, science."[51] Donna Haraway goes much further, arguing against the idea of standpoint theory itself, suggesting that it incorporates the very presumption that women are all in crucial regards the same that was one of the most damaging products of the essentialist reasoning predominant since the Enlightenment.[52] For Smith, as she argues in a reply to Harding, "such a degree of ontological tolerance defeats the essential character of inquiry as a project."[53] She is well aware of the imperfections of the truths we humans can claim, and of their imbrications in power relations, but she crucially affirms the practical importance of adhering to a stronger idea of knowledge. "We want to be able to know because we also want to be able to act and in acting to rely on a knowledge beyond what is available to us directly. We want to be able to have arguments about how things work that refer to an ontological ground in the world we have in common, and we want, therefore, to be able to arrive at an agreement on the basis of what is there for both of us."[54] Smith affirms, in other words, that she intends the feminist standpoint as an ontological position.

Smith writes, again in response to Harding, that "in assessing the products of inquiry," we want to ask: "Has she got it right? Is this how it really works? Is it accurate? Faithful to the character of the organization and relations investigated? Such questions can be asked only if there exists the practical possibility of another account that *can* invalidate hers. . . . So the epistemology must also be an ontology."[55] The last sentence simply does not follow. It is attractive, I think, partly because of the notion of finding a ground in the realm of concrete experience. Among other things, however, it misses the possibilities opened by Gadamer's rejection of both finalistic and historicist hermeneutics in favor of an account of judgment enabling us to move from a worse to a better position (within some practical frame of reference) without claiming essential truth.[56] Taking this approach encourages a more historically situated approach to knowledge without yielding to a sharp relativism.

At issue here is the potentially incapacitating result of affirming an incommensurability of experiences and understandings so complete that rational-critical discourse cannot bridge the gap.[57] Where this is the case, there is no reason why feminist claims – e.g. that spousal violence is wrong and intolerable – should be persuasive to those who do not share the original "interpretive tradition." Instead of an argument as to why violence against women *should* not be tolerated, we are left with a declaration that such violence will not be tolerated by those who speak the slogan – a declaration that is not truly a critique of either the discourse or the physical actuality of power but rather an attempt to oppose it with a contrary power.[58] Given the way power is structured in the world today, however, if material power cannot be opposed by rational-critical discourse but only by alternative powers – and if those alternative powers have the same theoretical status – then we are in an even worse position than what I take to be our sorry state when faced with sexual violence, racist attacks, and genocidal versions of nationalism.

V

In different ways and with varying degrees of clarity, a number of feminist theorists have turned to the notion that better observation and reasoning will come not from invoking a fixed subject position but rather from recognizing the contradictions in many – perhaps all – subject positions. Julia Kristeva, for example, introduces her own polar distinction between characteristically male attributes to which women might aspire and unjustly devalued characteristically female attributes. She then argues that "one must try not to deny these two aspects of linguistic communication, the mastering aspect and the aspect which is more of the body and the impulses, but try, in every situation and for every woman, to find a proper articulation of these two elements. . . . I think that the time has come when we must no longer speak of all women. We have to talk in terms of individual women and of each one's place inside these two poles. One of the gravest dangers that now presents itself in feminism is the impulse to practice feminism in a herd."[59] This is close to Smith's starting point, with her notion of women's bifurcated consciousness. After initial doubts, Harding has embraced an even stronger version of this idea: "the subject of feminist knowledge – the agent of these less partial and distorted descriptions and explanations – must be multiple and even contradictory. . . . the logic of the standpoint directive to start thought from women's lives requires starting from multiple lives that are in many ways in conflict with one another and each of which has its own multiple and contradictory commitments."[60] With such arguments, as Smith herself complains, standpoint theory has been relativized dramatically. Nonetheless, they seem logical outgrowths of the attempt to invoke women's concrete experience(s) as the source of the feminist standpoint.

Smith's "bifurcated consciousness" contrasts women's direct experience to the abstract systems and ruling apparatus characteristic of hegemonic, androcentric thought. As we have seen, Harding and other feminists have tried more systematically to suggest that feminist theory must mediate such experience before it can constitute the standpoint of critique. I want to ask whether even in such mediated senses, the category of experience is entirely adequate to what is being asked of it.

Appeals to experience easily slide into appeals to a kind of phenomenological immediacy that has been popular in counter-rationalist arguments from the earliest Romantics. Enlightenment thought seems excessively distant from lived experience (and, for many of the critics, reason triumphs over will). In many Romantics, as in Nietzsche, appeals to an aesthetic consciousness (especially a sense of the sublime) against a more scientific-rational consciousness invoke this same sense of immediacy. This is a problem not only for the dominant currents of Enlightenment thought, but for many so-called postmodernists. It is at the heart of the "metaphysics of presence" that Derrida criticizes in many versions, and which he sees as an almost transhistorical intellectual problem dating from Socrates, not from the anti-Enlightenment. His critique of this cult of direct experience sets him apart from others in the Nietzsche–Heidegger lineage with whom in other regards he shares much.[61] He argues, for example, that Heidegger's discourse is dominated by "an entire metaphorics of proximity, of simple and immediate presence, a metaphorics associating the proximity of Being with the values of neighboring, shelter, house, service, guard, voice, and listening."[62] As anti-Heideggerian as Habermas is, somewhat similar ideas underpin his distinction of an attractively immediate lifeworld of interpersonal experience from the abstract, potentially threatening world of systemic integration.[63]

Nancy Fraser has made Habermas's version of the appeal to (more or less) unmediated experience the object of feminist reconsideration.[64] In a good illustration of the intellectual advantages in starting analysis from consideration of women's lives (but without hardening this into a fixed standpoint), she points out how Habermas's idealization of the lifeworld is rooted in a conception of the family in which all communication is egalitarian, violence nonexistent, and labor equitably shared. Such a view is only possible, we might suggest following Smith, not just because Habermas is a man who doesn't see the ill-treatment of women in real-world families, but because failing to reason or observe from the standpoint of women's lives, he doesn't see the extent to which women's labor is marshaled to make possible the (putatively gender-neutral) systems of money and power.

At the same time, Smith's appeal to concrete experience seems important as a locus of agency. Here we need to distinguish between two dimensions that she sometimes conflates. On the one hand, she invokes the notion of women's direct experience. This has two faults. First, it is hard to see how one can get from the necessarily highly divergent experiences of different women to the categorial construct of a standpoint of women. Taken as the subjects of direct experience, women must appear immediately not only as different from each other, but as linked in different partial and particular solidarities: lesbians, for example, Christian women, mothers, or women of color. The last of these terms itself is a locus of difference that is too often denied – as when "women of color" is used to invoke a largely imagined or proposed solidarity among women very different in their experiences – and indeed in their colors.[65] Second, the idea of experience commonly suggests a passive subject; women's experience, thus, is disproportionately presented in terms of action on women rather than women's active construction of their own worlds. One of the advantages of locating the "feminist standpoint" not in the experience of female subjects but in particular sorts of practices – e.g. those of the women's movement – is that it avoids this implication of passivity.

The other dimension of Smith's appeal to direct experience is more promising. Along with other feminist thinkers, she points us towards a recognition of everyday life as commitments to specific others in rich, concrete social relationships, to specific places and senses of place, to specific activities and organizations of the rhythm of life. These commitments are relatively neglected by sociology, even though they are a very large part of what most human beings focus their attention on. They are also a crucial source of a sense of agency, crucial loci for resistance and opposition to the dominance of abstract systems or ruling apparatus, and crucial antidotes to the apocalyptic panic sometimes engendered by the sense that the "larger world" of corporations, nation-states, capitalism and the like has become senseless. Much of the "politics of identity" is rooted in commitments to place and in general settings for meaningful direct experience.

In recovering an emphasis on everyday life, however, we need to be cautious about recreating the public/private dichotomy somewhat uncritically within feminist thought. This comes with equating everyday life (as Smith among others sometimes does) with the local as against the supralocal, the global, or the systemic. It is, first of all, not sharply distinct from any of these. To take a simple example, television and broadcast media are now inescapably part of everyday life and experience for nearly everyone in nearly every country on the globe. The

workings of broadcast media certainly involve indirect social relationships as against the directly interpersonal, but they cannot be opposed so
neatly to either the notion of everyday life or of experience. One might be
tempted to say that they can be opposed to "immediate experience," but
though that makes a nice pun, I think it is wrong. In a weak sense, our
experience of television itself is felt as immediate, even though it includes
a highly mediated experience of that which television programs are
putatively about. In a strong sense, little or no experience is unmediated,
for nearly all – at least this side of madness and utter absorption in pain
– involves language and cultural construction.

Relatedly, we need to be alert to oversimple and misleading comparisons to smaller-scale societies, a thin appropriation of anthropology that
Smith shares with some other feminists and for that matter with
Habermas.[66] Thus she offers an example of Kalahari Bushmen in which
all members of a small band are present when hunters distribute the meat
they have brought home. She concludes, "the determinations of social
existence are fully present to the experience of its members and are
coterminous with it."[67] This is at the very least a major overstatement.
Not only are there links among Kalahari bands, including networks of
kinship, descent, and economic exchange, but even in this small-scale
society it is problematic to suggest that surface visibility is equivalent to
a sort of unmediated presence to experience, as though the sheer sensory
materiality of that experience could overcome the role of culture in
constituting its specific forms.

Smith is cognizant of the complexities involved in the articulation
between what she calls the "actual and immediate organization of the
experienced world" and the "extended social relations" created by capitalist economic life, political-bureaucratic power, and the like. I think I
am trying to push further in the same direction, not in a contrary one,
when I push for distinguishing the dimensions of directness or indirect-
ness of relationships (including their spatial reach) from the pattern of
organization of knowledge (including as "experiential" vs. "abstracted
conceptual"). The two are interdependent but not identical.[68] Smith's
basic model of the ruling apparatus emphasizes the reliance on an impersonal, conceptual mode of representation that disguises the actual personal agency involved in systems of power. This is clearly of central
importance. Yet it leaves us with important questions. I shall raise two.

First, Smith's binary opposition of the world of direct experience to
the world of abstracted relations and conceptualized knowledge relies on
a problematic understanding of the "supralocal" world of social integration and systemic power. Smith shares here – and not in an extreme
degree – a byproduct of the general and generally valuable feminist point

about the importance of learning from experience. This is the opposition of experience (however it is understood) to a too simple notion of the regimes of knowledge and power that have marginalized and split women's experience. Thus the ruling apparatus for Smith includes at once and without clear distinction (1) corporations and other complex organizations that enter into the social world as putative agents or collective actors, (2) capitalism and other systematically organized processes, and (3) the abstracted, specially codified discourses by which social scientists and others address and speak of each of these.[69] Aside from general issues of conceptual clarity, it is important to differentiate these different aspects of ruling apparatus if we are to develop a strong sense of how human agency may be deployed in action to change or resist any or all of them.

A second question concerns how we are to deal with those occasions where ordinary experience systematically misleads us about influences over our lives, especially because of the way the world is organized by supralocal powers. In Pierre Bourdieu's language, the potential for misrecognition is built into virtually all situations of social action.[70] How we understand these issues has major implications for how we think about possibilities for agency and opposition. Flax has pointed out the possibility that our experience may actually undermine our ability to grasp what is going on, or to take appropriate action. The notion of a feminist standpoint, she suggests, "assumes that the oppressed are not in some fundamental ways damaged by their social experience."[71] Even where subjects are in no sense "damaged," we need to ask about the possibility that hegemonic cultures systematically distort – or simply shape – the experience and even the self-recognition of subaltern groups. This is, of course, why (as Harding suggests perhaps in most detail) the feminist standpoint requires not just the existence of women, but both the women's movement and feminist theory. These enable a challenge to dominant ideologies and hegemonic cultures.

Smith recognizes that the everyday world is structured by forces it does not make immediately apparent. She rejects, for example, the notion that making the everyday world the locus of a sociological problematic is the same as making it an object of study:

> In constituting the everyday world as an object of sociological examination, we cut it off methodologically from the ways in which it is actually embedded in a socially organized context larger than may be directly known in that mode. . . . For the everyday world is neither transparent nor obvious. Fundamental to its organization for us in this form of society is that its inner determinations are not discoverable within it.[72]

Or, a few pages later, "the present structure of local social relations is organized by social relations external to it."[73] This is right, I think, but as I suggested earlier, it implies a sharper spatial separation than is plausible. The relations of large-scale administrative power, of abstracted discourse, of capitalism work within the most local of relations as well as beyond them. Neglect of this dimension has undermined a variety of attempts to ground a critique of those larger systems in the standpoint of "lifeworld" or locality. It is especially problematic for efforts to locate the standpoint of critique in the direct experience concrete groups have of such lifeworlds.

VI

If neither an appeal to immediate experience nor an appeal to the established putatively universalistic discourse is satisfactory, is there a standpoint from which to recognize misrecognition? Harding argues for reasoning from the multiplicity and contradictions that characterize our "subject positions" and our very existence as human agents. As Teresa de Lauretis suggests, "differences among women may be better understood as differences within women."[74] This makes sense, though only if reasoning from multiplicity and contradictions does not entirely displace recognition of struggles for more coherent individual and collective identities. Harding misleadingly tries to equate such a perspective with standpoint theory and claims simultaneously to achieve a rapprochement between standpoint theory and postmodernism. To combine gender with race, language, sexual orientation, concrete interpersonal relations, and a host of other dimensions of identity is no easy or uncomplicated thing. But it is from the recognition of this complexity and these contradictions that we must start.

Critical theory grasps its objects not in their simple identities but in their internal tensions. The idea of an immanent critique suggests that conditions in the world open possibilities for critical analysis. Capitalism only appeared to be – was historically constituted in the appearance of – an "identical, self-moving subject-object;" this afforded Marx the opening for his critique of classical political economy. To recognize and analyze this, Marx started not from labor as simply the class of workers or as the transhistorical phenomenon of work, but from labor constituted by capitalism as a category in an essential tension between the concrete particularity of the human beings whose lives were used up in it and the commodification process that rendered it an abstract form of social mediation (value). Similarly, the purchase of feminist theory derives in large part from the bifurcated female consciousness that Smith describes – and more generally from a range of contradictions not only in "objectively given" subject positions but in subjectively constructed identities and commitments.

This distinguishes critical theory – at its best – from the sorts of appeals to an Archimedian point that many feminists have rightly criticized in the theories generated by men and generated in part from the standpoint of large-scale systems of power and money. The Cartesian claim to a "view from nowhere" is to be avoided not just by invocation of the excluded other, nor even by the location of subjects within the realm of concrete experience and social relations, but by the recognition of a tension that opens up the possibility of critique and change. Read in this way, the invocation of a standpoint of women need not be an invitation to a new foundationalism, but rather an aspect of a knowledge-forming process. It can help us to recognize how gender may operate as a category constituting relations of inclusion and exclusion, of visibility and invisibility, particularity and generality even where it is most resolutely denied and the illusion of gender-free universality maintained. The historical constitution of putatively genderless but in fact exclusively or overwhelmingly male discourse of scientific understanding, public sphere, and economy is a contradiction literally engendering not only women's personal experience of split consciousness and struggle, but the categorial possibility for a critical challenge to the ways in which the institutions shaping our lives appear as immutable and impersonal forces.

The gendered construction of social life not only reflects but helps to produce a discourse in which the ruling apparatus, the economy, the state, etc., appear as though they were actorless systems – in other words, as though they could be studied as objective or even natural phenomena requiring neither a reflexive attention to the experience and knowledge-forming interests and processes of the observer, nor an account of how human agents exercise power in and through such modalities of ruling apparatus. The attempt to unmask the false impersonality of such putatively impersonal systems is of vital importance, and not just for the purpose of grasping the gendered nature of the world, but more generally for recognizing such systems of reification.

Notes

1 This distinction is explored briefly in chapter 3.
2 Rousseau, "The Social Contract."
3 See paragraph 40 of Kant, *Critique of Judgment*. As we saw in the introduction, in the case of judgment, universality for Kant implies universal communicability.

4   Kant, *Critique of Judgment*, p. 161 (para. 40).

5   Or man as embodiment of creative labor power; see especially Marx, "On the Jewish Question."

6   Marx and Engels, *The Holy Family*, p. 37.

7   See the essay "Reification and the Consciousness of the Proletariat" in Lukacs, *History and Class Consciousness*.

8   Postone has shown this nicely with regard to Lukacs and most varieties of traditional marxism, and developed an alternative reading of Marx that attempts to escape the subject-object problematic. See Postone, *Time, Labor*, esp. pp. 88 and 175 on Lukacs.

9   In Hegel, *Phenomenology of Spirit*.

10 See the various volumes of *Subaltern Studies*, and especially Spivak's provocative essay, "Can the Subaltern Speak?" Compare Gilroy's useful reminder of the fact that Hegel was, after all, speaking of slavery (*Black Atlantic*, ch. 1).

11 Use of the Kuhnian term incommensurability reminds us that this attention to the possibility of deep differences in cognitive and/or ontological orientations was part of a broader intellectual current. It was, of course, also central to poststructuralist thought and is one of the bases for the affinity between poststructuralism and many varieties of feminist theory (see Nicholson, ed., *Feminism/Postmodernism*).

12 Flax, "Gender as a Social Problem," quoted from Harding, *The Science Question in Feminism*, pp. 28–9.

13 Harding, *Whose Science? Whose Knowledge?*, p. 121.

14 Smith, *The Conceptual Practices of Power*, p. 13. Two other feminist theorists began to develop standpoint epistemologies relatively early when Smith's work was still not widely known outside Canada. See Hartsock, "The Feminist Standpoint," and Rose, "Hand, Brain and Heart."

15 Smith, *The Everyday World*, p. 81.

16 On the issue of multiplicity of publics, see chapter 8.

17 The issue of essentialism is addressed in the next chapter. Perhaps the most important pioneering effort to show the historical production of a "sex-gender system" is Rubin's "The Traffic in Women." Rubin's approach does not identify the range of variations in the working of gender as a category in different historical epochs or cultural contexts. Foucauldian accounts of the production of the individual "self" and sexuality suggest that a more historically specific modern form of gender needs to be explored.

18 Smith, *The Everyday World*, p. 4.

19 Postone, *Time, Labor*. Flax does not see that Marx can be read this other way, but sees how the transhistorical reading causes problems in socialist feminism: "Marxists (including socialist feminists) uncritically apply the concepts Marx should have used to describe a particular form of the production of commodities to all areas of human life at all historical periods. . . . In Marxist theory labor (defined as the transformation of natural or other objects into things with use or exchange value) is treated as the 'essence' of history and human 'being.' Under the influence of such assump-

tions, socialist feminists end up making reductive claims like the following: 'The family is definable exactly as property relations between men and woman, and the social relations of the family are those property relations in action.' Among other problems, such claims ignore the existence and sensuous activities of real people in families (e.g. children, for whom at least part of their formative and familial experiences have nothing to do with production). Few women would describe their experiences of pregnancy and childrearing solely in terms of the production of commodity labor power for the market" (Flax, *Thinking Frangments*, p. 154, quoting Kuhn, "Structures of Patriarchy and Capital in the Family").

20   Harding, *Science Question in Feminism*, p. 158.
21   Harding, *Whose Science?*, p. 167.
22   Ibid., p. 121, n. 19.
23   Ibid., p. 123; italics in original.
24   Flax, *Thinking Fragments*, p. 227.
25   It was precisely for failing to distinguish consensus based on persuasion from that based on truth that Habermas faulted Gadamer's hermeneutics; Habermas, *On the Logic of the Social Sciences*, ch. 8.
26   Lyotard, *Postmodern Condition*; see esp. p. 30.
27   Though the phrase sounds very strange, Lyotard is basically an anti-Enlightenment neo-Kantian. In addition to *The Postmodern Condition*, see *The Differend* and esp. *The Inhuman*.
28   I shall not attempt to trace the development of the history and sociology of science. The ideas noted above have become fairly commonplace since the 1960s, and especially since Kuhn's famous *The Structure of Scientific Revolutions*. Many were, however, already implicit in the empirical work of historians of science since at least Sarton, though not thematized or theorized as such.
29   Recall the extent to which the Enlightenment, as a narrative and rhetorical construction, relied on the image of a superstitious, mystified, shadowy past – exemplified by many enlighteners by Roman Catholic Christianity. Developments in what we now consider diverse fields of natural and physical science, philosophy, and human or social science were not sharply differentiated and shared a broadly similar orientation. Gay, *The Enlightenment*, remains perhaps the best single introduction for those not familiar with this narrative.
30   Along with the closely related standards of publicity, this argument carried potentially anti-authoritarian political implications; see Laursen, "The Subversive Kant."
31   Kant, *Critique of Judgment*, p. 160 (para. 40). Both the Kantian and the Habermasian perspectives assume that the various different standpoints to be included in the potentially universally communicable discourse will all be commensurable, and indeed have no strong theoretical account of differences among subjects. Indeed, both regard such differences as something to be bracketed and kept out of the discourse of science – and for that matter the public sphere – rather than as a productive source of knowledge. This is

one of the problems that other sorts of standpoint theories set out to remedy.

32 Haraway, *Primate Visions*.

33 Dietz, "Context is All."

34 One can see similarities to a variety of similar arguments for dialogical approaches in other fields of study. A version of this was, for example, central to the "interpersonal school" of psychoanalysts for whom Harry Stack Sullivan and Clara Thompson were pioneers. Indeed, many other breaks with orthodox Freudianism emphasized the dialogic relationship between analyst and analysand and challenged the scientific objectivism of Freud as much as they differed over more obstract theoretical matters; Karen Horney is another example in the American context. The relationship between psychoanalysis and feminism has become, I think, overly fixated on the great European fights: over object relations vs. ego psychology in England and especially between Lacanian structuralists and more orthodox analysts in France.

35 Smith, *Everyday World*, pp. 111–16.

36 There have been a variety of attempts to explicate what such a dialogic approach to scientific investigation (generally not called that) might look like, and how it might produce knowledge in various fields of research. Evelyn Fox Keller's study of Barbara McClintock's work, *A Feeling for the Organism*, is perhaps the most prominent.

37 Rorty, "Pragmatism." See also Rorty, *Philosophy and the Mirror of Nature*, where he argues powerfully against correspondence theories of knowledge, but sees the Enlightenment heritage and modern science entirely in terms of such claims to mirror nature. I think this tendency to see as something new and radically threatening the discovery that science is discourse may be the result of understanding science too exclusively through the philosophy of science rather than the history of science or the actual practice of scientists.

38 Harding finds herself straddling precisely this "either/or," as I suggested above, when she decides to claim objectivity for a feminist standpoint while simultaneously claiming the postmodernist infinity of standpoints. In the latter chapters of her book she makes some steps toward the more promising idea of seeing a feminist standpoint as rooted not in certain subjects, or the lives of the category of women, but in practices historically advanced by the women's movement, but she does not relate this as an alternative approach to the unresolved duality of Dorothy Smith and Derrida that she has embraced.

39 Harding, *Whose Science?*, pp. 146–7.

40 In this, Harding follows directly on Horkheimer's claims for critical as distinct from traditional theory; "Traditional and Critical Theory."

41 Harding, *The Science Question*. p. 138.

42 Ibid.

43 Harding, *Whose Science?*, pp. 284ff.

44 See the essay "Situated Knowledges," which responds directly to Harding, in Haraway, *Simians, Cyborgs and Women*.

45 Smith's account of feminist standpoint also shares much with readings of

Marx's work as a social ontology, e.g., Gould, *Marx's Social Ontology*. In addition, Smith reads Marx's work as an approach that affords researchers a "method of exploring everyday social relations without constructing an alienated world of abstractions" (Smith, *Conceptual Practices of Power*, p. 61). This reading leaves unclear how Smith thinks we are to recognize the "real" abstractions of capitalism (as discussed in the first chapter of *Capital*) since these are not to be grasped through simple exploration of everyday social relations as she implies.

46 This reliance on concrete experience is central, for example, to what Aptheker and her colleagues construct as a feminist standpoint; see Aptheker, *Tapestries of Life*. It is also shared with a number of feminists who do not enter into epistemological debates.

47 Lukacs, *History and Class Consciousness*.

48 See Harding's more general considerations of such postmodernist arguments against feminist standpoint theories in *The Science Question*, chs. 6 and 7 and especially *Whose Science?*, ch. 7. A thoughtful attempt to bring standpoint theory into relationship with postmodernist insights is Flax, *Thinking Fragments*.

49 Dietz, "Context Is All."

50 Harding. *Whose Science?*, p. 286. See also Dietz, "Context is All."

51 Harding, *Whose Science?*, p. 298.

52 Haraway, *Simians, Cyborgs, and Women*; see especially Haraway's "Cyborg Manifesto."

53 Smith, *Conceptual Practices*, p. 34; the reply is to Harding's *Science Question*.

54 Smith, *Conceptual Practices*.

55 Smith, *The Everyday World as Problematic*, p. 122.

56 Gadamer, *Truth and Method*. This is what Taylor has nicely described as the process of seeking "epistemic gain," *Sources of the Self*; see discussion and other citations in chapters 1 and 2 above.

57 See chapter 2 above.

58 The most sophisticated version of this approach to a discourse in which positions are taken without arguments being developed is offered by Derrida; see esp. *Positions*.

59 Baruch and Meisel, "Two Interviews with Julia Kristeva."

60 Harding, *Whose Science?*, pp. 284–5. Much the same sort of issue – including the same tension between need for theoretical mediation and appeals to direct experience – arises with regard to DuBois's concept of double consciousness and ideas of race and identity more generally. See discussion in Gilroy, *Black Atlantic*.

61 See Megill's analysis of Derrida's relationship to this lineage in *Prophets of Extremity*, which is fairer and more sympathetic than Habermas's in *Philosophical Discourse of Modernity*.

62 Derrida, *Margins of Philosophy*, p. 130.

63 Habermas, *Theory of Communicative Action*.

64 Fraser, "What's Critical about Critical Theory"; see also her "Rethinking

the Public Sphere."

65 This is an issue more often alluded to than discussed seriously. Perhaps the best treatment lies in the work of Collins (*Black Feminist Thought* and *Fighting Words*), despite her tendency to assume that acknowledgement of overlapping "both/and" dimensions of difference adequately addresses rather than merely recognizes the underlying theoretical issue (and for that matter, despite her suggestion of an epistemological frame of reference as adequate to solving this problem).

66 See, for example, Harding's very troubling account of how the African world view is like the feminist world view – based heavily on a single, extremely non-authoritative source, and failing to distinguish such categories as "Africans," "Africanists," and "African-Americans"; *The Science Question in Feminism*, ch. 7.

67 Smith, *Everyday World*, p. 92.

68 Compare Smith's formulation in *Everday World*, p. 75.

69 Smith and feminists taking similar positions are in famous if slightly surprising company here, for they are making equations similar to those effected by Parsons in *The System of Modern Societies* and Habermas (*Theory of Communicative Action*) in speaking of money and power as "non-linguistic steering media" organizing cybernetic systems of economy and administration that are logically on the same order (and that are mirrored in the systems theory and other abstracted discourses used to speak of them).

70 See Bourdieu (*Outline, Logic*) and chapter 4 above. "Misrecognition" is more apt than notions like false consciousness because it suggests (1) that reality is partially grasped not completely falsified, and (2) that the phenomena in question are more pervasive than the relations of subordinates to ideologies that serve the interests of superiors.

71 "On the contrary," Flax continues, "this position assumes that the oppressed have a privileged, unitary, and not just different relation to and ability to comprehend a reality that is 'out there' waiting for our representation" (*Thinking Fragments*, p. 141). Hartsock's version of feminist standpoint theory relies heavily on the notion of women's direct experience, and fits the epistemological privileging that Flax criticizes by turning Hegelian dialectic into a rather too simple notion of reversal. When experience is structured in fundamentally opposing ways for two groups, she says, "one can expect that the vision of each will represent an inversion of the other, and in systems of domination the vision available to the rulers will be both partial and perverse" (Hartsock, "The Feminist Standpoint," p. 285). Note how little room such an account leaves for the analysis of hegemonic culture or misrecognition.

72 .Smith, *Everday World as Problematic*, pp. 90–1.

73 Ibid., p. 94.

74 De Lauretis, "Feminist Studies/Critical Studies," p. 14.

7

The Politics of Identity and Recognition

I

Plurality, as Hannah Arendt observed, is basic to the human condition.[1] We are distinct from each other, and often strive to distinguish ourselves further. Yet, as Arendt emphasized much less, each dimension of distinction is apt at least tacitly also to establish commonality with a set of others similarly distinguished. There is no simple sameness unmarked by difference, but likewise no distinction not dependent on some background of common recognition.[2]

Concerns with individual and collective identity, thus, are ubiquitous. We know of no people without names, no languages or cultures in which some manner of distinctions between self and other, we and they are not made. Though the concern may be universal, however, the identities themselves are not. Gender and age seem to distinguish people nearly everywhere, pedigree or parentage are of almost equally wide significance. Yet it is no accident that discourse about identity seems in some important sense distinctively modern – seems, indeed, intrinsic to and partially defining of the modern era.

This has to do both with intensified effort to consolidate individual identities, to increase identification with social and cultural categories, and to reinforce self-sameness. These efforts respond to social changes that both made the production and recognition of identities newly problematic and gave new opportunities to those who wished to change the contours of identities. This intense modern concern for identity is neither simply positive nor simply negative. Different aspects are grasped by Michel Foucault's analysis of how discipline produces a new sort of individual self, Charles Taylor's presentation of the sources of the self in transformations of religious thought and new valuations of ordinary happiness, and more conventional treatments of the rise of individualism as a narrative of freedom.[3] A crucial common denominator is recognition of a new kind of stress on identity, that is, on the notion that self is integrally and immediately being and consciousness, name and voice. Descartes' *cogito* is a crucial index of the novel stress on identity: "I think, therefore I am." Not only does the person become a disembodied cognitive subject, knowledge is presented as dependent on this subject. In Fichte, the simple equation "I am I" is elevated to a philosophical claim to the self-sufficiency of identity, and in other parts of the German idealist tradition this is joined to an emphasis on the fundamental formative power of will. As the knowing and recognizing self is made to carry this philosophical weight, it is also more commonly seen as fixed, as reflecting itself in simple identity rather than complex relationship. The stage is set for Hegel's dialectical transformation of this tradition and for later thinkers, like Freud, Vygotsky, and Bakhtin, to rediscover notions of internal dialogue and contestation. Even as they and their successors have questioned simple self-sameness, however, most have retained a focus on identity in a relatively strong sense, on integral individuality.

At the same time, modern selves are called on to carry new sorts of moral weight. This weight was already assigned to the self in Augustine's *Confessions*. Augustine joined Judeo-Christian concerns with an individual god and individual salvation to Greek forms of intellectual exploration and ideas of recognition to create a new sort of morally charged introspection. Not until a thousand years after Augustine, however, did a similar synthesis re-emerge as part of the configuration of modern self-understanding. The same sorts of moral sources informed the crucial movements, largely on Christian motivations, to rethink the nature and significance of subjectivity in the era from the Reformation to the Enlightenment.[4] That this morally charged subjectivity is not in all respects uniquely modern does not stop it from being distinctively modern.

The discourse of self is distinctively modern, and modernity distinctively linked to the discourse of self, not just because of the cognitive and moral weight attached to selves and self-identity. Modern concerns with identity stem also from ways in which modernity has made identity distinctively problematic. It is not simply – or even clearly the case – that it matters more to us than to our forebears to be who we are. Rather, it is much harder for us to establish who we are and maintain this own identity satisfactorily in our lives and in the recognition of others. This is why what Adorno called "the jargon of authenticity" has been so distinctive of the modern era in everyday life and in politics as well as in aesthetics and certain schools (especially Heideggerian-existentialist) of philosophy.[5] Recall the form of Zola's intervention in the Dreyfus affair, his famous letter, "J'accuse," which presented not so much an argument as an intense expression of personal conviction.[6]

Both self-identity and recognition can pose challenges and difficulties. Self-knowledge – always a construction no matter how much it feels like a discovery – is never altogether separable from claims to be known in specific ways by others. But the two dimensions may not always be equally problematic. Many aspects of constructing or achieving identity, for example, can be fraught with obstacles without making the identity itself problematic for others to recognize. Upward mobility, say through the Church from the ranks of the common clergy to the episcopate, has always been hard to achieve and harder for some aspirants than others. But only rarely and intermittently have the identities of bishops been subject to dispute. Moreover, the Church offers – or at least has seemed through much of its history to offer – an all-encompassing scheme of identities. Bishops need not be validated in isolation but are consecrated through ceremony based on tradition and ideology and invested not only with the symbols of their office but with implicit recognition by a range of authoritative others. But this kind of clarity, rooted not only in cultural or ideological consensus but in the reinforcement offered by systematically organized networks of social relations is precisely what is challenged for most sorts of identity in the modern era. If the clarity of earlier identity schemes has never been quite perfect, and often characterized by more anomalies, doubts, and deceptions than we retrospectively imagine, it has nonetheless commonly underwritten a level of unquestioned acceptance of the apparent order of social categories that we no longer experience. In Bourdieu's terms, it has allowed schemes of understanding and normative order to appear as *doxic*, as simply given, rather than merely *orthodox* or authoritatively defended, let alone *heterodox* and implicitly contested.[7]

Modernity has meant in significant part the breakup – or the reduction to near-irrelevance – of most all-encompassing identity-schemes. Kinship still matters to us as individuals; we invest it with great emotional weight, but kinship no longer offers us an overall template of social and personal identities. When we meet strangers in an airport, we are unlikely to be able to place their relationships to us as part of a singular, overall system of kin relations which would offer clarity about both who we are in relation to each other and how we should behave. This distinguishes us from, say, Nuer who might meet while tending their cattle at a watering hole in the Nilotic region of Southern Sudan in the 1920s or 1930s.[8] The Nuer might have faced complexities – they might have shared clanship yet come from rival villages, for example, or been joined affinally while consanguinally opposed – but though they had a multiplicity of identities to sort out, and quite actively to manage, they had a minimally disputed set of shared rhetorics for both self-identification and recognition of others. Without attaining perfection, they had a very high level of systematicity to their scheme of identities. This was problematic primarily at the fringes – and of course patterns of migration, intergroup conflict, and communication were complex and important throughout the African continent. I do not mean to suggest that all issues of identity were simply and stably settled for the Nuer, but rather that most appeared within a range of activity where a limited range of common rhetorics could organize the struggles for identity and recognition. Now, of course, as Southerners within an ethnically, religiously, and politically diverse Sudan, members of a tribe implicated within a secessionist rebellion (itself internally divided), occasional Christians and widely labeled animists, construction workers in an increasingly city-centered economy, Nuer no longer can treat the categories of Nuer identity as doxically given but must face the modern challenge of deciding how to fit them into projects of collective and individual identity that presuppose inscription in a multiplicity of often incommensurable identity schemes. The change is not only one of scale; it is also one of complexity and especially of the extent of contestation over salient identities.

Kinship systems are not the only kind of all-encompassing identity-scheme the world has known. Within European history, despite the considerable heterogeneity of institutions and local identities, the notion of a "great chain of being" long offered a kind of doxic background to contests over more specific identities.[9] More generally, the point is not to contrast extremes of all-encompassing systematicity to the illusion of complete absence of pre-established rhetorical systems of identity, but rather to recognize a variable. The modern era brought an increase in the multiplicity of identity schemes so substantial that it amounted to a qualitative break, albeit one unevenly distributed in time and space. (Or, perhaps it is better to say that this transformation of identity construction helped to constitute the modern era as we know it.) In the modern era, identity is always constructed and situated in a heterogenous field and amid a flow of contending cultural discourses. In Cascardi's terms, summarizing an argument equally Weberian and Habermasian, "the modern subject is defined by its insertion into a series of separate value-spheres, each one of which tends to exclude or attempts to assert its priority over the rest."[10] The motif is apparent in Kant's distinction of the realm of pure reason (truth), from practical reason (morality) and both from aesthetic judgment (taste) [especially when judgment is not seen as mediating truth and morality]. This is basic to the Hegelian idea of the diremptions of modernity, and to the search for reunification transmuted into remythologization for Schlegel and Nietzsche and "fundamental ontology" for Heidegger. When postmodernists focus their attention on the rationalist Enlightenment, they borrow critical force from this tradition, but generally refuse its quest for reunification. The tension and even incommensurability among the various value spheres and discourses constitute not just a disunity of the larger social whole or "external" difficulties for individuals but also a series of contradictions within the "subject-self."

If George Herbert Mead was right, in other words, that our sense of self is constituted in relations to both significant specific others and a more generalized social other, we are presented with a serious challenge when it is impossible to assume congruence among the significant others or singularity of the generalized other.[11] Since the story is one of self-formation and internalization of images and capabilities, it is not just our environment but our selves that are made more complex. This sort of complexity, let me be clear, is by no means uniquely modern; aspects of it inform identity-projects in a variety of highly internally heterogenous societies – like those of most of South Asia. It may be that family life is less marked traditionally by these inconsistencies among others, both significant and generalized, than is public life. Nonetheless, an Enlightenment understanding of both individual and collective selves in terms of a project of unification and integral wholeness combined with the reality of such multiform, contested, and potentially incommensurably heterogenous contexts makes a distinctive modern issue.

II

A sociologist is apt to think that the new, poststructuralist rhetoric of "subject-positions" and "enactments" is an unnecessary reinvention of the familiar vocabulary of status and role. This is one result of the fact that so much of the most prominent recent social theory has been generated outside sociology and too often in ignorance of sociological theory. Nonetheless, while the older sociological approach to "roles" did provide a way to note that individuals bear multiple identities, it commonly obscured the full impact of this. Most versions of role theory tacitly posited a kind of ontological independence of the individual from her/his various roles. Individuals, thus, might experience "stress" stemming from the tensions among their roles.[12] In strong versions of role theory, persons might be understood as partially constituted by their roles. But even within its own rhetoric, role theory did not adequately address the complexity of the problem of relating multiple roles to each other – or more precisely, of reconciling the expectations (including self-expectations) based on multiple statuses. Attention was focused on how well (or poorly) individuals played socially prescribed roles – doctor, father, etc. There was correspondingly little attention to (1) the discourses which lent value to or withdrew it from various possible role-performances, (2) dissent from or political contestation about those roles, (3) the kinds of performances through which actors went beyond or outside roles and/or created new ones, or (4) the possibility that a kind of fragmentation of self was a common, possibly ubiquitous, byproduct of apparently successful role-performance.[13] The sociological analysis of roles was nonetheless a step beyond the essentializing of biological or psychological human identity; it facilitated recognition of the construction of self in social life.

Social constructionism has become extremely widespread, well beyond sociology. It challenges at once the idea that identity is given naturally and the idea that it is produced purely by acts of individual will. At their best, social constructionist arguments also challenge "essentialist" notions that individual persons can have singular, integral, altogether harmonious, and unproblematic identities.[14] And by the same token subtle constructionist arguments challenge accounts of collective identities as based on some "essence" or set of core features shared by all members of the collectivity and no others. Thus, for example, Dyson writes of the need to move "beyond essentialism" in "expanding African-American cultural criticism":

> Of course, I don't mean that there are not distinct black cultural characteristics that persist over space and time, but these features of black life are the products of the historical and social construction of racial identity. . . . These distinct features of black life nuance and shape black cultural expression, from the preaching of Martin Luther King to the singing of Gladys Knight. They do not, however, form the basis of a black racial or cultural essence. Nor do they indicate that *the* meaning of blackness will be expressed in a quality or characteristic without which a person, act, or practice no longer qualifies as black. Rigid racial essentialism must be opposed.[15]

Essentialist invocations of races, nations, genders, classes, persons, and a host of other identities nonetheless remain common in everyday discourse throughout the world. Pointing to the social and cultural histories by which they have been constructed has become the main way of trying to challenge the grip these essentialist identities have over us and the problems they create. Thus Hobsbawm and Ranger seek to weaken the grip of nationalist thinking by showing it to be based on "the invention of tradition."[16] Simply showing a process of construction, however, may fail to grapple with the real, present-day political and other reasons why essentialist identities continue to be invoked and often deeply felt. At the same time, the language of construction minimizes the role of power and implies a multidirectional flow of influence and agency. This may be the case with regard to many identities, but it misleads where the imposition of stereotypes and labels is especially one-sided.[17] It also implies a process happening "out there" in social life and not in the work of social science (and other science) itself. But ideas like racial difference – and indeed the special connection of racial difference to sexuality – flourished precisely on the basis of prestigious nineteenth-century evolutionary science; and in the present era too, labeling and the construction of identities and the demarcating of differences have hardly been social processes from which sociologists have kept their distance.

There is also risk that the "social constructionist" story will become a social determinism, too easily paired with an overly fixed, "essentialist" notion of society or culture. Thus sociologists who challenge essentialist approaches to individuals willingly speak of "the essence of community"[18] and sophisticated role analysts unselfcritically employ terms like "deviance" to describe persons who do not fit normatively sanctioned roles.[19] Within sociology, as Hewitt puts it, "the fundamental reference of identity is social location."[20]

Recent approaches to issues of identity have stressed the incompleteness, fragmentation, and contradictions of both collective and personal existence. They have shown how complex is the relationship among projects of identity, social demands, and personal possibilities. And in order to do so, they have commonly started with the deconstruction of "essentialist" categories and rhetorics. These discussions have been widespread and bear the general stamp of poststructuralism.[21] Derrida's challenge to essentialism is perhaps the most influential. But the exploration of this theme has been most far-reaching and sociologically substantive within the discourses of feminist and gay theory.[22]

This is not because feminists, gay men, or lesbians have settled the issue. On the contrary, each group remains deeply divided but the concerns are widely understood to be basic and therefore have drawn substantial theoretical attention. In a sense, the debate stems from a collision between the core practical political theme of both movements – claiming, legitimating, and valuing identities commonly suppressed or devalued by mainstream culture – and the poststructuralism that emerged as the theoretical discourse of choice for leading-edge feminists and gay or lesbian thinkers. Poststructuralism's attack on essentialism and "decentering of the subject" came into conflict with thinking and politics rooted in the standpoint of women or the experience of gays. This was not simply a conflict between theory and popular political practice, however, for the theoretical discourse was deeply involved in and shaped by political practice, and the practice often fissured along the same lines as the theory. The claim that a standpoint of women "essentialized" gender identities, for example, came not only from abstract or academic deconstructionist critiques, but from women of color and lesbians who argued that presumptions of white, heterosexual (and for that matter middle-class) experience structured both the women's movement and academic feminist analyses.[23] As hooks' recent restatement of this point reveals, however, the issue runs deeper than simply biasing theory or practice towards one group or excluding others; it strikes at core matters of conceptualization:

> The concept "Woman" effaces the difference between women in specific sociohistorical contexts, between women defined precisely as historical subjects rather than *a* psychic subject (or non-subject). . . . For . . . only as one imagines "woman" in the abstract, when woman becomes fiction or fantasy, can race not be seen as significant.[24]

Behind this argument over "essentialism" lie a number of longstanding approaches to identity. Philosophical arguments rooted most importantly in Aristotle, for example, pursued identity in terms of the relationship between "essence" and "appearance," or between the true nature of phenomena and epiphenomenal variations. This appeal to nature was reinforced and transformed with the rise of both modern arguments about the biological roots of human identities and Romantic demands for individuals to express and be true to their inner natures.[25] Nietzsche extended and radicalized Romantic naturalism, but also made the person more complex by showing how repressed human nature could turn against itself. Freud pushed Nietzsche's insight further, and psychoanalysis both constituted the individual in a newly complex way and showed that identity had to be achieved in development rather than merely discovered in direct reference to nature. At the same time, psychoanalysis continued a version of naturalizing discourse in its widespread approach to difference as pathology, and of essentialism in its argument that individuals must pursue a project of integral identity – e.g. must work to achieve an essentially coherent gender identity despite the ambiguities of early experience. Functionalist sociology participated in the naturalizing language of "pathology" and even non-functionalists pursued theories of "deviance" that reproduced essentialist notions of both normal and deviant identities. It was a crucial part of Derrida's intellectual project to challenge all such essentializing moves as reproductions of an illegitimate and imprisoning metaphysical tradition which needed to be contested even if it was not quite possible to escape through this contest.[26]

Critiques of aspects of these naturalizing and/or essentializing discourses did not have to wait for Derrida's radical formulation, however, but were developed early on, and in each case the discourse itself was amenable to reformulation away from essentialism. Thus psychoanalysis was reproduced as a theory of the social construction of seemingly natural identities and characteristics (as in Karen Horney's work and that of interactionists more generally) and later became (especially in "object relations" and Lacanian versions) a theory of fragmented and incomplete selves and one of the principal sources of the feminist critique of essentialism. Even sociologists who continued to use labels like "deviance" often committed themselves to radical social constructionist theories that insisted that unmediated nature had little influence on individual or collective identities while "socialization" processes were all-important.

Social constructionism proved, however, an ambiguous ally in the attempt to oppose the devaluing of various identities. Social constructionist approaches could be just as determinist as naturalizing approaches, for example, when they denied or minimized personal and political agency by stressing seemingly omnipresent but diffuse social pressures as the alternative to biological causation. The emphases on early socialization and on the power of social structure also led many social constructionists to treat identities in terms nearly as "essentialist" as those of biological determinists. The origins of various identities were seen as constructed and therefore potentially mutable, thus, so that in principle socialization processes and social structure could be changed. Boys might not brought up to be violent, or girls might be brought up to excel at math. But such programs of social change only operated on "sex-roles," rather than on gendered thinking as such. More specifically, one-sided social constructionism suggested variability in the correlates of "male" and "female," "homosexual" and "heterosexual" but then often treated the people addressed under these labels as essentially similar – i.e. similar to each other in terms of some true underlying identity or standard of equivalence. bell hooks made this point sharply in arguing against the term "sexual orientation."[27] By the time she wrote, this was displacing the alternative "sexual preference."[28] But hooks suggested that the notion of a singular sexual "orientation" was a reification. It suggested that individuals were somehow sexually open to or desirous of sexual interaction with all members of one sex or the other, minimizing both the autonomy of the individual and the differentiation of people within genders.[29] In the same vein, Eve Sedgwick showed the implicit narrowing of agency in strong versions of constructionism – those that emphasize not what individual people construct for themselves, nor the histories which some construct for others, but the massive though diffuse impact of impersonal social processes – and Diane Fuss argued that "constructionism (the position that differences are constructed, not innate) really operates as a more sophisticated form of essentialism."[30]

In one of the most decisive arguments as to why merely labeling an opposing view "essentialism" settled little in this debate, Donna Haraway showed how the opposition between essentialism and constructionism had often been deployed in such a way as to reinforce a nature/culture division that should instead be deconstructed.[31] Reference to biology was commonly dismissed with the accusation "essentialist." Among other effects, this freed critics from the obligation to learn enough biology to engage it in really serious critique. It presented biology as itself, ironically, an essentialized category, neglecting the internal differentiation of positions, the possibilities for critical intervention and new thinking – including thinking with concepts that had been deployed in essentialist fashion but against the grain of the theories in which they had previously been invoked. Perhaps most incisively, Haraway showed how a rejection of all biological thinking as essentialist contributed to difficulties in taking biology seriously on the part of the very women's movement that played such a large role in returning the body to social and cultural discourse.

Rather than a simple opposition between essentialism and constructionism, it is important to see a field of possible strategies for confronting issues of identity. Several feminist thinkers, for example, have argued that it may sometimes be crucial to "risk essentialism."[32] They do not have in mind a simple return to uncontested categories or uncritical assumptions of the biological determination of true identity. Rather, the point is to see that under certain circumstances – mainly identified as political but I think arguably also intellectual – self-critical claims to strong, basic, and shared identity may be useful. At its simplest, the argument suggests that where a particular category of identity has been repressed, delegitimated, or devalued in dominant discourses, a vital response may be to claim value for all those labeled by that category, thus implicitly invoking it in an essentialist way. Thus in the early years of the women's movement, it may have been vital for resistance to male domination and even for creative initiatives to construct a standpoint of women as such, to essentialize *écriture feminine*, to appeal to the presumed commonalities in the embodied experience of women. How much this need has been reduced is basic to strategic debates. But ironically, even the critique of how reliance on the general category "woman" obscured the variations among "women" itself has depended on the evocation of more specific quasi-essentialist categories – e.g. black women, lesbians, etc. In short, it may not be helpful to allow the critique of essentialism to become a prohibition against the use of all general categories of identity.

It is misleading to see essentialism as simply a historical stage, as though it is an error of eighteenth- and nineteenth-century thought out of which all "advanced" thinkers have grown. In the first place, the eighteenth and nineteenth centuries were somewhat more complex than that. The roots of social constructionist arguments, after all, lie in Lockean behaviorism and such nineteenth-century inheritors as Owenite socialism (in which context some of their early applications to gender issues arose) and were in many ways extended by nineteenth-century social theory.[33] It is common to speak as though essentialism reigned throughout Western history until a new Enlightenment freed us in the postwar era. Sometimes the contrast is narrower – essentialism is seen as modernist and postmodernism has saved us from it. In many cases such views are supported by rather simplistic reflection theories of knowledge suggesting that successive stages of capitalism or of communications technology have unequivocally produced their fitting complements in the realm of knowledge.

A more accurate historical story might start by recognizing the special force essentialist reasoning gained during the modern era as part of several different but related intellectual and practical projects. It reinforced and was reinforced by the rise of individualism, the rhetoric of national identity, and appeals to nature as a "moral source."[34] It participated in both the advance of universalistic moral reasoning – as for example the notion of human rights was grounded on a presumed essential commonality of human beings – and the advance of relativistic social explanation and moral construction – as from Montesquieu on the laws and mores of different peoples were understood as specific to their contexts. But this essentialist reasoning did not disappear. In the current clash between promoters of Western democracy and advocates of a neo-Confucian authoritarianism in Asia, for example, the competing essentialisms just mentioned come to the fore again as proponents of democracy are described as "human rights imperialists." Within the women's movement the matter is no clearer. For every critique of liberal "rights talk," there are two defenses of women's choice regarding abortion and childbirth that are rooted in essentialist claims to rights. There is no easy and clear-cut answer to Fuss's question, "How do we reconcile the poststructuralist project to displace identity with the feminist project to reclaim it?" Her question is addressed most immediately to Luce Irigaray, a French feminist theorist who absorbs much from Lacanian psychoanalysis but who also insists on a distinctive female imaginary rooted in female bodies. Irigaray's materialism has seemed simply an essentialism to many critics. Toril Moi, for example, reads Irigaray as fixing the representation of women in the metaphysical project of defining "woman."[35] Others are troubled by her insistent focus on genital physiology. Yet Irigaray herself argues against an order in which only men have full subjectivity and therefore essential identities while women are defined by their lack and presumed non-self-sufficiency.[36] Her work is full simultaneously of deconstruction of essentialist male logic and qualified, strategic claims to female essence. This can be read negatively for its seeming inconsistencies, or positively for the suggestion that it is not productive to be simply for or against essentialism.

The road forward from the early predominance of essentialist approaches to identity lies not in simple reversal. Rather, it lies – historically in the last hundred plus years of Western thought and prospectively for each of us – in a proliferation of the theoretical and practical tools with which we can confront problems of identity and difference. To essentialist reason we *add* constructionism and to this dualism we add the possibilities of both deconstructing and claiming identities.[37] Moreover, we can see that essentialism itself need not be essentialized, that there are a plethora of claims to "basic" or "root" or essential identities that stand on different grounds, that cohabit with different political bedfellows (or their female gendered equivalents), that open (or foreclose) different insights or coalitions or conflicts.

One implication of this is that the challenges posed by projects of identity cannot be averted simply by asserting that those projects are embedded in essentialist thinking. We cannot really stop thinking at least partially in categories – and therefore in at least something rather like an essentialist manner. Just as Derrida suggests we can never entirely escape from metaphysics however critical of it we may become, our task must be to remain seriously self-critical about our invocations of essence and identity. This means among other things paying attention to the agonistic, fractured, problematic aspects of identity. The politics of identity – politics either starting from or aiming at claimed identities of their protagonists – have to be taken seriously. The struggles occasioned by identity politics need to be understood, however, not as simply between those who claim different identities but within each subject as the multiple and contending discourses of our era challenge any of our efforts to attain stable self-recognition or coherent subjectivity.

III

The background to identity politics thus lies not only in ideological and cultural changes but in transformations of social structure and societal integration. These change not only the nature of our individual and collective projects – as for example careers in global business corporations and worldwide mobilizations of environmentalists to save rain forests become possible – but also the nature of our relationships to each other. Theoretical attempts to grasp the new scale and forms of societal integration have often combined interest in "rationalization" with attention to structures of relationships themselves. But this can lead to some confusion and a relatively uncritical packaging together of aspects of social life – and the constitution of identities – that do not have to move precisely together. We can see the issue in Habermas's distinction of system from lifeworld. Grasping something basic to modern social life, this nonetheless leads Habermas into a problematic treatment of identity as basically prepolitical and correspondingly only a weak recognition of the importance of collective identity, into an idealization of the lifeworld and a presentation of movements of identity politics primarily as reactions to systemic incursions into lifeworlds, rather than as attempts to improve upon or respond to tensions and contradictions within lifeworlds, and into an emphasis on rationality and the differentiation of modes of life by cognitively defined forms of action that undermines adequate attention to structures of social relationships and the formation of practical projects.

It would be a mistake to give up on projects like Habermas's attempt to theorize the transformation and differentiation of modern life. Simply to deny the issues he tries to grasp with the opposition of system and lifeworld undermines the capacity of critical theory to come to terms with the structural background that frames the possibilities for contemporary action. The divergence between direct interpersonal relationships and of large-scale apparently autonomous social systems is basic to the modern era. But it works not just as an objective distinction of realms or modes of social organization; it is also constitutive of our modes of experience of and action in the social world. Weber sought to grasp this as a part of the general process of rationalization in which (identity based) communal action (*Gemeinschaftshandeln*) was replaced by (rationally regulated) social action (*Gesellschaftshandeln*).[38] Though Weber did not focus much on patterns of concrete relationships as such (in the way that, for example, Simmel did), the *Gemeinschaft/Gesellschaft* distinction provided the rudiments of a relationally concrete background to the general phenomenon of the differentiation of value spheres. Habermas suggests a further split within the realm of rational action into "action oriented to reaching understanding and action oriented to success."[39] It is on the basis of the former that he attempts to rescue the Enlightenment project of rationalization from entrapment in the Weberian iron cage of domination.

A key challenge for Habermas's critical theory is to find a way to maintain the momentum of communicative rationality in the face of systemic, instrumental rationality on the one hand and recidivistic calls for a return to some premodern form of community and traditional authority on the other. But Habermas runs into four difficulties.

First, as McCarthy has indicated, he tends to appropriate systems-theory and sociological functionalism rather too completely for the sake of the critical edge of his theory and its relevance to action.[40] Though indebted to the marxist tradition he virtually abandons analysis of class and other fundamental social divisions.[41] Power relations play little constitutive role in his conceptualization of society. Relatedly, he does not make conflictual collective action a significant part of his account of social change.

Second, the Enlightenment rationalism underlying Habermas's project leads him to reject too completely the importance of tradition to intellectual life generally, and traditional communities as bases for progressive popular action. His accounts of human action and reason are always abstracted from cultural or social particularities and identities. Sociologically and hermeneutically it is necessary to give greater weight to the unchosen foundations for action if we are to envision either a stable society or a deeply motivated radical challenge to established patterns and tendencies; this is one of the reasons why Bourdieu's theory appears in the present discussion as an important complement to Habermas's.[42] If any form of lifeworld activity is to be defensible in the face of system world challenges, it will need to depend on strong social commitments, not simply contingent individual choices, however rational.

Third, Habermas's notion of pure communicative action, idealized in his account of the rationalized lifeworld, derives from institutional arenas that are hardly realms of perfect communication and freedom, including for example family relations that have generally been patriarchal.[43] While Habermas's conceptual opposition between action oriented to understanding and action oriented to success makes sense, in other words, the idea that the lifeworld and system can be concretized as spheres of life (e.g. family and community vs. bureaucracies and markets) is seriously problematic. Habermas presumes a lifeworld that is (1) separable in principle from systemic organization (e.g. not also constituted and given its specific organization by capitalism), and (2) somehow free from the reign of power and oppression and constituted – even in principle – by pure communicative action. In a world of compulsory heterosexism, family violence, and legal, economic, and cultural pressures that reduce women's choices about marriage and childbearing, it is hard to see the lifeworld – or the sphere of intimate and family relations that Habermas takes as its archetype – as unambiguously the locus of quality human relationships or to see all the problems of personal life as stemming from colonization by the system. Two forms of understanding may be involved – one more concrete and phenomenological, the other more abstract – but neither constitutes a realm free of power relations. And if power relations, however personal and direct, involve an instrumental or success orientation, so real-world bureaucracies involve meaningful social bonds and communicative action.

Fourth, Habermas's account of system and lifeworld lacks an adequate social structural foundation.[44] Not only does it not provide for an analysis of class conflict and power relations, it takes changing orientations to action as both the primary causes and primary results of the large-scale social changes of modernity. Little independent role is ascribed to demography, patterns in networks of concrete relationships, or capitalism's relentless expansion. Habermas takes changes in orientation to social action as primary, rather than seeing them as arising dialectically in relation to such social structural factors as the transformation in scale of social organization. It is in some part material changes in the scale and form of social relationships that necessitate adoption of instrumental or systemic orientations to action.

Habermas's theory posits two forms of societal integration, and indeed is important partly because it returns the issue of societal integration to the center of theoretical discussion in an innovative, not altogether functionalist way. But Habermas is ambiguous about whether system and lifeworld are to be understood as two spheres of life, or as two ways of looking at a social world which is always the result of constructive human action. The latter seems to me the more defensible view. There is no sharp demarcation between lifeworld and system. Rather, our experience in modern society leads to divergent ways of trying to understand the social world, and to an experiential and intellectual split between lifeworld and system (or such common sense analogs as "the people" and "the system," "everyday life" and "the big picture," etc.). This view is easier to maintain if we introduce a distinction between directly interpersonal social relationships (whether primary or secondary in Cooley's terms) and the indirect relationships which are formed when social action affects others only through the mediation of complex organizations, impersonal markets, or communications technology. Indirect relationships permit a societal scale unimaginable on the basis of direct relationships, and simultaneously encourage objectification and reification of their origin in human action.[45] They are much more likely to be approached solely with an orientation to instrumental success than are directly interpersonal relations (though the latter may be similarly degraded).

Rather than focusing on kinds of relationships as such, Habermas begins with a qualitative distinction of forms of rational action: instrumental (oriented to success in relation to objectified goals) and communicative (oriented to reflective understanding and the constitution of social relations).[46] In this view, both of these develop naturally in the course of human history. They come into conflict when they give rise to competing forms of societal integration – system and social (lifeworld):

> Thus there is a competition *not between the types of action* oriented to understanding and success [which Habermas sees as complementary], *but between principles of societal integration* – between the mechanism of linguistic communication that is oriented to validity claims – a mechanism that emerges in increasing purity from the rationalization of the lifeworld – and those de-linguistified steering media through which systems of success-oriented action are differentiated out.[47]

Money is the paradigmatic example of the "de-linguistified" steering media to which Habermas (following Parsons) refers, but a wide range of statistical indicators (e.g. of productivity, public opinion, etc.) share many relevant features. These media allow social systems to be "steered" as though they were independent of human action. Through systems theory they may be understood in the same way. Indeed, the real complexity of very large-scale social processes may dictate that they can be grasped better in cybernetic and other relatively abstract academic terms, than in terms of the ordinary discourse of the lifeworld. Accordingly, Habermas uses systems theory in his analysis of system integration even while he attacks the reifying (and anti-democratic) tendencies of systems theory. What is unclear is whether or how he maintains in his theory the ability to show that such large-scale indirect phenomena remain nonetheless human social activities and relationships.

Heavily influenced by Niklas Luhmann, Habermas comes very close to losing the "unmasking" moment of a putatively critical theory and allowing the reifications of cybernetic theory – which actual social arrangements make convenient and predispose us to use – to be accepted as fully satisfactory accounts of social systems.[48] It seems to me preferable to

argue that very large-scale social organization based on indirect relationships is difficult of to understand without recourse to the kind of
understanding Habermas describes as typical of the system world. This is
a way of looking at social action well suited to large-scale phenomena,
but nonetheless it is an intellectual choice. In other words, when relationships are directly interpersonal we are unlikely to fail to recognize the
extent to which they are human social creations. But when they are
highly indirect, mediated by technology, markets, and complex organizations, we are more likely to lose sight of their constitution out of human
action – and thus their inherently political character. Indirect relationships sometimes assume a solidity that is less typical of those direct
relationships in which action is more often and more clearly visible.
Arendt remarked on the "notorious uncertainty not only of all political
matters, but of all affairs that go on between men directly, without the
intermediary, stabilizing, and solidifying influence of things."[49] Large-
scale systems of indirect relations appear as relatively stable partly because we – more or less of necessity – grasp their operation through
aggregate statistics and systemic conceptions like those of cybernetic
theory. These will tend to make it look as though the large-scale systems
were somehow autonomously functioning entities rather than creations
of human social action.

We see this each time economists talk about the economy as though it
were a natural system to be predicted and understood in the same
manner as the weather (and indeed, economists are increasingly called
upon to play a role similar to that of weather forecasters on the television
news). It is almost impossible to see the manifold ways in which human
actions create large-scale markets, for example, and certainly to understand complex economic processes on the basis simply of aggregation
upward from those specific relationships of buying, selling, making,
using, etc. A categorial break is intellectually necessary in order to look
at these holistically, on a collective level of analysis. This break is not a
break in reality, however, but in our approach to understanding it. A
critical theorist needs continually to remind herself or himself that it is
provisional; it must be unmasked recurrently to reveal the actual human
activity creating the larger system. "System" is not, then, a sphere of life
so much as it is a mode of understanding (one which is particularly
relevant to certain spheres of activity). That mode of understanding is
made convenient (if not necessary) for considering societal integration by
the proliferation of indirect relationships on a very large scale.

A result of this, however, is that the economy, the state and other very
large-scale institutions are likely to appear to most citizens as alien
forces: bewildering, powerful beings rather than the abstractions critical

thinkers may see them to be. They are reified, and the baffling way in which they confront us makes this reification not an easily escapable form of false consciousness but an almost unavoidable condition of practical thought in the modern world. Their functioning can be grasped well only through statistics, theories, cybernetic concepts, and other intellectual tools which are both poorly distributed among the population, and also at odds with the direct understanding which people gain of their immediate surroundings. The lifeworld, by contrast, can be understood intuitively; it is a "lived reality," not an abstraction.

Many of people's most basic values concern attachments within the lifeworld – family, home, standard of living, religious experience, etc. The fact that people have such deep commitments to lifeworld attachments is an important reason why they resist the encroachments of large-scale institutions which seem to threaten them.[50] Habermas does not confront this issue very directly because he focuses on an extremely rationalized ideal of communicative action when considering the lifeworld, rather than on anything approximating contemporary lived experience.

The same immediate understanding of and high value on much of the lifeworld that supports communitarian, populist resistance to encroachments of impersonal systemic organization of everyday life is also a crucial source of the temptation to try to understand systemic integration through simple extension of lifeworld categories. As Castells puts it, "when people find themselves unable to control the world, they simply shrink the world to the size of their community."[51] This is a fundamental misrecognition built into the bulk of localist, populist politics today.[52] It also shapes and challenges movements and processes of identity politics. Not only may they misperceive the structural factors helping to reproduce culture or behavior they seek to change. More basically, the difficulties and opportunities to which they respond stem largely from the mutual implication of lifeworld and system in the social projects in which they are engaged. A feminist politics that stresses that "the personal is political" does not just defend the realm of the personal against colonization by systemic forces, but takes up the power relations constituting the most intimate and personal arenas of life. Some of these power relations are inextricably rooted in systemic patterns of social organization; so, however, are many of the resources – like law courts – by which personal power relations can be contested. Similarly, it makes no sense to see religious fundamentalisms as simply traditional or defenses of primordial lifeworld values or relationships; they arise precisely out of the simultaneous embeddedness in multiple projects that are hard to reconcile under existing conditions: economic advancement and family solidarity, moral rectitude and political power, clarity of identity and exchanges across lines of cultural difference.

The temptation to misrecognize a complicated and frustrating world is played upon by many politicians who offer illusory accounts of and solutions to social problems – accounts which make sense only on the basis of the denial of any basic difference between large-scale organization of social systems and everyday organization of directly interpersonal relationships. President Reagan, for example, told American television viewers that balancing the federal budget was really no different from balancing a family's checkbook. He capitalized on both the spurious intimacy of the television medium which made possible a jocular informality, and on the appeal of an account which falsely reassured his viewers that the workings of the federal government and the national and international economies were not deeply complex and difficult to master, but potentially as manageable as a routine of everyday life. The apparent complexity, he implied, was only obscurantism on the part of elites; the danger people sensed, while real, was only the result of stubborn foolishness on the part of a few people with highly particular vested interests. Though this sort of catering to public desires for a reassuring misunderstanding of systemic affairs may be particularly typical of mass-mediated executive branch politics, a similar mode of thought is important to much oppositional, populist politics.[53] It is because populist politics are in this sense a response to the divide between system and lifeworld that they are endemic to modern and modernizing societies. In modern societies, state and economy require and continually extend indirect relationships. The most powerful determinants of the general shape of society and of the web of relationships within which individuals will operate thus cannot be understood through extension of lifeworld ways of understanding to systemic social organization.

At the heart of Habermas's project is recognition that a future without instrumental rationality and impersonal systems of money and power based on it is fundamentally implausible. The lifeworld cannot be autonomous. If democracy rather than rule by experts is sought, the lifeworld must provide for some organization of analysis and discourse that enables people to understand and exert some control over the systems they have created. Habermas's understanding of the lifeworld, however, places the central emphasis on people's presumably primary orientations towards communication which is at least potentially full, free, and undistorted. It is not the lifeworld in general which he wishes to defend, but an idealized, purified form of communicative action aimed at interpersonal understanding. He conceptualizes this through the notion of an idealized speech situation, in which certain validity claims (to comprehensibility, truth, appropriateness, and sincerity) which are always implicit in speech are universalized. All real historical societies fall short of this ideal, but they may be compared to it and evaluated in terms of an evolutionary scale of undistorted communication.[54] Something closer to the ideal emerges from the lifeworld through a process of rationalization:

> Correspondingly, a lifeworld can be regarded as rationalized to the extent that it permits interactions that are not guided by normatively *ascribed* agreement but – directly or indirectly – by communicatively *achieved* understanding.[55]

"Communicatively achieved understanding," for Habermas, refers mainly to communication among individuals who already have identities, and the removal of blockages that normatively sanctioned culture may offer to common understanding, but not to the production of meaning or the creation of culture and identity. The work of rationality is, in part, to allow rational challenges to established agreements maintained by cultural hegemony. It provides for critique. But it does not bring culture-forming and identity-forming processes to the forefront of attention. Rather, Habermas focuses on the ways in which people who have already constructed identities organize their action in relation to each other. Do they pursue further mutual understanding through communicative action, or do they pursue only instrumental action, especially in relation to systems of money and power?

Neglect of the culture-forming dimension of human activity places the matter of achieving common understanding under the guiding model of translation (as discussed critically in chapter 3 above). It diverts our attention from the ways in which histories of mutual engagement produce new culture and new identities such that shared understandings are easier or harder to achieve. It also diverts our attention from the ways in which the pursuit of identity – and recognition of identities – is commonly a matter of politics, not only normative ascription or communicative understanding.

IV

Recognition is at the heart of the matter. No matter when and where one looks, subjectivity is perhaps best understood as a project, as something always under construction, never perfect. In varying degrees for different people and in different circumstances it may be more or less challenging, but it is never automatic. A crucial aspect of the project of subjectivity is identity. Identity turns on the interrelated problems of self-recognition and recognition by others. Recognition is vital to any reflexivity, for example, any capacity to look at oneself, to choose one's actions and see their consequences, and to hope to make oneself something more or better than one is. This component of recognition may be the aspect of identity made most problematic by the social changes of modernity.

Recognition may never have followed immediately on socially derived and/or sanctioned identities. There has probably always been some room for manipulation, some need for management or at least for successful presentation or performance. But with enormous nation-states, international diasporas, wide realms of personal choice, unstable and heterogeneous networks of social relations, mass media for the proliferation of cultural transmission, and the sheer multiplicity of discourses attempting to name or constitute persons, the social basis for recognition has come under particular challenge. The sheer scope and complexity of recognizable identities and competing social projects and identity-schemes makes recognition problematic and in need of specific establishment in various institutional and interactional settings.[56]

Problems involving recognition – or nonrecognition – by others are integrally related to issues in personal self-recognition. This is one of the reasons why the sometimes abused and increasingly criticized feminist slogan, "the personal is political," still merits attention. It is not just that others fail to see us for who we are sure we really are, or repress us because of who they think we are. We face problems of recognition because socially sustained discourses about who it is possible or appropriate or valuable to be inevitably shape the way we look at and constitute ourselves, with varying degrees of agonism and tension. These concerns frequently, though not uniformly, are expressed in and give rise to "identity politics."

These identity-pursuits are "politics" for several reasons. These go beyond the general assertion that "the personal is political," even though that slogan helped pioneer the feminist version of these identity politics. The slogan accepted the implicit division of personal or private and public or social systemic realms in order or challenge the notion that power and politics did not operate in the family, intimate relations, and other aspects of "personal" life. But almost immediately, feminist theorists also began to challenge that very division, showing for example how the distinction of public and private had operated to marginalize women and to distort both the realms it helped to constitute.

The pursuits labeled "identity politics" are collective, not merely individual, and public not only private. They are struggles, not merely gropings; power partially determines outcomes and power relations are changed by the struggles. They involve seeking recognition, legitimacy (and sometimes power), not only expression or autonomy; other people, groups, and organizations (including states) are called upon to respond. Indeed, one of the most problematic effects of the new age, pop psychological and self-help rhetorics with which many identity politics movements have articulated their concerns and programs is a tendency to obscure their necessarily social, political, and public character. Finally, identity-politics movements are political because they involve refusing, diminishing, or displacing identities others wish to recognize in individuals. This is familiar in rethinkings of both gender and racial identities – and made particularly visible in the latter case by the recurrent replacement of collective labels (negro, colored, black, Afro-American, African-American) that had come to impose identities at odds with the identity-claims of those labeled. It is given a sharp focus in the difference between critiques of homophobia and of compulsory heterosexism. The former accepts the category "homosexual" and challenges the fears, attacks, and delegitimations visited upon homosexuals. The latter resists the particular version of sexual identity (and for that matter sexualization of identity) that undergirds a host of social practices, opening a space for other practices or sexual orientations (including but not limited to those commonly labeled as homosexual) without being rooted in a specific identity-claim.[57]

The issue of resistance to imposed or fixed identities has encouraged in many quarters a shift from identity politics to a politics of difference. This focus on a critique of identity – often extended in poststructuralist and especially Derridian circles through a critique of identity as such rather than merely specifically problematic identities – is sometimes presented as though it marks a transcendence of identity politics. As Christina Crosby remarks, however, " 'differences' work now more or less as 'identity' did before."[58] Or, as I have suggested above, the choice between deconstructing and claiming identities (or identity as such) may be one that needs to be shaped by strategic considerations, not dictated by theoretical and normative first principles; to speak of identity is not always simply or only to repress. The operations of deconstructing and claiming coexist only in tension, but they may need nonetheless always to coexist and inform each other.

These various versions of identity politics have shaped and been shaped by a range of specific movements. Among the most commonly cited cases are the so-called liberation and lifestyle movements that have flourished in the relatively rich countries since the 1960s: women's movements, movements of gay men and lesbians, movements of African-Americans, Chicanos, Asians, youth and countercultural movements, deep ecology, and so forth. This list of examples is commonly associated with the idea of new social movements (NSMs).[59]

The new social movements idea is, however, problematic and obscures the greater significance of identity politics. Without much theoretical rationale, it groups together what seem to the researchers relatively "attractive" movements, vaguely on the left, but leaves out such other contemporary movements as the new religious right and fundamentalism, the resistance of white ethnic communities against people of color, various versions of nationalism, and so forth. Yet these are equally manifestations of identity politics and there is no principle that clearly explains their exclusion from the lists drawn up by NSM theorists.[60]

The NSM idea is rooted in an opposition of the movements that began to flourish in the 1960s to the labor and socialist movements that had putatively previously dominated activism. The older movements were allegedly governed by a single dominant identity structure rather than allowing for the open play and legitimation of many identities. Perhaps this was true of the 1950s, but it is historically myopic.[61] In the early nineteenth century, labor movements were engaged in identity politics, presenting the case that "worker" was an identity deserving of legitimacy, calling for solidarity among those sharing this identity, and demanding their inclusion in the polity. At the same time, socialism was dominated by utopian visions, calls for direct action, and attempts to reformulate fundamental ideas about human nature. NSMs have ebbed and flowed throughout modernity.

One could read the history of social movements as the story of efforts to bring "social" concerns into political contestation. As we shall see further in the next chapter, a key root to this was the claim that properly political concerns – and the legitimacy of political rule – could be determined "from the bottom up" and not only by rulers. In different ways, the Protestant Reformation, the struggles for liberal political institutions that brought both American and French Revolutions, and the struggles for socialism and democracy, all proposed to change the constitution of society dramatically and to use political means for novel pursuits. Identity politics have more generally been basic to a whole range of movements that sought to use the public sphere to challenge existing arrangements or bring forward new possibilities in religion, sexual relations, the human relation to nature, community life, work and economics, and a host of other dimensions of social life. To argue that wage rates or factory health should be a matter for state regulation was to bring "the social" into the political realm.

Different understandings and valuations of pressing social concerns were not just matters of fixed interests. They were – and necessarily are

– matters of the constitution of identities. Neither identities nor interests neatly come before the other; the struggle to achieve what we believe to be in our interest shapes our identities as much as the identities determine what we see as in our interests. The point is that neither is altogether fixed. Both are produced and altered in the course of everyday social projects and collective mobilizations of varying scale. There is always some politics to this process.

The notion that identity politics is a new phenomenon is, in sum, clearly false. The women's movement has roots at least two hundred years old. The founding of communes was as important in the early 1800s as in the 1960s. Weren't the European nationalisms of the nineteenth century instances of identity politics? What of the struggles of African-Americans in the wake of slavery? What of anticolonial resistance? Neither is identity politics limited to the relatively affluent (the "post-materialists" as Inglehart calls them), as though there were some clear hierarchy of needs in which clearly defined material interests precede culture and struggles over the constitution of the nature of interests – both material and spiritual.[62] Throughout the modern era, the capacity of ordinary people to bring their interests and their projects of identity formation into the public sphere and the political process has increased enormously. The expansion of the state, and the intensification of its reach into everyday life, is one powerful reason. The state suggests, among other things, that it is a practical possibility to act on the organization of everyday life, to change how it is constituted. It also occasions resistance. Moreover, the modern era has been enormously productive of movements partly because each wave of activism is productive of new potentials for activism – both because of demonstration effects and because of the nurturance of experienced leaders and participants (whose participation will not be limited to the same issues and identities that moved them in the past) and networks and organizations. Partly because of the very history of movements themselves, as well as because of changes in state power, capitalism, media, and other social forces, the production of identity politics is an expanding as well as a pervasive feature of the modern era.

Identity politics has been part and parcel of modern politics and social life for hundreds of years. But it has had to contend with various more universalizing, difference-denying, ways of thinking about politics and social life, and these have shaped the nature not only of our polities but of our academic thinking. Social science has paid only intermittent attention to issues of identity and identity politics. They do not figure in strong ways in classical social theory (though the construction of the generic, identity-bearing individual does). More recently objectivism, systemic determinism, and instrumental, interest-based understandings of motivation have kept social theorists from appreciating the importance of identity and identity politics.

Identity formation is commonly brought into consideration, if at all, as a prior condition of adult participation in social life – e.g. in socialization theory (and note the special place of socialization in, e.g., Parsons' functionalism). This is so even with regard to public life: in conceptualizing the public sphere, Habermas presumes that the private sphere provides it with fully formed subjects with settled identities and capacities.[63] Habermas discusses ways in which the literary public sphere helped to prepare the kinds of subjects needed for public political discourse, but once it has fulfilled its role as precursor to the political public sphere, the literary discourse drops out of Habermas's picture. He does not consider the continuing transformations of subjectivity wrought not only in literature but in a host of identity-forming public spheres.[64] Neither does he consider how identity might be transformed through public political activity. Upon entrance to the essentially liberal public sphere, he suggests following the idealized practices of the eighteenth-century bourgeois public sphere, differences of identity must be bracketed rather than thematized. On the other hand, of course, one of the problems that has led to the recent emphasis on a *politics* of the personal is that identity-forming discourses, even when carried out in public spheres of readers, cinema viewers, students, or self-help oriented radio talk shows, often fail to institutionalize attention to their own publicness and to recognize their implicit politics. Many of these discourses are "public" in the sense of being open to a variety of different participants, but not in the sense of thematically constituting themselves as *about* public matters. This has profound implications for the ways in which they can empower their participants and suggests an important politics about what discourses are either able or inclined to present themselves as being about matters of public significance.

Here Habermas's theory with its famous inattention to difference shares a problem with many forms of identity politics rooted in claims to difference. As Judith Butler puts it, "for the subject to be a pregiven point of departure for politics is to defer the question of the political construction and regulation of the subject itself."[65] This is a problem with the presumption of woman or women as subject just as with the implicitly male universal subjects of Habermas's public sphere. Social science suffers from this inattention (even incapacity) at all levels of analysis from individuals through such larger units as nations and even the globe or species. The problem reaches to significant practical political issues. There is generally no attention to the constitution of individual subjects in the discourse of human rights, for example, and in consideration of self-determination, nations are commonly understood as always already existing.

The constitution of identities has not only been kept off center stage. It has been presented as a more or less harmonious process resulting in a normally stable and minimally changing identity. Thus we have been led by our theories often to underestimate the struggle involved forging identities, the tension inherent in the fact that we all have multiple, incomplete, and/or fragmented identities (and sometimes resistances), the politics implied by the differential public standing of various identities or identity-claims, and the possibilities for our salient constructions of identities to change in the context of powerfully meaningful, emotionally significant events – like many social movements.

Just as conventional social theory misleads us, however, and obscures the importance of identity and identity politics, the contemporary advocates who have brought identity politics into the forefront of our attention often present the phenomenon in misleading and problematic ways. The false novelty of NSMs is an example of this. Many advocates and sympathetic analysts falsely oppose the struggle for identity to the demands of society; they accept far too sharp a separation between the individual as locus of interior feelings that need to be expressed in identity-claims, and society as exterior source of pressures for conformity.

This obscures the extent to which social life calls forth or demands identity-claims and provides opportunities (albeit biased ones) for their assertion. Among other things, our various claims and resistances to identities make sense only against the background of other identity-claims and social valuations. As Charles Taylor has argued, we need to be wary of a kind of "soft relativism" that suggests that all claims to recognition have the same standing, and that recognition can proceed without judgment.[66] To try to grant *a priori* equal recognition to all identity claims (or deconstructions) amounts to taking none seriously. Or as Rey Chow puts it, "since positions are now infinitely interchangeable, many feel that postmodernism may be little more than a recompensatory 'I'm OK, you're OK' inclusion or a leveling attribution of subversive 'marginality' to all."[67] Soft relativism also commonly obscures the extent to which identity claims are socially nurtured and constructed, not merely reflections of each individuals's inner (natural) truth. In some versions, it even and (somewhat ironically) reproduces tendencies to radically liberal individualism with its implied universalism. Those making identity-claims often present them within a rhetoric implying that everyone is equally endowed with identity, equally entitled to their own identity, and equally entitled to respect for it. But this liberal conception can at best provide a ground for tolerance, not for mutual respect or acceptance, and not for understanding the phenomenon of identity-formation itself.

A particularly troubling version of this impulse to find universally acceptable grounds for distinctive identities is the recurrent – and currently resurgent – urge to naturalize in the sense of finding a fixed biological basis for human identities. For all the critiques of essentialism that figure in gay theory, thus, many gay men are drawn to research suggesting a genetic foundation for homosexuality and to claims that gays should be accepted not because they are free to choose their own identities, but because they had no choice in the matter. While the naturalizing arguments advanced on the basis of genetic research and examinations of brain structure have been advanced by and I think have appealed mainly to gay men, a number of lesbian thinkers have advanced their own naturalizing arguments. These are more often rooted in phenotypic physiology than in posited underlying genetic or neural structures, and have been advanced with more theoretical sophistication (as for example by Irigaray with her account of natural female auto-eroticism based on the "two lips").[68]

Advocates of identity politics too commonly opt in the same arguments for a "soft relativism," a rediscovery of the philosophy of will that glorifies choice as such, and an exaggeration of difference. Such arguments cannot quite make sense of identity politics, however, since claims for legitimacy or recognition are more than claims for tolerance. It is crucial analytically to recognize that common frames of significance are implicitly claimed even in arguments emphasizing difference and denying shared moral discourse beyond the level of "you do your thing, I'll do mine."[69] This is so in two senses.

First, the significance of the identity struggled over is almost always claimed not just against other identities but within a particular field of shared relevance – e.g. a polity. Proponents of identity politics offer claims to have difference recognized as legitimate within a field like employment or legal treatment where people with many different identities are making similar claims. This is even so for the identity of nations, which normally involves a rhetoric of cultural difference yet is in large part a claim to equivalent standing with other nations – i.e. to be the same sort of thing that they are.[70]

Second, internal to the various identities on behalf of which political claims are made are various differentiated subgroups. Thus within the gay community there are gay men and lesbians, and many different sorts of communities of each. For identity politics to work, these must not all accentuate their differences but rather adopt a common frame of reference within which their unity is more salient. The claim that their shared identity is salient and even somewhat obligatory – as suggested by those who would "out" others – thus, cannot be entirely coherent with a tacit relativistic ethics as an account of how we ought to deal with difference.

V

Underlying much of the pressure towards repressive sameness and essentialist identities is a tendency to think in terms of what Harrison White has called categorical identities rather than either more complex notions of persons or networks of concrete social relations.[71] This is particularly pronounced where large-scale collectivities and mobilizations have been facilitated by new forms of systemic organization (capitalism, the modern state) and new infrastructures of transport and communication (from paved roads and railroads to telephones, TV, and computer networks). While telephones and sometimes computer networks may be used to transcend space within relationships that are still person-to-person (narrowcasting), many others are used primarily to address large categories of people constituted by their similarities and not by networks of interpersonal relations. Gun owners may know other gun owners, thus, but the National Rifle Association mobilizes them not on the basis of their network ties but by their membership in a category of people who will respond to common calls for action. The same goes for Muslims, to the extent that this category is invoked not just on a local or even a national but an international scale. And for national identities, class identities, and a host of others. The large-scale categories may be complemented in varying degree by local networks, and these may be crucial to some mobilizations, but at the level of the category as a whole, network density will almost by definition be low.

Most identity politics involves claims about categories of individuals who putatively share a given identity. This allows a kind of abstraction from the concrete interactions and social relationships within which identities are constantly renegotiated, in which individuals present one identity as more salient than another, and within which individuals achieve some personal sense of continuity and balance among their various sorts of identities. Categorical identities can be invoked and given public definition by individuals or groups even where they are not embodied in concrete networks of direct interpersonal relationships. Indeed, they are quintessentially objects of such public address. The abstractness of categories encourages framing claims about them as though they offered a kind of trump card over the other identities of individuals addressed by them. This encourages an element of repression and/or essentialism within the powerful categorical identities.

This struggle to achieve a "trump card" salience for a categorical identity – in the face of a modern world where there are always many possible salient identities – often encourages an ironic in-group essentialism. Such in-group essentialism is implied by the example given above of claimed biological determination of homosexuality, and the battles within the gay movement over this argument on the one hand and "queer theory" on the other would be well worth research.[72] In-group essentialism – ironically often juxtaposed to strident attacks on the essentialism of dominant categorizations of identities – is linked to portrayals of identities as more singular and/or fixed than they easily can be. Even while pointing to agonism about identity, in other words, such views often imagine their complete resolution: If only Serbia were autonomous and not subject to the threats of Croats, Catholics, and Muslims, thus, there would be no identity politics, only the one, true, correct model of Serbian identity. No Serbian women's movement, no Serbian gay movement, no Serbian debate about being inside or outside of Europe, or about pan-Slavic identities. In the American context too we can see how in-group essentialism is linked to suppression of some identities – like a distinct black feminist voice within black nationalism – and in general to pressures to conform to standard views of the identity in question and often to dependence or experts authoritative sources as to that identity.

As the previous two examples suggest, every collective identity is open both to internal subdivision and to calls for its incorporation into some larger category of primary identity. This is not only an issue for alternative collective identities, but for individuals who are commonly treated in this discourse as though they were unitary and internally homogenous. The capacity for an internal dialogicality is erased.

Tension between identity – putatively singular, unitary, and integral – and identities – plural, cross-cutting, and divided – is inescapable at both individual and collective levels. Individuals face the challenge of knitting together the different phases of their existence, their different social relationships and roles. Groups never wholly supersede the individuals who make them up (any more than individuals exist altogether apart from groups and social relations). Attempts to subsume any set of relations under a categorical identity or to invest any category with definitive meaning are always to some degree tendentious and invite resistance. To say that, as lived, identity is always project, not settled accomplishment points to the necessary temporality of existence, to the fact that in living we invest ourselves in identities not statically but with an orientation to the future and to action. Of course, various external ascriptions or recognitions may appear to be fixed and timeless. In the projects of our personal (or group) identities we may take on or resist the attempt to live up to such external idealization. Being Jewish, for example, is thus always a project (or an occasion for resistance) for every modern Jewish individual and community, even if stereotypes about how to be Jewish are maintained or presented as fixed by anti-Semites or the ultra-ortho-dox. Or, to change the example radically, "black unity" in South Africa can only be understood as a political project pushed at one level by the ANC, challenged at that level by Inkatha which claims a different unity, and both pushed and challenged by various factions within each. "Black" is not a settled, pre-theoretical or pre-political position from which to grasp practical affairs or achieve knowledge any more than Zulu is.

Rather than addressing this problem head on, much mainstream so-ciological theory tries to find a way to fix identity by appeal to some more "objective" underlying variable or factor. The most common candidate is rational self-interest. But identity cannot be collapsed satisfactorily into interest or made to reflect it except as part of a personal and/or political project. In the first place, identities can and to some extent, indeed, always do change.[73] More than merely externally determined change, one can seek to transform oneself – wanting, for example, to have better wants. Whether or not weakness of will hinders such a project, its very possibility necessarily means that we cannot understand individuals well as fixed bearers of interests. Finally, there are always internal tensions and inconsistencies among the various identities and group memberships of individuals. These are not always open to simple averaging solutions (as utilitarianism generally requires) because they often lack common denominators for such quantitative compromises. Thus acting on certain identities must frustrate others.

This is a key reason why the politics of personal identity and the politics of collective identity are so inextricably linked. In many settings it is not possible to make even an expressive, individual choice for the primacy of, say, an independent female identity (let alone to enter into active feminist politics) without running afoul of nationalist assumptions about gender. As Collins has pointed out with regard to black national-ism, this is painful because many women really understand themselves to be fundamentally – "essentially" – both feminist women and African-Americans.[74] They necessarily experience the hostility of conventional black nationalist discourse not simply as an external constraint but as an internal tension. Similarly, Bosnian Muslim feminists and other advo-cates of Bosnian women faced in 1993 a horrific version of the way nationalism and gender can collide. Serbian men raped thousands of

Bosnian women individually and in large, public groups as part of their project of ethnic cleansing. This was a specifically gendered violation equally specifically deployed against a nationally defined group. Yet some Bosnian men added to the calamity by treating the women who were raped as defiled and impure. They were defiled not only in the general sexist discourse of female purity, but in a specifically nationalist discourse in which they had been inscribed in proper roles as daughters, wives, and mothers. To think of themselves as either women rather than Bosnian Muslims or Bosnian Muslims rather than women made no sense. They were raped because they were both, and to condemn the Bosnian Muslim culture equally with the Serbian project of ethnic cleansing (as some American feminists rather shockingly have done) is to condemn those very women. Yet the obvious claim to be both women and Bosnian Muslims was only available as a political project (however implicit) to refigure the discourses of gender, religion, and nation within which their identities were inscribed and on the bases of which their bodies and their honor alike were violated.

To see identities only as reflections of "objective" social positions or circumstances is to see them always retrospectively. It does not make sense of the dynamic potential implicit – for better or worse – in the tensions within persons and among the contending cultural discourses that locate persons. Identities are often personal and political projects in which we participate, empowered to greater or lesser extents by resources of experience and ability, culture and social organization.

But the puzzles lie not just in invocations of strong collective identity claims. They lie also in the extent to which people (and not only in the West) are not moved by any strong claims of identity – or communality – with others and respond instead to individualistic appeals to self-realization. These two are not altogether mutually exclusive in practice. The same unwillingness to work in complex struggles for social transformation may lie behind both a preference for individualistic, psychologistic solutions to problems and a tendency to accept the illusory solutions offered by strong, simplistic identity claims on behalf of nations, races, and other putatively undifferentiated categories. In any case, as hooks puts it:

> Just as Nancy Hartsock's new work urges us to question why we are being asked to surrender a concern with the subject at this historical moment, when women have been struggling to move from object to subject, we must ask why it is women are being seduced by models of individual change that imply that no change has to occur in larger political and social realities.[75]

In other words, rather than being surprised by the prevalence of identity politics and seeking to explain it, should we not consider whether it is more remarkable and at least as much in need of explanation that many people fail to take up projects of transforming shared identities or the treatment accorded them? Should we really be more shocked by those who risk much to be true to high ideals and moral aspirations – by a Dietrich Bonhoeffer, say, or by Chinese students who defy their government – or by those who are complicitous in the myriad daily horrors of banal evil?

Our identities are always rooted in part in ideals and moral aspirations that we cannot realize fully. There is, therefore, a tension within us which can be both the locus of personal struggle and the source of an identity politics that aims not simply at the legitimation of falsely essential categorical identities but at living up to deeper social and moral values. Claims to the priority or dominance of large collective identities, therefore, are not only the stuff of manipulations by the Milosevices and Karadzices of the world, but sources of heroism and self-sacrifice that are as hard to understand in the conventional terms of social theory as in popular ideologies of purely individual self-fulfillment.

Notes

1   Arendt, *The Human Condition*.
2   Taylor, *Ethics of Authenticity, Multiculturalism*.
3   Foucault, *Discipline and Punish*; Taylor, *Sources of the Self*.
4   Taylor, *Sources of the Self*, is particularly strong on this theme.
5   Adorno, *Jargon of Authenticity*.
6   On the rhetoric of Zola's "J'accuse," see Sennett, *The Fall of Public Man*.
7   Bourdieu, *Outline, Logic*; see also chapter 5 above.
8   Evans-Pritchard, *The Nuer*.
9   Lovejoy, *Great Chain of Being*, offered a loving reconstruction of this scheme of identities. It was a crucial background to the medieval world that Weber (*Economy and Society*) took as an archetype of traditionality. One should note, though, that by taking medieval Europe as his archetype for traditional social organization and orientations to action, Weber failed to recognize the power of kinship in nonWestern societies and in general the much greater capacity for continuous social and cultural reproduction in a number of other settings.
10   Cascardi, *Subject of Modernity*, p. 3.
11   Mead, *Mind, Self and Society*.
12   See Haraway, *Simians, Cyborgs and Women*, on the vocabulary of "stress" as characteristic of functionalist-systemic formulations in biology as well as sociology.
13   This is one reason why Goffman's work (e.g. *Presentation of the Self*) stands

out as so distinctive, though even Goffman addressed these topics very unevenly.

14 The term "essentialism" has come to be used as a general label for arguments that posit fixed underlying sources of identity – essences (a label used by those who oppose such arguments, usually in favor of some notions of social construction and/or choice and contestation). These arguments vary a great deal, however, from claims to biological constitution of genders, races, or other categories to claims based on psychology, social structure, theology, or moral prescriptions. For the most part, the connection between these various "essentialist" arguments and the philosophy of "essences" in older metaphysics is extremely thin and distant at best. This is not an argument about souls or forms, or the four known essences and the possible quintessence of premodern metaphysics. It is an argument about claims to be able to specify unequivocally the conditions for membership in a category with clear and fixed boundaries, and what follows from membership in such a category. Popper coined the term in criticism of philosophies that looked to the "essence" of things for the "truth" behind concepts; see *The Logic of Scientific Discovery*.

15 Dyson, *Reflecting Black*, p. xxi.

16 Hobsbawm and Ranger, *Invention of Tradition*.

17 See Gilman's striking account of the interplay of sexuality and race in the construction of stereotypes of both women in general and African women in particular, *Difference and Pathology*, esp. ch. 1, "The Hottentot and the Prostitute."

18 Hewitt, *Dilemmas of the American Self*, p. 127.

19 See Merton, *Social Theory and Social Structure*.

20 Hewitt, *Dilemmas of the American Self*, p. 150.

21 Poststructuralism is certainly not the only source for this argument. It is also, for example, central to bell hooks' differently grounded attempts to develop a vision of "self-recovery" that is at once personal, social, and political (*Talking Back*, esp. ch. 5; *Sisters of the Yam*).

22 Though these theoretical discourses have been very sociological in many respects, they have seldom been the product of sociologists. Sociology, especially in the United States, has remained remarkably resistant to poststructuralist cultural discourse and to both feminist and gay theory (as distinct from empirical studies on gender or sexuality). One result of this has been that empirical sociological studies of women and homosexuals have often relied upon essentialist invocations of those categories; it has been exceptional – at least until very recently – for "mainstream" sociologists to participate in or even learn from the rethinking of the category of gender rather than simply relying upon seemingly manifest gender distinctions. If sociology has suffered from its resistance to the largely literary discourse of poststructuralism and cognate developments in feminist and gay theory, it should also be said that these interdisciplinary discourses – and that of "cultural studies" more generally – have suffered from a relatively underdeveloped understanding of the social dimensions of life and a ten-

dency to see – and dismiss – terms like social structure, organization, or integration as always and necessarily reified, totalizing, and/or reductionist. Nurturance of a better relationship between sociology and this interdisciplinary discourse is in order for both (or all) sides. For some recent steps in this direction, see Seidman (*Embattled Eros* and "Symposium: Queer Theory") and Collins (*Black Feminist Thought* and *Fighting Words*).

23   Collins (*Black Feminist Thought*) reviews and adds to the arguments developed by black feminists, the most important of which may be those of bell hooks (*Ain't I a Woman, Feminist Theory, Talking Back*). The lesbian critiques are discussed in Fuss, *Essentially Speaking*; Butler, *Gender Trouble*; and several of the essays in Butler and Scott, *Feminists Theorize the Political* and Rhode, *Theoretical Perspectives on Sexual Difference*. But it is important to keep distinct the general poststructuralist decentering of subjectivity from the specific challenges to totalizing accounts of collective subject-categories that efface the diversity of concrete individuals and groups. Hartsock ("Postmodernism and Political Change"), for example, has questioned the call to surrender a concern with the subject precisely at the historical moment when women have been meeting some success in moving from object to subject; see also hooks' assent (*Talking Back*, p. 34) and discussion in chapter 6 above.

24   hooks, *Sisters of the Yam*, p. 124.

25   The language of "nature" in these appeals, and later in the critique of "naturalizing" approaches to individual and social life, is not simply equivalent to the discourse of modern biology. The idea of nature that was imported into sociological and psychoanalytic discourse took a much more fixed view of evolution and human nature; it commonly ignored the fact that nature looked anything but fixed to most evolutionary biologists, and that a variety of different viewpoints could constitute appeals to nature as differently as appeals to social construction among sociologists. While evolution didn't figure in quite the same way for the Romantic tradition, its appeal to biology was also to a much more fixed and invariant notion than now seems useful to most biologists. In both the social science and the Romantic discourses, moreover, the nature/culture boundary was being constructed – and exaggerated – not simply recognized.

26   Aspects of this challenge appear throughout Derrida's work; *Writing and Difference* is perhaps as good a place as any to begin. Norris, *Derrida*, is a useful secondary source; Megill, *Prophets of Extremity*, nicely places Derrida in relation to Nietzsche, Heidegger, and Foucault.

27   hooks, *Feminist Theory*.

28   "Sexual orientation" was gaining the upper hand largely because it sounded more scientific and immutable. It fit with the construction of being gay as something over which individuals had little or no choice, something they merely recognized in themselves. This was reinforced by a growing sense that convincing the public that homosexuality was not subject to choice would reduce the extent to which it was morally condemned.

29   hooks' argument dovetails with the critique of "compulsory heterosexual-

ity," which shows how social norms have involved an implicit assumption that all members of each sex should have some level of sexual openness towards all members of the other. See Rich, "Compulsory Heterosexism" and discussion below.

30 Sedgwick, *Between Men*; Fuss, *Essentially Speaking*, p. xii.

31 Haraway, *Simians, Cyborgs and Women*.

32 See Fuss, *Essentially Speaking*; Schor, "This Essentialism Which Is Not One"; Spivak, *In Other Worlds*; Smith, *Discerning the Subject*; and several of the essays in Jardine and Smith, *Men in Feminism*.

33 Barbara Taylor, *Eve and the New Jerusalem*.

34 See Charles Taylor, *Sources of the Self* and *Ethics of Authenticity*, on the idea of "moral sources" and the specific modern importance of appeals to nature as a basis for moral claims and self-understandings.

35 Moi, *Sexual/Textual Politics*. See also Lundgren's suggestion that "the male language Irigaray wants to estrange is also constitutively decisive for being able to use the concepts of 'sameness' and 'difference' at all. . . . Irigaray violates the patriarchal norms for the development of metaphors, replacing a regulative rule (about visual, limited thinking) with a new regulative rule (about tactile, fluid thinking). But if, for example, the fundamental constitutive rule requires that gender always have a metaphorical (or perhaps rather symbolic) essence – irrespective of its content – then in being *regulatively subversive*, Irigaray is implicitly validating the constitutive;" Lundgren, "The Hand that Strikes and Comforts," pp. 149–50.

36 Irigaray, *This Sex Which Is Not One*.

37 And of course in claiming identities, as Collins (*Black Feminist Thought*) has argued, we are not obliged to make either/or choices. It is often our prerogative and perhaps our best strategy to insist on the option of "both/and."

38 Weber, *Economy and Society*; see also Töennies's *Community and Association*.

39 Habermas, *Theory of Communicative Action*, vol. I, p. 341.

40 McCarthy, "Complexity and Democracy," in *Ideals and Illusions*.

41 Similarly, Habermas's general Enlightenment universalism leads him to deny that difference as such – e.g. on gender lines – could be a significant positive social or intellectual value; see Benhabib, *Critique, Norm, and Utopia*.

42 See also Calhoun, "The Radicalism of Tradition."

43 Fraser, "What's Critical about Critical Theory?"

44 There was more attention to social structure in Habermas's early work on the public sphere (*Structural Transformation*); this continued in *Legitimation Crisis* and other works of the 1960s and early 1970s, but fell off after he embarked on the theory of communicative action.

45 See Calhoun, "Computer Technology, Large Scale Social Integration and the Local Community," and "Indirect Relationships and Imagined Communities."

46 There is also an intermediate from of strategic social action which is hard to treat as entirely collapsible into the binary scheme; see discussion in McCarthy, *Critical Theory*.

47 Habermas, *Theory of Communicative Action*, vol. I, p. 342.
48 Most of the relevant essays in Habermas's debate with Luhmann (in which Habermas both gave more ground and learned more) are collected in Habermas and Luhmann, *Theorie der Gesellschaft oder Sozialtechnologie*, which remains untranslated. There is a useful summary in Holub, *Jürgen Habermas*.
49 Arendt, *The Human Condition*, p. 182. Arendt seems to exclude from this potentially creative uncertainty the realm of the social production of the necessities of life.
50 Such threats may be perceived in a variety of ways, of course, and may be understood through the ideological categories of both left and right. The government may be feared and capitalism praised, for example, or corporate depredations seen as the major evil and government as a potential solution. Either way, people motivated by attachments within in lifeworld are led to embrace one of the major system world challenges to it, in order to resist the other. This reflects in part the underdevelopment of attention to associations in civil society on the part of both left and right.
51 Castells, *The City and the Grassroots*, p. 331.
52 Indeed, it appears even in the work of knowledgeable social scientists seeking to reach a broad public audience, as for example in *Habits of the Heart*, a best selling book by Robert Bellah and several colleagues. *Habits* calls for a renewal of communitarian commitments and a reigning in of American individualism, without seriously considering the political, economic, or social structural features of American society which fundamentally differentiate today's community life from that which supported New England town meetings. Problems of scale, the vulnerability of local communities to corporate and government decisions over which they have little control (or even potential for control), and the distance between most people and their political representatives are side-stepped in favor of an implication that getting involved in local organizations and community activities is sufficient to a major resocialization of American life. (Part of the basis for their notion of the sufficiency of such involvements is the authors' focus on the satisfaction which they believe individuals will reap from such commitments, as distinct from the practical efficacy of those commitments.) Despite the perceptiveness and readability of the book, one concludes that its avoidance of these hard issues raised by the tension between system-world and life-world was a condition of its reaching the extraordinarily broad audience it did. Bellah and his colleagues partially remedy the balance in *The Good Society*.
53 On the US case, see Lowi's analysis of *The Personal Presidency*, and Fishkin, *Democracy and Deliberation*.
54 See especially Habermas, *Communication and the Evolution of Society*.
55 Habermas, *Theory of Communicative Action*, vol. I, p. 340.
56 In this paragraph I am broadly following the lead of an argument offered by Taylor (*Ethics of Authenticity*) but qualifying it somewhat. Taylor assumes

that premodern and nonWestern social institutional arrangements offered grounds for more immediate, perfect, unnegotiated, and conflict-free recognition than seems plausible to me, and pays less attention to the specific of social organization and projects as distinct from culture and ideas than seems to me needed.

57 As Fuss (*Essentially Speaking*, p. 110) has rightly argued, seeing that the critique of compulsory heterosexism grasps something the critique of homophobia does not is not necessarily grounds for dropping the critique of homophobia. It is also worth noting that the critique of compulsory heterosexism grows out of feminist theory foregrounding lesbian experience (paradigmatically Rich, "Compulsory Heterosexuality," but also the work of Irigaray and Wittig) and that this division of two stances of theoretical critique has in many cases divided lesbians from gay men.

58 Crosby, "Dealing with Differences." The Butler and Scott collection, *Feminists Theorize the Political*, in which Crosby's article appears raises this issue in selection after selection, showing the centrality and currency of the problem however varied the proposed resolutions.

59 See, e.g., Melucci, *Nomads of the Present*; Touraine, "An Introduction" and *Return of the Actor*; and Cohen, "Strategy or Identity."

60 For the most part, this focus on the sort of movements sociologists like to study or find sympathetic is given no rationale, though the "sampling error" it produces may be quite significant. One study that does make clear the basis for such a distinction (though it still seems to me an arbitrary introduction of an evaluation) is Eyerman and Jamison, *Social Movements*, where the notion of social movements is definitionally limited to mobilizations that depend on and produce cognitive liberation among their members.

61 I have argued this in more detail in Calhoun, "New Social Movements."

62 Inglehart, *Culture Shift*.

63 *Structural Transformation*. See discussion in Calhoun, "Civil Society and Public Sphere," Calhoun. ed. *Habermas and the Public Sphere*, and chapter 8 below. In reaching beyond Habermas's narrow conception of the public sphere, however, it is important not to forget that his analysis is about what enables people to make collective political decisions by rational-critical argument and different publics vary widely in the extent to which they are able to maintain such standards of discourse.

64 This is one of the reasons why Negt and Kluge (*The Public Sphere and Experience*) use an appeal to the "horizons of experience" to criticize Habermas.

65 Butler, *Gender Trouble*.

66 Taylor, *Ethics of Authenticity, Multiculturalism*.

67 Chow, "Postmodern Automatons," p. 124.

68 Just how essentialist Irigaray's arguments really (essentially?) are is a matter of active contention as noted above. Spivak ("French Feminism Revisited," p. 74) has suggested that Irigaray is criticized as an essentialist mainly by those who do not see "the aggressive role of rhetoricity in her prose," while

Fuss (*Essentially Speaking*, p. 57) suggests that Irigaray uses essentialism as part of "a larger constructionist project of re-creating, re-metaphorizing the body."

69   Taylor, *Ethics of Authenticity*.

70   See, among many, Anderson, *Imagined Communities*, Chatterjee, *Nationalist Thought and the Colonial World*, Calhoun, "Nationalism and Ethnicity," and chapter 9 below.

71   White introduced the CATNET idea initially in an unpublished lecture nearly three decades ago. He has written about it more recently in *Identity and Control* (though his focus there is very different from mine here). See also the work of Nadel that (among other things) lies behind White's reformulation, especially *Foundations of Social Anthropology* and *Theory of Social Structure*.

72   On possible links between queer theory and social theory more generally, see Warner, *Fear of a Queer Planet*, and Seidman, "Symposium: Queer Theory."

73   Among other things this creates a host of problems about how to understand the relationship between present and future selves within rational choice theory. See Hollis, *The Cunning of Reason*; Calhoun ("Problem of Identity in Collective Action") develops this theme in regard to social movement participation.

74   Collins, *Fighting Words*.

75   hooks, *Talking Back*, p. 34.

8

Nationalism and Difference:
The Politics of Identity Writ Large

I

The politics of identity has often appeared as a new politicization of everyday life, a shift away from some more traditional politics of interests. Not only is the personal increasingly politicized, some analysts note, politics is increasingly aestheticized. It turns on dramatic performances rather than instrumental struggles.

These are fair observations about contemporary politics, but they are misleading insofar as they posit an "old" politics that stuck narrowly to instrumental struggles over interests, that was not in large part identity politics, that was not about the politicization of everyday life, that did not work in significant part by aesthetic production and performances. At least during the modern era, and arguably to some extent more generally, this has never been the case. That it could seem to be the case was the result of hegemonic ideologies differentiating the "properly political" – and therefore most explicitly contestable – dimensions of life from others, and accordingly obscuring the workings of power and power struggles in other realms of life.

The long modern history of increasing popular participation in political processes, rooted not only in early republicanism but in the political mobilizations and rituals of the absolutist era, has both brought everyday life concerns to the fore and made issues of identity basic. Though tied closely to the project of democracy, this increasing popular participation has not been limited to it. It has been manifest wherever regimes – even sharply undemocratic and dictatorial regimes – saw their legitimacy as based on serving the interests of ordinary people, improving the conditions of their everyday lives, and saw the conditions of their continued rule in terms of capacity to mobilize ordinary people for military, industrial, and civic projects. This was, for example, the rhetoric of all communist states, regardless of differentiations in how democratic they were and how well they seemed in fact to serve the interests of their citizens.

Where ordinary people are drawn into such mobilizations and into the discourse of legitimacy, politics must involve struggle over salient identities, as is manifest in the spread of the ideology of citizenship. Identities like "citizen" are in actual or potential tension with others, from "subject," through "worker," "woman," and "priest." Each of these can be equally ambiguous and equally subject to struggle (though the extent of ambiguity and struggle are both variables reflecting the stability and efficacy of hegemonic consciousnesses). To create the modern politics of class required identity struggle that persuaded workers that their common identities as workers should overshadow their differences on lines of craft or field of production, region, religion, gender, etc., and also should define a clear distinction from middle-class or elite identities. The quintessential politics of interest, in other words, was rooted in a politics of identity. It was also grounded in a politicization of everyday life, a call to see economic welfare and relations between employers and employees as matters of public, political concern rather than purely private interests.[1] This was in part an aestheticized politics from the outset, carried forward by dramatic performances and rituals from the mobilization of the traditions of the French *compagnonnage*,[2] to the political theater of the Luddites,[3] the spread of union songs, the retreat into factional identities, the idealization of workers' accents and styles where more broadly transformative politics were not available, and the replacement of active workers struggles by aestheticized images of the proletarian in communist societies.

In short, class politics was, partly but also necessarily, identity politics. Though it was rooted in very local workers' identities as well as the notion of class linked to the concentration of capital, it was carried out on a very large scale. But the politics of class was not the only or the most successful such venture in large-scale politics of identity. Indeed, it met its most decisive crises precisely in confrontation with commitments to national identities. Nationalists had produced, among other things, a more effectively aestheticized politics, a politics which could often appear as prepolitical or apolitical precisely in its aesthetic forms – national mythology and folklore, poetry and plays, folk music and grand symphonies, the very identification with the national language. Nationalism – the discourse and political programs of national identities – even shaped what was made of class identities, located workers' self-consciousness of themselves and conceptions of class politics generally within nation-states, despite the international organization of capital and calls like Marx's and Engels' for the workers of the world to unite. Nationalism showed its greater strength decisively in the disastrous era of World War I. If further evidence were needed of how the politics of everyday life, the aestheticization of politics, and the struggle over identities were already central to the modern era and not just waiting for invention in the 1960s, one would only have to look to fascism, national socialism, and the next world war.

It is not obvious what interests will move people in – or into – political struggles. Since each of us is typically involved in a range of personal commitments, projects, and aspirations, and each of us attempts to navigate multiple social worlds, we present at least partially indeterminate identities to the political process. But because our various identities may be contested, and because a range of agents seek to reinforce some and undermine others, there is always a politics to the construction and experience of identity, not just following from it. The present chapter explores this in relation especially to national identities, not just because they have so much impact but because they are so easily seen as natural and prepolitical in our contemporary world. They call, in other words, for critical theory precisely because the manner of their institutionalization and reproduction make them so commonly immune to critical re-examination.

Nationalism is not simply a kind of political policy or social movement. It is a rhetoric that has become enormously widespread and powerful in the modern world. It is used to shape and legitimate state policies, secessionist movements, and attempts to join existing states. It is the most prominent rhetoric for constituting or arguing over the "selves" at stake in political self-determination. It is thus implicated in the very idea of democracy, both as a claim about the internal integration of the political community and as a claim about its boundaries and relations to people and powers outside. The rhetoric of nationalism thus helps to constitute not only violent programs of ethnic repression or civil war but more commonly praised ideas of citizenship and patriotism.

Nationalist thinking also pervades social science, which is one reason why developing an adequate critical stance towards it is difficult. Our very ideas about what "a society" is are shaped by understandings developed under the influence of nationalism and European state-making. Not least of all, we make national identities seem natural, or at least primordial, by building them into our very sense of history. Modern history has been constructed first and foremost as national histories. Disciplines are organized and texts constructed in a way guaranteed to produced a Whiggish outcome – the idea that the nation was always already there to have its history written. Thus a recent Stockholm museum exposition on Swedish history began with fur clad cave dwellers who, it confidently assured its viewers, were Swedish cave dwellers. And as Benedict Anderson has noted, English history presents William the Conqueror as a founding father of England in a way that neutralizes his status as a foreign invader. Some national historiographical traditions are more self-conscious about acts of founding, especially revolutions, often presented in mythologized, heroic terms. But in America, which is one of the primary examples of this, it is still the case that colonists appear commonly (especially in popular history) as always already Americans and efforts at more inclusive history appropriate Indians ("Native Americans") to the same model. Even in Third World countries where the boundaries (and in some cases the very idea) of the state were imposed arbitrarily, history texts commonly claim the precolonial inhabitants of the territory as nationals.

How well these historiographical claims work may be one of the great, half recognized factors behind differences in how well democratic institutions work. The settled, established democracies of the world are – to a worrying extent – those countries where long processes of national integration preceded the establishment of democratic political institutions. If the United States of America seems an exception to this rule, consider not only the extent of genuine social, economic, and cultural integration among the founding colonies (compared, say, to precolonial Sudan), but the fact that national integration had to be ratified and strengthened by an extraordinarily bloody civil war.

Commentators like Samuel P. Huntington thus offer prime examples of uncritical theory when they claim that the potential for democracy is rooted largely in Western civilization and minimal in other broad civilizational categories.[4] They echo the claims of Asian authoritarian leaders who argue that they have no obligation to respect democratic ideals because that is not the Asian way. They give succor to African strong men at a time when many Africans hope for an end to the traditions of rapacious rule characteristic of the postcolonial states.[5] And they encourage us to accept quasi-naturalized categories of "civilizations" in place of genuine historical or social science analysis. Huntington fails to recognize, thus, how much the conditions for democracy were created in Western Europe by bloody repression and forced cultural assimilation, by projects of centralizing political power and state building that show few signs of being part of a civilization destined to support democracy, and by a history of military conflicts within as well as between states as disastrous as any anywhere. He is not alone in this, and it is indeed part of how the nationalist system of affirmative consciousness works. Nationalism is rooted not just in historical memory and myth, illusions of great continuity, and glorification of martyrs and heroes. It is, as Ernst Renan recognized in the last century, rooted also in the capacity not to remember those events and processes which would fester like sores and bring disunity:

> Forgetting, I would even go so far as to say historical error, is a crucial factor in the creation of a nation, which is why progress in historical studies often constitutes a danger for [the principle of] nationality. Indeed, historical enquiry brings to light deeds of violence which took place at the origin of all political formations, even those whose consequences have been altogether beneficial. Unity is always effected by means of brutality.[6]

The "brutality" Renan has in mind is exemplified in France by the massacres of Protestants and putative heretics, but the cultural or symbolic violence involved in forging unity could also be brutal. Forgetting could even be a part of it.

The point is not that we must encourage such forgetting in the interest of national unity, but that we need to see critically the problem any theory of democracy must face in giving an account of the constitution of the political community within which it is meant to apply. I do not in the following pages attempt to interrogate the concept of democracy more generally or to give a full-fledged theory of nationalism. Rather, I want to develop this issue of the creation of political community with an eye to how democracy has come – in theory and practice alike – to depend tacitly on nationalist constructions. This gives us a chance to explore the ways in which more critical theory can aid us in looking behind seemingly natural or primordial categories without falling into the opposite trap of imagining that showing those categories to be constructed settles much of anything, reduces their force, or provides us with an analysis of how they work or why they are reproduced. It gives us a chance also to see the politics of identity at work on a large scale, yet to note it is not within connection to the very self-recognition of individuals.

II

Political discussion commonly starts with the state. It is, indeed, the creation of states as quasi-autonomous organizations (or actors) that produces most clearly the differentiation of politics from other aspects of social life and of discourse.[7] As a result, it is not surprising that we are led to assume state-centered views of the constitution of political communities. Modern political communities are given their boundaries in the first instance by common subjection to a state. The outcomes of past struggles – conquests, inheritances, civil wars, revolutions, anti-imperial revolts –

are ratified through administrative centralization and integration. States define political communities not only domestically but in relation to other states, for example by issuing passports and visas, by sponsoring shared educational institutions that maintain linguistic homogeneity internally and heterogeneity externally, and by encouraging domestic and restricting foreign markets. Not all states are equally effective, but the effectiveness of some reinforces the assumption that states are the necessary objects of political communities, even where they are not their source.

There is, however, a paradox in the use of states to define political communities. States may distinguish political communities from each other in various ways, and states and their personnel may also occupy a great deal of the public sphere within each. Yet in modern usage, states are not in themselves political communities.

A state is not merely a country, but also a specialized apparatus of rule. A state is thus distinct from the people subject to its rule. The Roman state was not equivalent to the Roman people even in the Republican era, and still less was the state of imperial Rome equivalent to the peoples of the Roman Empire. In empires and in many other historical forms of rule, the relationship between state and people has commonly been distant and/or arbitrary. Hereditary elites were sharply distinguished from those they ruled. "Peoples" came under one or another state as a result of royal marriages, inheritance, or the conquest of the territories on which they lived, but neither their character nor that of the state that claimed them was necessarily altered by this. Some ethnic of other relative broad groupings within such states might have special claims on office or special capacity to influence rulers, as for example Romans did retain a special political access even as imperial Rome became more far-flung and multicultural. The Mughal state in India thus favored Muslims and Urdu speakers and indeed its British successor favored Englishmen and English speakers, but in neither case was being a member of the favored group a guarantee of jobs or power. These groupings were not coterminous with the state apparatus but had to relate to it through discourse and action; the state was not constituted by its relationship to any such broad category of people. In these and most other cases, the relevant political community was not "the people," nor even any very large segment of the people, but rather the networks of elites given voice and influence by heredity or military and administrative position.

This narrower political community gave identity to the state. Even where the state was tyrannical, some such political community existed and carried on some level of discourse, offering advice to the ruler and working out how to interpret his directives. Such political communities were always at least somewhat differentiated; courtiers and noblemen spoke with different backgrounds, interests, perceptions, and strategies.[8] But in and of itself, this sort of political community did not necessarily constitute a *public*. Take the scholar-administrators of imperial China. They acted neither to influence a state from which they were distinct (as did Roman citizens) nor in place of a differentiated state apparatus (as in certain periods the citizens of Athens constituted themselves as the government). Rather, this sort of political community was contained within the state.

In none of the cases mentioned was the relevant political community simply "the people," not even the people of the most favored ethnic classification. It was always a narrower elite. But the distinction could still be made between those settings in which the political community was basically contained within the state and those in which it included a public conceptually and practically outside the state apparatus (even if many of the members of this public were insiders to the state). The extent and kind of distinction between the political community and the state is thus a crucial variable.

Also important is the relationship between the political community and the broader population. Modern states distinguished themselves from empires and other earlier forms of state largely by claiming and building a more intimate relationship to the populations they ruled. This was partly a matter of changing patterns of taxation, military mobilization, trade and production, communications, and transportation infrastructure.[9] States penetrated more deeply into the daily lives of ordinary people, and did so more evenly throughout their territories. At the same time, three different sorts of ideological shift made the relationship of peoples to states seem more intimate.

The first, and most widely recognized in political thought, was the extremely broad influence of republicanism.[10] In this tradition, modern Europe saw itself as the heir of ancient Rome. Republicanism turned crucially on the notion of public, and granted public discourse a powerful role, though it often retained a limited notion of the range of people who constituted the political community that might carry on this public discourse.

Second, the Protestant Reformation encouraged a rethinking of the state that put the emphasis on the people – constituted first and foremost as God's chosen people or the people who shared religious revelation or understanding – rather than on the public. Here ancient Rome was not so much the proper ancestor of modern Europe as were the theocratic communities of the patristic era.[11] It is thus no accident that the Puritan influence on the English Civil War should offer us some of the first really modern invocations of the people as the source of legitimacy for the state.

Third, ethnic, cultural, and localist solidarities began to be invoked as the basis of political communities. Versions of this appeared alongside republicanism, as in the Florentine patriotism of Machiavelli, and alongside religious invocation of the chosen people, as in Cromwell's English nationalism (to some extent foreshadowed by Luther's letters to the German nation, though this was not quite "nation" in the modern sense). But this marked a distinct mode of claiming loyalty or legitimacy, as was evident in the successes both English and French kings found in using invocations of the alien other to help in the increasingly broad military mobilizations of the absolutist era.[12] In particular, nationalist rhetoric commonly employs certain tropes: The nation is presented as pre-political, as in any contemporary instance prior to political deliberation, as the basis for recognizing a public rather than as subject to constitution or redefinition in public (even when the roots of the nation are claimed to lie partly in glorious political acts). The individual is understood as directly and immediately a part of the nation, and undifferentiatedly so (membership being a status defined simply by in or out criteria rather than ranks and orders). National identity is understood to be inscribed, as it were, in the very body of the individual, and not the contingent result of membership in intermediate groups. The nation is understood as at once a unitary and integral being and a sharply bounded and discrete set of members.

In short, three different but interrelated modes of claiming a broader political community, one outside the state apparatus, became influential. I am designating these by the names people, public, and nation (though it should be noted that in everyday political rhetoric each of these terms has been used to refer to each of the three concepts I am trying to distinguish). Of these, "public" posited a differentiated citizenry; "people" emphasized a difference between rulers and ruled but the unity of the ruled; and "nation" implied a unity of the whole. Though neither ethnicity nor any other pre-existing similarity altogether explains nationalism, ethnic, linguistic, and other commonalities gave it a special force and aided those who would invoke it. It alone also provided an account of the boundaries of the polity, and it became the most influential of the three.

These new notions of political community reflected expansion in the nature of political participation and in the role of the state in various forms of social mobilization and regulation. They also figured centrally in a changed understanding of legitimacy. During most of previous European history, the notion that legitimate right to rule ascended from the people to the rulers had been subordinate to an understanding of power as descending from God and other authorities through the various ranks of the nobility to lower levels. Claims based on the "ascending theory" were generally claims against efforts to translate papal authority into state building or against the efforts of monarchs to institutionalize central states.[13] In the early modern era, a conceptual revolution helped to reconcile ascending theories of legitimacy, rooted in recognition of the political rights of the public, the people, or the nation, with centralized state-building.

This transformed understanding of the nature of political community and legitimacy depended in turn on the growth of ideas about non-political social organization. These were articulated prominently in the early discourse of civil society. This term, adapted in part from an image of free medieval cities, referred both to the capacity of a political community to organize itself, independent of the specific direction of state power, and to the socially organized pursuit of private ends.[14] This self-organization might be accomplished through discourse and decision making in the public sphere, or through the systemic organization of private interests in the economy. The Scottish moralists emphasized the latter in their account of early capitalist markets as arenas in which the pursuit of private ends by individual actors produced in aggregate an effective social organization not dependent on the intervention of the state. The market was thus a model for claims to the capacity for self-organization as well as the realm of specific interests to be protected from improper manipulations. Markets demonstrated, for thinkers like Adam Ferguson and Adam Smith, that the activities of ordinary people could regulate themselves without the interventions of government. Such claims were linked to rejections of the absolute authority of monarchs and assertions of the rights of popular sovereignty. Following Locke, these arguments placed a new emphasis on the social integration of society as such rather than merely on the aggregate of subjects. In such a view, the state no longer defined the political community directly, for its own legitimacy depended on the acquiescence or support of an already existing political community.

These changes powerfully shaped both political discourse and the most material sorts of politics for succeeding centuries, including our own. They were also crucial in the production of a discourse of "society," for they made politics increasingly a sociological problem rather than a matter of statecraft, princely wisdom, or sheer power understood solely in terms of relations among members of the state apparatus or its competitors. The political community had escaped the bounds of the state apparatus as such, and a new tension between the broad ideas of people and nation and generally narrower ideas of who constituted the proper custodians of the public good came to constitute more and more of political struggle.

The close relationship between the ideas of public, people, and nation warrants further exploration. Each influenced the other from the time they took on their characteristic modern inflections. In looking at these ideas here, however, my emphasis will not be on the history of these ideas as such, but on the ways in which recognizing their interlinkage helps to shed light on the modern discourse of nationalism. Nationalism has appeared recurrently as one of the greatest challenges to the ideal of rational collective decision making through peaceful discourse that has joined the term public to the projects of republicanism and democracy. Yet in many ways nationalist ideas are presumed by the more "successful" democracies, and nation-building has been closely related historically to the very rise of public life that has helped make modern democracy possible.

Even in academic analysis, too easy acceptance of the view that nationalism is a problematic but fading inheritance from primordial history has obscured recognition of its centrality to our modern ideas of publics and more generally of politically salient identities.[15] Most basic is the notion that there is some one people that constitutes the proper referent of public discourse and the ground of democratic claims to self-governance. On such a view, American public discourse is – or ought to be – about the public goods appropriate to the American people. This implies, among other things, that this people is sufficiently unified that it can be adequately represented by a single, authoritative public discourse. Such views work to privilege certain definitions of the public at the expense of others. Not only are certain speakers given wider attention, recognition, or influence; certain topics are defined as properly public and others as merely private. At stake throughout this discussion is the issue of difference – that is, of the extent to which discourse involving the notion of public or the identity of nation recognizes or represses the plurality of identities that shape the lives of individuals and the constitution of communities, societies, and even civilizations. Nationalism becomes the most frequently troubling instance of identity politics writ large, thus, but it is not the only one. Similar issues are involved in many invocations of legitimate publics and non-nationalist representations of peoples.

III

The very distinction of public from private took on new meaning in the early modern era with the notion that outside the immediate apparatus of state rule there existed both the private affairs of citizens that were legitimately protected from undue state regulation or intervention and a realm of public discourse and action in which citizens might address or act on the state. Persons existed in dual aspects, just as the private affairs of office holders came increasingly to be distinguished from their public roles.[16] The notion of a public realm is accordingly almost always ambivalent, referring to the collective concerns of the political community and to the activities of the state that is central to defining that political community. This two-edged notion of the public inscribes its parallel notion of the private. The private is simultaneously that which is not subject to the purview of the state and that which concerns personal ends distinct from the public good, the *res publica*, or matters of legitimate public concern.

The idea of "public" is central to theories of democracy. It appears both as the crucial subject of democracy – the people organized as a discursive and decision-making public – and as object – the public good. This has become a focus of intense critical theoretical attention recently, especially in the English-speaking world, partly because the English translation of Jürgen Habermas's major book on the subject coincided with the fall of communism and attendant concern for transitions to democracy.[17] As Habermas develops the theoretical problematic of the public sphere, for example, the basic question is how social self-organization can be accomplished through widespread and more or less egalitarian participation in rational-critical discourse.

Yet, as analyses of the exclusion of women from public life have shown most sharply, the conceptualization of public has also worked in anti-democratic ways. In the first place, women were simply excluded from the now-idealized public spheres of the early bourgeois era. They were excluded from the English Parliament and the French National Assembly in ways they had not been excluded from aristocratic salon culture and were not excluded from popular political discourse.[18] The issue of "democratic inclusiveness" is not just a quantitative matter of the scale of a public sphere or the proportion of the members of a political community who may speak within it. While it is clearly a matter of stratification and boundaries (e.g. openness to the propertyless, the uneducated, women, or immigrants), it is also a matter of how the public sphere incorporates and recognizes the diversity of identities which people bring to it from their manifold involvements in civil society. It is a matter of whether in order to participate in such a public sphere, for example, women must act in ways previously characteristic of men and avoid addressing certain topics defined as appropriate to the private realm (the putatively more female sphere). Marx criticized the discourse of bourgeois citizenship for implying that it equally fitted everyone when it in fact tacitly presumed an understanding of citizens as property-owners. The same sort of false universalism has presented citizens in gender neutral or gender symmetrical terms without in fact acknowledging highly gendered underlying conceptions.

All attempts to render a single public discourse authoritative privilege certain topics, certain forms of speech, and certain speakers. This is partly a matter of emphasis on the single, unitary whole – the discourse of all the citizens rather than of subsets – and partly a matter of the specific demarcations of public from private. If sexual harassment, for example, is seen as a matter of concern to women, but not men, it becomes a sectional matter rather than a matter for the public in general; if it is seen as a private matter then by definition it is not a public concern. The same goes for a host of other topics of attention that are inhibited from reaching full recognition in a public sphere conceptualized as a single discourse about matters consensually determined to be of public significance.

The alternative is to think of the public sphere not as the realm of a single public, but as a sphere of publics. This does not mean that the flowering of innumerable potential publics is in and of itself a solution to this basic problem of democracy. On the contrary, democracy requires discourse across lines of basic difference. It is important that members of any specific public be able also to enter into others. Political efficacy in relation to highly centralized states requires some organization of discourse and action on a very large scale. But even the most centralized states are not unitary; different branches of their bureaucracies can be addressed independently and often are most effectively addressed by publics organized on a narrower scale than the polity as a whole. Thus an environmentally focused public discourse better monitors what governmental regulatory agencies do with regard to the environment than could an altogether general public discourse. This does not eliminate the need for a broader discourse concerned among other things with the balancing of different demands on states or different interests. But this discourse can be conceptualized – and nurtured – as a matter of multiple intersections among heterogenous publics, not only as the privileging of a single overarching public.

Once we begin to think in terms of such alternative understandings of publics, however, we confront resistance stemming from the way notions of the public sphere have been rooted in the discourse of nationalism. Ideas of the public commonly draw from nationalist rhetoric both the capacity to presume boundaries and an emphasis on the discourse of the whole. As a way of conceptualizing political communities, nationalist rhetoric stresses, among other tropes, an understanding of the individual as directly and immediately related to the nation, so that national identity is experienced and recognized as personally embodied and not the contingent result of membership in intermediate groups. Because the nation is understood as unitary and integral, nationalist thought discourages notions of multiple and multifarious publics; it typically rejects claims to the quasi-autonomy of subnational discourses or movements as divisive. To the extent that our commonplace and politically effective understandings of public life depend on nationalist presumptions, a bias towards a homogenizing universalism is apt to appear. Where nationalism or any other cultural formation represses difference, however, it intrinsically undermines the capacity of a public sphere to carry forward a rational-critical democratic discourse.

The problem arises largely from an inadequate appreciation of the extent to which difference – what Hannah Arendt called "plurality" – is basic not only to human life in general but specifically to the project of public life and therefore to democracy.[19] Plurality is not a condition of private life or a product of quotidian personal tastes, in Arendt's view, but rather a potential that flowers in creative public achievements. Arendt accepted the classical Greek restriction on public participation precisely because she thought few people could rise above the implicit conformity imposed by a life of material production to achieve real distinction in the realm of praxis. But we need not agree with this exclusionary premise in order to grasp that the reason for a public discourse lies partly in the potential that various members will bring different ideas into intellectual consideration.

Part of the point of linking the distinction of public from private to that of praxis from mere work or labor is to present the public sphere as something more than an arena for the advancement or negotiation of competing material interests. This image is carried forward in Habermas's account with its emphasis on the possibility of disinterested rational-critical public discourse and his suggestion that the public sphere degenerates as it is penetrated by organized interest groups. To presume that these will proffer only different policies for achieving objectively ascertainable ends – let alone ends reducible to a common calculus in terms of a lowest common denominator of interest – is to reduce the public sphere to a forum of Benthamite policy experts rather than a vehicle of democratic self-government. This is clearly not something Habermas intends to praise. Yet it is not as sharply distant from his account of the public sphere as it might at first seem. One reason is that Habermas does not place the same stress as Arendt on creativity. He treats public activity overwhelmingly in terms of rational-critical discourse rather than identity-formation or expression, and somewhat narrows the meaning of and significance of plurality and introduces the possibility of claims to expertise more appropriate to technical rationality than communicative action.[20] Part of the background to this problem lies in the very manner in which public was separated from private in the eighteenth- and early nineteenth-century liberal public sphere which is the basis for Habermas's ideal-typical construction.

The liberal model of the public sphere pursues discursive equality by disqualifying discourse about the differences among actors. These differences are treated as matters of private, but not public, interest. On Habermas's account, the best version of the public sphere was based on "a kind of social intercourse that, far from presupposing the equality of status, disregarded status altogether."[21] It worked by a "mutual willingness to accept the given roles and simultaneously to suspend their reality."[22] This "bracketing" of difference as merely private and irrelevant to the public sphere is undertaken, Habermas argues, in order to defend the genuinely rational-critical notion that arguments must be decided on their merits rather than the identities of the arguers. This was as important as fear of censors for the prominence of anonymous or pseudonymous authorship in the eighteenth-century public sphere. Yet it has the effect of excluding some of the most important concerns of many members of any polity – both those whose existing identities are suppressed or devalued and those whose exploration of possible identities is truncated. In addition, this bracketing of differences also undermines the self-reflexive capacity of public discourse. If it is impossible to communicate seriously about basic differences among members of a public sphere, then it will be impossible also to address the difficulties of communication across such lines of basic difference.

The public sphere, Habermas tells us, is created in and out of civil society.[23] The public sphere is not absorbed into the state, thus, but addresses the state and the sorts of public issues on which state policy might bear. It is based (1) on a notion of public good as distinct from private interest, (2) on social institutions (like private property) that empower individuals to participate independently in the public sphere because their livelihoods and access to it are not dependent on political power or patronage, and (3) on forms of private life (notably families) that prepare individuals to act as autonomous, rational-critical subjects in the public sphere. A central paradox and weakness (not just in Habermas's theory but in the liberal conception which it analyzes and partially incorporates) arises from the implication that the public sphere depends on an organization of private, prepolitical life that enables and encourages citizens to rise above private identities and concerns. It works on the hope of transcending difference rather than the provision of occasions for recognition, expression, and interrelationship.

The resolution to this issue depends on two main factors. First, the idea of a single, uniquely authoritative public sphere needs to be questioned and the manner of relations among multiple, intersecting, and heterogeneous publics needs to be considered. Second, identity formation needs to be approached as part of the process of public life, not something that can be fully settled prior to it in a private sphere.

Recognizing a multiplicity of publics, none of which can claim a completely superordinate status to the others, is thus a first step.[24] Crucially, however, it depends on breaking with core assumptions that join liberal political thought to nationalism. It is one of the illusions of liberal discourse to believe that in a democratic society there is or can be a single, uniquely authoritative discourse about public affairs. This amounts to an attempt to settle in advance a question which is inextricably part of the democratic process itself. It reflects a nationalist presumption that membership in a common society is prior to democratic deliberations as well as an implicit belief that politics revolves around a single and unitary state. It is normal, however, not aberrant, for people to speak in a number of different public arenas and for these to address multiple centers of power (whether institutionally differentiated within a single state, combining multiple states or political agencies, or recognizing that putatively nonpolitical agencies like business corporations are loci of power and addressed by public discourse). How many and how separate these public spheres are must be empirical variables. But each is apt to make some themes easier to address and simultaneously to repress others, and each will empower different voices to different degrees. That women or ethnic minorities carry on their own public discourses, thus, reflects not only the exclusion of certain people from the "dominant" public sphere, but a positive act of women and ethnic minorities. This means that simply pursuing their equitable inclusion in the dominant public sphere cannot be either an adequate recognition of their partially separate discourses or a resolution to the underlying problem. It is important to organize public discourse so that it allows for discursive connections among multiple arenas.

Recognizing the existence of multiple public spheres thus is not an alternative to asking many of the questions Habermas asks about *the* public sphere, i.e. about public discourse at the largest of social scales and its capacity to influence politics. It simply suggests that these questions need to be answered in a world of multiple and different publics. It is a political exercise of power to authorize only one of these as properly "public," or of some as more legitimately public than others which are held to be "private." In other words, determining whose speech is more properly public is itself a site of political contestation. Different public discourses commonly invoke different distinctions of what is properly "private" and therefore not appropriately addressed in the public discourse or used to settle public debates. There is no objective criterion that distinguishes private from public across the range of discourses. We cannot say, for example, that either bank accounts or sexual orientations are essentially private matters. Varying public/private distinctions are potential (and revisable) accomplishments of each sphere of discourse.

A great deal of the discourse that takes place in public, and that is accessible to the broadest public, is not about ostensibly public matters. I do not mean simply that people take very public occasions such as television appearances to talk about what is customarily considered private, like their sex lives. I mean that many topics of widespread concern to the body politic – like childbearing and childrearing, marriage and divorce, violence of various sorts – are brought into discussions that are public in their constitution but that do not represent themselves as public in the same way the newspaper editorial pages do, and are not taken equally seriously by most participants in the more authorized public sphere. These matters are discussed in churches and self-help groups, among filmgoers and on talk-radio, among parents waiting for their children after school dances and those waiting for visiting hours to commence at prisons. How much the discourse of these various groupings is organized on the rational-critical lines valorized by Habermas's classical Enlightenment public sphere is variable – as is the case, of course, for any other public discussion. But it would be a mistake to presume *a priori* that one can only be rational-critical about affairs of state or economy, and that these necessarily comprise the proper domain of the public sphere. Conversely, relegation to the realm of the private can be in varying degrees both a protection from public intervention or observation and a disempowering exclusion from public discourse.

The differences among public spheres are important. Simply to treat all these different more or less public discourses as public spheres in Habermas's sense would be to miss the center of his theoretical project, to treat as entirely arbitrary his emphasis on discourse that attempts to work on a rational-critical basis, to include people different from each other while making arguments rather than the identities of arguers the basis of persuasion, and to address the workings of the state. It would fundamentally undermine the contribution of the analysis of public spheres to democratic theory. Habermas invites some of this problem by employing a problematic distinction of public from private. Intimate relations, family life, and civil society are all located on the private side of this too-sharp dichotomy. The arenas and discourses in which people form identities and constitute or recognize interests are all thus presented as separate from the potentially rational-critical discourse of the public sphere. In biographical terms, Habermas implies that they are temporally prior. But rational-critical public discourse can work only if people are adequately prepared for it through other aspects of their personal and cultural experience. Thus Habermas briefly discusses how the rise of a literary public sphere rooted in the rise of novel-reading and theater-going publics contributed to the development of the political public sphere, but he does not follow through on this insight. He drops discussion of the literary public sphere with its nineteenth-century incarnation, that is, as soon as it has played its role in preparing the path for the rise of the Enlightenment political public sphere. He does not consider subsequent changes in literary discourse and how they may be related to changes in the identities people bring into the political public sphere.

More generally, Habermas does not adequately thematize the role of identity-forming, culture-forming public activity. Though he treats identity-formation as intersubjective and hence social, he keeps it separate from rational-critical deliberation. If, however, we abandon the notion that identity is formed once and for all in advance of participation in the public sphere, we can recognize that in varying degrees all public discourses are occasions for identity formation. This is central to the insight of Negt and Kluge in their appropriation of the phenomenological notion of "horizons of experience" as a way of broadening Habermas's approach to the public sphere.[25] Experience is not something exclusively prior to and only addressed by the rational-critical discourse of the public sphere; it is constituted in part through public discourse and at the same time continually orients people differently in public life.[26] We can distinguish public spheres in which identity-formation figures more prominently, and those in which rational-critical discourse is more prominent, but we should not assume the existence of any political public sphere where identity-formation (and reformation) is not significant.[27] Identity-formation and topical debate are hard to keep entirely separate.

Excluding the identity-forming project from the public sphere makes no more sense than excluding those of "problematically different" identities. Few today would argue (at least in the broadly liberal public spheres of the West) against including women, racial and ethnic minorities, and virtually all other groups clearly subject to the same state and part of the same civil society. Yet many do argue against citizenship for those who refuse various projects of assimilation. It is not just Germans with their ethnic ideas about national citizenship who have a problem with immigrants. The language of the liberal public sphere is used to demand that only English be spoken in Florida, for example, or that Arabs and Africans conform to certain ideas of Frenchness if they wish to stay in France. And for that matter, many other arguments – e.g. that only heterosexuals should serve in the military – have much the same form and status. They demand conformity as a condition of full citizenship. Yet migration continues, making it harder to suppress difference even while provoking the urge. In a basic and intrinsic sense, if the public sphere has the capacity to alter civil society and to shape the state, then its own democratic practice must confront the questions of membership and the identity of the political community it represents. These cannot be left to the "prepolitical."

Once we acknowledge that the definition of a political community is not immutably given by nationality or any other putatively natural or historically ancient factor, then we may approach it as a matter of civil society – that is, of the actual construction of social relationships (alternatively, it becomes a matter of pure will). But we must be clear that this always involves culture and choice; civil society does not simply exist prior to the construction of meaning and the politics of identity.

Nor is it enough that we criticize "bad nationalism." Participation in a democratic public sphere obligates us to develop a good account of the identity of our political communities that faces up to necessary problems of inclusion and exclusion. This is not just a matter of letting "them" mingle with "us." A public sphere, where it exists and works successfully as a democratic institution, represents the potential for the people organized in civil society to alter their own conditions of existence by means of rational-critical discourse.[28] As a result, participation always holds the possibility not just of settling arguments, or planning action, but of altering identities. The "identity politics" common to "new social movements" is thus a normal and perhaps even intrinsic part of a successful, democratic public sphere. Even the very identity of the political community is at least partially a product, not simply a precondition, of the activity of the public sphere of civil society.

IV

Throughout much of European history, discussions of legitimate rule focused on arguments about divine or natural right, on questions of succession, and on debates about the limits which should be imposed on monarchs. When this was the case, the question of national identity either did not arise or was marginal. Reference might be made to a monarch's rule over a "people" or various "peoples," but only rarely before the modern era was any attempt made to treat sovereignty as "rising" from the people.[29] Calling such peoples "nations" initially carried no particular political significance. But when questions of sovereignty began to turn on appeals to the rights, acceptance, or will of "the people," this changed. Though the term "nation" (rather than "people") was not necessarily invoked, the modern notion of a popular will always assumed the existence of some recognizably bounded and internally integrated population.[30] This led political theory to depend on social theory; it was necessary to conceive of the society which a monarch ruled, not just the territory or feudatories.[31] Arguments turning on some notion of people or popular will were not introduced simply in response to the pre-existing "nationhood" of various peoples – e.g. as a result of their high extent of common ethnicity – but rather were linked to increasing state administrative capacity in the "absolutist" era, decline in the acceptance of spatially dispersed (as opposed to compact and contiguous) territories, and the growth of market relations.[32] They were also the products of political struggle and political thought.

The new sorts of claims on behalf of peoples figured prominently in and around the English Civil War, a conflict distinctively productive of theory. Just before the war, Hobbes offered a sharp and novel version of the argument that absolute monarchy was justified by the fact that it served the interests of the people rather than solely by inheritance or divine authorization.[33] *Leviathan* was a book about the commonwealth, by which Hobbes meant the *res publica* of Roman law. There was no public to enjoy public goods, Hobbes argued, without the pacifying rule of a monarch. This transformed the several and separate individuals who were originally doomed to incessant war among competing private interests into a socially organized body, a people. So while monarchy served the interests of the people, the latter had no status as a society without the monarch and hence no group claims against the monarch.

Similarly, in the language of this chapter, Hobbes had little interest in the discourse among the people that might qualify them as a public. This does not mean that Hobbes had no conception of the unity of the people, their existence as *a* people. Hobbes is commonly misrepresented as a completely asociological thinker appealing only to the interests of discrete individuals. But he did have a notion of the body politic that both anticipated functionalism and reflected the organization of the cosmos as a system of resemblances in the manner that Foucault has described as typical of the period.[34] This is embodied not just in the text of *Leviathan* but in its remarkable frontispiece in which the Great Body of the State is depicted, down to the chain mail armor of hundreds of tiny people.

Hobbes thus recognized social differentiation; he simply saw it as deriving its overall meaning and potential for peaceful continuity from the state. Similarly, Hobbes clearly recognized the existence of families, and local relationships like the hierarchies linking small farmers to gentry, squires to knights. Social life at this level did not depend on the monarch in the same way as the social organization of large-scale collectivities: counties, regions, nations. Influenced like many others of the early modern era by the traditions of Roman law, he distinguished those sorts of relationships that might be established by private contract or connection from those entirely conditional on the institution of a public realm. The monarch or state might provide enforcement for the directly interpersonal relationships of the private realm, but it crucially brought into being the indirect relationships of the public realm; these existed only through its mediation. They were public, thus, not because of discourse among the different members of the political community, but because the state itself made them so.

Hobbes' argument transformed from within a tradition of seeing political community defined entirely by subjection to a common ruler. Instead of locating that subjection in a hierarchy of intermediate authorities (e.g., as the inhabitants of a given region might fall into a different political community with the conquest or shifting allegiance of a superordinate nobleman) Hobbes treated each individual as directly a member of the state.[35] The political community thus became the whole people, though this people was deprived of the political capacities offered to the publics of most republican theory.

Hobbes' arguments were challenged almost immediately by others that, despite their predominant liberalism, appear in retrospect to anticipate nineteenth-century ethnic nationalism. They attempted to show the priority of political community to particular power structures. The theoretical device of social contract thinking, for example, was expanded with the idea of a "dual contract" in which a first contract bound prepolitical agents into a political community and a second bound that community (more contingently) to a ruler or a set of laws. The main initial development was to locate more and more of the political initiative and basis for evaluation in the socially organized people. In the long run, such arguments were often integrated with claims to ancient, even primordial peoplehood as parts of nationalist political programs of various stripes. But "the people" at this juncture meant mainly the politically active elites. After the Civil War, for example, Locke published a political theory (written earlier) that appealed not only to the interests of the people as a collection of discrete individuals with different roles to play in the body politic (Hobbes' image), but to the citizenry as a body laterally connected through communication, a public.[36] This prefigured aspects of democratic theory, but was also well suited to the context in which Locke published it: a monarchical restoration (which the English perversely call their Revolution) which in fact accorded a leading role to a revitalized, open, and internally communicative aristocracy. It was arguably among this aristocracy that English nationalism had its origins, encouraging a conception of a political community strongly distinct from and able to challenge the monarch.[37]

With the rise of claims to popular sovereignty and republican rule, the notions of "nation" and "people" were increasingly intertwined. In the first place, claims to nationhood offered a cultural basis for the demarcation of potentially sovereign political communities. The importance of this was not always explicit in democratic theory. Locke, for example, took the existence of discrete "peoples" more or less as a given. His treatments of conquest focused on the legitimacy of the subjection of conquered peoples not the possibility of their absorption into an enlarged nation. In general, democratic theory was written as though its province was simply to formulate procedures and arrangements for the governance of such communities, not to address their constitution as particular peoples. Discussions of constitution in democratic theory tend either to imagine a world without established communities or to imagine that the boundaries of a political community are not problematic. In the real world, however, peoples were and are always constituted as such in relation to other peoples and out of the refractory stuff of pre-existing communities and claims to loyalty and peoplehood. Democratic theory could ignore this only because it tacitly assumed what certain nationalist ideologues (like Fichte) explicitly asserted: that everyone is a member of a nation and that such nations are *the* relevant political communities. In practice, however, there is often no obvious or uncontested answer as to what the relevant political community is. Nationalism then is not the solution to the puzzle but the discourse within which struggles to settle the question are most commonly waged (too often with bullets and bombs as well as words). As such a discourse, it marks nearly every political public sphere in the contemporary world as an inescapable, if often unconscious, rhetoric of identity-formation, delimitation, and self-constitution. Nations are discursively constituted subjects, even if the rhetoric of their constitution is one that claims primordiality or creation in the distant, seemingly prediscursive, past.

It is only as nationalist discourse becomes institutionalized in a public sphere that "nation" or "people" are constituted as such. Thus nationalist rhetoric shapes the internal discourse of nearly every state, not just those marked by empire, alien rule, or ethnic conflict; it operates to constitute the nation (the public, the people) as a putative actor – the claimant to ultimate sovereignty – in relation to the state. "Nationalism," Gellner has thus averred, "is primarily a political principle, which holds that the political and the national unit should be congruent."[38] But as Durkheim noted long before, it is usually the apparent disjunction of people and state which brings the category of nation and the phenomenon of nationalism into play.[39] Grounding political legitimacy in notions of the people allows nationalists to assert a disjuncture between even a domestic government and its society if that government fails to serve the putative needs or interests of the nation. Thus in Eastern Europe during the last years of communist rule, a rhetoric appeared for speaking of the state (or government) as sharply separate from society (or civil society). This both conceptualized a realm in which people could organize their activities untainted by a corrupt and corrupting state, and a basis for challenges to the legitimacy of that state. This understanding, indeed, marks a stronger similarity to the great modern revolutions than any of the actual processes of political transformation in 1989 or just after.[40] This rhetoric grows in the sphere of public discourse within which intellectuals help to produce the national identity and engage arguments about the public good. But (as the post-1989 transformations have shown) it is also linked to the sorts of nationalism that distinguish society from state but represses rational-critical public argument in favor of conformity to the national mission, destiny, or identity.

The issue arose sharply in the French Revolution of 1789. The development of an active public sphere, a strong exemplar of both rational-critical discourse and creative thought about matters of the public good, was a crucial precursor to revolution and it flowered enormously in the early phases of the revolution itself, as public debate spread from salons and the National Assembly to innumerable neighborhood clubs and public gatherings.[41] Flourishing in print as well as oral debate, this public sphere presented "the people" as a capable political force to be counterposed to the king and to *ancien régime* elites more generally. But the very invocation of the people also threatened the institutions of the public sphere. It fueled both the illusory ideal of direct democracy and the rise of Jacobinism. The ideas of nation and sovereign people fused, encouraging the notion that the people ought to speak with a singular voice. Similarly, the people as assembled in public gatherings displaced both broader ideas of representation and occasions for reflective discussion.

Article 3 of the 1789 Declaration of the Rights of Man and Citizen declared "The principle of all sovereignty resides essentially in the Nation. No body, no individual can exercise any authority that does not expressly stem from the nation."[42] Though the crucial term changed, the discourse of nationalism continued to dominate the construction of the comparable article in the Constitution of 1793: "Sovereignty resides in the people. It is one and indivisible, imprescriptible and inalienable."[43] Such ideas linked the revolution directly to the tradition of Rousseau and the idea of general will.[44] Rousseau (like Ferguson in another tradition) also developed ideas of the social cohesion of the members of a nation far beyond Locke. His *Considerations on the Government of Poland* emphasized patriotic education capable not only of binding citizens to each other and imbuing each with love of *la patrie*, but also of making each a distinctively national person, giving each mind a "national form."[45] Montesquieu's appeal to the "spirit" of laws had presaged a modern discourse of national cultures and characters.[46] In the French Revolution, especially as it was interpreted on the European continent and celebrated in successive French political struggles, the nation had actively constituted itself as a sovereign being. One catch was that appeals to this sovereign being could often be deployed as "trump cards" against other loyalties and against critiques rooted in various internal differences among the members of the nation. Only the properly national interests could be legitimate or authoritative in the public realm; more specific identities – e.g. those of women, or workers, or members of minority religions could at best be accepted as matters of private preference with no public standing. Too often the pressure for national unity became a pressure for conformity even in private life.[47]

V

The rhetoric of nationalism is sometimes described as inherently "collectivistic" rather than "individualistic," but this is a misleading opposition. In its most characteristic modern employments, the idea of the nation depends very much on individualism. It establishes the nation both as a category of similar individuals and as a sort of "super-individual." As a rhetoric of categorical identity, nationalism is precisely not focused on the various particularistic relationships among members of the nation. But here a crucial differentiation among nationalisms arises. To what extent do nationalist rhetorics depend on the recognition of differences among members of the nation (both as individuals and as members of smaller collectivities) and thereby gain constitution through the discourse of this differentiated public? Or, conversely, to what extent do nationalist rhetorics posit the nation as a singular people in which the identity of each is merged into that of the whole? As Arendt put it (with a somewhat different example in mind):

This unitedness of many into one is basically antipolitical; it is the very opposite of the togetherness prevailing in political or commercial communities, which – to take the Aristotelian example – consist not of an association (*koinonia*) between two physicians, but between a physician and a farmer, "and in general between people who are different and unequal."[48]

The equality attending the public realm is necessarily an equality of unequals who stand in need of being "equalized" in certain respects and for certain purposes. It is citizenship that produces an "artificial" equality among the members of a public who are natural unequals as private persons. Nationalism may, thus, draw on and reinforce the classical division between a public realm in which individuals are equivalent as citizens and a private realm in which they are distinguished by various differentiations of family, contractual relations, or personal characteristics.[49] But, conversely, where nationalist rhetoric stresses oneness at the expense of a notion of a differentiated public, it becomes repressive not just of minorities, but of all citizens. One or the other pattern need not be a perduring characteristic of different national traditions; it may also reflect experiences forged in different practical circumstances. Generations less worried about the basic sovereignty and identity of the nation – perhaps because of the very success of earlier nationalist struggles – may find it easier to accept differentiated identities and even new sorts of identity politics.

Modern individualism (to which I can hardly do justice here) is tied to distinctive conceptions of the world, conceptions that abandon the notion of an implicate order or encompassing hierarchy as the basic source of identity.[50] It is also tied to material reductions in the extent to which identities constructed in webs of direct interpersonal relations are sufficient to organize people's lives.

In the main modern Western view, individuals exist in and of themselves. This modern idea of the individual as the locus of indissoluble identity – at least potentially self-sufficient, self-contained and self-moving – is a powerful factor in nationalism. It is no accident that the modern notion of nation arises in tandem with modern ideas of the "punctual self" or individual.[51] The modern idea of the person was forged partly in the context of political philosophy and law. It was closely linked to the notion that certain social conditions prepare individuals for entrance into the rational-critical discourse of the public sphere. Thus when Locks asks under what circumstances people can be autonomous citizens, he is probing the nature of responsible personhood at the same time as he is exploring how sovereign power might be distributed among citizens.[52] Rousseau's idea of the general will presumes a social whole, like a nation, and at the same time embodies his radical idea of the integrity and freedom – the absolute inalienability – of the individual.[53]

However paradoxical it has seemed to later analysts, Rousseau captures something basic to the discourse of nationalism in asserting simultaneously the indivisibility of the individual person and of the whole community, and in claiming the possibility of an immediate relationship between the two. The links between the histories of individualism and nationalism are perhaps most strikingly clear in Fichte.[54] Fichte's notion of self-recognition, of the person who seemingly confronts himself (or herself) in a mirror and says "I am I," is inextricably tied to the notion of the nation as itself an individual.[55] Just as persons are understood as unitary in prototypical modern thought so are nations held to be integral. In general, each nation is understood as indivisible (literally, thus, individual) and as the bearer of a distinctive identity. As Anderson has indicated, the unitary conception of the nation involves a special sense of time as the history through which the nation passes.[56] This renders the nation a perduring and singular being rather than one with a differentiable internal history. Marx's contemporary, Friedrich List, "pronounced nations to be 'eternal,' to constitute a unity both in space and time."[57] Yet List also thought that modern nations made themselves – a kind of collective *Bildungsprozess* that produced true individuality out of heterogeneous constituents and influences.

To be a "historical nation," in Fichte's phrase, was to succeed in this process of individuation and to achieve a distinctive character, mission, and destiny. Other nations lacked sufficient vigor or national character; they were destined to be failures and consigned to the backwaters of history. Not surprisingly, this is typically how dominant or majority populations thought of minorities and others subordinated within their dominions. This showed another side to the Springtime of Nations. It was the period when France took on its mission *civilisatrice*, Germany found its historical destiny, and Poles crystallized their Romantic conception of the martyr-nation.[58] Each nation had a distinct experience and character, something special to offer the world and something special to express for itself. "Nations are individualities with particular talents and the possibilities of exploiting those talents."[59] Individualism is important not just metaphorically, but as the basis for the central notion that individuals are directly members of the nation, that it marks each of them as an intrinsic identity and they commune with it immediately and as a whole. In the discourse of nationalism, one is simply Chinese, French, or Eritrean. The individual does not require the mediations of family, community, region, or class to be a member of the nation. Nationality is understood precisely as an attribute of the individual and the whole, not

of the intermediate associations. This way of thinking reinforces the idea
of nationality as a sort of trump card in the game of identity. While it
does not preclude other self-understandings, within most nationalist
ideologies it is held to override them at least in times of national crisis
and need. In Foucault's sense, therefore, nationality is understood as
inscribed in the very body of the modern individual.[60] A person without
a country must therefore be understood to lack not only a place in the
external world but a proper self.[61]

The discourse of nationalism not only encourages seeing identity as
inscribed in and coterminous with the individual body; it also encourages
seeing individuals as linked through their membership in sets of equivalents – classes, races, genders, etc. – rather than their participation in
interpersonal relationships.[62] It promotes categorical identities over relational ones. The constitution of such categories depends in part on
adopting quasi-universalistic standpoints such as those discussed in chapter 6. These offer the capacity to grasp society from a decentered point of
view rather than from within webs of interpersonal relations and local
groups.

Categorical identities flourish in nationalist discourse partly because it
addresses large-scale collectivities in which most people could not con-
ceivably enter into face-to-face relationships with most others. The increasing reliance on categorical identities manifest in nationalism
reverses, at least to some extent, the weight of competing loyalties from
the premodern era (and those contemporary settings where social integration is accomplished more through directly interpersonal relationships). National identity, thus, in its main Western ideological form, is
precisely the opposite of the reckoning of identity and loyalty outward
from the family. Where the segmentary lineage system suggests "I against
my brothers; I and my brothers against my cousins; I, my brothers, and
my cousins against the world," the discourse of nationalism suggests that
membership in the category of the whole nation is prior to, more basic
than, any such web of relationships.[63] This suggests also a different
notion of moral commitment from other modes of understanding existence. The discourse of nationalism offers the chilling potential for children to inform on their parents' infractions against the nation precisely
because each individual is understood to derive his or her identity in such
direct and basic ways from membership in the nation. This is sharply
différent from the discourse of kinship and the ideology of honor of the
lineage. There children derive their membership in the whole only
through their relationships to their parents.

Of course nationalist ideology can extol the virtues of the family and
nationalist movements can be rooted in the manifold interpersonal rela-

tions of traditional society. Indeed, as we have seen following Chatterjee, anti-colonial nationalists in India emphasized the family and local community in order to constitute the indigenous nation outside the officially political realm dominated by the colonial state.[64] Likewise, the idea that the Chinese are not individualistic but family-oriented can be an internal claim to national distinctiveness as well as an external attribution. And though seemingly endless discussions of "Chineseness" sometimes point to the power of tradition, programs for saving or strengthening the nation have also involved a stress on forging a new kind of Chinese person.[65] Once again, even in the case of nations, culture-forming and identity-forming discourses are inextricably part of, not simply preconditions to, the creation of a political public sphere.

In some versions, the account of the nation continues to include strong favorable references to family and community. These are not necessarily contradictory to the idea that nationalist discourse addresses a large category of equivalent individuals. Family and community can be treated rhetorically as things that all members of the nation have. On the other hand, many nationalists have found the grip of traditional patriarchal families and kinship groups too powerful, and sought to free individuals from their grasp both for their own benefit and so they could better serve the nation. Where the claimed priority of the nation confronted other categorical identities – race, class, gender, religion – there has almost always been conflict. Each of these raises the prospect of a fundamentally divided nation in a way that relational identities like family and community need not. On the Indian subcontinent, thus, Hindu and Muslim especially, and in some places Sikh, Christian, and other religions, have appeared as large-scale categorical identities, not just social networks. They could be invoked even by people only loosely woven into webs of interpersonal relationships with their coreligionists. The communities coincident with these religions have split the posited nation and become the basis for competing nationalisms. The situation in Northern Ireland has some similarities. By contrast, where family and community relations are organized in accord with divisions of categorical identities – that is, where category and network coincide, in the sense of Harrison White's term "CATNET" – this gives each collectivity greater capacity to mobilize and reduce the chances of bringing them harmoniously together.[66]

While nations can also be CATNETs – and to a small extent generally are – their very scale means that they are first and foremost categorical identities. Indeed, they become prominent in the construction of identity partly because of the dramatic expansion in the scale on which social life is organized. In other words, more weight is placed on the individual actor precisely as the organizing capacity of his or her direct social relationships – e.g. family, community – is rendered inadequate by large-scale, seemingly distant structures of indirect relations.[67] Local relations may remain important to people; communities are still often vital. But these local relationships are not capable of organizing the large-scale activities wrought, for example, by capitalism. Capitalism, as Marx argued, pulls individuals out of constitutive communal bonds and declares them to be autonomous. But of course the autonomy is illusory; people find themselves subject to forces – like global markets – operating on a very large scale, and must confront these as individuals not only as members of communities. Reliance on large-scale categorical identities like nation is partially a response to this. Similarly, the individual experience of movement among nations, and among territorially circumscribed states, reaffirms that significance of belonging to a nation (whether the movement is a matter of tourism, migration, or military mobilization).

Capitalism expanded the importance of very indirect social relations on a large scale – paradigmatically through the market, but also through large administrative organizations like multinational corporations. Capitalism also facilitated and encouraged, though it does not by itself explain, the development of other forms of communication. Both Anderson and Habermas, for example, have called attention to the importance of such early business and business-supporting ventures as newspapers, journals, and eventually novels – print capitalism as Anderson calls them.[68] These not only supported the emergence of public spheres, but facilitated nationalism by helping to spread nationalist ideology and culture. In addition, both their very form and the practice of reading them helped to reinforce a notion of social interconnection among the members of large-scale categories linked by only weak and not very dense social relationships.[69] Thus, as Anderson notes, readers of newspapers could imagine themselves as engaging in an activity which they shared with thousands or even millions of others. By helping to create public spheres joining diverse members of the putative nation such media provided for a whole range of discourses that were not explicitly about the nation nonetheless to reproduce it culturally. Small-scale businesses, adjuncts usually to the main dramas of capitalism, thus played an important role in promoting nationalist discourse by providing important bases for public life: coffee houses, publishing houses, etc. Communications infrastructures facilitated space-transcending linkages which encouraged people to give up the narrow outlooks of their native villages for an understanding of themselves as (individually) members of the nation.[70] Through such a sense of categorical identity people could situate themselves in relation to the enormous, distant, impersonal forces (economic above all) that shaped their lives, establishing a sense of commonality without tracing specific connecting relationships.

VI

Nationalist rhetoric has generally stressed the essential similarity of the nation's individual members.[71] It is rare to find comparable emphasis on the constitution of the nation through the discourse of a public of highly differentiated members.[72] This is a crucial implication of the rhetorical appeal to presumed ancient ethnicity or peoplehood that was invoked in struggles over political sovereignty. But of course this is not "mere rhetoric," it reflects significant social changes in the modern era. The rise of the state and the capitalist transformation of trade and production relations had brought increasing integration to large collectivities of people. The raising of citizen armies had not only reinforced national identity against the nation's enemies, but brought together soldiers from different regions and occupations. Roads and later railroads provided an infrastructure that both joined the various parts of the nation and linked regions more strongly within state borders than across them. Proliferation of print (and later broadcast) media, schools, and administrative offices all encouraged linguistic standardization and both directly and through common language helped to produce national patterns of culture and behavior. This notion is rooted in positive historical developments; it is not ideologically arbitrary. Tocqueville, for example, wrote of how the eighteenth-century expansion of state administration had paved the way for the French Revolution by rendering France "the country in which men were most like each other."

> Behind such diversities as still existed the unity of the nation was making itself felt, sponsored by that new conception: "the same laws for all." . . . Not only did the provinces come to resemble each other more and more, but within each province members of the various classes (anyhow those above the lowest stratum) became ever more alike, differences of rank notwithstanding.[73]

This extended even to such putatively private matters as childbearing. Fertility rates, which once varied from locality to locality, became strikingly uniform within nineteenth- and twentieth-century European nation-states.[74]

All these changes helped to create a new discourse of public affairs, the affairs that represented the interests of the integrated nation. It was in this discourse, not in any material reality of exchange networks, that national economies, for example, were constituted. The description of the economy as a self-regulating system of exchanges, thus, did not in itself constitute the unity of domestic vs. foreign trade. Such inner/outer distinctions were produced in a public discourse organized at the level of states, and then reproduced in state administrative policies and accounting procedures. In maintaining boundaries in this way, states were innovating, not simply protecting the interests of long-established national communities. So long as discourse (and identity) remained overwhelmingly local, most people invested relatively little in large-scale boundaries.[75] Concepts like "the wealth of nations" or "trade surplus or deficit" could only be developed in a supralocal public sphere. It was precisely on the basis of the perspective afforded by the constitution of the British and French publics, and in works addressed to those publics, that Adam Smith and the physiocrats could constitute their competing accounts of how national economies work and relate. In these discourses, the national and the international were always intertwined. The eighteenth and nineteenth centuries indeed saw an increasing organization of exchange relations and capital accumulation at the national level. But as mercantilist arguments suggest, this came at the expense of some international organizations and processes as well as at the expense of local autonomy. The innovation was driven largely by the emergence of spheres of public discourse which addressed the relationship between aggregated private interests and state institutions.

Not all states were in comparable positions to exercise central power, and not all could claim to have integrated "their nation" within their borders. The dominant modern story of state formation, that epitomized by French history, is thus not typical. There, over an extended period of time, disparate duchies and other feudal territories were transformed into provinces and knit into an increasingly effective centralized power structure concentrated in a primate city. Ironically, the very successful integration of the French nation-state may have predisposed France to its succession of republican revolutions – all of which not only claimed popular legitimacy but were made possible by the concentration of state power in a handful of spatially centralized institutions that could be seized by revolutionaries.[76] To the east, the process of state formation worked out somewhat differently. Only late in the nineteenth century did German state-builders achieve even partial integration of the culturally similar German peoples, and only briefly under the Nazis did this unification reach nearly completely throughout German Europe.

In France, a growing national integration was spearheaded by a central state of long standing. In Germany, the central state was added fairly late on top, as it were, of a variety of regions more or less widely understood as "German" in their language and culture. But despite their differences, both French and German stories thematize nationalism as an aspect of amalgamation of disparate regions into a superordinate state. In the territories of the declining Austro-Hungarian Empire, by contrast, nationalist discourse was generally invoked by separatists against the more central power. This is in part because the Habsburgs self-consciously maintained an empire of the old style; they did not attempt to integrate their dominions into a modern nation-state. That is, they did not attempt to treat their subjects as more or less interchangeable members of the polity, to impose linguistic uniformity, to build an infrastructure rendering communication and commerce easy throughout the realm, to replace narratives of conquest with those of primordial ethnic commonality, or to base claims to legitimacy on the interests or will of "the people."

Imperial rule – in the Austro-Hungarian case or those of most of the rest of the world – is precisely *not* the attempt to forge a unity between nation and state. Empires are organized through the coexistence – albeit often hierarchically structured – of a number of distinct "peoples" or "communities." These need not enter into any public discourse with each other, nor indeed into many collective activities. Their economic relations are typically matters of market exchange, not cooperation in production, and while imperial armies may mobilize members of different ethnic groups, they are generally organized more on the model of mercenaries than citizen-soldiers.

Parts of empires can be transformed into nations by the creation of quasi-autonomous public spheres. This is as characteristic of metropoles as peripheral regions. As the Ottoman empire declined, for example, it was just as novel a project to engender a national consciousness and project of state formation in Turkey as in Egypt, and early projects for pan-Islamic nationalism grew in the same soil. Among the most problematic settings are the frontiers between former or declining empires. The disastrous contemporary situation in the Balkans, thus, is not simply the result of ancient ethnic hatreds, nor entirely produced by the forced integration of Yugoslavia under communism, nor conjured out of nothing by the ideological and military manipulators who have turned the discourse of nationalism into the project of ethnic cleansing. It is rooted in the long history of the region as a frontier in which neither of the relatively stable imperial regimes – Ottoman or Habsburg – achieved clear hegemony. Local ethnic groups were not only divided by religion and military enlistment, they were in some cases resettled precisely to serve as buffers and prevent both socio-political and military consolidation. As empires receded from this frontier, they left behind not spatially compact and socially integrated nations but fragmented and interspersed ethnic communities. Pockets of Serbs, for example, were located in the middle of Croatian farm districts because their reputation as fighters made the Habsburgs think they would stiffen defense against the Turks. Even tiny cities like Mostar were miniature metropolises, housing a range of religions and ethnicities. Once they were no longer ruled from distant imperial centers, however, the members of these different ethnic groups were called upon to form their own public discourses to organize collective affairs. In such cases, elites who were previously subordinates in larger imperial hierarchies helped to promote national culture (including language and literature as well as nationalist ideology) partly as a project that would put them on top of the new or newly independent nation. Either the new public spheres would incorporate diverse cultures into regionally compact polities – as attempted most recently by Bosnia-Herzegovina – or the public spheres would be defined on ethnic lines and offer implicit bases for projects of ethnic nationalist reorganization of territory and population – as in the Serbian counterpart. But note that in either case the institutionalization of a public sphere was at the heart of the project of defining the nation, whether in terms of the civic institutions of a territorial polity or in terms of ethnic unity.

In many other cases, imperial rule involved the appropriation or development of subordinate state institutions that encouraged nationalism by making the contrast between alien, imperial rulers and indigenes powerful. Such contexts frequently nurtured ideologies that represented the colonized as unitary peoples joined by common membership in a single national category (not least because colonizers so frequently justified their rule by claiming that the locals were internally disunified and needed outside help to keep the peace). This representation of "natives" as a single category combined with the stunting of careers in the imperial bureaucracies to make ideas of legitimation by consent or participation of the governed attractive to colonized elites, thus further reinforcing links between the project of instituting a single public sphere and gaining national autonomy. Rendered subalterns in such a situation, for example, non-imperial elites might find attractions in the political strategy of forging closer links with peasants and others whom they could claim to represent as a nation against the imperial power. Displaced by new regimes, traditional elites who might otherwise have supported other, more elitist, doctrines of legitimacy often adopted and/or reinvented the notion that legitimacy should depend on the will of those governed. This happened in both India and China, for example, and in varying degrees in much of Latin America and Africa.

The "modernizing" elites who were active in the development of both early public spheres and anti-colonial nationalist movements pursued similar projects in a variety of settings – increased literacy and freedom of publication, for example. In a wide range of late nineteenth- and early twentieth-century contexts, they pursued nationalism and internationalism simultaneously in a way reminiscent of Europe's "Springtime of Nations," and as part of a project of replicating Europe's Enlightenment. This was true of such otherwise diverse movements as Spain's "generation of 1898," Turkey's "Young Turks" and secular nationalists under Ataturk, and China's student and intellectual protesters of May 4, 1919 and the "New Thought" movement. These examples suggest (1) how nationalism thrived as a modern discourse, not simply an ethnic inheritance, (2) how nationalism and the creation of cultural publics and political public spheres went hand in hand, and (3) how much global discourses and material factors affected these processes, helping to produce such similar movements nearly simultaneously in widely dispersed and culturally diverse settings.

At the same time, anti-colonialism and anti-imperial secessionism depend on the internal organizing capacity of the would-be independent nation. They cannot be understood as attempts simply to protect or restore traditional arrangements, even where that is their manifest ideological purpose, for they pursue a new, national form of mobilization as a more or less necessary concomitant of anti-imperial struggle. Such anti-colonial movements also often rebel against domestic elites who have entered into accommodationist agreements with imperial powers (as was the case in Korea's March First movement and China's May Fourth movement, both of 1919).

In both Korea and China, nationalist discourse remained extremely state-centered despite movements that attacked both traditional elites and imperial powers. There were only halting efforts in each case to develop national integration outside the purview of state power. In India, these efforts went much further. Indian nationalists brought forward in both ideology and practice a nation that was defined in social-relational and cultural terms as against the political terms monopolized by the colonial state.[77] In different but comparably dramatic ways in all three cases, the extent of material (social-relational, economic, infrastructural) as well as cultural national integration was insufficient to sustain completely the integrity of the nation after the departure of imperial powers and/or the collapse of accommodationist domestic regimes. The partition of India and Pakistan (and later independence of Bangladesh as well as communal separatism in India), the division of the two Koreas, and the warlords era in China all suggest the limits to the national integration that could be accomplished in opposition to the prevailing state power.

In each case, one of the key problematics of the post-independence states was to resume the struggle for national integration, equating the nation now increasingly with the state.

If one major source of nationalism is the new levels of national integration forged, it is also true that secessionist nationalisms are often forged from failed projects of broader national integration. Several East European countries and the former Soviet Union offer enough examples.[78] The post-colonial states are particularly vulnerable to challenges from subordinate national groups, since these can employ the very rhetoric that the anti-colonialists used in winning their independence struggles. This is why the discourse of nationalism encompasses both fissiparous or secessionist movements and unificationist or "pan-"nationalist movements.[79] Croatian or Ukrainian nationalism and pan-Slavic nationalism arise from the same discursive formation. Neither secessionist nationalisms from India to Ethiopia nor attempts to reunite divided nations from Germany through Yemen or Korea can claim clear precedence. Efforts to forge a more unified national state often inspire contrary efforts on the part of subordinate groups or neighbors. The formation of a larger unity is accompanied by rearrangements of national identities that create new lines of tension while overcoming some established ones. Thus programs for the unification of Europe draw on new histories that emphasize the commonality of the European experience and identity; the specificity of Europe is counterposed to the rest of the world, rather than the specificity of France being counterposed to Britain or the Netherlands. At the same time, fringe nationalist movements (and claims for regional autonomy) flourish within the European Community. Conversely, the pressure to break up the former Soviet Union came not just from pre-existing national groupings, the loss of legitimacy of the central regime, or the evolving regional structures of alliances (all important), but from the fact that there was never a strong national integration capable of sustaining economic and social transactions on a very large scale in the absence of the coercive force of the central state. In this sense the appellation "Soviet empire" was apt.

VII

No state or nation ever existed entirely unto itself. European states grew and intensified their administration in the context of a web of interstate rivalries.[80] These were played out in economic as well as military and diplomatic arenas (though the politics of dynastic kinship and inheritance did not disappear until fairly late in the process). A European public sphere, larger than that of any constituent state, debated the identities, rights, and relationships among states, the implications of multinational economic activity, and the prospects for peace and justice of wars. From even before the Enlightenment, the public spheres of different European countries were always embedded within this broader European (and eventually Euro-American) discourse. This international discourse established nationalist rhetoric as the crucial basis for addressing questions of identity and legitimacy. Those who would establish claims to sovereignty or self-determination staged performances before an international public sphere including not only diplomats and policy makers but the consumers of international news and culture. Representatives of other states and certain international organizations held the capacity to bestow formal recognition; the broader public offered a more diffuse but not insignificant prospect of recognition and support. The expansion of the international media has only expanded the role of this international public sphere.

From early in the era of nationalist discourse, the world was in principle divided into formally equivalent national states, each of which was or should be sovereign. The discursive principle became normative well before the Hapsburgs and Romanovs were finally forced to abandon their very different sorts of states, and paved the way for the still problematic efforts to align states and nations within their former domains. But gradually, at least, older political organizations like empires, quasi-autonomous principalities, and free cities did give way to a more standardized system. This was effected by international public discourse, as well as military power or diplomatic negotiation. By the second half of the twentieth century, it was clearly anomalous for any state to remain under the explicit political tutelage of another, and where such relations existed they were commonly subjected to campaigns to undo them. But of course the equivalence of the national states recognized in this international public sphere was a formal property of the discourse not matched by material equivalence of power, internal organization, or loyalty of citizens. The discourse of nationalism demands that San Marino, two dozen square miles with 24,000 citizens, be seen as formally equivalent to China or the United States. It is, for example, a full member of the United Nations. The equivalence of states is emphasized especially in arenas like the UN, not only because the discourse of nationalism predominates, but because attention is paid to the whole system of states at once. Even in interstate relations where disparities of power and scale matter substantially, however, the rhetoric of equivalence is commonly observed. This establishes, among other things, a new version of the old public/private division.[81] The international affairs of the presumptively equivalent states are public and addressable in the international public sphere while their internal, domestic affairs are treated as private. Attempts to challenge the formal equivalence of states by suggesting that international recognition should be linked to democratic institutions or by condemning domestic human rights abuses are as problematic within this division of public and private as attempts to intervene in families on behalf of the rights of children or spouses have been. Appearing as actions of the powerful against the weak, they have often backfired and rallied popular nationalist sentiments to the cause of elitist governments.

At the same time that formal equivalence confers a certain dignity on a nation, this is unlikely to substitute for power and stature among nations; nationalism can turn to militarism, economic insularity, and concerns for slighted honor.[82] This can of course lead to war, and to a cycle of injuries, resentments, and new conflicts (such as that in the Balkans). But the domestic, largely discursive, consequences of such international pursuits should not be ignored. International conflict generally, and military mobilization in particular, can help to confer (or enforce) unity on a disparate domestic population. As Sheehan writes of Germany after World War I, "military defeat brought national humiliation and called into question the very existence of the nation which many in the middle strata saw as the ultimate political value and the last hope for political cohesion."[83] The claim to a singular match between each state and its nation, reinforced by international jealousies, humiliations, and fears, has often been the basis for both repression of difference within the nation and attempts to exclude or subjugate all "foreign" elements within the state. The language of national humiliation (or international abuse more generally) provides a discourse in which people can respond to felt problems, like impoverishment, without recognizing the extent to which their interests conflict with others of their countrymen. This misrecognition (in Bourdieu's sense) is not simply manipulated from above but built into the discourse of nationalism.[84]

Even the pan-Islamic or pan-Shia nationalist variants of contemporary Islamic fundamentalism are products of a global production and reshaping of culture and movements; they are not simply local reactions. Not only do they knit together various predominantly Islamic countries, they are nurtured in part by the experience of life in Islamic enclaves within parts of the West. Thus the message of the Ayatollah Khomeini was honed in French exile as well as in the holy city of Qom; his messages spread more widely through the world by tape recordings and travelers than those of the *Communist Manifesto* even did in Marx's lifetime, or than the arguments of "Young Europe." They found, for example, receptive audiences in South Asian Muslim enclaves in Britain as well as in Islamic countries from Sudan to Pakistan. Khomeini's addresses reached an international Islamic public sphere – and in doing so threatened national governments in some predominantly Islamic countries. The message was perhaps reactionary in relation to much of the modern West and to the forms Westernization had taken in Iran and the rest of the Islamic world. But it was also universalizing and in some ways cosmopolitan *within* the Islamic world. It addressed Muslims as individuals wherever they might be, and as members of the great community of Islamic faith, but not primarily as members of intermediate ethnicities or local polities. Though Islamic fundamentalism challenges existing national boundaries, and challenges many Western ideas about what is proper to the relationship between state and religion, it does not break with nationalism so much as promote a redefinition of the crucial categorical identity or political community for devout Muslims.

That the discourse of nationalism is available in an international public sphere for adoption in disparate settings is made clear by the history of anti-colonial nationalisms. As Anderson has argued, nationalism may even have originated in colonial experience – that of Spanish America – but wherever it started it was immediately "modular," transportable into very different material and ideological contexts.[85]

Colonialism was a great source of nationalism for several reasons. In the first place, the presence and power of the colonial regime placed a premium on the affirmation or development of a national identity as its counterweight and a basis for resistance. In many cases, colonial ideology also carried the view that the colonized were essentially disunited (except for the peace maintained by the colonizers) and incapable of self-organization; nationalism was both the visible evidence against this and in some cases part of the actual achievement of capacity for self-organization on a large scale.[86] Third, colonial rule was itself more sharply incapacitating, in a crucial sense, once the world was organized in a system of states. Regardless of the difficulties in achieving either international efficacy or domestic self-organization, both opportunities were effectively limited to those who could mount a successful claim to state sovereignty. Whatever the actual form of government claimants anticipated, no matter how elite the anti-colonialists and how elitist their agendas for post-colonial rule, their claims to sovereignty came by definition from "below," from "the people," rather than from the rulers above. Nationalism was (and remains) the most readily available discursive form for such claims. Though it is in part imported from an international discourse, the very colonial situation leads also to its indigenous reinvention and reinforcement.

In anti-colonial movements it is easy to see the deep mutual interdependence of culture-forming, identity-forming, and political discourse.

This challenges the separation of these realms suggested in Habermas's account of the public sphere, and invites us to wonder whether the European experience may not have been more similar to many of the anti-colonial replications of the Enlightenment than to subsequent European idealization of it.[87] Much of the early activity of nationalists has been focused not on directly contesting state power but on efforts to reform culture, to undo traditional family forms and communal loyalties, and to create a "new person" combining aspects of Western individualism with distinctively indigenous cultural content. Such projects have commonly involved the production of a public sphere, even while much of the discourse in the public sphere invoked a rhetoric of essentialist national identity.

In attempting to account for the strength of imperial powers while demonstrating the continuing importance of indigenous national culture, many anti-colonial nationalisms produce or reproduce a split between spiritual and material life.[88] This resulted, in China, in the famous "Ti-Yong" dictum: Chinese studies for spiritual essence; Western studies for practical use.[89] In India too, nationalist ideology declared the "domain of the spiritual its sovereign territory" and sought to restrict colonial interventions into this realm.[90] This rationale for selective Westernization continues to operate as part of the program of nationalist modernization in India and China today, despite other dramatic changes in each country. It shapes, for example, Deng Xiaoping's promotion of some capitalist economic reforms while simultaneously condemning the spiritual pollution brought by Westernization.

Though much of this is distinctively a response to colonialism, Western history also involved struggles over cultural identity and the constitution of a citizenry.[91] Even Hobbes' justification of the absolute sovereignty of kings, as we saw, required first a body of citizens – a nation – capable of granting the right to rule in explicit or implicit social contract. In colonial (and post-colonial) settings as in the West, the crucial question remains to what extent the constitution of a citizenry and the idea of nation reflected the notion of a differentiated public or that of a unitary people.

What occasioned the issue was engagement with each other in common projects – those of self-rule or those of resistance to colonialism. Colonial rule, like that of empires generally, allowed groups of people quite different from each other to co-exist and interact partly because it called on them to undertake no common projects not initiated by the state.[92] The creation of a political community called for a new kind of interrelationships, and something more than a "live and let live" urbanity. Faced with the challenge of either anti-colonial movement or post-colonial government diverse populations could follow, sometimes in combination, various paths: to separate along the lines of their difference, to repress their differences, or to constitute their unity through discourse across the lines of their differences. The competition among these different approaches is painfully evident in the twentieth-century history of India. One of the crucial questions of the modern era is how often and under what circumstances the third option – meaningful, politically efficacious public discourse without fragmentation or repression of difference – can be achieved.

Leaders in many anti-colonial or secessionist struggles often see strategic advantages in either repressing internal difference or persuading their adherents that claims for recognition of and attention to other identities (gender, subordinate ethnicity, etc.) must be abandoned or postponed. Even in parts of the West where nationalist struggles did not have to be waged against colonial powers, the path of repressing or denying internal difference was commonly taken. As we observed at the beginning of the chapter, quoting Renan, the history of nationalism is largely a history of forgetting the many acts of both material and symbolic violence by which the unity of the nation was forged. It is precisely on the basis of such unsavory pasts, however, that many West European and North American nations achieved their tacit sense of unity and boundaries. And ironically, it has been where internal unity and external boundaries could be substantially taken for granted that democracies found it easiest in later generations to grow tolerant of a new sort of politics of diversity based on gender, subnational ethnicity, and the like.

Where and when the sovereignty of the nation appeared more in doubt, it seems to have been easier for nationalist movements to play nationalism as a trump card against other identities. But though nationalist self-descriptions generally emphasize mass participation and cross-class unity, nationalism is often an elite project structured in ways that maintain or institute patterns of domination. This is nowhere more true than in those post-colonial states where it is most vociferously denied. As Markakis remarks, "anti-colonial nationalism was not, as often depicted, a massive popular crusade driven by the desire to undo what imperialism had wrought. In fact, its constituency was socially circumscribed and its aims concrete."[93] Nationalism was commonly a project of groups linked to the colonial state and to vested interests in the colonial economy. Yet, one of the impacts of pursuing independence and elite interests through a specifically nationalist agenda was that the discursive frame led elites both to couch their claims in terms of a broader category of people and to attempt to forge links with a variety of less elite groups. Since anti-colonial nationalists challenged the legitimacy of colonial rule on the grounds that it did not represent the indigenous people, they helped lay the rhetorical foundations for more popular claims to political participation and restructuring. At the same time, the social relations elites forged outside their own ranks, and the "modernizing" educational and social reform projects they undertook among "the masses," often led precisely to a "de-massification" of ordinary people. Where colonialists claimed that their power was necessary to keep the peace and secure economic progress, indigenous elites sought to create or demonstrate the existence of an indigenous nation adequate to the modern era. They also relied on expanded public spheres in which the nation and its needs were crucial topics of discourse. In doing so, they provided ordinary people with increased means of mobilizing for their own projects and their own public discourses in competition with those of the initial nationalist elites.[94]

Nationalist elites, of course, then faced the challenge of defending their conception of the nation. Where the nation was not conceptualized as constantly in the making through public discourse (and it seldom has been so conceptualized) this generally meant defending a view of the essential similarity among the people. To bring forward a claim on behalf of a subsidiary category of the nation – peasants, women, a racial or ethnic minority – appeared implicitly to challenge the presumptive goodness and unity of the nation. It is not that nationalist ideology *per se* was intrinsically hostile to the substance of any such claims. Rather, the tension was rooted in the rhetorical tendency for the demands of such subordinate groups to appear as challenges to the unity of the nation (as defined, generally, by elite groups).[95]

Thus class-based claims could be supported by nationalists primarily when they were directed against colonial or international imperialists. Claims on behalf of women were often particularly problematic for anti-colonial nationalist groups. First, Western colonial powers often seized on the "traditional" treatment of women as evidence of the inherently oppressive nature of the entire cultural tradition of the colonized (and thus of the virtues of colonial rule as modernization).[96] Second, the effort to defend the "spiritual essence" of the nation often involved emphasizing the national identity found in social life outside the realms of economy and public administration. Home, family, and gender relations were particularly national (and attempts to introduce new forms of employment for women and other putative "freedoms" appeared as encroachments). Even beyond these specific contexts, nationalisms have been overwhelmingly male ideologies, not simply in the sense that men have been more nationalist than women, but rather in the way that national strength is defined so often as international potency, and men are treated as potential martyrs while women are mainly their mothers. Thus in 1989–90, one of the most prominent posters of the Magyar Democratic Front consisted of Béla Aba's painting of a pregnant woman above the slogan "For a Hungarian Future." Nationalisms are especially sexist in ideological content – militarism, for example, and the appropriation of patriarchal traditional culture. In form, nationalist appeals to the equivalence of individual members of the nation offer a potential basis for women to claim greater rights (as indeed they have done within many polities, and by no means only in the West). But, as in the classical Enlightenment public sphere, this formal equivalence poses the danger of the erasure or suppression of discourses of difference at the same time that it offers the potential for recognition of equal rights. Thus, women excluded from a nationalist discourse by practices that tacitly fail to recognize them as full members of the nation appear as anti-national when they attempt to claim women's voices and concerns within the national public sphere.

Ironically, even while nationalist ideologies repress individual differences, they generally address people precisely as individuals, rather than as members of intermediate groups. Indian nationalists, thus, have attempted not only to create a historical narrative of Indian unity, but to address individuals directly as Indians rather than first and foremost as members of different linguistic or regional groups, castes, or genders. In China too, communist ideology has been fundamentally nationalist (even more than that of the Guomindang) in demanding the direct and unmediated allegiance of each individual and challenging the independent claims of parents over children (most notoriously in the Cultural Revolution). As noted above, contemporary Islamic nationalism, however "fundamentalist" and "traditional" in content, shares a good deal of the same discursive form, positing a direct connection between the individual Muslim and Umma Islam. This is part of what makes fundamentalist Islam appear as so threatening to various formally more traditional governments like the monarchies of the Gulf states. These Arab states are precisely *not* nationalist and not organized around modern ideas of citizenship. Kuwait is ruled by an Emir, as the head of a royal lineage, within a tribal kin group that comprises a minority of the inhabitants of its territory and an even smaller percentage of those involved in material production or rendering services. Both Iraq's Baathist nationalism and the broader Islamic nationalism promulgated by Iran start from the premise of universal citizenship, at least for men. Both officially empower individuals through elections (whether or not all observers consider these to be free and honest), something Kuwait emphatically does not do. Fundamentalist Islam offers an ideology much closer, in this respect, to that of the French Revolution than purveyors of common stereotypes like to admit (drawing as they do on oppositions of the Western Enlightenment to both fundamentalist religion in general and the Islamic East in particular).

As these examples suggest, it would be silly to claim nationalist ideology as a species of liberal individualism. But it is worth seeing how nationalist discourse typically invokes a kind of individualism – in form more than content and perhaps almost despite itself – which sometimes can be mobilized for appeals to the rights of those individuals. And again, we see here how nationalist discourse implicitly depends on the creation of a public sphere, however far from ideal such public spheres may be. In turn, the introduction of discursive publics as part of the basis for modern political organization and legitimacy grew in significant part out of or in close relation to the discourse of nationalism. This has left important markings on both how actual political public discourse is organized and how theorists have analyzed it. Not least has been the normalizing power prediscursive nationalist assumptions exert over the way democratic public spheres deal with problems of difference.

VIII

The history of nationalism, in short, is not a story of the inheritance of primordial ethnic identities. Nor is it a narrative in which purely arbitrary boundaries are imposed by sheer force of will on indifferent populations. It is, rather, an aspect of the creation of socially integrated political communities in which a large-scale, identity-forming collective discourse was possible.

This was partly a matter of ideological transformation, as the meaning of categories like "the people" changed with transformed understandings of the sources of political legitimacy. It was partly a transformation of material infrastructure, as new transport and communications technologies enabled people in disparate parts of polities to stay in closer touch with their compatriots. It was obviously a matter of economic integration and perhaps above all it was a matter of growing state administrative capacity. But it is crucial not to see the rise of large-scale collective identities like "nation" as simply a reflection of the growth of specific states or of state power generally.

The discourse of nations and nationalism was from its beginning linked to the creation of political publics. Such political publics took on their important modern character when they ceased to be contained within the realm of state administration, yet retained the capacity to influence the state. These publics were multifarious, not singular and integral at the level of states; to modify Habermas's term, thus, we should understand the public sphere to be a sphere of publics. The identities of members were formed and revised partly through their participation in the public sphere, not settled in advance. It is this, above all, that complicated the relationship of nationalism to democracy. For nationalist ideas fixed the most basic of collective political identities in advance of public life, and could and often have become sharply repressive of claims to various competing identities. Yet in so doing, nationalism was at least partly complicitous with democracy, not in simple opposition to it. For nationalism allowed the domestic public life of democracies to proceed with a tacit assumption of the boundaries of the political community, and democratic theory and discourse had – and has – little coherent answer to why such boundaries should exist. The rise of new forms of identity politics often seems a challenge to democracy instead of an enrichment of democracy precisely because it places the very constitution of the political community at issue. Our thinking about democracy has left us lacking in intellectual resources for dealing with this issue because even though democrats commonly deny nationalism, democratic theory includes few coherent answers to the question of why a political community has these members, with these boundaries, that do not depend on a heritage of nationalist discourse. This is turn implies the need for a prepolitical sameness among members of the nation.

These issues come to the fore only on the basis of a critical-theoretical re-examination. It is necessary to overcome the naturalizing of notions of ethnicity and nation, for example, and to approach the themes of peoples, publics, and nations with attention to a world of possibilities and inner tensions, not just one of static entities. Such a re-examination forces us not just to question the categories of politics or everyday historical understanding but of social and cultural theory itself. Our whole approach to issues of large-scale identity and difference has been informed by naturalist presumptions usually left tacit. To take categories of nation and people as the givens of political discourse, without complicating them either by critical history or attention to internal contradictions and possibly divergent futures, is a prime example of what Horkheimer and Adorno challenged as altogether affirmative discourse, that which affirms the present as all there could be.

Notes

1 Behind this lay the more general moral valuation of "ordinary happiness," as Taylor describes a crucial shift in European consciousness during and after the Protestant Reformation. In order to produce political commitment

to such identities as "worker" it was crucial that the temporal pursuit of material well-being (and the other values linked to it like happy family life) be represented not as distractions from an otherwordly ideal but as moral goods in their own right. See Taylor, *Sources of the Self.*

2 See Sewell, *Work and Revolution.*

3 See Thompson, *The Making of the English Working Class.*

4 Huntington, "Clash of Civilizations." Note also Huntington's assumption that civilizations are more or less discrete, integral, and enduring units, not ambiguously distinct, internally contested, and constantly changing.

5 See Davidson, *Black Man's Burden*, on the way in which the importation of the very nation-state model from Europe has been one of the problems of modern African history, and has actually undermined indigenous democratic traditions and institutions, which might have been the basis for better politics – even after the violence and other evils of colonization – had there not been such an attempt to follow the European model.

6 Renan, "What Is a Nation?", p. 11. Forgetting is not unique to nationalism, but is a crucial part of the politics and constitution of identities at all levels, including the personal (as Freud recognized in his account of repression).

7 Different definitions of politics would make this statement problematic. If one followed Hannah Arendt, for example, in extolling politics as a vital part of the *vita activa* and denigrating administrative authority as the mere management of the necessities of life, one would avoid linking politics too strongly to states, and one would see politics sharply differentiated from the social. By the same token, the social would then appear as a very inferior and unfree dimension of life – and this raises all the questions about the politicization of the social that have been at stake in the social movements of the modern era. See Arendt, *The Human Condition.*

8 It is a mistake to imagine that either tyranny or its modern successor totalitarianism depended on complete elimination of difference. Despite the frequency of retribution for excessive independence, both Hitler and Stalin had diverse advisers. What such regimes, like many revolutionary movements, have generally demanded is the internalization of all difference, acceptance of the discipline of collective or authoritative decision, and the presentation of a strictly united front to the outside.

9 Tracing these transformations in the nature and underpinnings of states has been one of the central tasks of historical political sociology, in different generations preoccupying among many others Weber (*Economy and Society*), Deutsch (*Nationalism and Social Communication*), and Mann (*Sources of Social Power*, vols 1, 2). Of course, the extent to which the categories of "the people" or "the public" become locally meaningful depends on other factors: internal connections among people, occasions for collective action, ideologies that root citizenship in popular consent or in the capacity of rulers to serve the interests of the people, etc.

10 For a compelling account of the role of republican ideas in a crucial early moment of modern political transformation, see Pocock, *The Machiavellian Moment.* Even modern monarchical states have been shaped by republican

ideas. Of course, republicanism is not altogether new, as the example of Rome reminds us; Rome reminds us also that transitions from republic to empire are also possible, and these have also occurred in the modern era, as for example, the Union of Soviet Socialist Republics without announcement constituted itself in significant ways as an empire, both internally (with relation to the non-Russian republics) and externally (with relation to Warsaw pact dependencies).

11 And in this sense, we see more of the modern notion of the people in relation to the state in the early histories of both Judaism and Islam than in either the Greece or Rome of classical antiquity, however beloved of early modern political theorists these were.

12 Shakespeare's paradigmatically English King Henry IV, for example, devotes a good deal of effort to constituting the unity of his quarreling Scottish, Welsh, and regionally diverse English followers by reference to the undeniable foreignness of the French.

13 See Gierke, *Natural Law*; Ullman, *Political Theories*.

14 Hegel looms too large in the most prominent recent general account of the political theory of civil society (Cohen and Arato, *Political Theory of Civil Society*). This obscures the importance of both Scottish English and French analyses, and of the extent to which the discourse had from the beginning an emphasis on capacity for non-state social organization. This discourse was, of course, a crucial forerunner to the constitution of sociology.

15 Thus Carr (*Nationalism and After*, p. 1) observed that "since the 16th or 17th century, 'nation' with its equivalents in other languages has been the most natural word throughout western Europe for the major political unit: this explains the paucity of derivatives from the word 'state' and its equivalents and the use in their place of words like 'national' and 'nationalization'." This may have overstated the matter a little, considering for example the number of derivatives of the word state in common use in German. Nonetheless, Carr rightly reflects the basic political significance the notion of nation gained with the idea that a people, existing separately from the state and deriving their identity from their own historical existence and social organization, might be the source of the state's legitimacy.

16 Like the separation of family finances from business finances, this is of course part of the Weberian story of modernization as rationalization. See also Kantorowicz, *The King's Two Bodies*.

17 Habermas, *Structural Transformation*; see also Calhoun, ed., *Habermas and the Public Sphere*.

18 See Landes, *Women and the Public Sphere*, and Eley, "Nations, Publics and Political Cultures."

19 Arendt's exploration of the idea of a public sphere in *The Human Condition* both influenced Habermas and stands as an important (and importantly different) contribution to this line of theory in its own right. See the comparison in Benhabib, *Situating the Self*.

20 The last phrase of course borrows terms from Habermas's later work that are not in use in *The Structural Transformation of the Public Sphere*.

21   Habermas, *Structural Transformation*, p. 36.
22   Ibid., p. 131.
23   Though Habermas is influenced by Arendt, thus, he differs sharply when he situates the public sphere in civil society. She had seen public life as sharply opposed to private (which in general she devalued as a realm of mere reproduction of life's necessities), and, idealizing the Greek polis, had not much considered the relation of the public realm to modern state structures; see Arendt, *The Human Condition*.
24   Eley, "Nations, Publics, and Political Cultures"; Fraser, "Rethinking the Public Sphere."
25   Negt and Kluge, *The Public Sphere and Experience*.
26   This formulation differs not only from Habermas but from those "new social movements," in which experience is made the pure ground of knowledge, the basis of an essentialized standpoint of critical awareness. In recent work, Habermas uses language as the paradigm of intersubjectivity, showing identity to be dialogical and structured by social meanings, but still locating it prior to rational-critical discourse.
27   Habermas's sharp exclusion of identity-formation from the public sphere is one reason why he is left with no analytic tools save an account of "degeneration" and "refeudalization" when he turns his attention to the mass-mediated public sphere of the postwar era. Unfortunately, even in his recent work on immigration and other issues that lead him to take differences more seriously, he continues to rely heavily on a notion of prepolitical formation of collectively salient identities. See "Struggle for Recognition" and "Citizenship and National Identity."
28   In an era when political economy is in relative eclipse and discourse analysis and cultural studies are ascendant, it is worth reminding ourselves that the public sphere represents only potential, because its agreements must be brought to fruition, or at least brought into struggle, in a world of practical affairs where power still matters.
29   It was perhaps in medieval Germany that the disputes between "ascending" and "descending" theories of sovereignty were strongest (Gierke, *Natural Law*; Ullman, *Political Theories*). Descending theories were epitomized by divine right legitimations of sovereignty. Ascending theories, on the other hand, foreshadowed the birth of the more modern idea of nation or people with their notion that sovereignty was a grant of the people to the ruler. Claiming that this was crucial to ancient Germany, and invoking Althusius, Gierke used this as a rationale for arguments against absolutist rule and the domination of state over society. In general, the emerging ideas of nation and public both drew heavily on Roman Republican legal ideas and the discourse of natural law.
30   As Chatterjee has argued (*The Nation and Its Fragments*), this became a crucial issue in the way in which Europeans conceptualized the peoples they subjected to colonial rule. The British in India, for example, found it very important to claim that indigenous India did not constitute a single society but rather a melange of heterogenous and conflict-prone communities. This

view legitimated the Raj, but it also provided one of the incentives for Indian elites interested in opposing British hegemony to develop nationalist claims about the unity of India (which, in turn, are among the factors that have exacerbated Hindu–Muslim and other communal tensions).

31 This is not, of course, the only condition for conceptualizing rule in more sociological terms. Confucian understandings of Chinese imperial authority emphasized an account of patriarchy which knit together an entire society through kinship and descent. Particularly in periods when the imperial bureaucracy and *junxian* market system were ascendant over *fengjian* militarism and feudal lords this meant conceiving of the emperor as ruling an integrated society (see Schrecker, *The Chinese Revolution*).

32 Anderson, *Lineages of the Absolutist State*; Giddens, *The Nation State and Violence*; Mann, *The Sources of Social Power*, vol. 2; Polanyi, *The Great Transformation*.

33 Hobbes, *Leviathan*.

34 Foucault, *The Order of Things*.

35 Paradoxically, Hobbes' account also anticipated the tradition of civic nationalism associated most commonly with the French Revolution. Though Hobbes' theory supported monarchy rather than revolution, it suggested that any individual conforming to the institutions of political rule could be a member of the body politic. It was assimilationist rather than ethnicist.

36 Locke, *Two Treatises on Government* (the Second Treatise is most relevant here).

37 Kohn (*Age of Nationalism*) remains perhaps the best treatment of this dimension of the origins of English nationalism. See also Greenfeld (*Nationalism*), though note that she gives remarkably little attention to the extent to which the aristocratic proponents of nation against king were opponents of the more democratic assertions of the rights of Englishmen by levellers, diggers, and others. The notion of nation was not only elitist but repressive at its origins.

38 Gellner, *Nations and Nationalism*, p. 1.

39 Durkheim, *Textes*, pp. 179–80.

40 See Cohen and Arato, *Political Theory of Civil Society*.

41 Interesting uses of Habermas's public sphere concept to inform analysis of the French Revolution can be found in Baker, *Inventing the French Revolution* and "Defining the Public Sphere in Eighteenth-Century France"; and Landes, *Women and the Public Sphere in the Age of the French Revolution*.

42 Godechot, *La Pensée Revolutionnaire*, p. 116.

43 Ibid., p. 214.

44 Rousseau, "The Social Contract".

45 Rousseau, *Considerations on the Government of Poland*.

46 Montesquieu, *The Spirit of Laws*.

47 See, for example, the insightful discussions of the ways in which nationalist ideologues have tried to impose certain standards of proper sexual behavior in Parker, et al., *Nationalism and Sexualities* and Mosse, *Nationalism and Sexuality*.

48 Arendt (*Human Condition*, pp. 214–15) quoting Aristotle from the
    Nichomachean Ethics, 1133a16.
49 Though again, note that Arendt's (*Human Condition*, pp. 175–6) emphasis
    on equality in the public realm does not mean that citizens were conceptu-
    ally or in reality the same as each other even in public (and certainly not that
    equality should prevail outside the restricted public realm). The very idea of
    being equal as citizens depended on distinctions among persons which gave
    them different things to say as members of the public. Compare Habermas,
    Structural Transformation, where Habermas follows Arendt's emphasis on
    the way public life proceeded as though citizens were equal despite their
    inequality in civil society, though he is not equally attentive to the positive
    importance of their differences.
50 Dumont, *Essays on Individualism*; Taylor, *Sources of the Self.*
51 See Taylor's discussion of Locke in *Sources of the Self.*
52 Locke, *A Treatise of Government.*
53 Rousseau, "Social Contract."
54 Fichte, *Addresses to the German Nation*; see also Meinecke,
    Cosmopolitanism and the National State.
55 Schwarzmantel (*Socialism and the Idea of the Nation*, pp. 37–40) somewhat
    misleadingly portrays Fichte's idea of the nation as simply a domination and
    total absorption of the individual, rather than seeing the sense in which
    Fichte sees self-recognition and self-realization as having non-contradictory
    individual and national moments.
56 Anderson, *Imagined Communities.*
57 Szporluk, *Communism and Nationalism*, p. 115.
58 Kohn, *Age of Nationalism*; Walicki, *Philosophy and Romantic Nationalism*;
    Skurnowicz, *Romantic Nationalism and Liberalism*; Meinecke,
    Cosmopolitanism and the National State.
59 Fichte, quoted in Meinecke, *Cosmopolitanism and the National State*, p. 89.
60 Foucault, *Discipline and Punish*, *Power/Knowledge*, *History of Sexuality*;
    see also Fanon's attempt to grapple with this, *Wretched of the Earth.*
61 See related discussion in Bloom, *Personal Identity.*
62 Calhoun, "Indirect Relationships."
63 As Ekeh ("Social Anthropology") has noted, there has been a move to
    abandon the use of tribe in social anthropology and African studies, and to
    replace it with "ethnic group." But this has the effect of imposing a categori-
    cal notion – a collection of individuals marked by common ethnicity – in
    place of a relational one. Where the notion of tribe pointed to the centrality
    of kin relations (all the more central, Ekeh suggests, because of weak African
    states from whose point of view "tribalism" is criticized) the notion of ethnic
    group implies that detailed, serious analysis of kinship is more or less
    irrelevant.
64 In this sense, anti-colonial nationalisms use an opposition pioneered by
    Locke, but give it the opposite valence. Locke sought in the *Second Treatise*
    to distinguish family from state in order to establish the special ways in
    which political authority could be constituted as a realm of reasoned choice.

65 See Chow, *The May 4th Movement*, and Schwarcz, *The Chinese Enlightenment*.

66 See discussion of the category/network distinction and idea of CATNET in chapter 7 above; White's seminal paper on "CATNETs" remains unpublished, but related ideas are discussed in White, *Identity and Control*.

67 The extent to which networks of direct relationships can in fact organize large-scale social processes of course varies from one setting to another. Thus a number of observers have held Japanese society to rely more on complex webs of personal relations to coordinate large-scale processes than other relatively large, industrialized societies. The point is that scale matters, not that it predicts perfectly the balance of reliance on categorical and network identities.

68 Anderson, *Imagined Communities*; Habermas, *Structural Transformation*.

69 Calhoun, "Indirect Relationships."

70 Deutsch, *Nationalism and Social Communication*, *Nationalism and Its Alternatives*; Schlesinger, "On National Identity."

71 Nationalist rhetoric often employed organic metaphors like "body," of course, but even when doing so tended to emphasize both the direct bond between individual and nation and the similarities among individuals. Emphasis on organic unity was employed largely to suggest the ways in which the differentiations of private statuses produced mutual interdependence rather than to suggest fundamental differences vis-à-vis the nation. See, for example, the way in which Michelet is at pains in *The People* to show how the peasant, factory worker, artisan, manufacturer, shopkeeper, official, and bourgeois all suffer their distinctive forms of bondage that can be released only through the action of natural love among the people as a whole.

72 Liberal variants were distinct from more extreme, repressive ones largely by the greater scope they granted to a private realm in which individuals might pursue different sorts of lives, and the lesser justification they saw for the nation to transgress this boundary between public and private.

73 Tocqueville, *The Old Regime*, pp. 103–4.

74 Watkins, *From Provinces into Nations*.

75 Obviously, the limits of empires and even religions or civilizations like Christendom figured earlier in people's mental maps. Their salience might ebb and flow (e.g. as the Crusades brought the fact Christendom abutted the lands of the infidels into European consciousness) and always involved some sense of a frontier. But most of the time, few traveled or engaged in practical projects that made these boundaries very clear or effective in social organization.

76 Calhoun, "Classical Social Theory."

77 Chatterjee, *The Nation and Its Fragments*.

78 Chirot, *Crisis of Leninism*; Tilly and Walker, eds, "Special Issue."

79 Alter, *Nationalism*; Smith, *National Identity*.

80 Tilly, *Formation of National States*, *Coercion*; Mann, *Sources of Social*

Power.

81   For many nationalists, moreover, it would appear that in a serious sense the sorts of politics that are domestically illegitimate because they prize interpersonal differences over national unity are legitimate in the international public sphere, since the differences among nations are as essential as the similarities of persons within nations.

82   Greenfeld ("Formation," *Nationalism*) has analyzed the prominence of a nationalism of resentment in Central and Eastern Europe. Eley (*Reshaping the German Right*, esp. ch. 5) shows this pattern vividly in the German case. Arab and Islamic nationalism have likewise been motivated by a sense of the injuries perpetrated by those with strong states (Anderson et al., eds, *The Origins of Arab Nationalism*; Farah, ed., *Pan-Arabism*; Tibi, *Arab Nationalism*; Balibar and Wallerstein, *Race, Nation, Class*).

83   Sheehan, *German Liberalism*, p. 279.

84   See especially Bourdieu, *Logic of Practice*, and discussion in chapter 4 above.

85   Anderson, *Imagined Communities*.

86   The idea that Third World, nonWestern peoples were incapable of self-rule through nation-states has been widespread – together with its corollary that these "underdeveloped" countries needed some manner of tutelage for a time (Blaut, *The National Question*). This idea figured not just in the open ideologies of colonialists but in aspects of modernization theory, and even in some of the approach of Great Russians towards Asian peoples in the Soviet Union. Chatterjee (*Nationalist Thought* and *Nation and Its Fragments*) discusses this dimension of colonial ideology and nationalist response in the context of Indian history. The claim of disunity seems immediately more plausible in the case of India (and various African colonies) than in China, for example. Nonetheless, even though Western imperialists in China confronted an indigenous imperial regime capable of organizing administration in far-flung provinces, the theme of indigenous disunity and incapacity for self-organization was not entirely absent. It was given force by various peasant rebellions in the nineteenth century, including that of the Taipings, and by the internal conflicts among elites during the declining years of the Qing dynasty (including especially those between Han Chinese and their Manchu rulers). In the years of the Republic and warlords after 1911, the reality of internal division and consequent weakness impressed and shaped Chinese nationalism as well as imperialist opinion. Among other things, this intersection of imperialist ideology and domestic concern may have joined with ancient fears of chaos and faith in unity to reinforce nationalist desires for a strongly unified rather than a federal China. See discussion in Duara (*Culture*, "Rescuing History").

87   Some Enlightenment thought presaged such a separation of culture or identity-formation from politics, but by no means all. If Kant seems clear on this, Rousseau is ambiguous. On the one hand he insists on the separation of Emile's education from the social and political world in which he will live as an adult. On the other hand, Rousseau recurrently undercuts notions of the

autonomy of politics or the sufficiency of rational-critical thought or discourse, insisting on appeals to "truer" senses of self, often naturalized notions of inner identity but also aesthetic ideas that prefigure Romanticism and Nietzsche as much as Kant. Certainly much of the practice of the protagonists of the European Enlightenment belies the notion of a separation of public and private realms invoked by later theorists including Habermas.

88 This opposition allows a variety of different plays on the public/private distinction. The indigenous realm of the "spiritual," for example, may be simultaneously private in relation to the public sphere dominated by the colonial state and constitutive of the nationalist public discourse. The material realm is that in which the military and technical strength of foreign powers is evident. The spiritual realm is that in which the moral and cultural strengths of the subject nation can be celebrated.

89 Chow, *The May 4th Movement*; Schwarcz, *Chinese Enlightenment*; Spence, *In Search of Modern China*.

90 Chatterjee, *Nation and Its Fragments*, p. 5. In fact, as Indian nationalists in the late nineteenth century argued, not only was it undesirable to imitate the West in anything other than the material aspects of life, it was even unnecessary to do so, because in the spiritual domain the East was superior to the West. What was necessary was to cultivate the material techniques of modern Western civilization while retaining and strengthening the distinctive spiritual essence of the national culture (Chatterjee, *Nation and Its Fragments*).

91 Chatterjee (*Nation and Its Fragments*) writes sometimes as though the development of the concept of "nation" in Western thought had remained more completely within the realm of specifically political discourse than it did. Thus he argues that the "suppression in modern European social theory of an independent narrative of community . . . makes possible both the posing of the distinction between state and civil society and the erasure of that distinction" (p. 283). This overgeneralizes, however, since the narrative of community has been a widespread and basic constituent of European social theory. Until the recent development of "communitarianism," however, this was one of the main distinctions of *social* theory from political theory, especially in the English-language literatures. Political theory often suppressed consideration of communities other than the nation (a community of the whole), in favor of accounts relating individuals to states. Political theory lacked a strong account of social integration other than that accomplished by states; this paved the way for the recent "rediscovery" of civil society as a theme in liberal political theory (see, e.g., Cohen and Arato, *Political Theory*).

92 As Weintraub puts it, in the cosmopolis or empire, since "heterogeneous multitudes were not called upon to be citizens, they could remain in apolitical coexistence, and each could do as he wished without the occasion to deliberate with his neighbors" ("Theory and Politics").

93 Markakis, *National and Class Conflict*, p. 70.

94   The extent to which anti-colonial nationalist elites in fact relied on the creation of domestic public spheres (as distinct from connections forged in metropoles or secret societies or the mobilization of ascriptive loyalties through narrower means of communication) may be an important variable shaping the prospects for post-colonial democracy. India seems to have benefited from its substantial public spheres, forged significantly in anti-colonial struggles, to help it weather threats from communal and other less democratic movements. South Africa may similarly benefit from the extent to which a public sphere contesting the authority of apartheid developed despite the censorship laws of the old regime.

95   This is just as true when the nationalist discourse is still insurgent as when it is linked to a recognized state. "Black nationalism" in the United States, thus, has generally had little capacity to recognize black women or black feminist thought (Collins, *Black Feminist Thought*). Though feminist discourse was initially unselfcritically white, and perhaps too often remains somewhat so, feminists have moved much more rapidly to embrace the voices of black women than have black nationalists. This may be precisely because the feminist public sphere, though it has certainly employed essentialist rhetorics on occasion, has never been marked by the rhetoric of nationalism.

96   Chatterjee, *Nation and Its Fragments*.

Conclusion

I

"Life," observes Jonathan Weiner with Darwinian biology in mind, "is always poised for flight. From a distance, it looks still . . . but up close it is flitting this way and that, as if displaying to the world at every moment its perpetual readiness to take off in any of a thousand directions."[1] One of the ironies of modern social theory is that the "natural" has come to seem the realm of the stable and immutable, that which humans must accept as given. We think of the natural as the imagined truth and destiny of individual organisms, not the evolutionary change – speciation, variation, inheritance, natural selection – that makes life seem poised for flight in biology.

Still, Weiner's account of the flexible potential of nature recalls Hannah Arendt's key concept of natality – the potential for difference in every human birth and human act. Most "naturalizing" views of the social world attempt to fix it within preset categories and rob it of its potential to be other than it already is.

Donna Haraway has challenged this fixity not just by noting how untrue it is to "nature" as well as human society, but also by showing how permeable and unfixed are the boundaries between the natural and the artificial, the human and both the technical and the biologically nonhuman.[2] Just as we are not radically isolable individual creatures whose beings end at our skins, so our humanness is not sharply separable from the broader biological world or from the technologies we have created. To recognize this as an opening of possibilities rather than their foreclosure requires challenging received views of technology and biology as constraints by which the nonhuman world impinges on the human. Each needs to be seen as evidence for the many ways in which the world can be other than the way it already is. And then each can be approached within a critical theory, and looking at each can also inform the ways in which we grasp the nature of our own social relationships and lives.

We can note, for example, that one of the most basic and powerful of social technologies is that great "automaton" that Thomas Hobbes termed the state.

> Nature (the Art whereby God hath made and governes the World) is by the *Art* of man, as in many other things, so in this also imitated, that it can make an Artifical Animal. For seeing life is but a motion of Limbs, the beginning whereof is in some principall part within; why may we not say that all *Automata* (Engines that move themselves by springs and wheeles as doth a watch) have an artificiall life? . . . *Art* goes yet further, imitating that Rationall and most excellent worke of Nature, *Man*. For by Art is created that great LEVIATHAN called a COMMON-WEALTH, or STATE (in latine CIVITAS) which is but an Artificiall Man; though of greater stature and strength than the Naturall, for whose protection and defence it was intended.[3]

If Leviathan has come to symbolize the very opposite of liberation and openness to human potential, that does not make it natural and beyond the reach of human action for it is only in human action that it is created and recreated. Critical theory takes on the task not just of criticizing Hobbes or criticizing the state in any of its particular incarnations, but of critically grasping both the ways in which our categories of thought make the world what it is, and the possibilities for change in those existing conditions.

None of this means, of course, that anything and everything is possible, that we are somehow free for self-realization without constraint, or that social construction can make us into just any sort of beings. To see the many-directional openings in biology is not to suggest that biology does not give us certain capabilities and potentials and not others. The openness of biology is pronounced mainly at the level of evolutionary change not the experience or intentions of individual beings, while new technologies such as genetic engineering can introduce radical interventions into the processes of evolutionary change, creating new species and modifying old; moreover, if the lived adaptations of individuals are inherited, it is still mainly through culture. And the interaction between "nature" and "culture" is such that the influences of each can never be sharply sorted out from those of the other.

One crucial implication of taking the radical possibilities of human natality seriously is to reveal that most possibilities go unrealized. All sorts of ethnic groups, linguistic communities, and polities might plausibly have grown into recognized nations with autonomous states. Few have (though many more since 1989). Culture and history are the grounds of our existence in part because they – as much as nature – foreclose possibilities or render them very improbable. To recognize that there could in principle have been a Burgundian nation does not make it a viable project today, but it does remind us that France is neither an ancient nor an immutably natural category. If it is experienced as "primordial," that is because culture and social life have made it seem so in relation to contemporary individuals.

So too outside the realm of nations. The variations that we can see in culture and history are only a fraction of the possible differences among ways of life and social groups. Facing up to those differences does not mean abandoning ourselves to an orderless infinity of possibilities because our very acts of understanding take place within practical projects and bounded human lives shaped by their own culture and history. Critical theory is a call to take the project of knowledge seriously from within such contexts and to see it as a project rather than an accumulation of finished truths. This is a qualification on certain sorts of discourse of "natural" truth, but as I have tried to show, recognizing that we enter into the struggle for understanding within bounded, culturally and historically specific contexts, and oriented by practical projects, does not preclude taking that struggle seriously. We are able to assess our understandings as better or worse even when we cannot judge them sharply and absolutely true or false. This is why, in the realm of science, there is constant and necessary discourse among scientists, contests and struggles over ways of understanding, and not simply the conduct of purportedly conclusive experiments and observations and their summary in textbooks. And in public life too our struggles can reshape the objects of our understanding and our normative judgment, including even ourselves.

II

However much critical theorists have criticized the Enlightenment and challenged its universalism based on sameness and rationalism, they have also presumed it as background to every theoretical move. The challenge of postmodernism lies in the suggestion that the Enlightenment may be losing its force. This is not a challenge that would make equal sense in many Third World settings, though First World critics somewhat ironically claim a moral force based on presumptuous identification with Third World suffering and struggles. In Chinese struggles for democracy, in Indian struggles to avoid communal violence, in Eritrean struggles for self-determination it would seem that Enlightenment categories have not lost their force in the contemporary world. Yet at the same time, the stress on difference characteristic of "new social movements" and a range of related political concerns in the First World and throughout the world leaves Enlightenment-rooted social theory straining for a response that does not require a strong presumption of sameness.

There is a sense, as Allan Megill has noted, that the very presumption of crisis on which "postmodernist" and similar theories trade contains a certain incoherency. "The notion of a crisis in history presupposes what it sets out to destroy – the idea of history as a continuous process, history with a capital *H*. Crisis theorists attack the historicist notion of directionality in history. But in postulating a crisis or turning in history, they assume just such a directionality."[4] The notion of postmodernity – or the practice of postmodernism – thus presumes a linear transcendence of the modern; it presents history as a linear series of stages even while denying this sort of representation.

But if postmodernism of this sort is current in academic circles, the postulate of an end to history received its most popularly influential invocation from a different quarter. Francis Fukuyama's conservative-Hegelian article and book seized on the transformations of 1989 – the fall of communism – as the occasion for a remarkably facile but no less remarkably widely disseminated account of the happy overcoming of the dualism constitutive of cold war and more generally modern history.[5] Fukuyama's account is unappealing because of its naïveté, and because it lends itself to appropriation for reactionary political purposes. But consideration should not end there. We need to ask what it means that from such different quarters as poststructuralist Paris and post-cold war Washington there should be an eagerness to declare the end of an era – in each case without anticipating the recurrence of such enduring if unattractive modern motifs as the resurgence of nationalism and ethnic conflict. Part of the answer lies in the desire to invoke difference without taking seriously the problems it poses.

Though the formulations and rhetoric of many postmodernists lend themselves to such a reading, this misses the important extent to which postmodernism – like Levinas's antimodernism – has brought the themes of alterity and difference to our attention. More specifically, coherently presented or not, the challenge has revealed a weakness in the theoretical discourse of modernity. Just as the reproduction of ethnic nationalism and identitarian violence was unanticipated after the collapse of the Soviet Union and the Eastern Bloc, so modernist theorizing has failed to make sense of the ubiquitous politics of identity – and difference – in the West.

Indeed, if there is a clear predecessor to postmodernism, it is perhaps the pursuit of immediate experience characteristic of the 1960s and early 1970s student and youth protests.[6] Against the abstract culture of capitalism, the disciplines and deferred gratifications of market society and mass higher education, and the bureaucratization of social institutions, one of the central themes of the protests was an attempt to recover immediate interpersonal contact in social relations. Yet this pursuit of immediacy proved not only difficult in the face of large-scale capitalist and bureaucratic social organization, it proved also to mask the problems posed by the differences among the putative protagonists of the movement and the potential beneficiaries of their actions. Links between this dream of immediacy and ideas of total critique helped to precipitate the postmodern response.

The ideal of immediacy was not, of course, new to the 1960s. It has ancient roots; it was central to Romanticism; it shaped existentialism; and it has long figured in the thrill and appeal of the notion of revolution. Critical theorists have both appealed to the desire for and experience of immediacy and criticized the failure to see beyond the immediately apparent to more basic organization of social life. The ideal has two moments. On the one hand, it seems to refer to pure communication between human beings, a oneness based on the elimination of all obstacles of difference, imperfections of language, and instrumental agendas. On the other hand, it seems to refer to directly interpersonal relations as distinct from more mediated, indirect relations in which other people or even large-scale social systems stand between us. Neither is fully realizable; each can be misleading even as a regulative ideal. Yet to simply refuse them outright would be to deny a basic pathos of modern life. Angst over our awareness of the complexity and imperfections of our relations with each other is no more eradicable than that complexity. And of course there is more to the mediations among people than mere reference to the everyday complexities of social relations reveals. Language, power, markets, categories of thought, and forms of relations construct us and connect us in ways we have a hard time seeing.

In undertaking the task of seeing these ways in which the creatures of our own action become the apparently uncontrollable shapers of our lives, critical theory takes on a risk. It risks being unable to recover the positive sense of possibilities. This is what happened to Horkheimer and Adorno after the holocaust and the war and the radically normalizing reconstruction of postwar Germany. As social theorists they became pessimists, and they imagined ways out no longer in critical theory nor social action but in spiritual and aesthetic pursuits. Heidegger avoided this problem by not being critical, and by invoking an ideology of immediacy (the one crucial feature of Heidegger's thought that has attracted the most opposition from postmodernists otherwise deeply influenced by him). Heidegger, said Levinas, held unacceptably that Being must always be prior to beings, that the same must always triumph over the other.[7] This is how Heidegger constructed the appealing but dangerous claim to immediacy and the sense of being at home in the world without having to address the contradictions and violence of the world.[8]

Though Derrida is sometimes more manifestly political, he also seems often to withdraw from the challenge of orienting positive practice in a world conceived as unredeemable. One can read Derrida, for example, as articulating a plea for silence before the unrepresentable terrors and brutalities of modern history, like the holocaust. All discourse, he has said, essentially retains within it space and the Same; all discourse is originally violent.[9] Such a reading places Derrida alongside Elie Wiesel and George Steiner, at least narrowly with regard to the holocaust. But such a reading is hard to reconcile with such a copious production of verbiage as Derrida has offered, even though his tone is nearly always ironic, if not outright parodic or even self-parodic, and even if it speaks around but never fully on the issues of the day.

Yet, in his latest work, (even) Derrida returns to Marx (and to a more manifest politics).[10] Marx had seemed, not just for Derrida but for most postmodernists and a wide sweep of other intellectuals, to be on the verge of displacement from vital public discourse, about to be in some combination thrown on the rubbish heap created by the collapse of communism and relegated to the dusty prestige of canonical texts in the history of social theory. Marx's theory was too total, too invested in the idea of revolution as a radical social transformation, too rooted in the nineteenth century, too reliant on images of material (including biological as well as technological and economic infrastructures). Marx's theory appeared complicitous with the totalitarian horrors perpetrated partly in its name. Yet certain themes in Marx retain their purchase and make a return to his work very productive. Marx attempted seriously to link political, economic, social, and even cultural analysis, sometimes reproducing the notion of the differentiation of spheres, sometimes challenging it creatively. Most importantly for present purposes, Marx developed an account of capitalism as an historically specific but basic structuring of social life, constituting much of the modern world and activity within it through the categories of labor and commodity, bringing a relentless dynamism and transformative pressure for capital accumulation. We need not follow Marx's occasional reductionism and believe that all aspects of social and cultural life follow the patterns of capitalist change to see how important it is in establishing conditions of life and action.

Marx never managed a full integration of his own ideas on politics, culture, and for that matter psychological anthropology with his economic theory. He claimed coherences where these were, at least, not manifest. Today it seems clearer than it did in Marx's day that though these realms may be linked and mutually conditioning, there is no reason to expect them to move precisely together. Many of the political quagmires of the present era, taken as evidence of modernity's incipient collapse, are joined historically not to crises of capitalism but to increasing global organization of capitalism.

Marx took much more seriously than most postmodernists what it would mean to transcend an epoch. We need not follow every specific of his theory to learn from him a similar seriousness. And even the most cursory juxtaposition of Marx's theory of capital to the quasi-theoretical understandings of modernity and postmodernity that are current suggests the difference between a critical theory and a conceptualization that fails to challenge the existing constitution of the world, however negative those using it may be about various features of that world. Marx's theory of capital includes an account of the constitutive categories that make capitalism possible, an account of the historical processes by which capitalism came into being, an account of the dynamic pressures that make capitalism expand and intensify, and an account of the internal contradictions that jeopardize its long-term stability and point to possibilities for its supercession. Marx also offered theoretical accounts of the nature of human life that made capitalism possible and the nature of political practices that both affirmed and potentially challenged capitalism, though these are not in a strong sense internal to his account of capitalism.

Most theoretical attempts to account for modernity and postmodernity, by contrast, are hampered by difficulties in giving specific historical meaning to their objects. Modernity is a label for a conjuncture of different kinds of social changes and patterns, differently motivated, produced, and reproduced, not for a theoretically determinate transformation. It has characteristic features, but not an analytic unity. The politics of identity is endemic to the modern era partly because human action is embedded in so many different projects and these are not altogether integrated or even commensurable. The crossing of cultural boundaries may be significantly driven forward by capitalist expansion, but the reification of those cultural boundaries under the influence of nationalist categorical thinking is not simply the product of capitalism but of the constitution of capitalism within a world system of states (and indeed the flourishing of a specific way of thinking about the political communities of those states).

Modernity, thus, should not be equated with capitalism (a too-common marxist mistake). But likewise we need to see the profound way in which the modern era has been produced by and remains conditioned by capitalism. Capitalism is a relatively coherent theoretical object, and to encourage seeing it as nothing but a multiplicity of differences would be senseless. At the same time, the modern predicament is not simply or only that of human beings living under capitalism and it does involve a multiplicity of differences, including the cross-pressures of different, more or less coherent "systems" like capitalism and state power.[11]

We cannot solve all puzzles at once with a "critical theory of modernity"; we need more modestly to conceptualize the role of critical theory in modernity. This includes helping to make sense of these multiple projects and our lived relations to them, showing the ways in which, however powerful, these projects are not inevitable, identifying not only contradictions among but contradictions within such projects, trying to bring into sensible relationship the different intellectual discourses and perspectives through which people have tried to come to terms with this heterogeneous world, suggesting the political implications of such approaches, and the possibilities for transformative action. By taking seriously the question of what it would mean to transcend the current epoch, critical theory opens more space for considering the possibility that the world could be different than it is than does any simple affirmation of existing differences or claim that postmodernity is just a matter of perspective.

The ideas of modernity and its purportedly opposite twin, postmodernity, are parts of this world, themselves in need of critique, not autonomous ideas for grasping it. Marshall Berman writes, for example, that modernism is "any attempt by modern men and women to become subjects as well as objects of modernization, to get a grip on the modern world and make themselves at home in it."[12] Berman's vision is humane, politically serious, and in many regards compelling, but we should also be wary. Continuing to think within this modern consciousness can be debilitating. Partly because of the influence of capitalism, the modern epoch has been devoted to novelty, in art and high culture as well as in technology and economic products. Ironically, this constant succession of everything by a putatively new successor makes it hard to be challenged by any idea of radical novelty. Berman evokes modernity as a "maelstrom" in which:

> To be modern is to find ourselves in an environment that promises us adventure, power, joy, growth, transformation of ourselves and the world – and, at the same time, that threatens to destroy everything we have,

everything we know, everything we are. . . . To be modern is to be part of a universe in which, as Marx said, "all that is solid melts into air."[13]

This expands one of Marx's crucial insights, focusing on the problems the modern world poses for the constitution of stable horizons of experience. It is an account, ultimately, from the perspective of the experiencing subject. As such, it participates in the recurrent modern search for an authentic personal voice, a capacity for authentic experience, and a way to grasp the largest-scale phenomena of social life in terms of categories that viably make sense of individual involvement in lifeworlds. But the modern era is also constituted by indirect social relations constituted outside the consciousness of individuals through their mutual involvement in capitalist production processes and markets, in states and electronically mediated communication.[14] A critical theory able to make sense of it, and able to orient action in relation to it, must offer the ability to grasp these more "experience-distant" social relationships as well. This requires going beyond the categories offered us immediately by modernism itself.

Modernity is the self-conception of an era idealizing change and especially progress. Perry Anderson captures this well in his appreciative critique of Berman's attempt to resuscitate modernism:

> the idea of modernization involves a conception of fundamentally *planar* development – a continuous-flow process in which there is no real differentiation of one conjuncture of epoch from another, save in terms of the mere chronological succession of old and new, earlier and later, categories themselves subject to unceasing permutation of positions in one direction as time goes by and the latter becomes the earlier, the newer older.[15]

This understanding of modernization is the capitalist epoch's self-understanding, but it will not do for a critical theory of the epoch. Nor can the constant reformation of everything, the instability of all practices, cultural forms, and objects amount to revolution. Anderson is concerned to restore revolution to its "precise meaning: the political overthrow from below of one state order and its replacement by another."[16] Even beyond this specifically political sense of revolution, however, the indeterminate, multidirectional succession of everything by something new implies only flux, not transformation of underlying order. Postmodernists who declare allegiance to this version of novelty and "everything is possible" are both eminently modernist and unable to offer any idea of real societal transformation. There is, thus, a positive as well as a negative way to become closed to the possibilities of radical transformation in social life.

Yet, as Robert Musil wrote, "If there is such a thing as a sense of reality, there must also be a sense of possibility."[17] Any of us can, of course, become closed to the sense of possibilities in life. Sometimes, however, the sense of possibilities rushes in on us with the force of passion. We affirm it not only because we can employ reason and observation to see the possibilities in the world but because certain basic experiences orient us to the existence of possibilities. This orientation may be a condition of critical theory, however much critical theory also seeks to expand it. As with middle-aged lovers who had forgotten why the expression *falling* in love was invented, various experiences offer us the possibility of epiphanies, though usually modest and unoriginal ones. These are not solely the province of aesthetic productions as against practical activity or the pursuit of truth. Possibilities open in each.

This is not a call to collapse the distinctions among these "value spheres." It is a call to see that as knowers, doers, and reflexive thinkers we are embedded in collective and personal projects. The social interrelationship among these projects provides a genuine basis for coming to understand each other – never without some distortion – even across the most basic lines of cultural difference. Our mutual understanding, in other words, is made possible by mutual engagement with practice in the world; it is not a purely cognitive project, an exercise in translation and consensus formation that takes place prior to our potential collaboration. Moreover, because we each engage multiple projects and inhabit multiple social worlds, we cannot arrive as simply self-identical beings at the outset of any social encounter. The possibilities for changing the world and the potential for mutual understanding across lines of difference are always present in our internal dialogicality and the dependence of our self-constitution on our relations with others; they are always possibilities for self-transformation as well.

III

The recognition of difference, this book has argued at some length, need not be seen as an occasion for surrender to relativism or the impossibility of communication. It is true that more or less relativistic fragmentation seems the order of the day in many arenas. New nations are carved out of old states and then face secessionist movements of their own. Social movements proliferate, many claiming privileged epistemological standpoints as well as personal commitment to projects of identity and social change. Not only is the left deeply fragmented in practice, the very idea of a unified left is under deep challenge from those who see such organization as intrinsically repressive.[18] At the same time, fundamentalist and integralist movements attempt new and often repressive unifications to empower nations and religions. Asian political leaders like Lee Kwan Yew and Mahathir Mohamed argue that there is an "Asian Way" based on a generalized (but selectively interpreted) Confucian culture that makes "Western" talk of human rights and democracy inappropriate.

Difference, in short, is not a virtue about which one can feel unambiguously easy at heart. As plurality, it is basic to human life; as the basis for asserting unbridgeable divides it makes us unnecessarily pessimistic about future relations; when invoked as the vehicle for claiming that all those who differ from others in one way must be essentially the same within their group, it is pernicious and repressive. Fortunately, we do have resources for living more happily with difference and forming social relations across its distinctions.

A crucial resource is our capacity to talk with one another. We do not have to agree with all the implications of Habermas's theory of communicative action to see how attractive it is to be able and willing to give reasons for actions. Those prepared to enter into reasoned discussions, to explain why they are angry or resentful or suffering from hurt pride are immediately less likely to act out their passions in violent and destructive ways. They may learn something from their conversations with others; indeed, they are apt to learn not just about the others but about themselves as they reflexively assess their own rationales and narratives. But as I have suggested in several parts of this book, we would be in even more serious trouble than we are if our only resource for living with difference lay in formal communication, coming to cognitive agreements based on translations of our different views. Thinking only in terms of cognitive, discursively articulate agreements as the basis for life together relies on a very intellectualistic view of human nature.

In fact, we are able to live with differences not only because we engage in explicit communication but because we join in practical projects together, organized in part by habitual, inarticulate, embodied knowledge that enables us to coordinate our actions even when we cannot discursively describe them, give adequate reasons for them, or explain why we have a sense of what others are about to do. Beyond – or perhaps before – formal communication, then, we rely on physical sensibilities and shared practical orientations to help us live together and even to understand each other. This is not just a matter of how we understand those very different and very distant from ourselves. It is also how we bridge differences large and small in our most intimate relations. With our children, our spouses, our lovers, our friends we not only speak but touch; we inhabit shared physical spaces oriented to the others' presence; we clear the dishes from the table, give massages, change the baby's diapers. Our ability to carry out these sorts of social relations prepares us for the challenges of entering into other relations where cultural differences may be sharper. Is it a mistake to try to take our dishes into our Chinese host's kitchen? We will, if we are somewhat open, sense this. More basically, when we undertake actually to *do* things together, we can use not only words but physical, embodied sensibilities and the demands of the practical task itself to guide our interaction. This creates the occasion for learning that may be partly mediated by words, but would be unlikely if we relied only on words.

This matters not just in directly interpersonal relations but in the largest scale of social cooperation and communication. We watch each other – on films and television as well as in person. We enter into limited forms of practical collaboration and from them both learn more about each other and build up habituated ways of working jointly that control some of the differences between us so that it becomes practicable to explore the others. We feel intuitively at home in certain settings largely because so much of our habituated and prediscursive knowledge works well without confronting the irritant of challenges. This is a key part of the sense in which we inhabit our "national characters," a way attitude surveys have a hard time grasping. Conversely, the *aussren habitus* of immigrants and foreigners impedes our mutual understanding. Indeed, this puts the matter too neutrally. Our embodied and cognitive senses of identity and of "how things should be done" not only enable us to feel at home in certain settings, they encourage us to see deeply different habituses as disturbing and problematic. More bluntly, in Sander Gilman's words, "the Other is always 'mad' . . . the Other's 'madness' is what defines the sanity of the defining group. The group is embodied with all the positive associations of the self. The Other is the antithesis of the self and is thus that which defines the group."[19] The construction of "our" identities is never, therefore, without implication for the construction of "their" identities, and vice versa; neither is this play of identities kept at a cognitive level where the deepest senses of danger and lust do not play a role. The challenge of coming to mutual understanding with those very different from ourselves is always thus a challenge to our visceral sensibilities, not just our minds and vocabularies.

But though a habitus is not easily changed, it is not perfectly fixed either. It is adjusted in the course of adapting to new situations and engaging in new practical tasks. Moreover, there is no reason to think of any habitus as internally self-consistent, as though it were a perfectly logical, structuralist system.[20] Our embodied practices, like those mediated more by discursive consciousness, change in part because they are rent by internal tensions and we try to work those out. We remake ourselves, in response to internal issues as well as external pressures, better or worse, often with more difficulty than we would like. Our knowledge of ourselves and others, thus, is situated not only in relationship to our external contexts but to our internal states and biographical contexts.

Recognizing that all knowledge is situated and shaped by embeddedness in projects of practical action, both individual and collective, does not mean that there can be no room for rational-critical discourse or scientific inquiry. Rather, it entails recognizing that we deal in better and worse understandings, not clear-cut truths; statements that achieve the effect of truth only by dependence on discourses that cannot be simply true or false. Discourse in which we give reasons for what we do and what we think remains a crucial response to the challenge of fundamental difference. But if this is to support a Habermasian theme in one sense, it should also be clear that it is not a suggestion that we can proceed asymptotically towards ever fuller and freer communication or that we should take as an adequate regulative ideal universal presuppositions of communication. On the contrary, we have to take much more seriously the extent to which our understandings with other human beings are rooted in shared physical activity; in tacit, nondiscursive recognition of commonalities; and in joint participation in practical activities based only partly on prior coordination through communication. When critical theory is too fully focused on the discursively rational, it makes poor sense of the politics of identity from gender to nationalism; it makes the distinctions among cultures seem much harder to bridge than they are; it encourages the mirror-image response of an idealization of the nonrational.

When we say, then, that critical theory engages not only the externally existing world but the conditions of theoretical knowledge itself, we need to hear ourselves saying that theory is produced by people with bodies, with investments in specific webs of interpersonal relations and categorical identities, with their orientations shaped by their cultural and historical contexts. We need to take on critical theory in a spirit of reaching out from those bodies, those relations, those identities, and those contexts, but not in a spirit of imagining we can universalistically transcend them.

Notes

1 Weiner, *The Beak of the Finch*, p. 331. Translating Darwin into sociology (and preDarwinian social thought on which Darwin had drawn *back* into sociology), Spencer visualized social evolution on the ambivalent image of a tree. "Social progress," he wrote, "is not linear but divergent and

redivergent" (*Sociology*, quoted in Peel, *Herbert Spencer*, p. 157). This could lend itself to grasping manifold differences among human social forms, but also to an ultimately classificatory, taxonomical approach. The key issue is not linear vs. multilinear evolution, but whether the manifold differences among human social forms are temporalized, as though they were all historical differences, or understood in terms of more genuine histories that address their contemporaneous relations with each other. See Fabian, *Time and the Other*.

2 See Haraway, *Simians, Cyborgs and Women* and *Primate Visions*.

3 Hobbes, *Leviathan*; p. 3; italics and capitalization in original.

4 Megill, *Prophets of Extremity*, p. 346.

5 Fukuyama, *The End of History*.

6 This is well noted in Negt and Kluge, *Public Sphere and Experience*. See also Gitlin's *The Sixties*.

7 See Levinas, *Totality and Infinity*, esp. pp. 43ff.

8 One can also wonder why Derrida seems to defend Heidegger against Levinas – or at least to deconstruct the latter's non-ironic argument against the former – given Derrida's own critical stance towards a philosophy rooted in presence and immediacy.

9 Derrida, *Writing and Difference*, p. 116.

10 Derrida's *Spectres of Marx*, released in Paris just as this book is going to press.

11 Conversely, there is no reason to equate possible socialist – and indeed democratically socialist – futures with the production of sameness and equivalence among all human beings, as though there were a single underlying anthropological condition of fulfillment in life together. As Anderson suggests, the problem stems largely from the idealization of simplicity and transparency in the utopian tradition, from which it is incorporated into the socialist imagining of *a* better society (as distinct from many better societies or forms of social life). I would add that rationalism of various forms, including but not limited to the technocratic, reinforces the same orientation to transparency which then becomes an issue even for theories like Habermas's. As Anderson says, optimistically but attractively, "It seems perfectly clear that if you had a socialist society in which production, power, and culture were genuinely democratized, you would have an enormous multiplication of different ways of living" ("Modernity and Revolution," p. 336).

12 Berman, *All That Is Solid Melts Into Air* (Preface to the Penguin edition), p. 5.

13 Ibid., p. 15.

14 See Calhoun, "Indirect Relationships" and "The Infrastructure of Modernity."

15 Anderson, "Modernity and Revolution," p. 321.

16 Ibid., p. 332. Though note that this may amount to an implausible narrowing of usage to the most specific of modern political meanings (abandoning not only metaphorical usages like "industrial revolution" but earlier

understandings of revolution as returning full circle that inform, for example, the English idea of the Glorious Revolution).

17 Musil, *The Man Without Qualities*, p. 11.
18 See Gitlin's discussion of this problem in "The Fragmentation of the Left."
19 Gilman, *Difference and Pathology*, p. 129.
20 As chapter 5 discussed briefly, the structuralist roots of Bourdieu's thinking remain in various ways strong despite his challenge to them. One continuity with the earlier structuralist project that is perhaps still too strong in his later work is a tendency to see culture and physical practice as too completely logically integrated.

References

Abbott, Andrew 1990: "Conceptions of Time and Events in Social Science Methods: Causal and Narrative Approaches," *Historical Methods*, 23 (4), pp. 140–50.

Abbott, Andrew 1992: "From Causes to Events: Notes on Narrative Positivism," *Sociological Methods and Research*, 20 (4), pp. 428–55.

Adorno, Theodor W. 1973: *The Jargon of Authenticity*. Evanston: Northwestern University Press.

Adorno, Theodor W. 1973: *Negative Dialectics*, trans. F. B. Ashton. New York: Seabury Press.

Adorno, Theodor W. et al. 1950: *The Authoritarian Personality*. New York: Harper.

Adorno, Theodor W. et al. 1976: *The Positivist Dispute in German Sociology*, trans. Blyn Adey and David Frisby. New York: Harper & Row.

Alexander, Jeffrey 1982: *Theoretical Logic in Sociology*, vol. 2: *The Antinomies of Classical Social Thought: Marx and Durkheim*. Berkeley: University of California Press.

Alter, Peter 1989: *Nationalism*. London: Edward Arnold.

Anderson, Benedict 1991: *Imagined Communities: Reflections on the Origin and Spread of Nationalism*, rev. edn. London: Verso.

Anderson L., R. Kahlidi, M. Muslih, and R. Simon (eds) 1991: *The Origins of Arab Nationalism*. New York: Columbia University Press.

Anderson, Perry 1974: *Lineages of the Absolutist State*. London: New Left Books.

Anderson, Perry 1988: "Modernity and Revolution," pp. 317–38, in Cary Nelson and Lawrence Grossberg (eds), *Marxism and the Interpretation of Culture*. Urbana: University of Illinois Press.

Aptheker, Bettina 1989: *Tapestries of Life; Women's Work, Women's Consciousness, and the Meaning of Daily Life*. Amherst: University of Massachusetts Press.

Arendt, Hannah 1958: *The Human Condition*. Chicago: University of Chicago Press.

Arendt, Hannah [1951] 1973: *The Origins of Totalitarianism*. New York: Harcourt, Brace, Jovanovich.

Arendt, Hannah [1954] 1977: *Between Past and Future*. New York: Penguin.

Arendt, Hannah 1982: *Lectures on Kant's Political Philosophy*. Chicago: University of Chicago Press.

Baker, Keith Michael 1990: "Defining the Public Sphere in Eighteenth-Century France: Reflections on a Theme by Habermas," in Calhoun (ed.), *Habermas and the Public Sphere*. Cambridge, Mass.: MIT Press, pp. 181–211.

Baker, Keith Michael 1990: *Inventing the French Revolution*. Cambridge: Cambridge University Press.

Bakhtin, Mikhail 1981: *The Dialogical Imagination*. Austin: University of Texas Press.

Balibar, Etienne and Immanuel Wallerstein 1991: *Race, Nation, Class*. London: Verso.

Barthes, Roland 1982: *Empire of Signs*. New York: Hill & Wang.

Baruch, Elaine M. and Perry Meisel 1984: "Two Interviews with Julia Kristeva," *Partisan Review*, 51 (1), pp. 120–32.

Baudrillard, Jean 1975: *The Mirror of Production*. St Louis: Telos Press.

Baudrillard, Jean 1977: *Oublier Foucault*. New York: Semiotext(e).

Baudrillard, Jean 1981: *For a Critique of the Political Economy of the Sign*. St Louis: Telos Press.

Baudrillard, Jean 1983: *In the Shadow of the Silent Majorities*. New York: Semiotext(e).

Baudrillard, Jean 1989: *America*, trans. Chris Turner. London, New York: Verso.

Bell, Daniel 1973: *The Coming of Post-Industrial Society*. New York: Basic Books.

Bellah, Robert N. et al. 1985: *Habits of the Heart: Individualism and Commitment in American Life*. Berkeley: University of California Press.

Bellah, Robert N. et al. 1991: *The Good Society*. New York: Knopf.

Benhabib, Seyla 1985: "The Generalized and the Concrete Other: The Kohlberg–Gilligan Controversy and Feminist Theory," in S. Benhabib and D. Cornell (eds), *Feminism as Critique*. Minneapolis: University of Minnesota Press.

Benhabib, Seyla 1986: *Critique, Norm, and Utopia: A Study of the Foundations of Critical Theory*. New York: Columbia University Press.

Benhabib, Seyla 1992: *Situating the Self*. New York: Routledge.

Benhabib, Seyla and Fred Dallmayr (eds) 1990: *The Communicative Ethics Controversy*. Cambridge, Mass.: MIT Press.

Berman, Marshall 1982: *All That Is Solid Melts Into Air: The Experience of Modernity*. New York: Penguin.

Bernstein, Richard 1983: *Beyond Objectivism and Relativism*. Philadelphia: University of Pennsylvania Press.

Bernstein, Richard 1992: *The New Constellation: The Ethical-Political Horizons of Modernity/Postmodernity*. Cambridge, Mass.: MIT Press.

Bernstein, Richard J. (ed) 1985: *Habermas and Modernity*. Cambridge, Mass.: MIT Press.

Blau, Peter 1977: *Inequality and Heterogeneity*. New York: Free Press.

Blau, Peter and Joseph Schwartz 1982: *Cross-Cutting Social Circles*. New York: Academic Press.

Blaut, James 1987: *The National Question: Decolonizing the Theory of Nationalism*. Atlantic Highlands, NJ: Zed Books.

Bloom, William 1990: *Personal Identity, National Identity and International Relations*. Cambridge: Cambridge University Press.

Bourdieu, Pierre 1977: *Outline of a Theory of Practice*, trans. R. Nice. Cambridge: Cambridge University Press.

Bourdieu, Pierre 1980: "The Production of Belief: Contributions to an Economy of Symbolic Goods," *Media, Culture and Society*, 2 (3), pp. 261–93.

Bourdieu, Pierre 1983: "The Field of Cultural Production, or the Economic World Reversed," *Poetics*, 12 (Nov.), pp. 311–56.

Bourdieu, Pierre 1984: *Distinction: A Social Critique of the Judgement of Taste*. Cambridge, Mass.: Harvard University Press; London: Routledge & Kegan Paul.

Bourdieu, Pierre 1985: "Social Space and the Genesis of Groups," *Social Science Information*, 24 (2), pp. 195–220.

Bourdieu, Pierre 1986: "The Forms of Capital," in John G. Richardson (ed.), *Handbook of Theory and Research for the Sociology of Education*. New York: Greenwood, pp. 241–58.

Bourdieu, Pierre 1987: "The Force of Law: Toward a Sociology of the Juridical Fields," *Hastings Journal of Law*, 38, pp. 209–48.

Bourdieu, Pierre 1987: "The Historical Genesis of a Pure Aesthetics," *Journal of Aesthetics and Art Criticism*, special issue on "Analytic Aesthetics," Richard Schusterman (ed.), pp. 201–10.

Bourdieu, Pierre 1987: "What Makes a Social Class? On the Theoretical and Practical Existence of Groups," *Berkeley Journal of Sociology*, 32, pp. 1–18.

Bourdieu, Pierre 1988: *Homo Academicus*. Stanford: Stanford University Press.

Bourdieu, Pierre 1988: "Vive la crise! For Heterodoxy in Social Science," *Theory and Society*, 17 (5), pp. 773–88.

Bourdieu, Pierre 1989: *La noblesse d'État: grands corps et grandes Écoles*. Paris: Éditions de Minuit.

Bourdieu, Pierre 1990: *The Logic of Practice*. Stanford: Stanford University Press.

Bourdieu, Pierre 1990: *In Other Words: Essays toward a Reflexive Sociology*, trans. M. Adamson. Cambridge: Polity; Stanford: Stanford University Press.

Bourdieu, Pierre 1991: *Ce que parler veut dire*. Paris: Minuit.

Bourdieu, Pierre 1991: "Genesis and Structure of the Religious Field," *Comparative Social Research*, 13, pp. 1–44.

Bourdieu, Pierre 1991: *The Political Ontology of Martin Heidegger*. Cambridge, Polity; Stanford: Stanford University Press.

Bourdieu, Pierre and Jean-Claude Passeron 1967: "Sociology and Philosophy in France since 1945: Death and Resurrection of a Philosophy Without Subject," *Social Research* 34 (1), pp. 162–212.

Bourdieu, Pierre and Loïc Wacquant 1992: *An Invitation to Reflexive Sociology*. Chicago: University of Chicago Press.

Bourdieu, Pierre, Jean-Claude Chamboredon and Jean-Claude Passeron (eds) 1991: *The Craft of Sociology: Epistemological Preliminaries*, trans. R. Nice. New York and Berlin: Aldine de Bruyter.

Brown, Richard Harvey 1991: "Social Science and Society as Discourse: Toward a Sociology for Civic Competence," in Steven Seidman and David G. Wagner (eds), *Postmodernism and Social Theory*. Cambridge, Mass. and Oxford, UK: Basil Blackwell, pp. 223–43.

Butler, Judith 1991: *Gender Trouble*. New York: Routledge.

Butler, Judith 1992: "Contingent Foundations: Feminism and the Question of 'Postmodernism,'" in J. Butler and J. Scott (eds), *Feminists Theorize the Political*. New York: Routledge.

Butler, Judith and Joan W. Scott (eds) 1992: *Feminists Theorize the Political*. New York: Routledge.

Calhoun, Craig 1983: "The Radicalism of Tradition: Community Strength or Venerable Disguise and Borrowed Language?" *American Journal of Sociology*, 88 (5), pp. 886–914.

Calhoun, Craig 1986: "Computer Technology, Large-Scale Social Integration, and the Local Community," *Urban Affairs Quarterly*, 22 (2), pp. 329–49.

Calhoun, Craig 1987: "Class, Place and Industrial Revolution." in P. Williams and N. Thrift (eds), *Class and Space: The Making of Urban Society*. London: Routledge, pp. 51–72.

Calhoun, Craig 1988: "Populist Politics, Communications Media, and Large Scale Social Integration," *Sociological Theory*, 6 (2), pp. 219–41.

Calhoun, Craig 1989: "Classical Social Theory and the French Revolution of 1848," *Sociological Theory*, 7 (2), pp. 210–25.

Calhoun, Craig 1989: "Social Theory and the Law: Systems Theory, Normative Justification and Postmodernism," *Northwestern University Law Review*, 83, pp. 1701–63.

Calhoun, Craig 1991: "Indirect Relationships and Imagined Communities: Large-Scale Social Integration and the Transformation of Everyday Life," in J. Coleman and P. Bourdieu (eds), *Social Theory in a Changing Society*. Boulder, Colo.: Westview Press, pp. 95–120.

Calhoun, Craig 1991: "The Problem of Identity in Collective Action," in J. Huber (ed.), *Macro-Micro Linkages in Sociology*. Beverly Hills, Calif.: Sage, pp. 51–75.

Calhoun, Craig 1992: "Beyond the Problem of Meaning: Robert Wuthnow's Historical Sociology of Culture," *Theory and Society*, 21, pp. 419–44.

Calhoun, Craig 1992: "The Infrastructure of Modernity: Indirect Relationships, Information Technology, and Social Integration," in Neil Smelser and Hans Haferkamp (eds), *Social Change and Modernity*. Berkeley: University of California Press, pp. 205–36.

Calhoun, Craig 1993: "Civil Society and Public Sphere," *Public Culture*, 5, pp. 267–80.

Calhoun, Craig 1993: "Nationalism and Civil Society," *International Journal of Sociology*, 8 (4), pp. 387–411.

Calhoun, Craig 1993: "Nationalism and Ethnicity," *Annual Review of Sociology*, 19, pp. 211–39.

Calhoun, Craig 1993: "New Social Movements of the Early 19th Century," *Social Science History*, 17 (3), pp. 385–427.

Calhoun, Craig (ed.) 1992: *Habermas and the Public Sphere*. Cambridge, Mass.: MIT Press.

Calhoun, Craig and W. Richard Scott 1990: "Introduction," in C. Calhoun, M. W. Meyer and W. R. Scott (eds), *Structures of Power and Constraint*. Cambridge: Cambridge University Press.

Carr, Edward H. 1945: *Nationalism and After*. New York: Macmillan.

Cascardi, Anthony J. 1992: *The Subject of Modernity*. New York: Cambridge University Press.

Castells, Manuel 1983: *The City and the Grassroots: A Cross-Cultural Theory of Urban Social Movements*. Berkeley: University of California Press.

Chatterjee, Partha 1986: *Nationalist Thought and the Colonial World: A Derivative Discourse*. Atlantic Highlands, NJ: Zed Books.

Chatterjee, Partha 1994: *The Nation and Its Fragments: Studies in Colonial and Post-Colonial Histories*. Princeton: Princeton University Press.

Chirot, Daniel (ed.) 1991: *The Crisis of Leninism and the Decline of the Left: The Revolutions of 1989*. Seattle: University of Washington Press.

Chow, Rey 1992: "Postmodern Automatons," in J. Butler and J. Scott (eds), *Feminists Theorize the Political*. New York: Routledge, pp. 117–32.

Chow, Tse-Tung 1960: *The May 4th Movement: Intellectual Revolution in Modern China*. Cambridge, Mass.: Harvard University Press.

Clifford, J. and G. E. Marcus (eds) 1986: *Writing Culture: The Poetics and Politics of Ethnography*. Berkeley: University of California Press.

Cohen, Jean 1985: "Strategy or Identity: New Theoretical Paradigms and Contemporary Social Movements," *Social Research*, 52, pp. 663–716.

Cohen, Jean and Andrew Arato 1992: *The Political Theory of Civil Society*. Cambridge, Mass.: MIT Press.

Collins, Patricia Hill 1991: *Black Feminist Thought*. New York: Routledge.

Collins, Patricia Hill forthcoming: *Fighting Words*. Minneapolis: University of Minnesota Press.

Crosby, Christina 1992: "Dealing with Differences," in J. Butler and J. Scott (eds), *Feminists Theorize the Political*. New York: Routledge, pp. 130–43.

Davidson, Basil 1992: *The Black Man's Burden: Africa and the Curse of the Nation-State*. New York: Times Books.

Davies, Robertson 1968: *The Lyre of Orpheus*. Harmondsworth: Penguin.

Debord, Guy 1983: *The Society of the Spectacle*. Detroit: Black and Red Press.

De Lauretis, Teresa 1986: "Feminist Studies/Critical Studies: Issues, Terms, and Contexts," in Teresa De Lauretis (ed.), *Feminist Studies/Critical Studies*. Bloomington, Ind.: Indiana University Press.

Deleuze, Gille and Felix Guattari 1977: *Anti-Oedipus: Capitalism and Schizophrenia*. New York: Viking.

Derrida, Jacques 1967: *Of Grammatology*. Baltimore: Johns Hopkins University Press.

Derrida, Jacques 1972: *Dissemination*. Chicago: University of Chicago Press.

Derrida, Jacques 1973: *Speech and Phenomena*. Evanston, Ill.: Northwestern University Press.

Derrida, Jacques 1978: *Writing and Difference*. Chicago: University of Chicago Press.

Derrida, Jacques 1981: *Positions*, trans A. Bass. Chicago: University of Chicago Press.

Derrida, Jacques 1982: *Margins of Philosophy*. Chicago: University of Chicago Press.

Derrida, Jacques 1984: "Of an Apocalyptic Tone Recently Adopted in Philosophy," *Oxford Literary Review*, 6 (2), pp. 3–37.

Deutsch, Karl Wolfgang 1953: *Nationalism and Social Communication: An Inquiry into the Foundations of Nationality*. Cambridge: MIT Press and New York: Wiley.

Deutsch, Karl Wolfgang 1969: *Nationalism and Its Alternatives*. New York: Knopf.

Dews, Peter 1987: *Logics of Disintegration*. London: Verso.

Dietz, Mary 1992: "Context is All: Feminism and Theories of Citizenship," in Chantal Mouffe (ed.), *Towards a Radical Democracy*. London: Verso, pp. 63–85.

Dosse, François [1987] 1991: *L'Histoire du structuralisme*. Paris: Éditions la Découverte; translation forthcoming from University of Minnesota Press.

Duara, Prasenjit 1988: *Culture, Power and the State: Rural North China, 1900–1942*. Stanford: Stanford University Press.

Duara, Presenjit 1992: "Rescuing History from the Nation-State." Chicago: Working Papers and Proceedings of the Center for Transcultural Studies, no. 48.

DuBois, W. E. B. [1903] 1994: *The Souls of Black Folk*. New York: Dover.

Dumont, Louis 1982: *Essays on Individualism*. Chicago: University of Chicago Press.

Durkheim, Emile 1893: *The Division of Labor in Society*. New York: Free Press.

Durkheim, Emile 1950: *Textes*, vol. 3, ed. V. Karady. Paris: Éditions de Minuit.

Dyson, Michael 1993: *Reflecting Black: African American Cultural Criticism*. Minneapolis: University of Minnesota Press.

Ehrman, Bart 1993: *The Orthodox Corruption of Scripture: The Effect of Early Christological Controversies on the Text of the New Testament*. New York: Oxford University Press.

Eisenstadt, Shmuel N. 1962: *The Political Systems of Empires*. Glencoe, Ill.: Free Press.

Eisenstadt, Shmuel N. 1964: *The Decline of Empires*. Englewood Cliffs, NJ: Prentice-Hall.

Ekeh, Peter P. 1990: "Social Anthropology and Two Contrasting Uses of Tribalism in Africa," *Comparative Studies in Society and History*, 32 (4), pp. 660–700.

Eley, Geoff 1980: *Reshaping the German Right*. Oxford: Oxford University Press.

Eley, Geoff 1992: "Nations, Publics and Political Cultures: Placing Habermas in the Nineteenth Century," in Calhoun (ed.), *Habermas and the Public Sphere*. Cambridge, Mass: MIT Press, pp. 289–339.

Eribon, Didier 1991: *Michel Foucault*. Paris: Flammarion.

Evans-Pritchard, Edward E. 1940: *The Nuer*. Oxford: Oxford University Press.

Evans-Pritchard, Edward E. 1968: *Witchcraft, Magic and Oracles among the Azande of Southern Sudan*. Oxford: Oxford University Press.

Eyerman, Ron and Andrew Jamison 1991: *Social Movements: A Cognitive Approach*. Cambridge: Polity Press.

Ezrahi, Yaron 1990: *The Descent of Icarus: Science and the Transformation of Contemporary Democracy*. Cambridge, Mass.: Harvard University Press.

Fabian, Johannes 1983: *Time and the Other: How Anthropology Makes Its Object*. New York: Columbia University Press.

Fanon, Frantz [1963] 1968: *The Wretched of the Earth*. New York: Grove Press.

Farah, Tawfic E. (ed.) 1987: *Pan-Arabism and Arab Nationalism: The Continuing Debate*. Boulder: Westview Press.

Fichte, Johann Gottlieb [1807] 1968: *Addresses to the German Nation*. New York: Harper.

Fishkin, James S. 1991: *Democracy and Deliberation: New Directions for Democratic Reform*. New Haven: Yale University Press.

Flax, Jane 1990: *Thinking Fragments: Psychoanalysis, Feminism, and Postmodernism in the Contemporary West*. Berkeley: University of California Press.

Foucault, Michel 1965: *Madness and Civilization*. New York: Random House.

Foucault, Michel 1966: *The Order of Things: An Archaeology of the Human Sciences*. New York: Random House.

Foucault, Michel 1972: *The Archaeology of Knowledge*. New York: Pantheon.

Foucault, Michel 1977: *Discipline and Punish: The Birth of the Prison*. New York: Pantheon.

Foucault, Michel 1978–1988: *The History of Sexuality*, 4 vols. New York: Pantheon.

Foucault, Michel 1980: "Truth and Power," in Colin Gordon (ed.), *Power/Knowledge: Selected Interviews and Other Writings, 1972–1977*. New York: Pantheon.

Foucault, Michel [1977] 1984: "Nietzsche, Genealogy, History," in Paul Rabinow (ed.), *The Foucault Reader*. New York: Pantheon Books, pp. 76–100.

Fraser, Nancy 1989: *Unruly Practices*. Minneapolis: University of Minnesota Press.

Fraser, Nancy [1986] 1989: "What's Critical about Critical Theory: The Case of Habermas and Gender," in *Unruly Practices*. Minneapolis: University of Minnesota Press, pp. 113–43.

Fraser, Nancy 1992: "Rethinking the Public Sphere: A Contribution to the

Critique of Actually Existing Democracy," in Craig Calhoun (ed.), *Habermas and the Public Sphere*. Cambridge, Mass.: MIT Press, pp. 109–42.

Freud, Sigmund [1930] 1962: *Civilization and Its Discontents*, trans. James Stachey. New York: W. W. Norton.

Frisby, David 1985: *Fragments of Modernity*. New York: Blackwell.

Frisby, David 1985: "Georg Simmel, First Sociologist of Modernity," *Theory, Culture and Society*, 2 (3), pp. 49–68.

Fukuyama, Francis 1992: *The End of History and the Last Man*. New York: Free Press.

Fuss, Diana 1989: *Essentially Speaking: Feminism, Nature and Difference*. New York: Routledge.

Gadamer, Hans-Georg 1975: *Truth and Method*. New York: Seabury.

Gadamer, Hans-Georg 1976: *Philosophical Hermeneutics*. Berkeley: University of California Press.

Gadamer, Hans-Georg 1981: *Reason in the Age of Science*. Cambridge, Mass.: MIT Press.

Garnham, N. and R. Williams 1980: "Pierre Bourdieu and the Sociology of Culture," *Media, Culture and Society*, 2 (3), pp. 297–312.

Gay, Peter 1966, 1969: *The Enlightenment: An Interpretation*, 2 vols. New York: Simon & Schuster.

Gellner, Ernest 1983: *Nations and Nationalism*. Ithaca: Cornell University Press.

Giddens, Anthony 1977: *Studies in Social and Political Theory*. New York: Basic Books.

Giddens, Anthony 1984: *The Nation State and Violence*. Berkeley: University of California Press.

Giddens, Anthony 1990: *Modernity and Its Discontents*. Stanford: Stanford University Press.

Giddens, Anthony 1992: *The Transformation of Intimacy*. Cambridge: Polity.

von Gierke, Otto 1934: *Natural Law and the Theory of Society*. Cambridge: Cambridge University Press.

Gilligan, Carol 1982: *In a Different Voice: Psychological Theory and Women's Development*. Cambridge, Mass.: Harvard University Press.

Gilman, Sander L. 1985: *Difference and Pathology: Stereotypes of Sexuality, Race, and Madness*. Ithaca: Cornell University Press.

Gilroy, Paul 1993: *The Black Atlantic*. Cambridge, Mass.: Harvard University Press.

Gitlin, Todd 1988: *The Sixties: Years of Rage and Years of Hope*. New York: Simon & Schuster.

Gitlin, Todd 1994: "The Fragmentation of the Left," in C. Calhoun (ed.), *Social Theory and the Politics of Identity*. Oxford: Blackwell.

Gluckman, Max 1963: "Les rites de passage," in M. Gluckman (ed.), *Essays on the Ritual of Social Relations*. Manchester: Manchester University Press.

Godechot, J. (ed.) 1964: *La Pensée Revolutionnaire en France et en Europe 1780–1799*. Paris: Armand Colin.

Goffman, Erving 1959: *The Presentation of Self in Everyday Life*. New York:

Doubleday.

Goody, Jack 1967: *The Social Organization of the Lo Wiili*. Oxford: Oxford University Press.

Gould, Carol C. 1978: *Marx's Social Ontology*. Cambridge, Mass.: MIT Press.

Greenfeld, Liah 1990: "The Formation of the Russian National Identity: The Role of Status Insecurity and Ressentiment," *Comparative Studies in Society and History*, 32 (3), pp. 549–91.

Greenfeld, Liah 1992: *Nationalism: Five Roads to Modernity*. Cambridge, Mass.: Harvard University Press.

Habermas, Jürgen 1970: *Towards a Rational Society: Student Protest, Science, and Society*. Boston: Beacon Press.

Habermas, Jürgen 1971: *Knowledge and Human Interests*, trans. Jeremy J. Shapiro. Boston: Beacon Press.

Habermas, Jürgen 1973: *Theory and Practice*, trans. John Viertel. Boston: Beacon Press.

Habermas, Jürgen 1975: *Legitimation Crisis*, trans. Thomas McCarthy. Boston: Beacon Press.

Habermas, Jürgen [1969] 1976: "The Analytical Theory of Science and Dialectics," in T. W. Adorno et al. (eds), *The Positivist Dispute in German Sociology*, trans. Glyn Adey and David Frisby. New York: Harper & Row.

Habermas, Jürgen [1969] 1976: "A Positivistically Bisected Rationalism," in T. W. Adorno et al. (eds), *The Positivist Dispute in German Sociology*, trans. Glyn Adey and David Frisby. New York: Harper and Row.

Habermas, Jürgen 1979: *Communication and the Evolution of Society*. Boston: Beacon Press.

Habermas, Jürgen 1984: *Theory of Communicative Action*, Vol. 1: *Reason and the Rationalization of Society*. Boston: Beacon Press.

Habermas, Jürgen 1985: "Questions and Counterquestions," in R. Bernstein (ed.), *Habermas and Modernity*. Cambridge, Mass.: MIT Press.

Habermas, Jürgen 1987: *The Philosophical Discourse of Modernity*, trans. Frederick Lawrence. Cambridge, Mass.: MIT Press.

Habermas, Jürgen 1988: *On the Logic of the Social Sciences*, trans. Shierry Weber Nicholsen and Jerry A. Stark. Oxford, UK: Polity.

Habermas, Jürgen 1988: *Theory of Communicative Action*, Vol. 2: *Lifeworld and System: A Critique of Functionalist Reason*. Boston: Beacon Press.

Habermas, Jürgen 1989: "Morality and Ethical Life: Does Hegel's Critique of Kant Apply to Discourse Ethics?" *Northwestern University Law Review*, 832, pp. 38–53.

Habermas, Jürgen 1989: *The Structural Transformation of the Public Sphere*. Cambridge, Mass.: MIT Press.

Habermas, Jürgen 1990: *Moral Consciousness and Communicative Action*. Cambridge, Mass.: MIT Press.

Habermas, Jürgen 1991: "Modernity and Postmodernity," *New German Critique*, 22, pp. 3–14.

Habermas, Jürgen 1993: *Justification and Application: Remarks on Discourse Ethics*. Cambridge, Mass.: MIT Press.

Habermas, Jürgen 1994: "Struggle for Recognition in the Democratic Constitutional State," in A. Gutman (ed.), *Multiculturalism*. Princeton, NJ: Princeton University Press.

Habermas, Jürgen forthcoming: "Citizenship and National Identity," *Cardozo Law Review*.

Habermas, Jürgen and Niklas Luhmann 1971: *Theorie der Gesellschaft oder Sozialtechnologie*. Frankfurt: Suhrkamp.

Hannerz, Ulf 1988: "The World in Creolisation," *Africa*, 57, pp. 546–59.

Hannerz, Ulf 1992: *Cultural Complexity: Studies in the Social Organization of Meaning*. New York: Columbia University Press.

Haraway, Donna 1989: *Primate Visions: Gender, Race and Nature in the World of Modern Science*. New York: Routledge.

Haraway, Donna 1991: *Simians, Cyborgs and Women*. New York: Routledge.

Harding, Sandra 1986: *The Science Question in Feminism*. Ithaca: Cornell University Press.

Harding, Sandra 1991: *Whose Science? Whose Knowledge?* Ithaca: Cornell University Press.

Hartsock, Nancy 1983: "The Feminist Standpoint: Developing the Ground for a Specifically Feminist Historical Materialism," in S. Harding and M. Hintikka (eds), *Discovering Reality*. Dordrecht: Reidel.

Hartsock, Nancy 1989–1990: "Postmodernism and Political Change: Issues for Feminist Theory," *Cultural Critique*, 14, pp. 15–33.

Harvey, David 1989: *The Condition of Postmodernity*. Oxford, UK and New York: Blackwell.

Hegel, G. W. F. [1807] 1977: *The Phenomenology of Spirit*, trans. A. V. Miller. Oxford: Clarendon Press.

Hegel, G. W. F. [1801] 1978: *The Difference Between the Fichtean and Schellingian Systems of Philosophy*, trans. Jere Paul Sourber. Reseda, Calif: Ridgeview Publishing.

Hewitt, John P. 1989: *Dilemmas of the American Self*. Philadelphia: Temple University Press.

Hirschman, Albert 1983: *Shifting Involvements*. Princeton: Princeton University Press.

Hobbes, Thomas [1651] 1968: *Leviathan*. Harmondsworth: Penguin.

Hobsbawm, Eric and Terence Ranger 1983: *The Invention of Tradition*. Cambridge: Cambridge University Press.

Hollis, Martin 1987: *The Cunning of Reason*. Oxford: Oxford University Press.

Hollis, Martin and Steven Lukes (eds) 1982: *Rationality and Relativism*. Cambridge, Mass.: MIT Press.

Holquist, Michael and Katerina Clark 1986: *Bakhtin*. New Haven: Yale University Press.

Holub, Robert C. 1991: *Jürgen Habermas: Critic in the Public Sphere*. New York: Routledge.

Honneth, Axel, Thomas McCarthy, Claus Offe, and Albrecht Wellman (eds) 1993: *Philosophical Interventions in the Unfinished Project of Modernity*. Cambridge, Mass.: MIT Press.

hooks, bell 1981: *Ain't I a Woman: Black Women and Feminism*. Boston: South End Press.

hooks, bell 1984: *Feminist Theory: From Marton to Center*. Boston: South End Press.

hooks, bell 1989: *Talking Back: Thinking Feminist, Thinking Black*. Boston: South End Press.

hooks, bell 1993: *Sisters of the Yam: Black Women and Self-Recovery*. Boston: South End Press.

Horkheimer, Max 1947: *Eclipse of Reason*. New York: Oxford University Press.

Horkheimer, Max 1982: "Traditional and Critical Theory," in *Critical Theory*. New York: Continuum.

Horkheimer, Max 1993: *Between Philosophy and Social Science: Selected Early Writings*, trans. G. Frederick Hunter, Matthew S. Kramer, and John Torpey. Cambridge, Mass.: MIT Press.

Horkheimer, Max and Theodor W. Adorno 1972: *Dialectic of Enlightenment*, trans. John Cumming. New York: Herder & Herder.

Huntington, Samuel P. 1993: "The Clash of Civilizations?" *Foreign Affairs*, 72 (3), pp. 22–8.

Inglehart, Ronald 1990: *Culture Shift in Advanced Industrial Society*. Princeton, NJ: Princeton University Press.

Irigaray, Luce 1977: *This Sex Which Is Not One*. Ithaca: Cornell University Press.

Jameson, Frederic 1971: *Marxism and Form*. Princeton: Princeton University Press.

Jameson, Fredric 1991: *Postmodernism, or, The Cultural Logic of Late Capitalism*. Durham, NC: Duke University Press.

Jardine, Alice and Paul Smith (eds) 1987: *Men in Feminism*. London: Methuen.

Jay, Martin 1974: *The Dialectical Imagination*. Berkeley: University of California Press.

Jay, Martin 1985: *Marxism and Totality*. Berkeley: University of California Press.

Kant, Immanuel [1790] 1987: *Critique of Judgment*, Indianapolis, Ind.: Hackett (Pluhar translation).

Kantorowicz, Ernst Hartwig 1957: *The King's Two Bodies: A Study in Medieval Political Theology*. Princeton: Princeton University Press.

Keane, J. (ed.) 1988: *Civil Society and the State*. London: Verso.

Keller, Evelyn Fox 1983: *A Feeling for the Organism*. San Francisco: Freeman.

Kellner, Douglas 1989: *Jean Baudrillard: From Marxism to Postmodernism and Beyond*. Stanford, Calif.: Stanford University Press.

Kellner, Douglas 1990: "The Postmodern Turn: Positions, Problems, Prospects," in G. Ritzer (ed.), *Frontiers of Social Theory: The New Syntheses*. New York: Columbia University Press, pp. 255–86.

Kohlberg, Lawrence 1981: *Essays on Moral Development*, Vol. 1: *The Philosophy of Moral Development*. New York: Harper & Row.

Kohlberg, Lawrence 1984: *Essays on Moral Development*, Vol. 2: *The Psychology of Moral Development*. San Fancisco: Jossey-Bass.

Kohn, Hans [1944] 1968: *The Age of Nationalism*. New York: Harper & Row.

Kosseleck, Reinhart 1985: *Futures Past: On the Semantics of Historical Time*, trans. Keith Tribe. Cambridge, Mass.: MIT Press.

Kroker, A. and D. Cook 1986: *The Postmodern Scene: Excremental Culture and Hyper-Aesthetics*. New York: St Martins.

Kuhn, Annette 1978: "Structures of Patriarchy and Capital in the Family," in A. Kuhn and A. M. Wolfe, *Feminism and Materialism*. Boston: Routledge.

Kuhn, Thomas S. 1970: *The Structure of Scientific Revolutions*. Chicago: University of Chicago Press, 2nd edn.

Lakatos, Imre 1970: "Falsification and the Methodology of Scientific Research Programmes," in I. Lakatos and A. Musgrave (eds), *Criticism and the Growth of Knowledge*. Cambridge: Cambridge University Press, pp. 91–196.

Landes, Joan 1988: *Women and the Public Sphere in the Age of the French Revolution*. Ithaca: Cornell University Press.

Lasch, Christopher 1991: *The True and Only Heaven: Progress and Its Critics*. New York: Norton.

Lash, Scott 1990: *Postmodernist Sociology*. London: Routledge.

Latour, B. 1987: *Science in Action*. Cambridge, Mass.: Harvard University Press.

Laursen, John Christian 1986: "The Subversive Kant: The Vocabulary of 'Public' and 'Publicity'." *Political Theory*, 14, pp. 584–603.

Lemert, Charles 1992: "Subjectivity's Limit: The Unsolved Riddle of the Standpoint," *Sociological Theory*, 10 (1), pp. 63–72.

Lenski, G., J. Lenski, and P. Nolan 1990: *Human Societies*. New York: McGraw-Hill.

Levinas, Emmanuel 1979: *Totality and Infinity*. Pittsburgh: Duquesne University Press.

Locke, John [1690] 1950. *Two Treatises on Government*. London: Dent.

Lovejoy, A. O. 1936: *The Great Chain of Being*. Cambridge, Mass.: Harvard University Press.

Lowi, Theodore 1985: *The Personal Presidency: Power Invested, Promise Unfulfilled*. Ithaca: Cornell University Press.

Lukacs, Georg 1922: *History and Class Consciousness*. Cambridge, Mass.: MIT Press.

Lukacs, Georg 1976: *The Young Hegel: Studies in the Relations Between Dialectics and Economics*, trans. Rodney Livingstone. Cambridge, Mass.: MIT Press.

Luhmann, Niklas 1986: *Love as Passion: The Codification of Intimacy*, trans. J. Gaines and D. L. Jones. Cambridge, Mass.: Harvard University Press.

Lundgren, Eva 1992: "The Hand that Strikes and Comforts: Gender Construction in the Field of Tension Encompassing Body and Symbol, Stability and Change," pp. 131–58, in M. L. Eduards, I. Elgqvist-Saltzman, E. Lundgren, C. Sjöblad, E. Sundin, and U. Wikander, *Rethinking Change: Current Swedish Feminist Research*. Uppsala: Humanistisk-samhällsvetenskapliga forskningsradet.

Lyotard, Jean-François [1982] 1984: "Answering the Question: What Is Postmodernism?" Appendix to *The Postmodern Condition*. Minneapolis: University of Minnesota Press.

Lyotard, Jean-François [1979] 1984: *The Postmodern Condition*, trans. Geoff Bennington and Brian Massumi. Minneapolis: University of Minnesota Press.

Lyotard, Jean-François 1988: *The Differend*. Minneapolis: University of Minnesota Press.

Lyotard, Jean-François 1991: *The Inhuman*, trans. G. Bennington and R. Bowlby. Stanford, Calif.: Stanford University Press.

Mann, Michael 1986: *The Sources of Social Power*, Vol. 1. Cambridge: Cambridge University Press.

Mann, Michael 1993: *The Sources of Social Power*, Vol. 2. Cambridge: Cambridge University Press.

Marcuse, Herbert 1955: *Eros and Civilization: A Philosophical Inquiry into Freud*. Boston: Beacon Press.

Marcuse, Herbert 1964: *One-Dimensional Man: Studies in the Ideology of Advanced Industrial Society*. Boston: Beacon Press.

Markakis, John 1987: *National and Class Conflict in the Horn of Africa*. London: Zed Books.

Marx, Karl [1843] 1975: "On the Jewish Question," pp. 146–74, in *Karl Marx-Friederick Engels Collected Works*, vol. 3. London: Lawrence and Wishart.

Marx, Karl and Frederick Engels [1845] 1975: *The Holy Family or Critique of Critical Criticism against Bruno Bauer and Company*, pp. 5–211, in *Karl Marx Frederick Engels Collected Works*, vol. 4. London: Lawrence & Wishart.

McCarthy, Thomas 1978: *The Critical Theory of Jürgen Habermas*. Cambridge, Mass.: MIT Press.

McCarthy, Thomas 1991: *Ideals and Illusions: On Reconstruction and Deconstruction in Contemporary Critical Theory*. Cambridge, Mass.: MIT Press.

McCarthy, Thomas forthcoming: "Legitimacy and Diversity: Dialectical Reflections on Analytical Distinctions," in *Cardozo Law Review*.

Mead, George Herbert 1934: *Mind, Self, and Society*. Chicago: University of Chicago Press.

Megill, Allan 1985: *Prophets of Extremity: Nietzsche, Heidegger, Foucault, Derrida*. Berkeley: University of California Press.

Meinecke, Friedrich 1970: *Cosmopolitanism and the National State*. Princeton: Princeton University Press.

Melucci, Alberto 1988: "Social Movements and the Democratization of Everyday Life," in J. Keane (ed.), *Civil Society and the State*. London: Verso, pp. 245–60.

Melucci, Alberto 1989: *Nomads of the Present: Social Movements and Individual Needs in Contemporary Society*. Philadelphia: Temple University Press.

Merton, Robert 1968: *Social Theory and Social Structure*. New York: Free Press, 3rd edn.

Miller, Jim 1993: *The Passion of Michel Foucault*. New York: Simon & Schuster.

Mills, C. Wright 1959: *The Sociological Imagination*. Harmondsworth: Penguin.

Michelet, Jules [1846] 1973: *The People*, trans. John P. McKay. Urbana: University of Illinois Press.

Moi, Toril 1985: *Sexual/Textual Politics: Feminist Literary Theory*. New York: Methuen.

Montesquieu, C. [1748] 1978: *The Spirit of Laws*. Berkeley: University of California Press.

Mosse, George L. 1985: *Nationalism and Sexuality: Middle-Class Morality and Sexual Norms in Modern Europe*. Madison: University of Wisconsin Press.

Musil, Robert 1965: *The Man Without Qualities*, trans. E. Wilsins and E. Kaiser. New York: Capricorn.

Nadel, Siegfried 1951: *Foundations of Social Anthropology*. Oxford: Oxford University Press.

Nadel, Siegfried 1957: *Theory of Social Structure*. London: Cohen & West.

Negt, Oskar 1978: "Mass Media: Tools of Domination or Instruments of Liberation? Aspects of the Frankfurt School's Communication Analysis," *New German Critique* 14, pp. 61–80.

Negt, Oskar and Alexander Kluge 1993: *The Public Sphere and Experience*. Minneapolis: University of Minnesota Press.

Nicholson, Linda 1991: *Feminism/Postmodernism*. New York: Routledge.

Nicholson, Linda 1992: "On the Postmodern Barricades: Feminism, Politics, and Theory," in Steven Seidman and David G. Watner (eds), *Postmodernism and Social Theory*. Cambridge, Mass. and Oxford, UK: Basil Blackwell, pp. 82–100.

Norris, Christopher 1987: *Derrida*. Cambridge, Mass.: Harvard University Press.

Parker, A. et al. 1992: *Nationalism and Sexualities*. New York: Routledge.

Parsons, Talcott 1949: *The Structure of Social Action*. Glencoe, Ill.: Free Press, 2nd edn.

Parsons, Talcott 1968: *The System of Modern Societies*. Englewood Cliffs, NJ: Prentice-Hall.

Peel, J. D. Y. 1971: *Herbert Spencer: The Evolution of a Sociologist*. New York: Basic Books.

Plant, Sadie 1992: *The Most Radical Gesture: The Situationist International in the Postmodern Age*. New York: Routledge.

Pocock, J. G. A. 1975: *The Machiavellian Moment*. Princeton: Princeton University Press.

Polanyi, Karl 1944: *The Great Transformation*. Boston: Beacon.

Popper, Karl 1959: *The Logic of Scientific Discovery*. New York: Basic Books.

Popper, Karl 1968: *Conjectures and Refutations: The Growth of Scientific Knowledge*. New York: Harper & Row.

Postone, Moishe 1993: *Time, Labor, and Social Domination*. Cambridge: Cambridge University Press.

Postone, Moishe and Barbara Brick 1982: "Critical Pessimism and the Limits of Traditional Marxism," *Theory and Society*, 11, pp. 617–58.

Putnam, Hillary 1981: *Reason, Truth and History*. Cambridge: Cambridge University Press.

Redfield, Robert 1957: *The Little Tradition*. Chicago: University of Chicago

Press.

Renan, Ernst 1990: "What is a Nation?" in Homi Bhabha (ed.), *Nation and Narration*. London: Routledge.

Rhode, Deborah L. 1990: *Theoretical Perspectives on Sexual Difference*. New Haven, Conn.: Yale University Press.

Rich, Adrienne 1983: "Compulsory Heterosexuality and Lesbian Existence," in A. Snitow, C. Stansell and S. Thompson (eds), *Powers of Desire*. New York: Monthly Review Press, pp. 177–205.

Ricoeur, Paul 1984–86: *Time and Narrative*, 2 vols, trans. Kathleen McLaughlin and David Pellauer. Chicago: University of Chicago Press.

Rorty, Richard 1979: *Philosophy and the Mirror of Nature*. Princeton: Princeton University Press.

Rorty, Richard 1982: *The Consequences of Pragmatism*. Minneapolis: University of Minnesota Press.

Rorty, Richard 1987: "Pragmatism and Philosophy," in Kenneth Baynes, James Bohman, and Thomas McCarthy (eds), *After Philosophy: End or Transformation*. Cambridge, Mass: MIT Press, pp. 26–66.

Rorty, Richard 1989: *Contingency, Irony, Solidarity*. Cambridge and New York: Cambridge University Press.

Rose, Hillary 1983: "Hand, Brain and Heart: A Feminist Epistemology for the Natural Sciences," *Signs*, 9 (1), pp. 73–90.

Rosenau, Pauline Marie 1992: *Post-Modernism and the Social Sciences: Insights, Inroads, and Intrusions*. Princeton, NJ: Princeton University Press.

Rousseau, Jean-Jacques [1762] 1962: "The Social Contract," in E. Barker (ed.), *Social Contract: Essays by Locke, Hume and Rousseau*. New York: Oxford.

Rousseau, Jean-Jacques [1782] 1963: *Considerations sur le Gouvernement de Pologne*. New York: French & European Publications, Inc.

Rubin, Gayle 1975: "The Traffic in Women: Notes on the 'Political Economy' of Sex," in R. Rapp (ed.), *Toward an Anthropology of Women*. New York: Monthly Review Press.

Said, Edward 1976: *Orientalism*. London: Edward Arnold.

Schama, Simon 1989: *Citizens: A Chronicle of the French Revolution*. New York: Knopf.

Schlesinger, Phillip 1987: "On National Identity: Some Conceptions and Misconceptions Criticized," *Social Science Information*, 26, pp. 219–64.

Schluchter, Wolfgang 1981: *The Rise of Western Rationalism: Max Weber's Developmental History*. Berkeley: University of California Press.

Schor, Naomi 1989: "This Essentialism Which Is Not One: Coming to Grips with Irigaray," *Differences*, 1 (2), pp. 38–58.

Schrecker, John 1991: *The Chinese Revolution in Historical Perspective*. New York: Praeger.

Schutz, Alfred and Thomas Luckmann 1976: *Structures of the Lifeworld*. London: Longman.

Schwarcz, Vera 1986: *The Chinese Enlightenment*. Berkeley: University of California Press.

Schwartzmantel, John 1991: *Socialism and the Idea of the Nation*. Hemel Hempstead: Harvester Wheatsheaf.

Scitovsky, Josef 1980: *The Joyless Economy*. New York: Oxford University Press.

Scott, Alan 1990: *Ideology and the New Social Movements*. London: Unwin Hyman.

Sedgwick, Eve Kosovsky 1985: *Between Men: English Literature and Male Homosexual Desire*. New York: Columbia University Press.

Seidman, Steven 1992: *Embattled Eros: Sexual Politics and Ethics in Contemporary America*. New York: Routledge.

Seidman, Steven 1994: "Symposium: Queer Theory/Sociology: A Dialogue," *Sociological Theory* 12 (2), pp. 166–248.

Sennet, Richard 1977: *The Fall of Public Man*. New York: Knopf.

Sewell, William Jr. 1981: *Work and Revolution*. Cambridge: Cambridge University Press.

Sheehan, James J. 1978: *German Liberalism in the Nineteenth Century*. Chicago: University of Chicago Press.

Shils, E. 1981: *Tradition*. Chicago: University of Chicago Press.

Sica, Alan 1988: *Max Weber on Rationality and Social Order*. Berkeley: University of California Press.

Simmel, Georg 1967: *Conflict and the Web of Group Affiliations*, ed. K. Wolff. New York: Free Press.

Simmel, Georg [1903] 1971: "The Metropolis and Mental Life," in D. N. Levine (ed.), *Georg Simmel on Individuality and Social Forms*. Chicago: University of Chicago Press, pp. 324–39.

Skurnowicz, Joan S. 1981: *Romantic Nationalism and Liberalism: Joachim Lelewel and the Polish National Idea*. New York: Columbia University Press.

Smith, Anthony 1991: *National Identity*. London: Penguin.

Smith, Dorothy 1987: *The Everyday World as Problematic: A Feminist Sociology*. Boston, Northeastern Press.

Smith, Dorothy 1990: *The Conceptual Practices of Power*. Boston: Northeastern University Press.

Smith, Paul 1988: *Discerning the Subject*. Minneapolis: University of Minnesota Press.

Somers, Margaret 1992: "Narrativity, Narrative Identity, and Social Action: Rethinking English Working-Class Formation," *Social Science History*, 16 (4), pp. 591–630.

Somers, Margaret R. and Gloria D. Gibson 1994: "Reclaiming the Epistemological 'Other': Narrative and the Social Constitution of Identity," in Craig Calhoun (ed.), *Social Theory and the Politics of Identity*. Oxford: Blackwell Publishers.

Sorokin, Pitirim A. 1957: *Social and Cultural Dynamics*, rev. and abridged edn. Boston: Extending Horizon Books.

Spence, Jonathan 1991: *In Search of Modern China*. New York: Norton.

Spivak, Gayatri Chakravorty 1987: *In Other Worlds: Essays in Cultural Politics*. London: Methuen.

Spivak, Gayatri Chakravorty 1988: "Can the Subaltern Speak?" in Larry

Grossberg and Cary Nelson (eds), *Marxism and the Interpretation of Culture*. Urbana: University of Illinois Press, pp. 271–313.

Spivak, Gayatri Chakravorty 1992: "French Feminism Revisited: Ethics and Politics," in J. Butler and J. Scott (eds), *Feminists Theorize the Political*. New York: Routledge, pp. 54–85.

Steiner, George 1975: *After Babel*. Oxford: Oxford University Press.

Stinchcombe, Arthur 1968: *Constructing Sociological Theories*. New York: Academic Press.

Stinchcombe, Arthur 1978: *Theoretical Methods in Social History*. New York: Academic Press.

Strauss, Anselm 1978: "A Social World Perspective," *Studies in Symbolic Interaction*, 1, pp. 119–28.

Szporluk, Roman 1988: *Communism and Nationalism: Karl Marx vs. Friedrich List*. New York: Oxford University Press.

Taguieff, Pierre-André 1988: *La force du préjugé: Essai sur le racisme et ses doubles*. Paris: La Découverte; translation forthcoming from the University of Minnesota Press.

Tambiah, S. J. 1990: *Magic, Science, Religion and the Scope of Rationality*. Cambridge: Cambridge University Press.

Taylor, Barbara 1983: *Eve and the New Jerusalem*. New York: Pantheon.

Taylor, Charles 1975: *Hegel*. Cambridge: Cambridge University Press.

Taylor, Charles 1982: "Rationality," in M. Hollis and S. Lukes (eds), *Rationality and Relativism*. Cambridge, Mass.: MIT Press.

Taylor, Charles 1985: *Human Agency and Language: Philosophical Papers, I*. Cambridge: Cambridge University Press.

Taylor, Charles [1971] 1985: "Interpretation and the Sciences of Man," in *Philosophy and the Human Sciences: Philosophical Papers, II*. Cambridge: Cambridge University Press.

Taylor, Charles 1985: *Philosophy and the Human Sciences: Philosophical Papers, II*. Cambridge: Cambridge University Press.

Taylor, Charles 1989: *Sources of the Self*. Cambridge, Mass.: Harvard University Press.

Taylor, Charles 1992: *The Ethics of Authenticity*. Cambridge, Mass.: Harvard University Press.

Taylor, Charles 1992: *Multiculturalism and the Politics of Recognition*. Princeton: Princeton University Press.

Taylor, Charles 1993: "To Follow A Rule," in C. Calhoun, E. LiPuma and M. Postone (eds), *Bourdieu: Critical Perspectives*. Chicago: University of Chicago Press, pp. 45–60.

Taylor, Charles 1995: *Selected Essays*. Cambridge, Mass.: Harvard University Press.

Thompson, E. P. 1964: *The Making of the English Working Class*. New York: Pantheon Books.

Tibi, Bassam 1990: *Arab Nationalism: A Critical Enquiry*, 2nd edn, trans. M. F. Sluglett and Peter Sluglett. New York: St Martin's Press.

Tilly, Charles 1990: *Coercion, Capital and European States AD 990–1990*.

Oxford: Blackwell.

Tilly, Charles (ed.) 1975: *The Formation of National States in Europe*. Princeton: Princeton University Press.

Tilly, Charles and Lee Walker (eds) 1991: "Special Issue on Ethnic Conflict in the Soviet Union," *Theory and Society*, 20, pp. 569–724.

Tocqueville, Alexis de [1856] 1955: *The Old Regime and the French Revolution*, eds J. D. Mayer and A. P. Kerr. New York: Doubleday.

Todorov, Tzvetan 1993: *On Human Diversity: Nationalism, Racism and Exoticism in French Thought*. Cambridge, Mass.: Harvard University Press.

Tonnies, Ferdinand [1887] 1955: *Community and Association*. London: Routledge and Kegan Paul.

Touraine, A. 1985: "An Introduction to the Study of Social Movements," *Social Research*, 52, pp. 749–88.

Touraine, A. 1988: *The Return of the Actor*. Minneapolis: University of Minnesota Press.

Turner, Stephen 1986: *The Search for a Methodology of Social Science: Durkheim, Weber, and the Nineteenth-Century Problem of Cause, Probability and Action*. Boston Studies in the Philosophy of Science 92. Dordrecht: Reidel.

Turner, Stephen 1992: "The Strange Life and Hard Times of the Concept of General Theory in Sociology: A Short History of Hope," in D. Wagner and S. Seidman (eds), *Postmodernism and Social Theory*. Cambridge, Mass. and Oxford, UK: Basil Blackwell, pp. 101–33.

Ullman, Walter 1977: *Political Theories of the Middle Ages*. Harmondsworth: Penguin.

Vonnegut, Kurt 1968: *Slaughterhouse Five*. New York: Dell.

Wacquant, Loïc 1989: "Toward a Reflexive Sociology: A Workshop with Pierre Bourdieu," *Sociological Theory*, 7, pp. 26–63.

Wacquant, Loïc and Craig Calhoun 1989: "Intérêt, rationalité, et histoire: a propos d'un récent débat sur la théorie de l'action," *Actes de la Recherche en Sciences Sociales*, 78 (June), pp. 41–60.

Walicki, Andrezej 1982: *Philosophy and Romantic Nationalism: The Case of Poland*. New York: Oxford University Press.

Walker, Henry and Bernard P. Cohen 1985: "Scope Statements: Imperatives for Evaluating Theory," *American Sociological Review*, 50 (3), pp. 288–301.

Warner, Michael 1993: *Fear of a Queer Planet*. Minneapolis: University of Minnesota Press.

Warnke, Georgia 1987: *Gadamer*. Stanford: Stanford University Press.

Watkins, Susan Cott 1991: *From Provinces into Nations*. Princeton: Princeton University Press.

Weber, Marianne 1975: *Max Weber: A Biography*. New York: Wiley.

Weber, Max [1922] 1978: *Economy and Society*. Berkeley: University of California Press.

Weber, Max [1919] 1989: "Science as a Vocation," in P. Lasseman and I. Velodny (eds), *Max Weber's "Science as a Vocation."* London: Unwin Hyman, pp. 3–31.

Weber, Max 1991: "Politics as a Vocation," in H. H. Gerth and C. Wright Mills (eds), *From Max Weber: Essays in Sociology*. London: Routledge & Kegan Paul, pp. 77–128.

Weiner, Jonathan 1994: *The Beak of the Finch: A Story of Evolution in Our Time*. New York: Knopf.

Weintraub, Jeff 1990: "The Theory and Politics of the Public/Private Distinction." Paper presented to the annual meeting of the American Political Science Association.

Weintraub, Jeff 1994: "Introduction," in Jeff Weintraub and Krishan Kumar (eds), *Public and Private in Thought and Practice*. Chicago: University of Chicago Press.

Wertsch, James 1990: *Vygotsky*. Cambridge, Mass.: Harvard University Press.

White, Harrison 1992: *Identity and Control*. Princeton: Princeton University Press.

White, Hayden V. 1973: *Metahistory: The Historical Imagination in Nineteenth-Century Europe*. Baltimore: Johns Hopkins University Press.

White Hayden V. 1978: *Tropics of Discourse: Essays in Cultural Criticism*. Baltimore: Johns Hopkins University Press.

Wiggershaus, Rolf 1994: *The Frankfurt School: Its History, Theories, and Political Significance*. Cambridge, Mass.: MIT Press.

Wilson, Bryan (ed.) 1970: *Rationality*. Oxford: Basil Blackwell.

Winch, Peter 1958: *The Idea of a Social Science and Its Relation to Philosophy*. London: Routledge.

Winch, Peter 1964: "Understanding a Primitive Society," *American Philosophical Quarterly*, 1, pp. 307–24; reprinted in B. Wilson (ed.), *Rationality*. Oxford: Basic Blackwell, 1970, pp. 68–111.

Wolff, Robert Paul, Farrington Moore, Jr, and Herbert Marcuse 1969: *The Critique of Pure Tolerance*. London: Cape.

Wuthnow, Robert 1987: *Meaning and Moral Order*. Berkeley: University of California Press.

Wuthnow, Robert 1989: *Communities of Discourse*. Cambridge, Mass.: Harvard University Press.

Young, Iris Marion 1987: "Impartiality and Civic Virtue," in S. Benhabib and D. Cornell (eds), *Feminism as Critique*. Minneapolis: University of Minnesota Press.

Young, Iris Marion 1990: *Justice and the Politics of Difference*. Princeton: Princeton University Press.

Index

Abendroth, Wolfgang, 42n.72
action
  autonomy (freedom to act), 150, 164, 201, 258
  collective, 110, 123, 146, 206, 216
  concrete, 167–72, 179
  coordination of, 143–54
  modes of, 205–9
  social, 148, 154–5, 185
  sources of, 98, 144–5
  strategic, 141–2, 149–52, 160n.71, 178
  see also Bourdieu; communicative action;
    habitus
Adorno, Theodor, 194
  on difference, xv, 33, 75
  and Frankfurt School, xv, 11, 14, 40n.46, 134
  on relative enlightenment, 23–4, 40–1n.54
  views on empirical methods, 37n.10, 39n.40,
    42n.83
  see also Horkheimer and Adorno
aesthetics, 38n.20, 158n.30
  Bourdieu on, 143–4
  as critique of reification, 15–16, 39n.28
  in politics, 231–2
  in postmodernism, 99–100, 104, 113
  see also Kant; postmodernism
agency
  collective, 110–12, 123
  as continuing question, 98, 124
  as obscured in systems, 143–4, 183–4, 199–
    202
  transformative, 168, 185
Alexander, Jeffrey, 91n.2
Althusser, Louis, 121, 131n.81
Anderson, Benedict, 234, 255, 258, 267
Anderson, Perry, 291, 296n.11
anthropology, 156n.6
  evaluating interpretations in, 44, 60
  as model of understanding culture, 55, 81–2,
    84
  and view of similarities among cultures, xi, 44,
    58, 121, 136
Aptheker, Bettina, 191n.46
architecture, postmodernist, 99, 101, 121,
  126n.19
Arendt, Hannah, 209
  on creativity, 75–6
  on culture as value, 1, 36n.3
  on Hegel, xxiin.15, 28
  on history, 10, 38nn.16, 18
  on identity, 2, 75
  on natality, 11, 283–5
  on philistines, 1, 2, 36n.2
  on plurality, 12–13, 66n.12, 75–6, 193, 243–4
  on public sphere, 243–4, 253–4, 275n.19,
    276n.23, 278n.49
Aristotle, 28, 74, 200
"Asian Way" of nationalizing, 203, 234, 293,
  296n.11
Augustine, Saint, 194
Azande, 82, 94n.33

Bachelard, Gaston, 121
Bagehot, Walter, 149
Bakhtin, Mikail, 45, 50, 95n.43, 125n.10, 194
Barthes, Roland, 108, 128
Baudelaire, Charles, 101
Baudrillard, Jean
  on consumption relations, 102–8, 126n.17,
    154–5
  on Foucault, 107
  as postmodernist, 100, 124n.2, 125n.7,
    126n.16
Becker, Gary, 141
Bell, Daniel, 100, 102, 126n.14
Benhabib, Seyla, 40n.50, 92n.8
Benjamin, Walter, 14, 22, 34, 41n.59
Berman, Marshall, 290–1, 296n.6
biblical scholarship, 67–8n.27
  and hermeneutics, 48, 56, 58
bifurcated consciousness, 167–70, 181–6
  see also standpoint theory, feminist; standpoint,
    of women
biology
  in essentialist claims, 219, 226nn.14, 25
  in social theory, 195, 199, 224n.12, 283–4,
    295–6n.1
black nationalism, 222, 282n.95
Blau, Peter, 89, 90
  critiques of structuralism, 68n.33, 92n.14,
    95–6n.51
both/and, *see* difference
Bourdieu, Pierre, xvi, xviii, 12, 59, 65
  on action, 134, 160n.71
  on aesthetics, 143–4, 158n.26